Voices of the Village

Foreword

Many people in the Village have enjoyed reading the late Sylvia Saunders-Jacobs' book "West Chiltington in West Sussex". Following the death of Mac Steele, Parish Councillor and long-term resident of the village with a fund of stories and memories of village life, Councillor Roger Watts was concerned that other villagers with similar stories would take their tales with them when their time came. He therefore suggested to me and the Council that someone should bring Sylvia Saunders-Jacobs' book up to date as so much has happened since the early 1900s.

So when the Parish Council considered plans on how to mark the Millennium, one suggestion which received universal approval was to encourage the writing of a book on "West Chiltington in the 20th Century". At our Annual Parish Meeting in April 1997 Joan and Ron Ham spoke to us about how they had carried out similar work in Storrington and Sullington.

After that meeting we were able to gather a team of people (mentioned in the Acknowledgements) who all contributed research and input into the project. But all this would have been to little avail had it not been for the enthusiasm and dedication of our author Ann Salmon. She has spent endless hours interviewing people who lived in the Village over the last 80 years, tape recording for posterity and then preparing drafts of the various chapters of the book for comments. On behalf of the whole Village and of the Parish Council I wish to express our heartfelt thanks for all her hard work which has resulted in this production.

I hope you will enjoy reading this as much as those of us who have helped Ann have enjoyed working with her. Having lived in West Chiltington for 28 years I thought I knew quite a lot of its history. I now know how little I knew - and it is all thanks to everyone who has co-operated and to Ann who has put it into place.

We have lived in an age when so many changes have occurred in such a short space of time - through a revolution in fact, unlikely to have been experienced in any preceding century.

Douglas Andrews
Chairman of the Parish Council 1993 - 1999

Acknowledgements

West Chiltington Parish Council
wishes to acknowledge, in random order, its thanks to the following members of the parish
without whose invaluable help this history could not have been recorded

Douglas Andrews OBE - Chairman of the Parish Council.
Peter Evans - Clerk to the Parish Council.
Caroline Wells for research at the West Sussex Record Office and most of Chapter 1.
Margot Bonnett for collating Parish Records.
Sheila Baxter and Gladys Engledow for work on the Parochial Church Council Records.
All the Club and Society secretaries, chairmen or members who submitted reports for Chapter 13.
Rosemary Wills for starting the 'project'.
Elizabeth and Howard Aldridge, Sue Chapman, Elizabeth Cutler, Gladys Engledow,
Rev Gerald Evans, Laurie Hancock, Peter and June Knowles,
Ian Kemp-Potter, Martin F Mace, Dennis Mounstephen.

Shirley Adsett, Cheryl Berry, Heather Bibby, Valerie Hawkins, Samantha King, Jean Maile,
Ann Salmon, Sheila Smith, Nancy Towns, Sandra Weidenbach,
for transcribing over seventy audio tapes.

Bill Hutchinson and Alan Pauling for general help and research; Margot Bonnett,
Bill Hutchinson, Jean Maile, Caroline Wells, Reg Slater for endless checking of facts.

Marion Douglass for all the charming line illustrations, and everyone who has lent treasured
photographs, particularly the late Ena Howard and the late Dr John Swan.

Elizabeth Anderson for proof reading.

Not least to all the people mentioned in this book for their time and their memories.

From outside the parish the Parish Council would also like to thank

Elaine Dawson of Steyning Museum
Driver & Vehicle Licensing Agency
Horsham District Council
Guy Leonard & Co
Paul Hyman from Luton Museum
Heritage Lottery Fund, BP research, Victoria and Albert Museum
Ministry of Defence Archives
The Registrar at the Royal Archives
Lord Melchett and the ICI Archives
Peggy Cory Dixon
The Family of Reginald Fairfax Wells
West Sussex County Council
West Sussex Police Service
West Sussex Record Office

Author's Note

This book has been written as part of West Chiltington's millennium celebrations to catch the old ways before they are forgotten, and to record the new.

It is divided into three parts: the first is a tour around some of the buildings of the parish showing the people who lived there, the second shows the Parish Council's responsibilities and the third shows village life at work and play.

Some names occur frequently because those families *were* the village and I am grateful to them simply for being here through the generations, to keep this village alive and intact for us newcomers to enjoy. I make no apology for these names dominating the book, but I do apologise if I have got names wrong, missed people out, or omitted someone or some event.

Voices of the Village can be read in many ways:

As a series of stories of other people's lives, their houses, their clothes, their work and play.

As an historical record of this village and how it has adapted to change.

As a source for research into: social interaction;
the effects of farming on the community and governmental decisions on farming;
the break-up of the old feudal estates; to show the arrival and departure of families;
the creation and collapse of hamlets; the results of increased housing pressure; how we spend our leisure time.

It shows above all that the parish is made up of many diverse people and interests.

It can be dipped into, or read as a whole.

There is an index at the back so readers can look up the names of their friends and relations, and a Glossary.

The unabridged version stretched to over 225 pages of A4, excluding space for illustrations, so had to be reduced. The working archives are housed at the West Sussex Record Office.

It is meant to give pleasure; I hope it does.

Ann Salmon

Voices of the Village
A History of West Chiltington during the Twentieth Century

Books always have dedications and thanks to proof readers, editors and family.

This is your book. Without you, the people of the village, there would be no book, so the dedication of this one is:

To The Voices of the Village

Our Thanks

Village voices tell stories, some are true, some are embroidered, and some are pure fiction.
We have done our best to sort out which is which, but we cannot be held responsible if, after all our research, we have not told it as *you* remembered it.

Published by Ann Salmon,
Karibu, Grove Lane, West Chiltington, West Sussex RH20 2RD
and by West Chiltington Parish Council

Typesetting by Elite Typesetting Techniques, Eastleigh,
Hants SO50 4SR

Printed by Antony Rowe Limited, Chippenham,
Wiltshire SN14 6LH

Published December 1999

ISBN 0–9537702–0–6

All plans in this book are the sole copyright © of Caroline Wells.

The line drawings are the sole copyright © of Marion Douglass.

The illustration of Carver's Yard is the sole copyright © of
Gill Palengat.

The photographs of R F Wells, and his Tiles and Potteries offices are
the sole copyright © of the Wells Family.

No part of this publication may be reproduced, copied or transmitted
without the written consent of the publishers, in accordance with the
provisions of the Copyright, Designs and Patents Act 1988.
© Mrs Ann Salmon 1999 unless otherwise stated as above.

Contents

Chapter 1 – Introduction to the Parish - Page 13
Early history; Inclosures; Parish Perambulations; Roads; Manor Rent book; Sale of Land and subsequent building; The Local Plan; Boundaries and Changes; Geology.

Chapter 2 – West Chiltington Village - Church Street - Page 24
Residents' Memories of the Early Days; Stan Gooch and the Post Office; Walk down Church Street; Edith Green; The Village Pond; New House Farm.

Chapter 3 – West Chiltington Village - From the Cross Roads - Page 51
Hatches Estate and Bill Hampton; Scotlands; The Forge and Ted Crowhurst, Jack Phillips; Kings and Princes Farm, the Greenfields; The Mill; Fryars; Palmers and Palmers Lodge.

Chapter 4 – From Broadford Bridge Road to the North of the Parish - Page 75
Huntleys; Sparrows Farm and WC Golf Course; Woodshill Farm; Gobles; Knowetop and New House Farm; the Pavey Family; The Shops at the Cross Roads; Willetts Farm; The Water Garden Specialists; Cattlestone Farm; Harbolets; Coneyhurst.

Chapter 5 – The Common - Page 103
Herbert Short and Family; Railway Carriage Houses; Rosebank; The Garage; Melrose Stores; Ridpath/Haglands Stores; Cherilyn; Saturday Market; Ted Strudwick; Caravans and Romanys; Council Housing; Allotments; Kensington Close; The Barkworths; The Haven; The Grange; The Mustchins and Little Haglands; Monkmead.

Chapter 6 – Roundabout - Page 138
Roundabout Farm; R F Wells; The Roundabout Hotel; Heather Nook; Childhood in the 1930s-1950s, John Ascoli, Carol & Jeremy Fisher, Michael & Judith Fitzgerald; The Van Tromp Family; Meadowbrook; Colourful Characters; April Cottage; Pansala; Ann Salisbury; a Ghost Story; Meg & Gerry Judd; The Munitions Crates.

Chapter 7 – The Outskirts - Page 168
Marigolds; Sinnocks and Village Nurseries; The Bicknell's Smallholding; Farthings; Smugglers; Southlands Farm; Whales Farm; The Five Bells; Lordings Farm and Billy Shaw; New Barn Farm and the Drabble Family; Voakes and the Kensingtons; Gay Street; Lower Jordans Farm; Nyetimber Manor; Gay Street Farm.

Chapter 8 – Parish Matters - Page 209
The Parish Council; The Recreation Ground; Groundsmen and Roadmen; The Old Comrades Hall; Village Hall, New Hall; The Gymkhana and Dog Show, The Fayre, the Fete and Flower Show; The Recreation Ground; Groundsmen and Roadmen; Pubs; The Police; Nurse's Cottage; District Nurses and Doctors; The Parish Magazine; The Reading Room; The Museum and its Exhibits; Royal Events; The Juggs; Steele Close; The Hurricane, POTT and Replanting; Transport on Road and Rail; Public Utilities, Electricity, Refuse, Water, Sewerage, Refuse.

Chapter 9 – The Church -Page 272
The Congregational Mission; Miss Bolwell; The Viewlands Mission and Miss King; Sunday Schools and Youth Clubs; The Rectors and Events during their Incumbencies.

Chapter 10 – Schooldays - Page 301
First School; Memories from 1912 - 1939; Wartime; Post-war 1950s and 1960s; A 1972 'Adult's Eye View; Childminders; Private Schools: Mrs Dixon, Little Thatch, Fir Tree Lane, Felix Eames, Ireton House; The New School; 1999 Children's Contributions.

Chapter 11 – The World of Work - Page 333
Children's Work; In Service; Slater's; Carver's; Peter Penfold; Mustchin's Coalyard; The Laundry; Telegraph and Telephones; Churchfield Farm.

Chapter 12 – The War Years - Page 359
Letters from the First World War; Evacuees; Monkmead Camp; Memories of Canadian Soldiers, Parties and High Jinks; Boys' and Girls' Souvenir Hunting; Rationing; Home Guard, ARP, Special Police; Land Army; POWs; Eddie Shotnik; F C Belok.

Chapter 13 – Spare Time! - Page 388
Cubs and Brownies, Scouts and Guides; The Snowdrop Band; the XYZs; The Silver Band; The British Legion and Women's Section; the Women's Institute, its Handbell and Croquet sections; Stoolball; The Cricket Club; Football; The Dramatic Society; The Boys' Club; The Preservation Society; The Art Group; Horticulture; Probus; Bowls; Table Tennis; Walking; Mary How Trust; Children's Play Area; Tennis Club; Fjord Horses; Owls; The Lottery.

Chapter 14 – Future Fortunes - Page 422
The Computer Age and Sussex Rural Community Council; Effects of World Affairs; BBC Domesday Survey; The WI Collage; What is a 'Villager'?; Millennium Celebrations; Doug Golds; The Future.

Glossary - Page 430

Bibliography - Page 433

Index - Page 435

xi

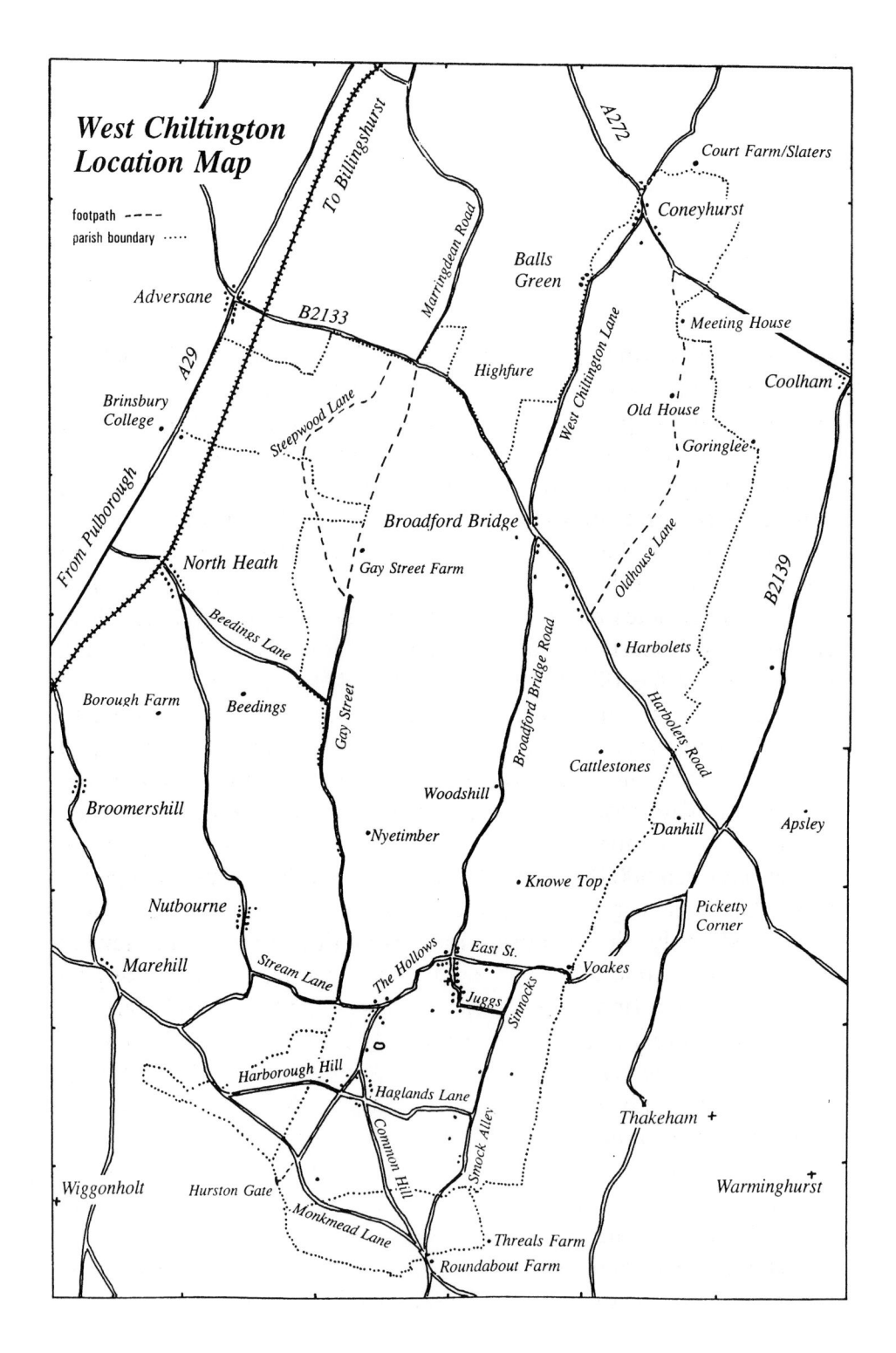

West Chiltington Location Map

footpath ----
parish boundary ·····

Chapter 1

Introduction to the Parish

"Has West Chiltington got a history?" asked a woman in the pub on hearing about this book. In fact several local people have written histories of the village in the past; Sylvia Saunders-Jacobs begins her book of the parish with the prehistoric times of round barrows and flint implements following through from the Romans, Saxons and the Domesday Survey to the more recent past; in 1917 the then vicar of West Chiltington, the Reverend Andrew Caldecott, wrote a history which was followed in 1955 by a short account by M Wilson. Both Lt-Colonel and Mrs G B Kensington kept notes and a "log book", as did Sheila de Burlet. There have also been at least two guides to the Church, published in 1947 and 1960, plus one in the 1970s so this book is the latest in a long line.

Although this is a history of West Chiltington during the twentieth century, this book has to be placed in time and space. Our present is rooted in our past, just as our future will depend on attitudes and decisions that prevail today. Our past goes back a very long way: Two palaeolithic handaxes testify to the presence of man here in the remote past, on occasions between 500,000 and 250,000 years ago. Just outside the parish around 32,000 years ago some people repaired their flint tools which were rediscovered early this century. Late Neolithic barbed and tanged arrowheads of c. 2,000 BC have been found in two places on Chiltington Common, and other finds of waste flakes suggest hunting or early farming peoples of Mesolithic, Neolithic or Bronze Age times used the land here.

The name of the parish has been discussed in other books, but as modern research advances new ideas evolve: the name Chiltington suggests a Saxon origin for the place-name. The –ing end is derived from –"ingas" – the people of. Place-name experts have interpreted Chilt as being derived from the Old English word cil meaning hill, thus Chiltington would be "the ton of the people of the hill".

The Old English origin of the word indicates that this was a place to be referred to when Old English was spoken, in the 6th-10th centuries. We know nothing of Middle Saxon West Chiltington, but by the later Saxon period (the 11th century) the village must have been well established. Domesday book, written twenty years into the Norman period, records that there was a church here. The parish has two entries in Domesday book because the dividing line between the Rape of Bramber (William de Braose) and the Rape of Arundel (Earl Roger) ran through the parish. The church was in Earl Roger's part. (The rapes were political divisions of the county peculiar to Sussex.)

The parish was part of three manors, the manor being the main administrative unit in medieval and post medieval Sussex. Part of the parish (Nyetimber Manor) was given to the Cluniac Priory at Lewes. The central parcel of land was also in the gift of the king in Tudor times; Henry VIII gave the Manor of Chiltington to Lord Bergavenny. This manor remained in the Nevill family for nearly four centuries and the last sale of Abergavenny land in West Chiltington took place in 1930. The history of the northern part of the village has not been traced in detail but where we pick up our evidence in 1840 much of the land from Coneyhurst in the north and down the eastern edge of the parish was owned by the Bysshop family which lived at Parham from 1601 until 1922.

The documentary evidence for nineteenth century West Chiltington comes from several sources. The most important and most useful is the tithe map of 1840. Produced to calculate the commutation of tithes from payments in kind (wheat or oats) to cash payments to support the rector, this document lists every house and cottage, field and coppice, its owner, its occupier, its acreage and tithe valuation. From this we can produce the maps that show the owners, and the farm units in 1840. Firstly there is a map showing the main landowners, and secondly a map showing the actual farms recorded in 1840.

The next document of use is the West Chiltington Inclosure Award. It is quite clear from the tithe map that the arable farmland was already enclosed by the nineteenth century and all that remained to be enclosed after the national Inclosure Act was "The Lord's Waste", in other words the common land, the heathy pasture that belonged to Chiltington Manor, Nyetimber Manor, and also, because our parish boundaries have changed, to South Heath Nutbourne Manor, now the area of Harborough Hill and Castlegate (see map of The Common Chapter 5). These Inclosure maps for the different manors show the fields or allotments that were enclosed in 1868 - or were officially enclosed; the Steward of the Manor in 1622 had complained that the commoners were enclosing the Lord's Waste much earlier! This map shows that the road network was well established even across the unenclosed heathland. The Common is the area of West Chiltington most affected by building development in the 20th century but a close look at our map of the Common in 1868 in comparison with a modern map will show that nearly all the field boundaries are preserved in our modern property boundaries. It has been said that the most enduring feature in a landscape is the property boundary. The maps demonstrate this to be correct.

Following the 1868 evidence for the enclosure of the common we can turn to a completely different document. This is the Perambulation. Most parishes had a tradition of "beating the bounds" when parish officers and others would walk around the parish and maintain some traditional activity (like beating choir boys) at the various bound stones. This does not seem to have been a frequent activity in our parish, but perambulations were organised in 1834, 1864 and 1871. Those participating were the church wardens, several farmers, and most importantly some of the younger parishioners, so that the parish boundary would be fixed in living memory. The route began in the south-west corner of the parish – by a bramble bush - and would proceed up the Pulborough parish boundary to the Roman road. On another day the Billingshurst boundary would be walked up to Coneyhurst, and later the Thakeham boundary, the Sullington stretch and the Storrington end would be covered. The presence or absence of neighbouring parishioners would be recorded. Used in conjunction with the tithe map the perambulations also tell us about who lived in the peripheral cottages, and when notable features had disappeared since the last visit. Walking the boundaries would be hard work today with uncut hedges and difficult access.

The public highways in West Chiltington appear in old Sussex maps and are clearly well established routes. Monkmead Lane is the old road from Storrington to Pulborough, crossing the bridge at Heath Mill as shown on Budgen's map of 1724. This was the route used before the turnpike road from Storrington to Pulborough, now the A283, was constructed in about 1817. Other routes have been preserved as bridle paths and footpaths, notably Oldhouse Lane, which is a stone paved trackway possibly used by the Quaker William Penn when riding from Warminghurst to worship at the Thakeham Meeting House. The footpath that crosses Haglands Lane, Crossways and joins Roundabout Lane is an old track from the village to the wasteland and on to Storrington via Threals Lane. Gay Street is a dead end now, but footpaths show the old route heading north to Billingshurst and joining Marringdean Road. Some of the tracks may have been footpaths or packhorse trails, others may have been wide enough for wagons. Heather Lane, Sunset Lane and Westward Lane were tracks across the heathland of Roundabout Common on the first edition OS map. Today in 1999 we call the road between the Queen's Head and the Mill 'The Hollows'. The WI book of the village collated in 1947 records that all five deep cut 'holloways' in the village were known as The Hollows.

Leaving the sources of information about the landscape we come to a document which gives us much detail about the village. This is the manor rent book for the Abergavenny properties in 1893, with amendments through to the 1920s. The manor lands were occupied as copyhold (rented) or as freehold. Even at the beginning of the twentieth century curious mediaeval customs remained in force with the practice of copyhold. When a copyholder died a heriot had to be paid, this was normally a beast such as a cow, or it could be a payment of money. The rent book gives the name of all the copyholders and the value of their rents. In 1900 the value of rents was £4. 4s. 8d., by 1906 this had dwindled to £3. 9s. 9d. because a few copyholders had been "enfranchised" whereby they had paid a figure to become normal tenants rather than continue with the old manorial customary dues. Other tenancies "had fallen in" on the death of named individuals. After 1833 it became possible to sell parts of old manorial land – no longer was there a risk that the Crown might claim it back again, and, as the income from copyholds was getting smaller there was a move to change to more modern systems of land tenure. Copyholds could be bought by the sitting tenants, this process was known as being "enfranchised". In other cases the copyhold properties were bought by speculators who then exacted much larger rents from the tenants. Finally the manorial land tenure system came to an end with the passing of two Law of Property Acts in 1922 and 1924 and the last of the big land-owning families who had owned most of the parish of West Chiltington in 1840 had sold up by 1930. But as will be seen at Nyetimber, the days of the country estate had not passed entirely.

In 1895 and 1915, Kelly's directory (a gazetteer of gentry and small businesses) records information about West Chiltington, listing the principal landowners, and some of the farmers, shopkeepers, licensed victuallers and so forth. This record of the village meshes in with a sadder record – that of the First World War, when those who gave their lives are commemorated on the brass plaque and individual plaques in the church.

Lord Abergavenny owned much of Nutbourne as well as West Chiltington and many fields were sold as separate lots, particularly in 1925. In what was then Pulborough parish, fields on either side of Harborough Hill and Monkmead Lane were sold by him and within ten years house building had begun as we can see from the 1937 OS Map. In The Chiltington Common area land was also sold by Abergavenny in 1930 and by Mary Ann Greenfield and others in 1933. However, the heathland and rough grazing pasture in the central part of the Common, once Nyetimber Common, remained as just that until after the Second World War. Used for a temporary army camp during the war, it was not developed intensively for houses until the 1960s. Building development increased exponentially through the twentieth century as exemplified by the population figures. The housing density gradually increased until now in the 1990's the trend is to build three or more houses in the gardens of the houses built in the 1930's. Hopes that the village expansion was stopping were shaken with a recent announcement from the Labour government of 1997 that West Sussex would have to accept 58,000 more houses in the next 17 years.

When asked why everyone in the village was not living in exotic places on the vast profits they must have made selling farm land, the point was made that it was in the 1980s that land prices really increased and prior to that land for agricultural use changed hands for very little profit, and no-one thought of change-of-use for housing.

Though we see the purchase and sale of agricultural land continuing, a new force arrives on the market in the 20th century and that is the property developer. Estate Agents were keen to advertise suitable sites for desirable residences. In 1895 Clay Farm and Solelands were on the market; the sale particulars mark several places with a cross and the note 'fine spot for a residence'.

The sale of land for development is discussed by the developers in Chapter 11; the map in this chapter is taken from the OS map of 1911.

To bring us into the period of this book, at the beginning of the twentieth century, West Chiltington was a more or less self sufficient country parish with shops and a post office, and work on the land in farming and its supporting industries, or in the building trades. Over the hundred years it has changed considerably with the enormous reduction of men on the land, the changes in farming often decreed by the European Union, the rise of the out-of-town shopping centres and the influx of new residents, who are often retired, or commute into London. The roads have been surfaced, the car has superseded two feet, the horse or the bicycle, life has speeded up. This change has not always been for the better; mains water and electricity make life easier, but we have paid for it by the loss of the freedom to pick primroses, walk slowly to admire our countryside, and allow our children to play in the woods and fields free from concerns about speeding traffic and preying adults.

There is a core of families in the village who can trace their ancestors back through generations that have lived here; sometimes brothers and sisters of one family would marry sisters and brothers of another family; sometimes they would marry 'outsiders' but often from only as far away as Storrington or Nutbourne. The First World War had begun to change all that with the arrival of the Land Army girls and prisoners of war who worked on the farms. During the Second World War the pace of change quickened with the arrival in the village of evacuees, Land Army girls and foreign billeted troops, and thereafter there was the great influx of the commuters and the increasing demand for houses caused by the results of the 'baby boom' (the increase in the birth rate from 1946-1950 following the return of the troops at the end of the war). The population figures show that in 1921 there were 1,244 persons, but by 1931 this had risen to 1,718. There were 1,558 in 1934 and 1,646 in 1940. By 1999 the electoral roll lists 2,926 voters but this figure does not include the under 18 year olds. The parish covers about 4,000 acres and most of its present day population of 3,500 people live not in the main village itself, but on the Common and outlying areas to the south.

As a consequence building construction has been going on all through the century in the parish and there has been a resigned acceptance of its inevitability. It was Reginald Fairfax Wells in 1925 who really began the development of the Roundabout area in this and adjacent parishes, with his weekend cottages for the London rich or artistic. This inevitably pushed up property prices so that by the end of the century the children of the local residents have to look elsewhere for their houses as West Chiltington is too expensive for them. Initially the 'weekenders' probably made little impact on village life, bringing with them in their cars all that they would need, but as the properties were sold as permanent homes, local shops noticed the change as did the garage, and private preparatory schools were patronised or set up. The Roundabout development had been born, and other developments were to follow through the years, producing an influx of new residents that has contributed to the retention of our village school, garage and shops.

The West Chiltington and District Local Plan was brought out in early 1969. The Draft Plan was prepared by the County Planning Department and was the statutory map for the area used as a basis for development control. The idea was to retain the character of the villages covered, to restrict development to sites within the limits, and to restrict housing density to between 1½ to 4 dwellings per acre. The Plan stated that there was to be a programme of land release for housing development; housing for the next six years had already been given planning permission, the next release of land was to be after seven years, and then there were areas where development would not be permitted for at least fifteen years. The future rate of population growth was estimated to be 1.7% per annum, which would result in an increase of 520 persons by 1981.

Four sections were then covered: the first proposed that part of the woodland on West Chiltington Common should be retained in its natural state; that 27 acres bordering Hurston Warren should be shown as Public Open space with a small area for car parking and a note that part of the area is a Site of Special Scientific Interest; that the belt of trees to the east of Martlets Estate be covered by a Tree Preservation Order and that the extensive network of footpaths and bridleways should be rationalised and clearly signposted. The second section covered the proposal for designation as a Conservation Area of the core of the village, plus the Hollows and the Windmill. The third section covered the provision for additional shops on a site opposite the present shops in Haglands Lane, and for the new school site in East Street, and the final section covered roads, noting that 'none of the roads in the area is expected to carry sufficient volume of traffic to warrant any major alterations' but indicated suggested roads for future residential development.

This plan was displayed in the Church Hall on 7 and 8 May 1969, and objections could be sent to the clerk of the County Council.

In the 1980s the Government set up a Boundaries Commission to consider whether any changes to civic parish boundaries were desirable in view of the extensive house building that had been taking place since the end of the Second World War. Our parish is bounded by Pulborough, Billingshurst, Thakeham, Sullington and Storrington, and houses had been built in the outlying areas of some of these parishes, but the residents in

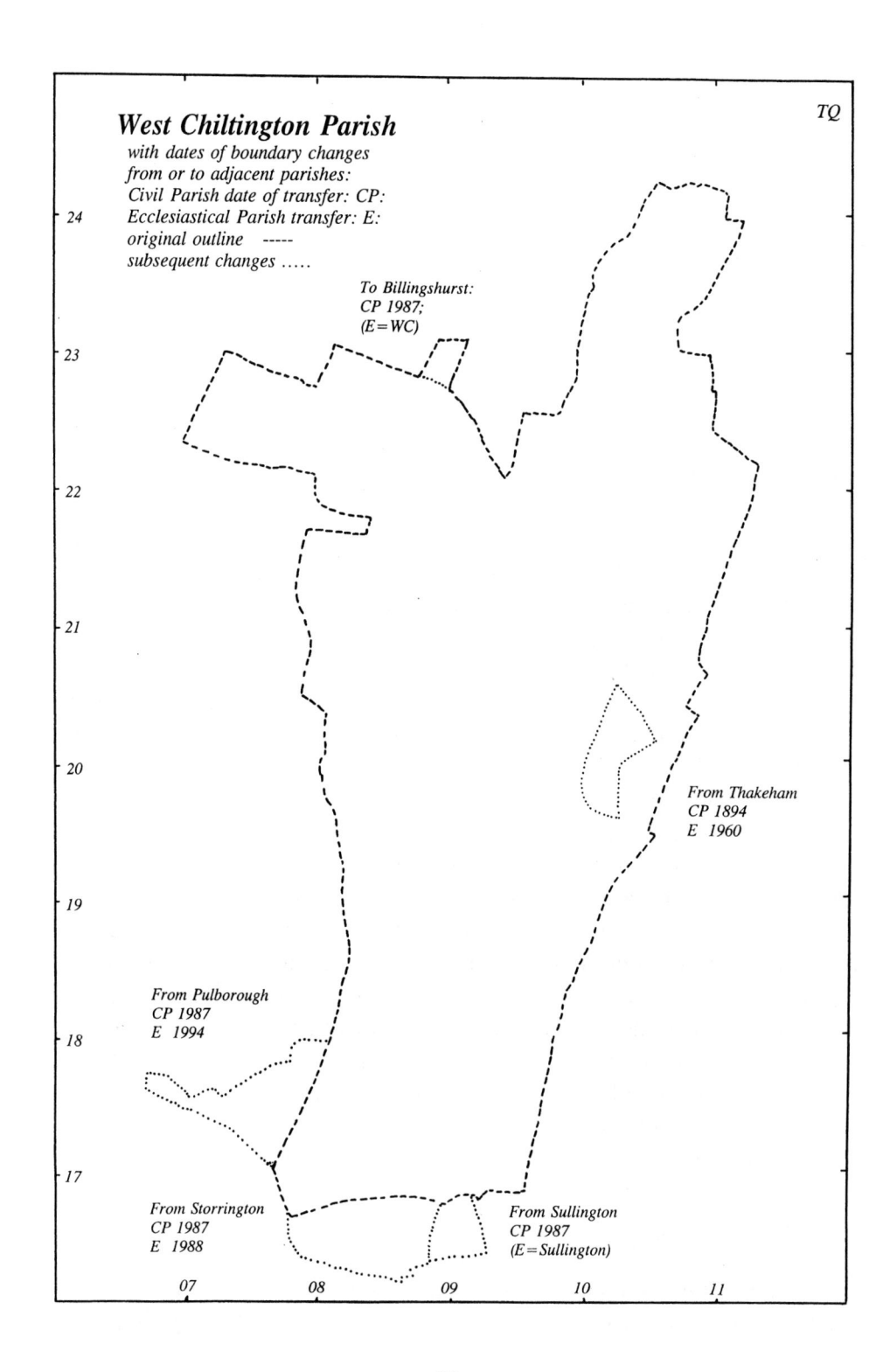

West Chiltington Parish
with dates of boundary changes
from or to adjacent parishes:
Civil Parish date of transfer: CP:
Ecclesiastical Parish transfer: E:
original outline -----
subsequent changes .....

To Billingshurst:
CP 1987;
(E=WC)

From Thakeham
CP 1894
E 1960

From Pulborough
CP 1987
E 1994

From Storrington
CP 1987
E 1988

From Sullington
CP 1987
(E=Sullington)

the south looked to West Chiltington as their natural centre. The Boundaries Commission therefore recommended that West Chiltington should include, for civil purposes:
A) From Pulborough Parish: the triangular section of land including Harborough Hill, Castlegate and Monkmead Lane
B) From Storrington Parish: Sunset Lane, Spinney Lane area
C) From Sullington Parish: Threals Lane, Grove Lane and Roundabouts area
D) They also considered whether Coneyhurst north of the A272 should be transferred to Billingshurst but the residents resisted the idea and only a small area of land further west, north of the B2133 was in fact transferred.

The parish boundary and its changes are shown on the map; this shows the old civil parish boundary plus the new intake areas.

The ecclesiastical boundaries have also changed: in 1960 the neighbouring parish of Thakeham was united with Warminghurst and at that time the Thakeham outlier, Cattlestone Farm wholly surrounded by West Chiltington parish, was transferred to the ecclesiastical parish of West Chiltington. Other changes took place later; these changes were effected by the Horsham (Parishes) Order 1986 which came into force in 1987, one consequence being that the number of parish councillors was increased to 13. This order affected only the civil parishes, but it made sense that the ecclesiastical parishes should also have the same boundaries; however, this required the consent of the respective Rectors and Parochial Church Councils. Storrington was in full agreement and the Sunset Lane area became part of West Chiltington in 1988.

The consent of the rectors of Pulborough and Storrington were not forthcoming at that time. However in the West Chiltington interregnum of 1993 the churchwardens were able to reach agreement with the new rector of Pulborough, so that the Harborough Hill area was transferred in April 1994.

The churchwardens were not successful with Sullington; although the new rector had no objection, his churchwardens had - on historical grounds. So that area remains in the ecclesiastical parish of Sullington, and any daughter of residents in this area who are not on the West Chiltington electoral roll should expect to be married in Sullington Church assuming she wishes to have a Church wedding!

The local geology is interesting and still influences how we use the land: at the southern end, from the village hall northwards up Gay Street to

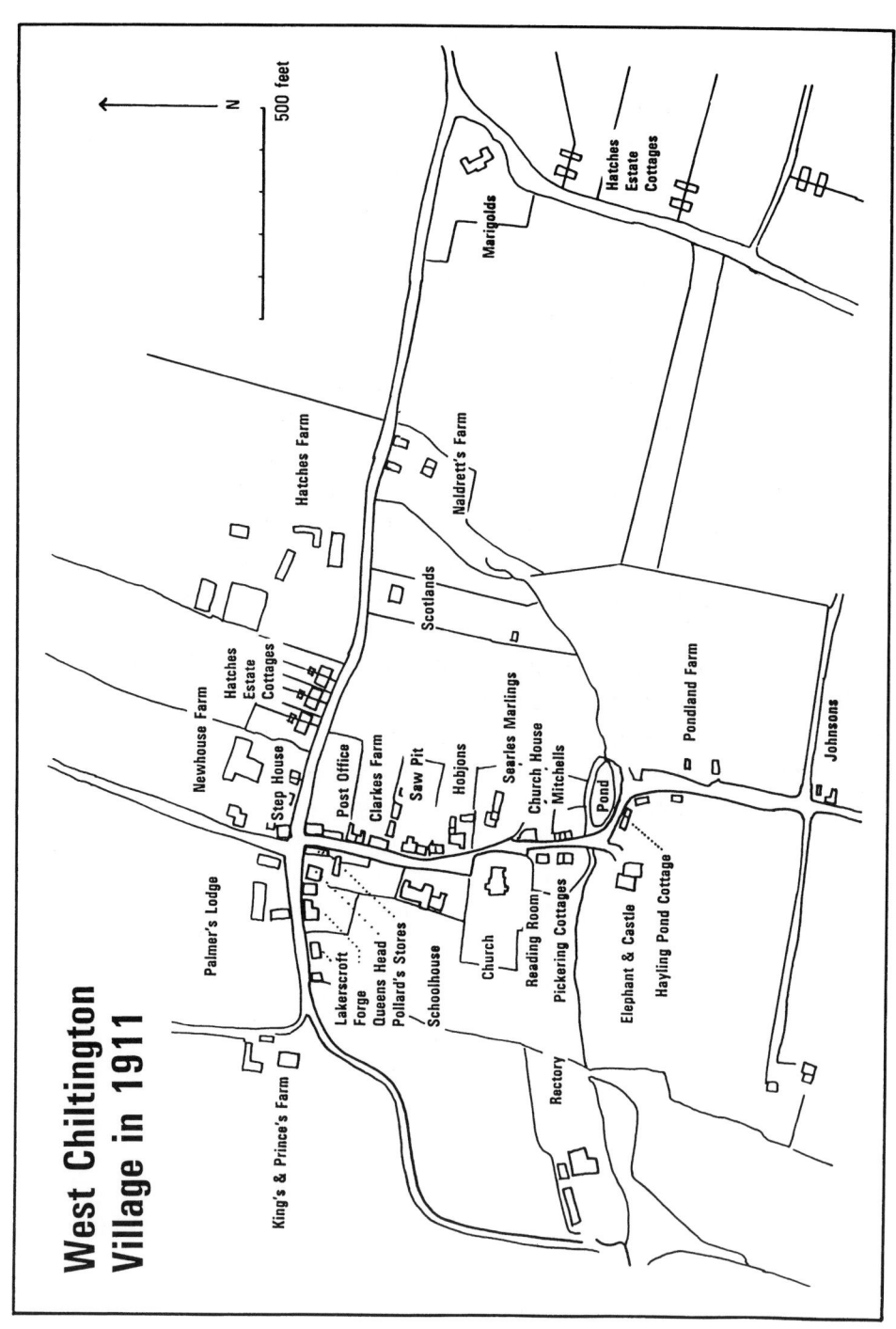

Village in 1911

Crowell Farm, and from Whales Farm north to Woodshill, the geological formation is the Lower Greensand Hythe beds giving highly productive land. Here are the orchards and strawberry fields, the vineyards and maize; good arable land cultivated for at least a thousand years. Land Sales Particulars from the 1920's list the apple trees, pear trees, strawberries, turnips and swedes being grown in various fields by various landowners.

Further north at Woodshill we can stand on the crest of the hill; to the south the South Downs are spread out from east to west, to the north the land falls away across the low Weald, across acres of green pasture, some arable, and every field fringed with oak trees and hedges, so that as the eye travels north the whole landscape seems to become one vast oak forest. Of course it is not a vast oak forest now as it was in Roman times when the Weald was Anderida. The northern part of West Chiltington parish is on the Weald clay; wet and stiff in winter, hard and dry in summer with wet ditches along the field edges. In this part of the parish there are dairy cows and beef animals, some sheep, and to the surprise of the modern walker, large numbers of alpaca! This part of the parish has seen the least change as Broadford Bridge and Coneyhurst have not expanded much. New bungalows and houses with temporary homes for farm workers have been built by some roads and near some farmhouses; the hovels and pigstyes of 1900 have been replaced by tower silos and huge prefabricated barns on some premises but on the whole the landscape would be very familiar to those who lived here in the last century.

Chapter 2

West Chiltington Village
The Street

Most of the village life centred around the cross roads by the Post Office and The Queens Head, and the road that is now called Church Street used simply to be The Street.

One of the earliest memories of the village is from Winifred Boyd (née Johnson) who left some writings of her early life: "I was born on December 25th 1909 in the house called Finches which was built in the sixteenth century by John Finch. Unfortunately a later owner thought it was named after a bird and re-named it 'Cleves Cottage' because of the Nyetimber connection with Anne of Cleves after whom the Queen's Head pub is also named. My parents were both from families of eight children,

The Village Cross Roads
This is one of the first photographs of the village

on my father's side the Johnsons and the Dukes, and on my mother's side the Figgs, and the Styles of Wiston.

There was no public transport, one walked, or later, rode a bicycle. A few people had a pony and trap, and I remember when there were only two cars: one at the Rectory and one at Voakes. The only tarred road was The Street (now called Church Street), the other roads were of flint and there was an old man who used to sit by the roadside breaking flints; every so often a steamroller came and rolled them in. It was very dusty in the summertime. There was no electricity or gas, just candles or paraffin lamps."

This theme is continued by Mrs Edith Pettitt (née Freeman) who gives a telling history of her early days in the village in 1910 "My parents lived at New House Farm, with all of us, six boys and six girls. My father was farm bailiff and managed the farm for a Mr Fladgate, he did a lot of the checking up to see that work was being done, rather than working on the land himself. My mother kept chickens, and I think she kept them for herself rather than for the farm; she did all the work and any money she made was hers. She also made butter in the dairy which was opposite the back door, which she sold along with the eggs, either in the village or at market. The farm was a general farm, and Dad would go to market in Pulborough or Steyning to buy and sell stock, and would either take Mum's produce or she would go herself if she wanted to go to the shops. Market day was a busy day. We grew all our own vegetables as everyone did, and when Dad killed a pig in the yard we would smoke it for bacon in the big old chimney from the kitchen range. We got our food as we needed it, so everything was very fresh or had to be preserved, it needed to be as we had no fridges!

All of us children went to the village school and I was told by my older brothers and sisters, though I don't know whether to believe it or not, that I was taken to school for the first weeks in a push chair! The only reason I can think of is that either I was very young, much younger than five, or I had something wrong with my legs. The boys and girls went into school through separate entrances, and we hung our coats up on numbered pegs. First there was prayers, an assembly it's called now, and we had religion, arithmetic, writing and reading; the headmaster, George Chad, did most of the teaching. We used books, but I can remember slates being around. The older girls did sewing, but I never got that far because we left the village just after the end of the Great War. One of my brothers went into farming, two of my sisters went into service, but the third down, she passed her exams and went to Steyning Grammar School and on to a two year teacher training course - I remember her as a pupil teacher.

There were a lot of children at the school, and although hoops were banned from the playground, we played with them in the road; there were no pavements then, we just played in the middle of the road. Out of school the older children in the family helped look after the younger ones, and we all had to take a turn with the jobs, the boys worked in the garden and we girls washed up and helped prepare the meals. We all sat down together for meals, we didn't start to eat until everyone had their plate in front of them, and we didn't dare speak! There was a lot of work in the house and we all had to help, I mean there were even open fires in all the bedrooms though we didn't light them very often. The coal came in from a shed, we didn't have a coal bunker, and we had a scuttle beside every fire. At harvest time everyone helped; the binder was pulled by the horses, as were the rakes, and we followed behind stacking up the stooks that had been tied by a machine. It was chokingly dusty work, and hard. During the Great War we had four German Prisoners of War who came from the big house in Ashington where they were being held, to work on the farm. Ethel, my older sister became quite friendly with them, though I don't know how they managed to communicate! I remember seeing soldiers in khaki home on leave in the village. The experiences abroad must have been a dreadful shock to them.

Sundays were all about Church. When we were little we went to Sunday School, and only into the church for the service when we were a bit older, the rector was Mr Caldecott. Once a year the Sunday School would take us by farm wagon to Bognor or Littlehampton, on alternate years, and the most important thing was to have enough pocket money for a 'hokey pokey', a very white ice cream in a paper wrapper. We talked about our day out on the beach with our bucket and spade for weeks, for this was almost the only occasion when we left the village. I'm 89 now, and have seen such a lot of changes."

Perhaps the most important building on this corner is The Post Office and Village Stores. Bill Hampton left school at 14 on a Friday in the really hot summer of 1921 and began work on the following Monday at the West Chiltington Village Post Office for which he was paid 12/- per week. He worked for Mr Robson for about $3\frac{1}{2}$ years, still at the same wage, delivering groceries, telegrams and paraffin round the village on his

The Street – 25 April 1908 – it snowed

bicycle with a big container on the front. Bill remembers "There were no tarmac roads they were just old flints, and after a vehicle had gone by you couldn't see for the dust! I'd get three or four punctures a week on the flints. Mr Robson sold out to Mr Gooch, who had a son, Stan. I stayed for three more months to let Stan take over my job; I remember a little chubby boy of about 14 years old, with knickerbockers. I was the first person Stan knew in the village, and he stayed for 40 years then!"

Edith Green was born in Laurel Cottage in East Street in 1934, and, after four years working at Melrose Stores, she started work at The Post Office. She tells her story: "I worked at the Post Office Stores for twenty four years until I retired four years ago; before that I was running the family's market garden. Everyone calls it Gooch's shop because it was owned for a long time by Mr Gooch (from 1924 until his death in 1929) and then by his son and daughter in law, Stan and Connie, from 1929 until 1969. In those days the substantial house next door and the shop were separate and you couldn't get through from one to the other, the Jiggle family lived in the house, so Mr Gooch had Kithurst built in East Street, although it was called Innisfree then. For his retirement he had the bungalow Charbury built, between Kithurst and the shop, on the land that went with the shop.

In the years I worked there there were four owners, I started with J and F G Thompson, who had bought it from Mr Gooch. The Thompsons made some major changes, the upstairs room which had been a stock room, was made into a bedroom and knocked into the house next door, which the Thompsons had also bought as it had become vacant. The house was modernised and they lived in it, but not for long as they left a year later, selling it to H and J Cousens in September 1970. During the four years they were there they also made alterations; they built a stock and store room on the back behind the ceiling beam running across the shop. Dibble, the harness maker of Dibble and Curtis, used to go there twice a week to collect the leather goods for repair. When the Cousens left in May 1974, they turned their old stock room into a house, called it Saddlers after Mr Dibble's work, and moved into it, selling the shop premises to D B and E A Taylor who stayed for eleven years. The Wyles were there fourteen years before they left in April 1999. It was they who moved the post office into its present position, that room used to be the office. They even have computers in the shop now." Don and Peggy Mathieson came to the Post Office in 1999, from Copsale in Sussex where Don had worked as an insurance broker with interests in the Far East. When the Japanese economy collapsed he changed careers and took a ten day course on Post Office management, followed by a further ten days 'on-site' practical course. He expects to put his own stamp on the shop as time goes on in order to maintain a vibrant and busy business.

Edith continues "In Stan Gooch's time there were two long old mahogany counters, which stretched down each side, with the post office being just inside the door, on the right. Stan was helped in the shop by Connie, otherwise there would have been much running backwards and forwards between the two counters; they also had Arthur Warren to help in the latter years because there were the orders to put up and deliver. Goods could be ordered by filling in the book and handing it in, or by asking the delivery boy to take it, or later, by telephoning the order; and the account could be paid monthly. The delivery service continues up to the present time." This wonderful emporium sold everything and people remember buying a quart of paraffin over the counter with the butter, the sweets and the tea - a gallon of paraffin, a pint of methylated spirits and a quarter of tea! What people also remember is what a tower of strength and advice Edith was to each new owner, and how "some of them would never have made a go of it if it hadn't been for her!"

During and after the first world war, one village resident has written that she remembered the post office savings scheme: as children they were encouraged to get a form on which to stick twelve penny stamps. When this was full it was surrendered and one shilling entered in one's Post Office Savings book.

As far back as anyone can remember it has always been a post office, and before the postman came round in a van he used to come on a push bike from Pulborough. In 1909 the Parish Council received a letter from the Postmaster at Petworth stating that 'in future, 12 hours a day will be regarded as the maximum attendance for public business at the more-important sub-post-offices.' In reply it was stated that the attendance at the Post Office be from 8am-8pm. This side of Picketty Corner there was a copse where the postman, Mark Lelliott had a hut, locally known as Mark's Hut, in which he used to make a cup of tea and have a rest, because by the time he got back to Pulborough from delivering the letters it was time to come back again and empty the letter boxes. He delivered to the house, and in the very early days before the houses had names he knew where everyone was because there were so few people living in the village. Edith ends by saying "Dad used to say that he himself knew everyone in the village by their walk, so even if it was dark he would still know who he was meeting even if he couldn't see them."

Stan Gooch and Customer – 1960s

The village is remembered in 1924 in this extract from the Parish Magazine of July 1978 written by Stan Gooch: "We have everything that makes an English community here - beautiful countryside, a lovely old Church with a modern Church Hall, a new Primary School, three pubs, a selection of shops, friendly people, and a Village Hall which is the envy of a lot of Sussex folk.

Fifty-four years ago when I arrived from London as a boy of 14, life was totally different. The only organisations then were the band, the British Legion and the WI. All social life took place in the Nissen hut by the Elephant and Castle in the Village - mostly whist drives (weekly during the winter), dances occasionally and Concert Parties annually, provided by local talent.

The Village was a small community consisting mostly of farm labourers and market gardeners. No running water, sewerage or electricity, no buses, a car rarely seen. One either walked or, if you were lucky, cycled. Horse and plough tilled the land, the scent of strawberries filled the air in Summer, flint roads, little housing between here and Storrington.

This was 1924 when we had come down from London for my father to become the Postmaster and Village Grocer. There was a small shop at the crossroads on the Common, and the Village forge and blacksmith next to the Queens Head in the Village - that was all.

The Village School next to the Church took care of the education of the child aged 5 to 14. There were four important people who controlled the village in their different spheres - the Village Squire (Col Kensington), the Rector (the Revd Andrew Caldecott), the School Master who lived in the School House next to the School (Mr Mills), and the Sub-Postmaster (my father). They knew the villagers. The villagers knew them and they all consulted one another on various problems.

In 1925 The Marquis of Abergavenny auctioned his property in West Chiltington. This consisted of the entire left hand side of the Village Street from the crossroads down to the village pond beyond the Church. This took place in the Corn Exchange in Pulborough, which no longer exists. My father bought the shop, house, outbuildings and ¾ acre garden for £750. This was a lot of money in those days but I can still see the look of delight on his face. In 1927 he installed an electric light plant which modernised the whole house and shop from paraffin to electric lamps (a minor miracle in those days).

In 1928, in a small back room behind the shop occurred another minor miracle - the first telephone exchange in West Chiltington was installed with fifty subscribers. In 1928 he died, in my opinion because of this exchange which necessitated him getting up at all hours of the night to answer the calls. I was thrown in at the deep end, and ran the business until 1969 during which time I watched the Village grow and change to what it is today." He was helped by Phil Slater, another eighteen year old, for the first six years until he joined the Post Office at Pulborough.

Stan Gooch's earlier thoughts are echoed by various residents who remember the village in the 1930s as being a vibrant and busy place with delivery men with their ponies and traps, "There was some traffic on the roads, carts taking produce to market, and delivery men visiting the houses and farms. Dibble and Curtis, the harness makers, used to come up from Storrington once a week and spend all day repairing shoes; the harnesses would be taken back to Storrington to mend. Terrys the bakers delivered from Nutbourne with a horse and cart, Killicks came from Pulborough, and three or four other bakers also delivered."

Joy Adams (née Pullen) was born on the Common and adds "In the 1930s we also had our bread delivered, from Stilwell's at Pulborough; he used to come round in his covered wagon with the horse. He would come every other day with newly baked bread. The newspapers arrived at Pulborough station and were delivered from there by push bike, but I can remember my mum getting very cross because sometimes when it was raining, the papers were wet. The daily paper cost a halfpenny but the Sunday one was twopence. We used to get our milk delivered from Southlands Farm and there was a big grocery store, apart from Greenfields in Storrington, called Ivan Kellets and Childs, nicknamed IKCs, who also used to deliver; they had branches in Worthing and Storrington (about 25-30 years ago they were taken over and are now incorporated into Bookers). They came round in a horse and trap to collect your order on a Tuesday and deliver on the Saturday. It was a big round and often my friend and I would ask for a ride up the road 'Yes, missy, get up and I'll drop you at the top of the road', so we had to climb this high step thing to get up onto the seat that was on top of his trap. That was the highlight of our day." Others can remember Harry Fielder coming round with a big bath of fish on his shoulder, ringing his bell to announce his arrival, on Tuesdays and Saturdays. The herrings, from Worthing, were a shilling for fourteen and the housewives would go out to him with their own dishes to put the fish in. In due course he acquired a van to make his deliveries easier.

Even in 1951 when Meg and Gerry Judd with their two small sons came to live in a Wells cottage on their return from South Africa the village had not yet begun its period of rapid change. Many of the firms were still delivering, although some had had to alter their pattern of work. "As Gerry commuted to London from Pulborough station I was left without a car so was very glad of the good delivery services, which included a dry-cleaning service. They used to come round on Tuesdays and bring the clothes back on hangers on Thursdays; full dry cleaning took a week, but just sponging and pressing only took the two days." said Meg.

The coalman delivered every week, as did the paraffin man who delivered the oil for the paraffin lamps. From his van he would fill large 4 or 5 gallon drums which were fitted with a pump so that a smaller, quart container could be used to fill the lamps. Mail order catalogues were popular; Williams from Manchester used to send a catalogue from which clothes were ordered and 'the tally man' then came round every week for the money until the item was paid for.

The post office was not the only shop: the private residence on the south-west corner of the crossroads, now called The Village House, was described in the Abergavenny Estate Sale of 1925, as Lot 28 'a Freehold Residence and Shop known as Pollards. The house and garden were let on a weekly tenancy, and the shop on a quarterly tenancy to Mr Jesse Johnson at an aggregate rent of £16.18s.0d.' There was the 'Shop with fireplace 14' 9" x 13' 4"; Living Room with range, oven and cupboard under stairs; Pantry with shelves; Scullery with fireplace, copper, sink and Semi-rotary Pump; Cellar; Four bedrooms. Outside:- Wood House; Privy; Kitchen Garden. Water is obtained from a Well on the Premises by means of a Pump in the Scullery.' This was the place remembered as Mrs Bessant's Shop, and Elsie Pullen, who lived at Lower Jordans, Gay Street, remembers that the shop fronted onto the cross roads but if Mrs Bessant had closed they would knock at the house door which was round the corner in Church Street and she would open for them. There was a big square window on each side and in the corner was a chair. She sold sweets, and on the counter were chocolates, with the groceries down one side. The village people patronised both shops and schoolchildren remember going to Mrs Bessant's shop to buy a pennyworth of broken biscuits and liquorice sweets called blackjacks. Alf Akehurst had run the shop before Mrs Bessant took it on; he had owned the butcher's shop previously. There is an old photograph of about 1920 showing the shop owned by Jesse Johnson, Harness Maker of Storrington. By the 1950s it was owned by Mr Rolf, but seems to have closed by the 1960s.

General Stores – 1967

The Queens Head and Forge – 1905
Challen was both harness maker and cycle engineer

Mr Dibble, of Dibble and Curtis, used to lodge with Mrs Bessant; it is possible that they used the premises next door as their shop. They subsequently moved to the house now called Saddlers.

The property above is described as having a frontage 'to the Main Street and return frontage to road leading to the Church' as if Church Street did not have a name at that time, and Main Street ran from the cross roads towards the Hollows. This is borne out by minutes of the Parish Council for 3 December 1946 when the Clerk reported that the Parish Council had been asked by the Rural District Council to prepare a schedule showing the suggested names and what the council considered to be suitable lengths of streets for naming in the Parish. A schedule and map were prepared but there was a unanimous vote against the proposal on the grounds of unnecessary expense and that, in a small village, no benefits would result. There was strong criticism of what was called 'urbanisation' of villages, and even the weight of the Postmaster at Pulborough failed to convince the Council. A minute for 12 March 1957 agrees to take no action to signpost the village streets. We are still fighting against creeping suburbia today!

Just down The Street, is Clarkes Cottage. Many of the properties have changed and it is not always easy to tell what has been before. Sally

Clarkes Cottage

Carrott who lives in Clarkes Cottage explains that her house has had a chequered existence; it was part of the Abergavenny Estate, and on the 1840 tithe map the place was called Clarkes Farm and was one house although the land was perhaps more of a smallholding than a farm. Then it became known as 'Clawks Cottages' as the one house was divided into two labourer's cottages, until finally it achieved its present name as one house again. The Carrotts have had to retain both front doors as they are both listed, but the house is most noteworthy for its twisted chimney which was taken down during house rebuilding but had to be reinstated. The Queens Head used to have a similar chimney, necessary to make the fire draw, but that one was also removed when the bar was extended and the fireplace built up to form a wall in the middle of the room. It would seem that these chimneys, although originally purely functional, were also decorative and were copied in this locale; there are known to be one or two in Henfield.

Various villagers recall The Street in the 1930s: next to Clarkes Cottage there is a new house called Barncroft which has been built on the site of an old barn which was demolished.

Next there was the entrance to P Slater and Sons Ltd (the builders) yard, reached over an ironstone cobbled pavement, which had taken over from the brick pavement in front of Gooch's. At the turn of the century Walter Duke had been the village wheelwright whose garden and orchard, where village children used to play cricket has been built over; he is also remembered as having a cider press where the local people made cider. In the 1920s Bill Puttock was the wheelwright who worked together with Slaters; the relationship was a useful one as Bill was also a carpenter. In 1937 Bill Puttock went abroad and his business was taken over by Philip Slater.

Just beyond the entrance to Wheelwrights is Hobjohns, a private house; this property had been owned by the Greens but was bought by Slaters, and also used to be two cottages. Mr Callaway lived in one end from where he ran his Prudential Insurance Company business. He would set out on his bike with his case and collect the money every week, nobody banked in those days because no one had any spare money; people were paid on Friday and spent it on necessities almost immediately, any spare going into a tin box. His son who was deaf and dumb, worked for Puttock from the age of 16, and continued to work for Slaters when they took over, retiring at the age of 65; the last village Wainwright, Wheelwright and Coffin Maker.

The other end of the property was occupied by Tom Adams who was the foreman at New House Farm, now Churchfield Farm.

> **GREYHOUND RACING**
> AT
> **WIMBLEDON STADIUM**
> EVERY TUESDAY & FRIDAY at 3 p.m.
>
> The Evenin
>
> FRIDAY, SEPTEMBER 29, 1939
>
> IT'S QUIET DOWN in this Sussex village, where the only sign of war is the presence of evacuated children.

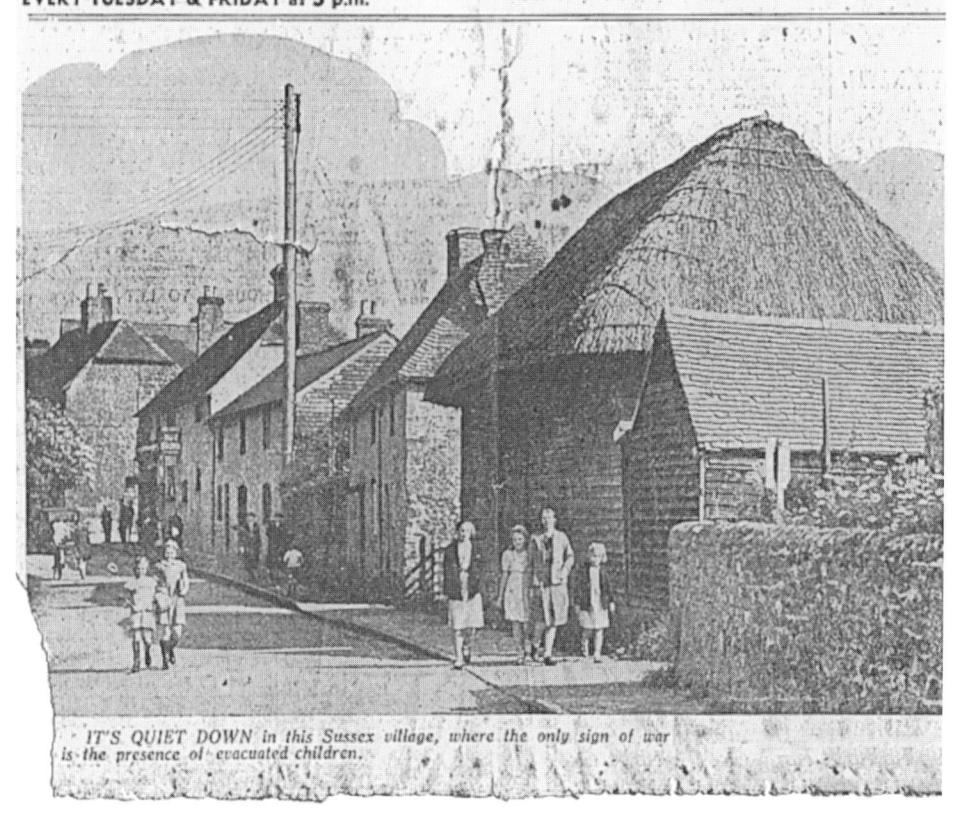

Church Street. The Barn – 29 September 1935

Continuing towards the Church is what is now called Stocks Cottage, but cottages used to be known by the name of the tenant, so this one was Brown's Cottage. No-one can now remember Mr Brown but in this century it was owned by the Greens and occupied by Billie Greenfield and Bill Rogers' families; it was Bill who drove the steam engines at the forge.

Opposite the Church entrance is Hobjohnscroft, now a hairdressers. At the turn of the century Bill Gumbrell had had the shop as a bakery and then as a pork butcher's but by the 1930s it was used as a general store; it was run by Mrs Kate Burchell, described as 'a funny old dear, very old fashioned'; her husband Sid left her to run the shop as he was a garden and farm worker. The children of the time remember going in for sweets although it was primarily a general store. In 1931, Mrs Kensington who lived at Voakes, founded a tiny museum which she housed initially in the old bakehouse at the rear of Hobjohnscroft; on payment of twopence the key could be obtained from a cottager who lived nearby. When Mrs Burchell died the store was taken over by Ted Charman, it, like much of Church Street being part of the Green's Estate at the time. Part of the shop, approached round the side, was used as a bicycle shop; Ted would mend bikes and sell bicycles, tyres and parts, latterly he added wellingtons and bits and pieces for the garden, and would charge the accumulators for wireless sets. Although it was rather small and cramped, the children were often invited in for a chat while the punctures were being repaired.

In 1959 the premises were rebuilt by Slaters and the lawn dug out; prior to this the property had been bounded by a 4' wall against the pavement, with a gate, behind which steps led up to the lawn and the path to the door.

Further down the hill, Searles Cottages have both been extended over the years; the Searle family first appear in the village records about 1300. In this century Bill Gumbrell lived in Number 2 having moved there from Lakerscroft in order to set up his bakery business. His son Tom, who had been born in the village about 1896, worked for Mr Meeten at the windmill as a carter before going on to general farm work and labouring at a local brickyard. He married Maud in 1919; she had been billeted in the village with the Land Army from London and had become friends with Tom's older sister; they lived in Number 1. Beryl Phippen, a WI member recalls "There's an old story that Tom told me about the time the hayricks in Juggs Field caught fire: it happened before the First War, when he was just a lad. One of the village boys was dispatched on his bike to Storrington to summon the Fire Brigade, but by the time the horsedrawn fire engine had arrived the ricks were just about burned down. To prevent the fire spreading, the pump was put into the village pond and the hosepipe taken up to the field. The firemen began to pump, and to encourage them the Chief stood by, shouting 'Pump yer buggers - pump… Pump yer buggers - pump…' and the lads of the village, standing around the pond all raised their voices and joined in wholeheartedly with the Chief's encouragement!" During his retirement Tom raised bedding plants for sale outside Searles Cottages and helped out on farms when required. Both he and Maud took care of the Church; for thirty years he locked it up every night and unlocked it every morning. He died in 1987 at the age of 90 and saw many changes in the village.

John Geal was the village snob (cobbler) in the 1920s. He lived in the western end of Searles from where he ran his cobblers, and he also rang the church bells.

The fig tree that was bearing figs in the 1930s is still healthy and fruitful in the front garden.

Pickering Cottages were occupied by Mercy Charman in Number 1 and Mr and Mrs Stoner in Number 2 after they had left Searles. The houses replaced an older cottage on the site, called Ledgegetters, and had been built for the use of the verger and sexton, by the Marquis of Abergavenny, and named for the Rector of that time, the Reverend J H Pickering (1872-1898); they appear from the outside to have hardly changed over the years. Mrs Charman was the church cleaner until 1905, when her daughter Mercy took over; for some fourteen years she had helped her mother with the cleaning. In 1926 the Parochial Church Council decided to pay her £1 extra a year for spring cleaning, and to stamp her insurance card at the cost of 1/1d per week. She retired at the end of 1947 in her eighties, when ill health forced her to stop. Mercy is remembered standing by her gate wearing a white lace apron, which always looked immaculate no matter what work she had been doing; her hair was done in a bun tied with a big velvet bow. For many years Dick Green lodged with Mercy.

Number 2 Pickering Cottages has had a succession of tenants and was often occupied by the Church gravedigger, most notable of whom was Marshall (Taffy) Horlor who had married Kitty Stoner. He had come to the village as an out-of-work Welsh miner and was employed in the Laybrook brick yard. He was a large man in every way: he drank hugely and sang superbly, was large in bulk and strong, being able to dig a grave in only a couple of hours, less than half the time it usually took. It is said he went one day to the fair in Storrington and pitted himself in the boxing booth against a professional boxer whom he knocked out in the first bout, so was not allowed to compete in future years!

Mr Tanner, another gravedigger lived in Pickering Cottages; he was followed by Frank Pullen. During the Second World War a Special Constable from London lived there.

These cottages had no hot water facilities or indoor sanitation, but in the 1950s the Church had no resources with which to rectify this so they were finally sold, still unmodernised, in 1960.

Beyond the pond the lane continued south; on the corner of Church Street and Juggs Lane is a pair of cottages, the Greens lived in one and Henry Geal and his family lived in the other. Opposite, on land known as

Johnsons Farm, there was a caravan where two men lived; one, Bill Pannell is remembered as being the tuba player in the village band, (his father Jack was the original drummer, succeeded some years later by Bert Ruff). The other was Charlie Puttock. On the opposite corner was Charles Winton's caravan; he had lived at East Wantley but sold it and bought the cabbage field that is now Holly Close. He lived here in a caravan while his bungalow was being built; this was the only property on that corner at that time. His land finished at the end of the original six bungalows, beyond which was Barnes Farm Field, used initially for strawberry growing. That is where Curbey Close, on the old maps called Curvey Croft, was built, prior to that it had been farmland owned by Mr Greenyer.

Hayling Pond Cottage has been extended. The Green family used to own it and Tom Downer lived there with his step-sister Lou Parsons (after Mr Downer died his widow remarried a Mr Parsons). Mrs Downer is remembered as a dressmaker.

Sarah Jane Bristow, Edith Green's paternal grandmother, was born in the village in 1869 and is buried in the churchyard. She married William

The Green Family outside Holland Cottage – autumn 1901
From left: WH Green, Dick Green, Bill Jr, Jim Green, Emily Green,
Sarah Jane Green, Alma Green

Henry Green and their six children were born in the village; George the fourth son, being born in Holland Cottage opposite the pond (now called Acorn Cottage). It seems that the pond was called both Holland pond and Hayling pond by different people in the village at that time. Edith (Jr) now lives at Juggs Cottage on the corner of Juggs Lane and Church Street, with her mother Edith, who married George in 1930. George and Edith lived first in Gay Street, but eventually moved to Laurel Cottage in East Street where, she says: "water came from the well, by pump, but the well was in next door's garden, not every house had its own. The bath was a tin affair in front of the fire, and the water was heated by a little boiler beside the old black kitchen range. The room was lit by paraffin lamps, which became very useful just after the war when we had all those power cuts. I used to make all the children's clothes with material bought from Storrington or Worthing; we used to go in on the bus, which in the 1950s ran once an hour. There was a double decker bus service which ran every day from Pulborough to Worthing with relief double deckers waiting on a Saturday at The Common because it would nearly always be full by the time it had been from Pulborough up to here. It hardly seems possible now, does it, that we needed relief buses. There were so few cars that the children used to play in the street at the cross roads quite safely. By the time Edith (Jr) was two, we had moved to Juggs Cottage. Colonel Kensington had the pair of Juggs Cottages built, and he also owned Laurel Cottage."

At first George Green worked for the Greenfields at Kings and Princes, as his father's market garden could not support both George and his older brother Dick. Eventually William Green left the market garden business to his sons, and George left Greenfields. Edith (Jr) explains about one aspect of land management: "Grandad used to own about 17 acres of land round here, all we've got left now is the original piece that he started with. What they now call Fly Farm, or Sinnocks Field, used to be owned in strips, a bit like allotment plots, and as each strip became available Grandad bought it so that in the end he had sufficient for a market garden." (This practice of farming in strips goes back to mediaeval times; the name is derived from Middle English-'innocks' meaning 'to take into cultivation'. It suggests a 13th or 14th century date for inception.) The Green brothers are remembered by many in the parish for their quality garden produce, sold and delivered around the village. Dick was well known for something else too, he sang country songs and sang them once on the wireless. Edith continues "After Grandad had died, my father and uncle took over the business until they too

Bill Green – between late 1800s and early 1900s

retired so I took over. I managed as best I could, but it was too much so I had to give up; unfortunately we didn't make enough money to be able to afford paid help and it was too hard for one person. Like everyone else in market gardening we had no guaranteed price for our produce; we could take a load to the wholesaler and if it didn't sell you got nothing. All your time and effort for nothing. We grew peas and beans, cabbages, lettuce, and lots of soft fruit, and Grandad's apples and pears. When I walk up to the shop from home here in Juggs Cottage sometimes I think of how it used to be, with the trees and the pond there. I remember there used to be a walnut tree; old Mr Gumbrell sat on a seat under it, and I loved scuffling through the leaves in the winter because they all scrunched. You didn't have to worry about dogs mess either because you never used to see any, the farm dogs stayed on the farms, there were more fields for them to use, and no one walked dogs. Dogs worked, like we all did. Then there were Gran's ducks, the white ones, swimming on Hayling pond. Although there were fewer people in the village in those days, there were far more shops and, because there were fewer people, everyone was more friendly. Nobody ever used the front door, everyone came in the back. Many of the cottages in Church Street which are now one house used to be two cottages; Clarke's and Stocks; and Step House was two cottages with two back doors but only one front door, as was Palmers. The other thing was that we didn't need to put the house names up, everyone knew where everyone else lived, and the cottages were often called after the people who lived there.

Opposite here, at the bottom of Juggs Lane, Grandad owned a field which used to have a two-up-and-two-down cottage called Johnsons, and some stables for the cart horses who also used to pull the plough and work in the fields. The cottage fell into disrepair and was demolished many, many years ago, and the stables fell down having become redundant. This field was the first that Grandad Green bought, and he planted an orchard of fruit trees and cob nut trees there, some of which are still standing and producing. A lot got blown down in the hurricane of 1987, but there are still one or two up there, which must be about a hundred years old by now. There's a cider press left up there too from the time when we used to make cider from the windfalls." (The Sales Particulars of 1906 show 'Johnson's otherwise Dyer's as a dwelling house with 2 front sitting rooms, large kitchen with range, scullery with copper and sink, pantry with good cellerage below, First floor has three bedrooms one fitted with stove. In the garden is a small timber and tiled coal house, and a privy.' Johnson's is the south-east corner of Juggs Lane and Church Street; Johnson and Pondlands (now Pond Rise) were once called Dyers, and it is possible that the name came from the tanning ponds that were below Naldretts.)

"Pond Rise has been built on part of our land, the other part of Pond Rise land we used to rent, but it wasn't ours to sell - the owner did that. We didn't get a lot for it even though it was building land because it is only recently that land prices have gone up so much. The road Pond Rise is so called because it is where the old village pond used to be, and the field behind the pond was called The Cucumber Field. All the fields had names and some of them can be remembered: Rocky Lane was the extension of Church Street, with Little Rocky and Big Rocky fields on one side and along the bottom. Even if the names have stayed the same, the roads have sometimes 'moved': Sinnocks Lane bent round at the top and continued down what is now known as Juggs Lane, until it met Church Street."

George and Dick Green had an unmarried sister, called Cis, who lived with her mother in Holland Cottage. She had had a job in London for three years but had returned to the village to look after her mother whom she nursed for 21 years. Although she would help with such tasks as fruit picking for the market garden the city experience had given her a taste for clean finger nails and a lady's life, and she was very different from her brothers. Her real moment of fame came in February 1958 when she won a competition in the Daily Sketch entitled 'If Only I had the Chance'. She

Mrs Green and Cis – 1920s

Holland Cottage and Pickering Cottages – about 1910
Those are quince trees behind the pond, and the trees out of view in the foreground were 100" tall

had written 'I've never had a party and if only I had the chance, I would give one for all the grandfathers of our village.' The party was held at the New Hall and 45 grandfathers arrived, to be greeted by Cissie for an afternoon of tea and entertainment. (There have been three main village halls in this century, they are discussed further in Chapter 8.)

The village pond was a necessary focal point for the village; here the big cart horses used to stop, drink and wash the working-day's accumulated soil and dirt off their legs by walking round and round in the water. It is remembered by many, many people, surrounded by white posts and used by children, dogs and horses. The stream, a tributary that ran into the river Nut, begins behind Naldretts and flowed into the pond from a waterfall; this constant stream of clear water allowed the most delicious watercress to grow wild for people to take home. There were stepping stones which enabled water to be drawn. With the rose tints of memory the schoolchildren of the time remember collecting the eggs from the ducks that swam there (a war-time evacuee girl remembers that if she found a duck's egg near the pond, she could take it to one of the cottages nearby and would be given a penny for it), and picking the watercress that flourished on its edges. The water then ran out beside what is now the drive into the Church car park continuing on its journey to the Hollows; at this point it flowed into a dipping well that the children fondly

The Pond and Hayling Pond Cottage
The haystack is where The Juggs is now

remember as the wishing well; it is described as being round, made of brick, with a slab of Horsham stone on the top; it was only about a foot deep as the stream ran through it. You could dip your hand into the slot and drink the clear spring water; it must have been a sizeable gap because Joyce Duffin remembers sitting young Bernard Crabb in the water! This well was situated to the right hand side looking up the drive of the house called Lavenham in The Hollows and was formed by Ned Slater in about 1880 over a spring that was the source of water for Gadds Cottages and the cottages at the Mill corner. It is thought that it was still there until the early 1960s.

Unfortunately, when the Water Board sank the bore at the Smock Alley water works in the 1960s some of these natural springs dried up as the water table fell.

The Dipping Well

In the 1930s the pond is remembered by two schoolchildren of the time: "We used to spend a lot of our lunch times down there and it was interesting because one of the old workers from the surrounding farms would come along with his horse and cart and he would go into the Elephant and Castle for a pint while the horse would wander into the middle of the pond with his cart still attached. The cows used to come down from Knowetop, too, meandering all over the road, and into the pond, and then wander back again. All along the back were these big Aspen trees rustling in the wind, and there were coots and moorhens."

"The pond came out to the present kerb line; there was a bank at the eastern end which had lovely daisies, it was really beautiful. The spring that fed it passed under the road that went into the field (which is now Pond Rise) and came out of a culvert to form a waterfall about three feet high in front of the aspen trees. On the northern boundary were quince trees hanging over from the garden of Searles; the Gumbrell family used to pick the fruit in waders, and in a boat. We used to sit on the bit of grass beside the pond and watch the Green's ducks, and sometimes we'd find an egg and give it to Mrs Green. The Green's market garden was up behind there, and so was the school garden where they taught us how to garden. My brother used to spend more time in that garden than anyone else! Some of the produce went to Harvest Festival at the Church, but I'm not sure what happened to the rest, we didn't need it because we had such a big garden at home. In those days we didn't grow flowers, just fruit and vegetables."

Unfortunately the Parish Council records show a slightly different picture: at a Parish Council meeting in 1913 complaints were made regarding the smell arising from the pond owing to the neglect of cleaning it out, a problem exacerbated by no-one appearing to know to whom the pond belonged. It was not until November 1915 that the situation became clearer when a letter from Mr Thomas Greenfield was received which stated that Holland Pond was part of his Pondland Tenement, that he was the present owner and that the property was life-hold in the Manor of Chiltington. Twenty eight years later, in 1943/4 problems with the pond were still being raised regarding its cleansing and the clearance of rubbish deposited therein. The condition of the pond continued to deteriorate and in May 1949 the Parish Council approached Chanctonbury Rural District Council with a request to *'remove the present eyesore of the Village Pond'*, because as the pond was probably on private property it had no authority to do this. Discussions of ownership continued until 1954 when the Parish

Council asked the RDC to clear up the matter once and for all. The problem was solved for them when in January 1956 a planning application was submitted for a proposed bungalow with an entrance across what used to be the old pond; there were no objections to the plan and it was hoped that an eyesore would be remedied as a result. By the end of 1966 the land, formerly the site of Hayling Pond was owned by the RDC; weeping willows were planted and the laying out of the site was completed in March 1967. In 1990 following a request from the Parish Council, Horsham District Council agreed to transfer ownership of Hayling Pond Green to the Parish Council for the sum of £1 plus legal fees; the occupiers of Braeside and Mitchells have a right of way over the land which cannot be used for any other purpose than *'amenity open space commonland for the enjoyment of the public at large and shall forever be kept as land open to the sky.'*

Which perhaps illustrates the fact that we are liable to romanticise the pleasant parts of our childhood experiences.

For many years the southern edge of the village was New House Farm, now Churchfield Farm. The earliest memory here comes from Elva Lipscombe who tells of a prank her father and one of his cousins got up to: their grandfather, Francis Figg, who lived at the farm was very fond of his nightly drink at the Elephant and Castle, so one winter night the lads put a sheet of ice from the water butt on the privy seat. They then hid behind some bushes until grandfather came home and they had the satisfaction of hearing his yell as he sat on the ice!

Later days are remembered by Joan Marlow: "In 1936 my family moved up from Goring when my Grandfather Greenyer bought New House Farm, which is not to be confused with New House Dairy Farm which is at the cross roads in the village. His land at Goring had been compulsorily purchased by the Council, and he and his son and daughter liked New House Farm as the fields faced south. Aunt May and Uncle Ernie Greenyer lived in the farmhouse, while grandfather built the two New House Cottages, one for himself and his wife, and the other for my parents Sybil and Cyril Hawkins, and me; the house which I still occupy. At that time, the field opposite (which was later developed as Holly Close) was owned by the Wintons who lived in a bungalow there, otherwise there were no other houses around. Grandfather grew a little of everything because in those days you grew something all through the season so that you had something to sell and an income all the time. We grew corn and all root crops, and Father took a lorry down to Worthing three times a week to sell fruit during and after the war. When Grandfather died the farm was left to my Uncle Ernie Greenyer, but unfortunately he only lived for a few years and it was sold to Mr and Mrs Champ and it was they who changed the name to Churchfield Farm. They converted the land from nurseries and a smallholding, and ran a successful Jersey dairy business for 10 to 12 years; they also extended the house.

Grandfather had also left a field (the one where Curbey Close is now) to my father, Cyril Hawkins, so in the 1950s Father decided to go into pigs because he had always been interested in them. During the war when things were short, we had kept a pig and boiled up the scraps to feed it. If I remember correctly, the government allowed us to keep one pig for our own use but a householder couldn't turn this into a business. When the pig was killed, as there were no freezers in those days, my father used to preserve the meat by rubbing salt into the flesh and hanging it in the larder (which is where my front door is now!) which was north facing and quite cold. It kept well. Mother used to salt beans into layers to keep them, and we pickled the eggs from the chickens we kept; father kept rabbits so we used to have rabbit once a week. Country people managed quite well for food, we were lucky because we also had the garden next door as extra space and we had all the fruit and vegetables from the farm. There were extra rations for the farm workers at harvest time, cheese and things, and people used to barter their rations; we didn't have sugar in tea or coffee but Pat opposite did, so they had our rations of sugar, and we had something of theirs.

Anyway, to get back to the pigs, there was nothing on the field when Father got it so he built styes for the sows, and a huge barn with an outside run where the young ones were kept. Gradually he built more styes, collected more equipment, and improved the site; at first he didn't have paths so he built concrete ones so that the wheeled bin with the food didn't keep getting stuck, and he didn't get so dirty. The pigs were part free range and rooted around on the ground in the field; they never had rings in their noses to stop them digging but they couldn't dig their way out as the styes were concrete. Forage was supplemented by meal from Muddles at Ashington and by scraps; Father had started with a small boiler when he had just the one pig and boiled up potatoes and scraps. Then he started getting contacts with different hotels and collected the swill from Roundabout Hotel and Abingworth and as far as Worthing; he collected twice a week and towards the end of the war he added the Canadian and

Polish camps to his list. In the beginning he had had a little Ford Prefect with a trailer to carry the bins for the swill, but we had a few snowy winters and it was pretty difficult. When he got the swill back it had to be boiled, partly to sterilise it; the little boiler was followed by a huge steam one which bubbled away for about an hour until everything was cooked through. All sorts went into it, vegetables, meat, bones and meal, and he had a contract with Knowles the bakers from Worthing which added bread and cake. There are some people in the village who remember collecting acorns for the pig during the war as children, and I expect that went on for a bit, too. The boiler room was warm and we collected about a dozen stray cats who came for the heat and the scraps, but were also useful in keeping the rats down.

The pigs aren't mucky like some people think, they soil in the corner and keep the rest clean, I've watched them fluff up their straw to make a bed just as I would do with a pillow. Father understood pigs and loved them, he would cherish them and nurse them. He could give them injections and that sort of thing when necessary, but not medicines to make them grow, which is why the meat was so good. He wouldn't hurry them, if they weren't ready for market he'd wait another week until they were. At first he took them live to Steyning market at a certain size and then he got a contract with the Horsham Bacon Factory; he would say 'I've got a hundred pigs ready' and they would come and collect them in a large lorry and take them away for slaughter. Towards the end he kept a boar, which was so gentle because he had never been shouted at or mishandled, but before that he used to borrow a boar which he used to collect in a trailer from a lady. Nowadays of course, there's AI. He would help with the farrowing and put the little piglets under infra-red lamps to keep warm, taking away the tiny ones to hand feed. The sow would just flop down for the piglets to feed, and she was so huge and the piglets so small that sometimes she did squash them, but we never used those iron cage things. It was sad if we lost a piglet but we just accepted it as the way of life, just as father, who loved his pigs, could send them off to market.

He had hundreds towards the end, but it was a seven-day-a-week job and Mother used to say that they couldn't come for Christmas or have holidays because he couldn't get away. He worked until he was seventy and then the offer came up that they wanted the land for building which was fortunate because Mother was in ill-health by then as well. The money that he made by selling the land to Federated Homes to build Curbey Close (it was they who took away the old hedge that divided the two fields that ran Holly Close into Curbey Close) allowed him a retirement because the pigs didn't make him that much; he'd started in a small way, from scratch, and everything he made was ploughed back into the pigs. It was funny when the land was sold - there was this huge pile of pig manure that the builders thought was marvellous and took home with them! That land must be pretty good for growing on, up there. Because Father didn't have any extra land to spread his manure on, he had someone come to take it away I think. He had a long retirement which was nice."

Chapter 3

West Chiltington Village From the Cross Roads

Much of the northern and eastern edge of West Chiltington parish was in the last century owned by Lord Zouche, owner of Parham. Hatches Estate comprised Hatches and Park Farms, Southlands and New House Dairy Farm. Between 1895 and 1905 the Hatches Estate had four owners, the last being Mrs Walter Fladgate with her husband, and mother Rebecca Harris. Over the years they acquired other pieces of land including Danhill Farm (Thakeham), plus Stanfords Farm in West Chiltington parish (on Harbolets Road), and a couple of other small plots. In 1916 Fladgate apparently owned Willetts Farm, in that he was leasing it for 5 years to Thomas Evershed, but this did not form part of the sale in 1920.

Bill Hampton is now in his 90s, and remembers his time as a boy working at Hatches in East Street: "Mr Freeman was the manager and I

Hatches Cottages in East Street – 1907

used to get a shilling pocket money from him while I was still at school, for the work I did on the farm. I started there when I was about eight, in 1915, because Mother, who lived up at Woodshill and Mrs Freeman were friends. I put in a lot of time up there while I was at school, and at weekends; we never worked on Sundays if it could be helped, except to collect two wagon loads of sheep for market at Steyning or Pulborough the next day.

Up on the Estate we were called in the morning when it was still dark in the winter. One of Mr Freeman's sons who had stayed at home managed the calf suckling herd; we had to take the bucket over there and he'd milk out nearly a gallon of milk to go back to the house, then he'd let the calves out for suckling and we would have to stand there to ensure the cows didn't knock the calves away. On other occasions Albert Freeman, who was Freeman's youngest, and I would spend the day ferreting, often right down at the far end of the estate. I used to enjoy the shooting days when I was beating; we'd get a good lunch! I longed for the time when I could carry my own gun, which I did do eventually. I bought my gun from Birmingham, sent away for it.

Albert Freeman ran the place. After Mr Harris had bought it the Freemans moved round the corner to New House Farm and that was where I used to spend my holidays and spare weekends.

We had eleven horses on the Hatches Estate that had to be fed, and all the cows. We only sold milk, didn't make any butter - Willetts did that. I can remember the separators up at Willetts screaming away; they made a terrific noise. We had a 5 hp oil-burning engine that ran the pump for the water, and a power line going through with a mill to grind the oats, wheat and barley, for feed. Everything was produced on the farm except the maize which we bought in. As I was a few months older than the others I had the job of bagging them up and standing the bags back at the end of the mill while someone else was on the cake crusher. That was for the linseed cake which we put between the two lots of rollers. We'd mix three parts linseed cake to one of cotton cake, and also, during the wartime, there was black treacle came in for the cattle, and dates, lots of dates, oh great packs of dates for cattle feed. Well we had seven cattle yards. The cows were all brought in for the winter, taken off the meadows so they didn't ruin the grass through the wet weather.

The sheep were also folded over for the winter; they had swedes, turnips and rape to eat. The sheep would often leave pieces of turnip on the ground, which would grow; we called them kilk. These kilk would flower at the same time as the corn that was planted in the field after the sheep had left, and it was the job of four of us boys to pull the kilk out of the corn because the threshing machine couldn't tell the difference between turnip seed and corn seed. We always had Southdown sheep and sometimes we had to help the shepherd drive them. We always went to Findon Sheep Fair and would walk the new sheep back from the Fair if Mr Freeman went there and bought some. Hurdles for the sheep pens were made on site with our own hazel, and we made all our own faggots from our own coppiced wood. At Christmas we were up early in the morning to drive four fat bullocks with horns to Pulborough market before we went to school, and if our bullocks took a prize we got part of the drover's prize from the auctioneer at Newland Tompkins and Taylor. Sometimes we had to stop until the cattle were sold and then drive them under the archway to put them on the train to butchers all over the place. Mr Freeman's son Bill was a butcher in Eastbourne, so I expect some went there.

At haying time there had to be a man and a boy and I usually had to be on the front of the wagon with the man loading at the back. It's quite easy to do if you have two good pitchers each side, they can do all along the side of the load and all I had to do was to tie that one in, and tidy that side, and fill up the middle until it got right up high. Mr Freeman's twelve year old daughter used to drive Polly, who was hitched to a sort of milk float thing, to Sandgate Camp to pick up the four or five German Prisoners of War who worked on the farm doing a lot of the pitching of the hay. Bruno was one I remember, he always came, and was a very educated man who could speak perfect English. We got on really well with them and during our lunch hour we would play games with them - sort of mounted tug of war where I 'rode' Schwier and Albert 'rode' Bruno 'Pull him off! Pull him off!' the men would shout. They had food brought out to them for lunch and were better off out of the war. They were good fellows, yes, and I was sorry I lost touch with them. The day the Armistice was signed I was working with them; in fact that morning, that Saturday on the 11th hour of the 11th day of the 11th month I was loading mangles up into the carts with them to be taken over to the farm buildings for the winter feed, when the church bells started. The men went, and we never saw them again. I would have loved to know how they were, and some 25 years later, during the Second World War, when I saw our bombers streaming out, loaded up, I hoped none of our bombs were destined for Bruno and Schwier. We were only ten or eleven, just children, and never thought to ask about their families or life in Germany; now I'm older, I wish I had, but children don't think like that."

The next time the property was on the market was in 1920. Walter Fladgate had died, his widow was selling the collected properties of Hatches and Park Farms, Southlands and New House, Danhill in Thakeham with Stanfords in West Chiltington. The purchaser was West Sussex County Council which bought the land for smallholdings, dividing the estate into its constituent farms. Schedules were prepared showing the state of the fields as left by the outgoing farmer; over the 3 farms there were seven fields of root crops (swedes, mangolds and turnips) which followed cereal crops the previous year, kale in two fields and tares and rape in another, all after barley or clover or peas in 1919. A number of fields were freshly sown with young seeds; there were eight fields of wheat and also listed were nine hay stacks, four being of meadow hay, two more of first cut hay, two of second cut hay. Galvanised iron water troughs in many places, the sack hoist and pulleys in the granary, even the fittings for the roller blinds in the house were itemised. The date fixed for completion had been 11th October but because the harvest in 1920 was late the sale was postponed to 14th and 15th of October and the County Council was not going to get possession until the 18th. An interest rate of 6% was to be charged for the delays.

WSCC began selling up the estate; in 1922 155 of acres of what had been New House farmland was sold as 'High Barn buildings and farmland'. High Barn formerly existed on the highest spot above the village but only the ruined barn can now be seen. However, Hatches House, five bedrooms and assorted outbuildings, was not considered suitable for a smallholder so that was sold separately for £2000 being purchased by William Clarke of Ewhurst, Surrey for the benefit of his wife Mary and his four children: two military sons, an unmarried daughter and Mrs Lillian Mary Kensington of West Chiltington. Villagers remember Hatches was later owned by Mr and Mrs Ritchie; they were 'gentry' and determined that the public should not use the private right of way across their fields to Knowetop Farm. Hatches has since been turned into two, with all of the farm buildings converted to homes most of which incorporate the word 'Granary' in their names.

Bill says that the County Council was very forward thinking in its investments. There was money to invest in the smallholdings from the rents, and money to be raised by selling the land off eventually. Bill remembers that some of Hatches meadows that were used for hay were sold off to Willetts Farm, and Harbolets Wood at the bottom of the meadow is now a livery yard.

Hatches Cottages were occupied by smallholders; many were local people. Mr Tipper the fishmonger used to live in one; he would go round the village calling "Thirteen a Bob, Thirteen a Bob" (13 fish for a shilling) and had an old van in which he came up from Worthing where he had bought the fish. He came from London, an ex 1914-18 war veteran who had lost a limb in the Royal Flying Corps. The second war put an end to his business as there were no petrol coupons for him, and he became a postman.

At the break up of the Estate, Bill then twelve, next earned his pocket money of 2/6d working for Bill Grace on Saturdays. Mr Grace owned a part brick building and two railway carriages on his land where Castlegate is now. When he reached fourteen, Bill left school and got a full time job at the Post Office. By the time he was eighteen he had gone to work for Gochers at Gentle Harry's Farm; he and his mother were already living in Gentle Harry's Cottage. Eventually he moved on to rent the field behind Naldretts, and met Mervyn and Pauline Webb. He lived in his caravan there with his little dog, "a Jack Russell bitch, which was the prettiest little thing you ever did see; she had a brown saddle mark, brown back against the tail and a brown and white face, and she used to sleep in the same bed as me!"

Opposite Hatches is the Rectory, beyond which is the house Scotlands. This is a large property which had been sold by the Abergavenny Estate on 9 July 1923, and was described on the Sales Particulars housed at the West Sussex Record Office, as 'very desirable small detached country residence and garden known as 'Scotlands'. Porch, hall, dining room, drawing room, cupboard, kitchen with range and oven, scullery, pump for well water, larder, three bedrooms, washhouse, store, stable, coach house and hovel, fowl house, nearly one acre.' Included in Scotlands boundary there was also a small cottage made from the stabling and the coach house, and orchards and woods. The main house, built about 1889, has the Abergavenny coat of arms on it because it was used by the family, it is said, as a hunting lodge, one of many across the county. Ada Alice Bellamy-Brettoneur bought the property in 1950 or 1951 but when her husband died she retired to Lancing finding the place too big for her. Her grandson Bill Van Tromp, who was living nearby in rented accommodation with his wife and small baby, acquired the house in 1968. He ran his plant hire business from there, because without his own premises his plant was still in the field behind his parents' home in Sunset

Lane. Behind the cultivated part of the Scotlands garden was the area that he used as the yard with workshops and barns, and storage for combine harvesters, diggers and pick up balers, this land has now been built on, but the stream still flows there.

Bill explains "We used to do all our own repairs on site; initially I was a farm contractor, just at the time when the earth-moving machine business was starting up, so I bought a bulldozer and a drag line crane and we went out onto Amberley Wildbrooks for Linfield's Nursery, digging peat for a couple of years. From there the company became established, W Van Tromp we were called, and I had two or three chaps working for me, but everyone you employ needs a machine so expansion was slow. I'm not sure now of the order of the contracts, but I was the one that cleared the woodland on the Thakeham side of Threals Lane; Threals Wood it was called. There's just a little bit of woodland I left at the bottom, the rest, right through to Thakeham I bulldozed and ploughed, and planted barley I think. I left some huge beech trees, but I don't know if they're still there because once you disturb their roots by digging around them they never really settle again and a severe wind will uproot them at a later date. I also filled in the village pond; now that was a shame but the contract had to go to someone; it was a lovely pond, a natural pond with a hard bottom. We also put in the main drains for the area over the 1960s and 70s; it took us about eighteen months to do as the sewer works for this area is on the other side of the Pulborough Road. We put in the mains and each house was left a special pipe with a connector; we had to leave white topped pegs in the hedge as markers, and then it was up to the householder to have the pipe connected as they had to pay a private contractor to do the work.

I remember on Christmas Eve 1962 we had this great blizzard which drifted; I was registered with the Council as I had three snowploughs, so I ploughed the village out and sat back waiting for the Council to ring and arrange to pay the men. When nothing happened, I rang them and asked what was happening, and they asked if I had a plough! I told them they had a filing cabinet with the names of all the farmers who had ploughs in the area, and as soon as they had that information we all went ahead. The farmers had snowploughs to tow behind their tractors to keep the lanes open; we seemed to have much worse weather then.

The children from The Juggs used to climb the wall and scrump our apples but we had very little theft from the yard. You could always spot the ringleader of the lads, so I used to give him a ride on the machines and we never had any trouble after that."

In the 1970s Bill retired and the house was sold, but he lived in the tiny one bedroom cottage, which the family used to call The Goat House because the previous people had kept goats in the stable at the back. Eventually even this house was sold as he went to live with his daughter in Wiltshire, and the new owners demolished the cottage and built a new place which they called Little Scotlands.

This has led to certain confusion because the house that is now the Rectory used to be called Little Scotlands. It was built by Percy Greenfield in 1920/21 while William Cobbett Greenfield and family were living at New Barn Farm on the Common.

Heading west from the cross roads there is The Forge Cottage. When Dave Griffiths bought The Forge Cottage in 1984 he was fortunate enough also to find included in the price a file and a folder giving the house's history, illustrated, where possible with documents and photographs. It is from those documents, compiled by Kenneth Neale, who bought the cottage with his wife Dorothy, in 1972, that some of these notes are taken.

The surviving components of the original timber frame suggest that it was built between 1550 and 1600, an Elizabethan cottage. It was extended and improved over the years of the seventeenth century suggesting a long period of stability, until the 19th century.

When the Abergavenny properties in the village were sold off, the freehold of the cottage and the forge was bought by John Hubbard in 1927; he had bought the copyhold in 1895 for £200 and was from a family of blacksmiths. It is he who made the railings round the old village stocks, and his name is on the top rail. He also repaired much of the local farm machinery and implements. He employed another blacksmith to help him, a Ted Crowhurst, who, with his new bride Kathleen lived

Ted Crowhurst – 1940s

in part of Huntleys which was also owned by John Hubbard at that time. Ted Crowhurst also came from a family of blacksmiths and he bought the business himself in 1929 when John Hubbard died, and moved into Forge Cottage with his family, a son and daughter. He was known as 'the sixpenny blacksmith' which was the price he charged for small jobs, but as well as being an excellent smith, he kept the farm horses' feet in good order, and good shoes, as well. The Church records show that in 1930 he made and installed the iron gate in the south wall of the churchyard at a cost of £3.5.0d. and it is thought he also made the weathervane on the church.

During the Second World War the forge was the headquarters of the village fire brigade, of which he was the Leading Fireman. After the war everything had changed and farm machinery became increasingly mechanised so in 1952 Ted Crowhurst sold the forge to Herbert Ellis Hall as the village could no longer support a blacksmith and farrier, in spite of his doing chimney sweeping and other odd jobs to make ends meet. Ted and Kathleen moved to Pickering Cottages where Ted continued as verger and sexton until his death in 1955. Kathleen died in 1987; interested in the village affairs she had been a founder member of the West Chiltington WI. When H E Hall bought the house and forge, for £2,500, it was very dilapidated and had been condemned; he also bought the sliver of land beside The Queen's Head. Slaters the builders restored the property and provided sanitation; one bedroom became the bathroom and the utility room was built on the newly purchased land, which had been the urinal for the pub. There is a story told that if you were on top of the double decker bus which turned round outside the pub, you could see into the gents, which had no roof! The Forge Cottage was purchased by Sir Hugh and Lady Molony, in 1970, without the old forge, which was, by then, a workshop, and a complete restoration and renovation was carried out, again, by Slaters. A new house 'Crowhurst' stands on the site of the old forge itself.

Forge Cottage is a building that has attracted interesting people; it was sold to Mrs Violet Galsworthy, sister-in-law of the novelist; later it was bought by Kenneth Neale, who himself has written books including one, published in 1975 called *Victorian Horsham*, and two articles on West Chiltington. Baron Willis of Chislehurst, better known perhaps as Ted Willis was the author of the 1960s television series *Dixon of Dock Green*. He lived in Chislehurst in Kent, but left home to find peace and quiet at Forge Cottage while writing, beginning work early in the morning and stopping about 2pm to go down to the pub for a steak and kidney pie and a whisky. Some years later the magazine *Woman's Own* ran a series of stories from Britain's top politicians, and Ted Willis' story concerned PC Dixon and his proposed retirement to 'a rose covered cottage in the country.' George Dixon, in an effort to amuse his grandchildren, had been showing them old family photographs, when one particular photo slipped out of the book, on the back it said 'George Dixon. The Forge. West Chilting…' He determines to visit his family's old home and the story revolves around a burglary in Forge Cottage. The house, the village, and the views of the countryside are identifiable in every detail.

Jack Phillips was a well remembered character who frequented the village. In 1844 John Hubbard had married Ann Phillips from Petworth, so it is possible that Jack Phillips was related to the family. It would appear that Jack was the black sheep, and had gone his own way in life ending up as a vagrant at Thakeham's workhouse which used to be where Rydon school is now. He disliked life there so much that he left and came back into the old village arriving at Crowhurst's the blacksmith one day. Old Mrs Bessant who ran the little shop on the corner next to the Queens Head used to give him a cup of tea in the morning, as did Mrs Tyrell from the Queens Head, and various villagers would add bread and cheese and a cup of tea during the day. He used to sleep rough beside the smithy and in return he used to 'bellows the fire'. It is generally accepted now that he had a sad life with his family refusing to own him, but life cheered up when the Canadians were here as he used to sit in the corner of the pub telling stories, while the soldiers bought him beers, until they took him home

Jack Phillips – about 1920

and put him to bed! His sister Lou Phillips was a professional needlewoman, living in a black wooden bungalow behind and between Church House and Mitchells (where Braeside is now), and is remembered as always wearing a man's cap. She worked for Mrs Kensington and it is possible that it was fear of Mrs Kensington's finding out who her relation was that caused her to disown Jack. When Colonel Kensington had two new semi-detached bungalows built, he allowed Lou to have one of them.

There are many stories told about Jack, one is that once when he went to the workhouse he got in a coffin to sleep. All was well until they came to collect the coffin when he sat up and terrified the people. He had a dreadful stutter but miraculously lost it when he had to swear at a local dog that had knocked him over! He used to do all sorts of odd jobs and was a recognised watch mender. He stayed wherever he could; there are many reports of his being accommodated in various sheds and barns, causing comment wherever he went with his big belt from which his belongings hung . He had a sort of sponge bag containing his soap, flannel and towel which he used to take down to the pond every morning for his wash before coming back for breakfast. Next to the forge under a huge oval shaped roof and beside where the ramp went up to The New Hall were all the carts and the farm implements that were waiting to be repaired, and beyond that was Jack's bed. He had an old chaise longue type of thing with heaps of blankets on it. When he died it was said that he was wearing twelve pairs of trousers and two overcoats, the top one shiny with dirt! The children used to torment him, and say that he smelled, and in return he was glowering and frightened them, but even they had to admit that he was superb at shaping a piece of iron.

The forge was a place of fascination to more than the children, and many can recall watching as Ted Crowhurst put the tyres on the old wagon wheels that Mr Puttock the wheelwright had brought to him. On the grass verge just in front of Palmers was a great metal plate with a hole in the middle which held a central hub that the wheel fitted onto to keep it steady. When the iron tyre was red hot in the fire three or four men would get hold of it with tongs and run across the Hollows to put it over the wooden wheel. Then, when the tyre was hammered into place, buckets of water were thrown over the wheel and tyre to shrink the metal and to prevent the wood catching fire or scorching. There was a lathe to shape the elm nave or box of the wheel (the central hub), but the spokes were all made with a draw knife and spoke shave from oak while the felloes were ash, and everything had to measured exactly before the tyre was heated. The hub and the tyre held the whole thing together, so although the tyre never wore out, it had to be maintained; in the very dry weather of summer the wood would shrink so the wheels were thrown in the stream or pond to swell them again. If the tyre came off for any reason, the whole wheel would collapse.

Kings and Princes Farm house in The Hollows is said to be 12th century with a cellar used for smuggling. Its history can be traced back to 1368 when there is a reference to a Thomas Kyng at West Chiltington; it is probable that this man gave his family name to the freehold estate. In John Rowe's survey of the Manor of West Chiltington in 1622 a Daniel Searle, who was one of the reeves of the manor, owned a field called Prynses. However, based on architectural features, the current house probably dates from the seventeenth century.

It is remembered by many from the days when milk and eggs were collected from the farm, which had belonged to the Greenfield family since Michael Greenfield (1794-1872) owned it; this was one of the biggest farms in the area. Tom Greenfield was the agent for the Marquess of Abergavenny (it is remembered that one of his jobs was to go around the roads and pay the unemployed who had been put to work breaking stones for the road surfaces), and after his first wife Elizabeth Moase died he had married Mary Ann. William Cobbett Greenfield (so called because his father married Priscilla Cobbett, a descendant of William Cobbett) was born in 1882 and had originally lived in Cuckfield but was brought up at Kings and Princes by his Uncle Tom and Aunt Mary Ann, who sent him to the village school at a cost of 4d a week. When William Cobbett Greenfield grew up he married Marion Barnes of Palmers Lodge, and they had three children: Mary Elizabeth, and two boys, Michael, born in 1923 at New Barn Farm and Percy, born in 1925. Mick Greenfield explains his family's history "The Barnes family moved to West Chiltington from Meopham in Kent; Walter Barnes

Kings and Princes

had married a Miss Gower and had been presented with a gift of £1,000 by his father. Ten children were born to the Barnes' at Palmers Lodge; five boys and five girls, my mother being one. Ted, one of the boys, married Sadie Meeten from the mill and subsequently moved to Huntleys; I believe that Ted's father-in-law was the last miller to use the mill to grind corn commercially."

Following the First World War and William Cobbett's experiences on the Somme he had a breakdown and it was suggested that he return to the countryside. He came back to Kings and Princes and became manager there. During the war market gardens prospered all over the country and Kings did well, but as foreign markets became established and foodstuff was imported English produce was not so sought after, and Kings Farm market garden had to be closed down.

Gladys Barrow (now Adsett) was 14 when she went to work for the Greenfields in 1926. Her father was the local road repair man who used to work with a traction engine. When Mrs Greenfield was looking for extra help someone who worked at the farm had mentioned that they knew Gladys' mother had a daughter who was of an age to work, so Gladys was employed and walked to work from home in Pulborough, until she learned to ride a bicycle. She helped Edith (who lived at Lintotts in Gay Street) in the house and describes her work: "I was a general dogsbody really, I did everything and anything, housework and dairy work. The house was owned by Mrs Greenfield, and her daughter who was also Mrs Greenfield - it could be rather confusing. We had a nursery garden, and cattle, pigs, chickens, turkeys at Christmas, and geese, and peacocks. The nursery produce went to market by lorry twice a week, and the cows were a dairy herd; we had two milk rounds, delivering the milk out of the churn, one round for the Village and one for the Common. Tom Downer did the morning milk round before he went to work on the land. The cowman used to separate the milk that was left over from the dairy and I sold it at the back door for 2d a quart, the cream was sold

Tom Downer in working clothes – 1920s – 1930s

round the village and we made our own butter in a wooden churn in the dairy. As there was no regular supply of water at the farm, the cattle used to be taken to the village pond to drink

Mrs Greenfield was ever so nice and did a lot for the village. She used to sit up in her bedroom and knit or crochet or sew; every curtain in that house was either knitted or crocheted by her. Round the mantelpiece was green velvet and over the top there were crocheted birds and butterflies to match the curtains. She made the tablecloths and doilies and she made lots of baby clothes for the WI in the village, vests and woollies - she was a one woman industry! She used to send away for the materials. Edith and I lived in with the family, we had breakfast together, Mrs Greenfield sat by the gun cupboard in the corner, Edith in the other corner and me by the little table at the back. The big arm chair was for the dog! There was a dining room and a conservatory, and a big kitchen which had a huge table, a grandfather clock, and a big dresser with old china; I remember the big blue and white soup tureen. The dairy was beyond the kitchen. Outside there was a shed where we kept the milk float and the churns, and past that there were the packing shed, the cart shed, a garage, and a big open part that was the store for all the boxes for the vegetables that went to market. The old boxes that were no longer any use, we used on the fire for the copper. In the far corner of the garden there was an enormous Bramley

Cattle drinking at the pond – about 1927

apple tree and we used to have massive apples from it. The garden was full of fruit, plums, pears, greengages - a real abundance of things.

I loved working there; when I arrived at 14 I couldn't do anything; Edith taught me how to make cakes and pies and bread, otherwise I just watched and learned. I had a half day off in the week, and all Sunday but I had to be back from Pulborough by 9pm. I had my 21st birthday there, but it was just like any other working day. I went home for Christmas Day, but the animals still had to be looked after, so it wasn't a real day off. Mrs Greenfield was very fond of animals, she kept a pet deer, and I used to feed anything up to twelve cats at night in the kitchen. I used to do my knitting while I watched the guinea pigs, lots of them on either side of the path out by the front door; outside the back door there were two cages: one had a Little Owl in it and the other had a talking magpie! All the farm animals were more like pets than serious farming, although the she bred the turkeys commercially. I left when I was about 16, for another job. After Edie left to get married, Mrs Greenfield asked me to go back to Kings and Princes; I was then 18.

A woman used to come in to do the washing once a fortnight; one of the men used to help us fill the copper with water from the well, and we had a stone sink, a great big washing line, and flat irons. I didn't like the washing, but I did like the cooking and I remember that I used to watch Edie icing her cakes so they bought me an icing set, one of those syringes; I'm still using it! I remember making this cake for my Dad's birthday; it was my first attempt at icing, and I put the cake in a box on the handlebars of my bike and started pedalling home down Watery Lane (Stream Lane). I hadn't been riding a bike long and I caught my knee on the box and fell off. I had to be rescued by a passing groom from Gay Street, but eventually the cake and I arrived home not too much the worse for wear! In the kitchen at Kings and Princes there was a large brick oven and every Friday we had a big baking session - bread, cakes, pastry and pies. We didn't smoke the bacon, but the

Tricycle riding!

people before did and the hooks that go up and down are still there. Just inside the dairy we had a coffee machine to grind the beans. Mrs Greenfield had a tricycle with a basket on the back which stayed in the kitchen - she'd had it out for cleaning one day and we all had a go on it.

We had a cowman, a lad, and two resident carters and an extra one who came in when he felt like it! The foreman, Mr Alan Laker, used to live in Meers Farm, and when he got too old Mr Howard took over and went to live in Meers Farm. Eventually he retired as well, and the cowman lived at Meers. One morning Mrs Greenfield Jr just didn't get up for breakfast and when I went up to see her, she was very confused. I rushed across to the Mustchins who called the doctor. She had had a stroke and the farm had to be sold in 1933; Mr and Mrs Thorpe bought it. I went with Mrs Greenfield in 1934 to live in Marian bungalow on the Common because she had got ill through having to sell Kings and Princes. In July 1935 I got septicaemia and was off work for a year - the very strong washing soda made my right hand come up in spots, and after weeks and weeks of this I was sent to hospital in Brighton where I was given a saline wash every 20 minutes to clean up the stuff coming out. It was awful; no antibiotics in those days. I lost track of the house after that."

The Sales Particulars from the auction in 1933 describe 'the market garden and fruit growing land of 9.02 acres', and list the produce grown there: 383 apple trees of 9 varieties, 102 pear trees, 282 plum trees, 180 cob nuts and 4 walnuts. There were nearly 1,000 gooseberry bushes and many currants, black and red. There was 'a charming old-world stone-walled garden, greenhouse with boiler and pipes'; an altogether desirable property.

Herbert Marcus and Octavia Adler bought Kings and Princes; their son Robin, a well known photographer still lives just outside the parish boundary at Flower Voakes, which used to be called Lower Voakes. He explained that his parents bought the property in 1939 with a view to retiring there. At that time it consisted of thirteen acres which supported two nut plats or groves, plums, all sorts of soft fruit, and, of course, strawberries. At one time the farm had sent a quarter of a ton of strawberries to Brighton market three times a week, by horse and cart, but by the time the Adlers bought it it was no longer a working farm. The farm kitchen which used to be the scullery has, he says, a very unforgiving stone floor, you can even see the fossils. Over the years they made changes to both the house, for example a second bathroom was added, and to the land. There was a very dilapidated barn which was falling down; Robin rescued it by getting together a team of friends who began to rebuild it. Being an historic building, he appealed to the council for funds to help in the restoration, but the money was unavailable, and the next purchaser of the house, the Johnson family, pulled it down. The Johnsons were responsible for a great deal of restorative work to the house and planted the delightful garden. They sold the house, but the new occupants did not stay long, being disturbed by the noise from the coal yard across the road, and the house changed hands again. Tim and Sarah Fooks, the current owners, bought the house in 1992 and have rediscovered the 35' deep well outside the back door and are continuing to restore and maintain the buildings and walled gardens. They have bought back from Meers Farm some of the land the Johnsons had sold including the nuttery which is now being coppiced again after an interval of thirty years or so.

Strawberry time at Kings and Princes

The windmill, described as a black smock-mill with fantail, was built on its present site about 1830 and appears on a tithe map of 1840. It is thought that the valuable working parts of the mill, the sweeps, cap, wheels, stones and gearing were brought from a site near Monkmead, and it is generally accepted that the base was built of local stone. It is octagonal with, in places, walls three feet thick, and has four floors plus cap; above the first floor there is a stage for servicing the sweeps. It is often referred to as Meeten's Mill, after Henry Meeten who was the last miller to work it; he had begun his three years apprenticeship as a miller in 1879. He was a founder member of the Parish Council and a Councillor for 38 years; an Overseer of the Poor until that ancient office was abolished; the People's Warden in 1920, having been elected in 1893; and was a school manager for about forty years. He died in October 1937 aged 78.

Before Mustchin's had started their coal yard, Mr Meeten had the coal pulled up from Pulborough by the carter. One person remembers "I used to take a pram or a truck to the mill for coal and a few pounds of mixed corn for the bantams. It was surprising that that mill stood up, when those big sweeps were going round it used to creak and groan, you'd think the place was going to fall to pieces!"

She (windmills are always "she") stopped work in about 1921 when the import of Canadian wheat flour had made many of our mills redundant, and was cleared of machinery in 1922 when Mr Powell of Coolham bought the stones. This importation of wheat was beginning to have an impact on the landscape, the wheat fields being given over to fruit growing.

The Mill – 1906
Note the catwalk, the haystack and the state of the lane.

In 1921 Henry Meeten left the Mill House where he had been a tenant and bought a cottage in Mill Road for his retirement; in 1923 the mill was converted into a house by William Hartley-Clark. The conversion removed all of the gearing and internal workings except its windshaft, winding gear and sweeps; four sections of the great wooden mill shaft remain in the garden. The front door remains where it was, with the present owners' sitting room being the area where the grain was stored. There is a catwalk at first floor level, and there used to be a bridge going from the first floor across the lane into the opposite field. It is said that one day this bridge came crashing down on the people below.

There is an auction leaflet from Harrods dated 5 May 1931 describing it as 'The Admirable Freehold, Hunting Box and Summer Residence' which had 'central heating. Hot water system. Electric light and telephone easily installable. Excellent water supply. Up-to-date sanitary fittings and arrangements'. Hunting with the Crawley and Horsham, and with Lord

Leconfield's hounds was advertised in the auction particulars, as were the Storrington beagles and Crowhurst Otter Hounds. There was good shooting in the neighbourhood, with golf, racing at Fontwell, Goodwood and Sandown Parks, tennis, boating and bathing. The conversion to a house had been so skilful that it was the subject of a special mention in *Britannia and Eve* issued July 1929. In 1938 the mill was sold to the literary critic Cecil Gray and it is interesting to speculate that he could have been drawn here by more than the mill: Hillaire Belloc the poet was living in the mill at Shipley, John Ireland the composer was living at the mill in Washington, and another composer Arnold Bax was living at the White Horse in Storrington; the Wells cottages were being built for London artistes and the area was very interesting for a critic.

Colonel Walter bought the mill at auction in 1952, thereafter it was sold to Peter and Pamela Crane in 1965 in a very run down state. It became 'Pamela's Project', she restored it, rewired it, rebuilt the outside staircase, replaced the kitchen and reorganised the bedrooms to include ensuite facilities. Unfortunately she and her husband died early; the present owners Colin and Kathryn Johnson purchased the property in 1981 having seen it advertised in Country Life. Over the years they have acquired the deeds and various documents relating to the mill so its short history is quite well recorded.

There used to be many mills, both wind and water-powered in this area; eventually people realised that on some days they could mill more than on others when the wind wasn't so good, and they began to install auxiliary engines. There are three main types of mill: a post mill where the whole mill moves on its king post to face the wind; a tower mill, and a smock mill which is so called because it looks like a shepherd's smock, where the cap turns to catch the wind. Many mills came to untimely ends because of storm damage when they were shaken to pieces, or because of fire caused by the explosive mixture of flour dust and the friction of the brake trying to slow down the sails in heavy weather. Another problem was 'backwinding' when the fantail which was meant to rotate the cap to face the sails into the wind, did not react fast enough and the cap was blown right off as the wind got underneath it. This did not usually destroy the mill but it was very expensive to repair and it was that cost that destroyed it. Repairs are carried out by a millwright; Colin Johnson continues "We had to employ one to replace our sweeps in 1990. We had an estimate from a firm in Lincolnshire but although different counties have different mill designs, the principles are the same. The mill had four sweeps originally, and then three after one came off in the gales of 1948; it remained like that until 1977 when the remaining three were too far gone and had to be replaced by just two. They're pitch pine which is a resinous wood and is supposed to be more rot resistant than other woods. When the company isn't working on mills they're agricultural engineers and steeplejacks and it's frightening to watch them walking out along the sweeps."

In 1933 Iso Elinson, a Russian Jewish refugee emigrated to this country. He was a concert pianist who had studied at the Petrograd (now St Petersburg) Conservatoire and he, his wife and two daughters lived at the Mill House (on the corner, next to the mill) during World War II. The girls went to a local private school in Fir Tree Lane. Iso later went to teach at the Royal Manchester College of Music and his being in the house adds further evidence to Colin Johnson's theory about the artistic coterie in the area.

On the diagonal corner opposite The Windmill, in The Hollows, stands Fryars, originally owned by Nyetimber Manor. It was sold to the Hartley-Clark family who restored it around 1920, and was then bought about 1968 by Stephen and Pam Brown, from an elderly gentleman called Mr Black. It consists of 12-14 acres whose boundary marches with that of Chris Lawson, a dairy farmer in the next parish, who has a little land in the parish of West Chiltington. There are stories in the village of secret tunnels and cellars; of children in the village, years ago, frightening themselves by going along the low, narrow passage, with only a candle or oil lantern for light, but no-one ever seems to have got to the end; it was supposed to be a very long passage! The Browns turned the cellar into a playroom and Reg Slater the builder adds that when they cut out walls and dug up the floor for Mrs Hartley-Clark there was no evidence of passages leading from Fryars nor any priest buried in the cellar.

The property was sold as one lot and included what had been known as Fryars Cottage at the bottom of the drive, where Mr Black's housekeeper lived. Mr Black did not farm the land, but now seven acres of blackcurrants are growing on the land that marches with the Churchfield Farm land, and Stephen continues the story of the blackcurrants that was started by James Mursell in Chapter 11: "I have a joint venture with James Mursell, and two years ago Ribena said that they could get blackcurrants for their cordial from Eastern Europe much more cheaply than from us, and other small producers like us, so 1997 would be our last year. We thought we were going to have to grub up the bushes, but lo and behold, as happens in the farming world, everyone started grubbing up and cutting back, including the Poles and East European farmers, because if prices are forced so low there's no point in continuing, so Ribena is now finding that there are fewer blackcurrants to be had in this country, and the price is going up again. No wonder farmers never know where they are!

I retired from business in London in 1980, and, after the children had grown up and left home, and I had found new homes for their horses, I was left with a five acre field, spare. In a wild moment I decided to plant grapes, the German varieties of Müller-Thurgau, Reichensteiner and Huxelrebe. We had our first harvest in 1986, encouraged by my very good and old friend who owns a vineyard in Steyning, but three or four years ago I reduced the acreage because my wild whim had become hard work, and I was finding it hard to sell the wine. I get it made, bottled and labelled with my labels in various places by good winemakers, but I found I was getting 15,000 bottles a year to sell, which was too much. So now I'm down to about an acre and still get 6,000 bottles, which I sell to friends and businesses. Even though I am only a small business, I still have to have a licence which I get from Petworth and I have to pay duty to the Customs and Excise people of £1.05p per bottle; yet you can go over to France and buy a whole bottle for less than I pay in customs duty. I need to get about £5 per bottle which is inexpensive for an English wine so I rely on locals, friends, and word of mouth." (It is important here to draw a distinction between English and British wines; English wine is made from freshly harvested grapes grown in England, whilst British wine is made in Britain from reconstituted grape concentrate which can have come from anywhere in the world.)

Stephen continues "Now the vines are established it's a bit easier, but they all have to be sprayed, pruned, tied in and trained, picked and so on. We spray against botrytis and mildew, and we watch for the wasps and destroy their nests because they can pierce the skin of a juicy grape and spoil the crop, and we wage constant war against the starlings. They sit on the sails of the windmill, waiting; I have a theory about them: I think they send out about a dozen scouts who come back and report, so if we can scare that first wave away a few times with the propane gas-powered bird scarer which creates a series of loud bangs they will go elsewhere for easier pickings. There are hoards of birds, they'll clean you out if they can, so we aim to drive the flocks away but have to put up with the odd few. It's surprising how attractive their plumage is when you have to look at it so often!"

Back at the crossroads opposite the Queens Head are Palmers and, round the corner, Palmers Lodge. The village seems to have a magnetic pull, Peggy Warren's great grandmother used to live in the village and is buried in the churchyard; her grandmother got married and moved away to Durrington which is where Peggy's father was born. Years later, in 1937, Peggy came from Goring with her aunt Charlotte Green, her cousin Eva and Eva's husband Bill Warren, to live at Palmers Lodge, and to run it as a market garden. In those days the farm included the orchard on which Orchard Dell was built, and continued almost to Gay Street behind Fryars where the horses were housed in a big field and barn on what is now the golf course, behind Fryars. The barn and stables were on the left hand side of the footpath and can be identified on the old OS maps. The horses were got ready mid afternoon to take the strawberries to market in Brighton; the journey would go via Steyning where they would stop for supper so that they got to Brighton for 4am when the market opened. If the load was too heavy they had to journey through Findon and along the bottom road, as the bridge at Beeding was too steep for the horses to pull a heavy load up.

Peggy married Arthur Warren, Bill's brother and she remembers how, before the children were born, they all used to walk across those fields to the pub at Nutbourne on a summer Sunday evening; it made a lovely walk. Bill and Arthur farmed together, growing potatoes, green vegetables and keeping pigs. Peggy and Bill eventually built the bungalow Dawn in Broadford Bridge Road, whose back garden is where the pig styes used to be, while Sunset, the bungalow next door was built for a distant cousin who was a family retainer.

In spite of now having a lorry, the early morning starts continued for the market in Brighton two or three times a week, to sell the produce which included apples, pears, damsons and plums from the orchard. Many of the trees in the orchard were over 100 years old but still cropped well, and along the cart track from the barn (now converted into a house called The Barn) to the orchard was a row of plum trees. The end of that cart track now forms the central road in Orchard Dell, and it is said the old well could still be found in the garden of Medburn, and there were two other wells in the garden of Palmers. Palmers had been the original farmhouse before Palmers Lodge was built in the 18th century and by 1931 had been converted into two workmen's cottages, although only one was inhabited and there was only one staircase for both parts. Palmers Lodge was considered more modern and convenient, although Peggy said "it was anything but modern when we arrived, with no bathroom and an outside toilet, although it was rather special being a double one, but we had four bedrooms so we converted one of them into a bathroom later on. We had no scullery, just a huge kitchen with a range on the stone flagged floor, and a gas cooker. We had a hand pump for the water, which pumped it up into a tank in the loft and then it fed down by gravity, and because we were too modern to have a copper, I did the washing in a huge saucepan and used the hand wringer which was kept outside, for the wet clothes. We used a scrubbing board and a scrubbing brush to get the real dirt out, and the condensation was terrible. With the soot and ash from the fires things did get dirty, but once a year we had a damn good spring clean, washed and even sometimes repainted the walls, washed the curtains and the chaircovers, cleaned and tidied the drawers. It was a once-a-year job, very thorough because we couldn't vacuum once a week as we do now, so it had to last.

    I was twenty four when we moved here, but by the time a girl was about eighteen she was wearing a corset, a very supportive garment, all boned, you could stand it up on its own on the floor! Most people had theirs made individually by such firms as Spirella, and then you didn't need a bra. When bras came in later they were very unsupportive, the flat chested girls used to pad them out with cotton wool as there was no padding and no underwiring. They had to be washed by hand because of the elastic, I remember we used Sunlight soap as we did for all the washing, except when things such as work clothes were really dirty and then we used soda. I can't really remember what we wore when we were very little, but I do remember the liberty bodices; made of cotton or linen they were a thickish cloth and shaped rather like a waistcoat with buttons up the front. They came down to your bottom, and we wore a vest underneath, and navy knickers for school with an elastic waist and elastic in the legs which were mid-thigh length. Even when I went to High School I was wearing socks, but had lisle stockings, with garters, a bit later. High School uniform was much the same everywhere, in the summer we had white socks with coloured tops, a white blouse and gym slip and a blazer, and in the winter we added a V-necked pullover and changed the socks to a darker colour. The gym slips were made from that heavy, slightly rough material serge, pleated from the waist and had a belt; they were supposed to be 1″ clear of the ground when kneeling, but we used to tie the belt tight and pull them up a bit to make them shorter. By the late 1920s skirts were very short, and I often wore shorts as I did a lot of walking, not short shorts you understand, but just above the knee. School shoes were black leather lace ups, but my indoor shoes had a bar with a button.

I loved my shoes, and when we came here I had about twenty pairs, all made of leather as there were no man-made materials, and many with high heels because I hated being short! Not very practical for the country, because I broke the heels on the ruts in the road many a time going to visit my sister-in-law! Mother was very old fashioned and would never have dreamed of having high-heeled shoes; she never had her hair cut, either. When my sister went into hairdressing it was a very new profession and she had to pay £50 - £100 for her training.

During the Second World War Bill was an ARP warden and Arthur was in the Home Guard; it was damn hard work getting up early, back from market, finishing the farm work and then off for war duties. We had a couple of horses as well as the tractor, and Arthur used to take them to drink at the village pond, and we would also fill the water carts with water to irrigate the greenstuff we were growing. My husband also did some contract ploughing with his old Ferguson tractor, the one with an iron seat and no cover, and would see the whole business through: the binder would throw out the sheaves which we would stook, six at a time, and after a week or so when they were dry they were piled onto a lorry to be taken to build into a rick. They would be thrashed later and he would build the rick again, this time more thoroughly as it had to last. The tractor went round and round the field so there was always a small stand left in the middle and we would all wait for the rabbits, during the war the rabbit pie was very welcome. There were mice and rats as well of course. In those days Harvest Festival Sunday was the last Sunday in September, although it isn't any more, but we never had the harvest in by then; if the weather was bad it could take up to three months to get in and there was the danger of the ears going mouldy, or heating up and self-igniting. The mill had stopped working by this time, so we sent the corn to Muddles in Ashington to be ground. Then we had to harvest the root crops of potatoes and swedes, but we did get 'harvest rations', extra cheese, margarine and sugar for the men for both the corn and the potato harvests, and if we were careful with the sugar I could make jam, bottle and can the extra fruit and there was still some for the wine Bill made. The kitchen at Kings and Princes was huge and had a stone flagged floor and an Aga, and the WI used to use it to can our fruit in cans provided by the government. For years after the war I used to preserve the fruit in Kilner jars, there was a 1lb and a 2lb size with glass lids and metal securing loops. My husband came from a large family and in the summer they would descend for the holidays - summer in the countryside with lots of free fruit! During the war we had Italian and German Prisoners of War to help us on the farm as all our young men were away; Bill and Arthur were exempted from serving as they were working on the land. We liked the Germans best as they worked hard and some of them had a smattering of English, in fact one young German, only in his early twenties, kept in touch with us for years afterwards. I used to take these cans of tea out to the POWs working in the field, so got to know them quite well. During the war Arthur used to boil up the peelings and bits for the chickens, ducks and geese that we kept; we also had goats and I used to make butter and cheese with the milk - you did it just like you would with cows' milk in a wooden churn, by hand, but it took longer to 'go' than cows' milk. I also kept up to a hundred rabbits; we used to sell the skins for gloves and so on, but we never ate them; we ate the wild ones Arthur shot. At least we did until there was that disease myxomatosis. There was a cellar in Palmers Lodge which Bill used for storing the wine made from the fruit in the orchard, and after we'd killed our pigs and sent them to Billingshurst to be smoked, we stored the meat in our loft so you could say the whole house was put to good use!

I used to do a bit of dressmaking on the side to make a bit of extra money, and during the war you wouldn't believe the things I made: a pair of dressing gowns; one from an army blanket and one from a navy one for the husband and son of a friend of mine, and blouses, nighties, slips from parachute silk. I don't know where they got the materials from, I just made them up and didn't ask!

In 1956 my aunt died and the farm was sold; the building of Orchard Dell began in 1957. Colonel Walter who owned the mill at the time bought it on a maiden bid because no-one had realised that there would be permission for building so he got it cheap. The bottom phase of Orchard Dell was built in 1957, up to the row of hornbeam trees that divided the orchard from the rest of the farm, and the top phase was built in the early 1960s. The first residents to move in were predominantly older, coming up to retirement age, and as long as they could drive, either to Pulborough to catch the train to London, or just to get about, they were happy, but eventually they stopped driving and moved away, or died and their places have been taken by a much younger group, with school-age children. We don't have the same friendly chat with them as we did with the older ones, we used to play darts in the pub on a Sunday and talk, but the younger ones don't do that. Mind you, even the pub's got posh now, it's got two bars!"

Chapter 4

From Broadford Bridge to the North of the Parish

Just beyond Orchard Dell on Broadford Bridge Road, stands Huntleys; Elsie Cattell who was born Elsie Slater recalls "When I was four in 1917 we moved to Huntleys in West Chiltington Village, on the Broadford Bridge Road. It was owned by Jack Hubbard the blacksmith who had a few pigs up there, although later it became a fruit farm. At that time our nearest neighbours were the Coles from Woodshill; they were gentry with a large house and servants. Huntleys was a lovely cottage, and so much bigger than we were used to because when we were in Whales Cottage we had had one half and my grandfather had had the other half. By the time we moved to Huntleys Granny had died and Father had gone to the war in France; we liked Huntleys so much we stayed for twenty years. But we still had to draw the water up from a well in the garden and there was no inside bathroom; we had a tin bath which we took turns to use, and the toilet was up the garden. We used oil lamps. We sometimes saw tramps passing through the village on their way to the workhouse in Thakeham. I remember one day Mother thought Jack Phillips had left the workhouse and thought he might be up at Sparrows (some buildings just above Huntleys) and sent me and my brother Ernest to find out. Sure enough, there he was, sitting in some straw, so we went back home and brought him a can of tea and a great slice of bread and cheese. He was an old man, and many people in the village provided for him. I left school at fourteen and went to work at Nutbourne Manor for a family who lived in London during the week, so I only had to work at weekends for them, and spent the weekdays at Huntleys looking after my family."

Sparrows Farm on the Broadford Bridge Road was sold in 1930 by the Abergavenny Estate as freehold arable land, and eventually came into the ownership of Clive Coulson, a New Zealander who hankered after farming, but in fact managed a pop group. In April 1987 the construction of West Chiltington Golf Course began on this pastureland, owned and

West Chiltington
larger farms before 1900

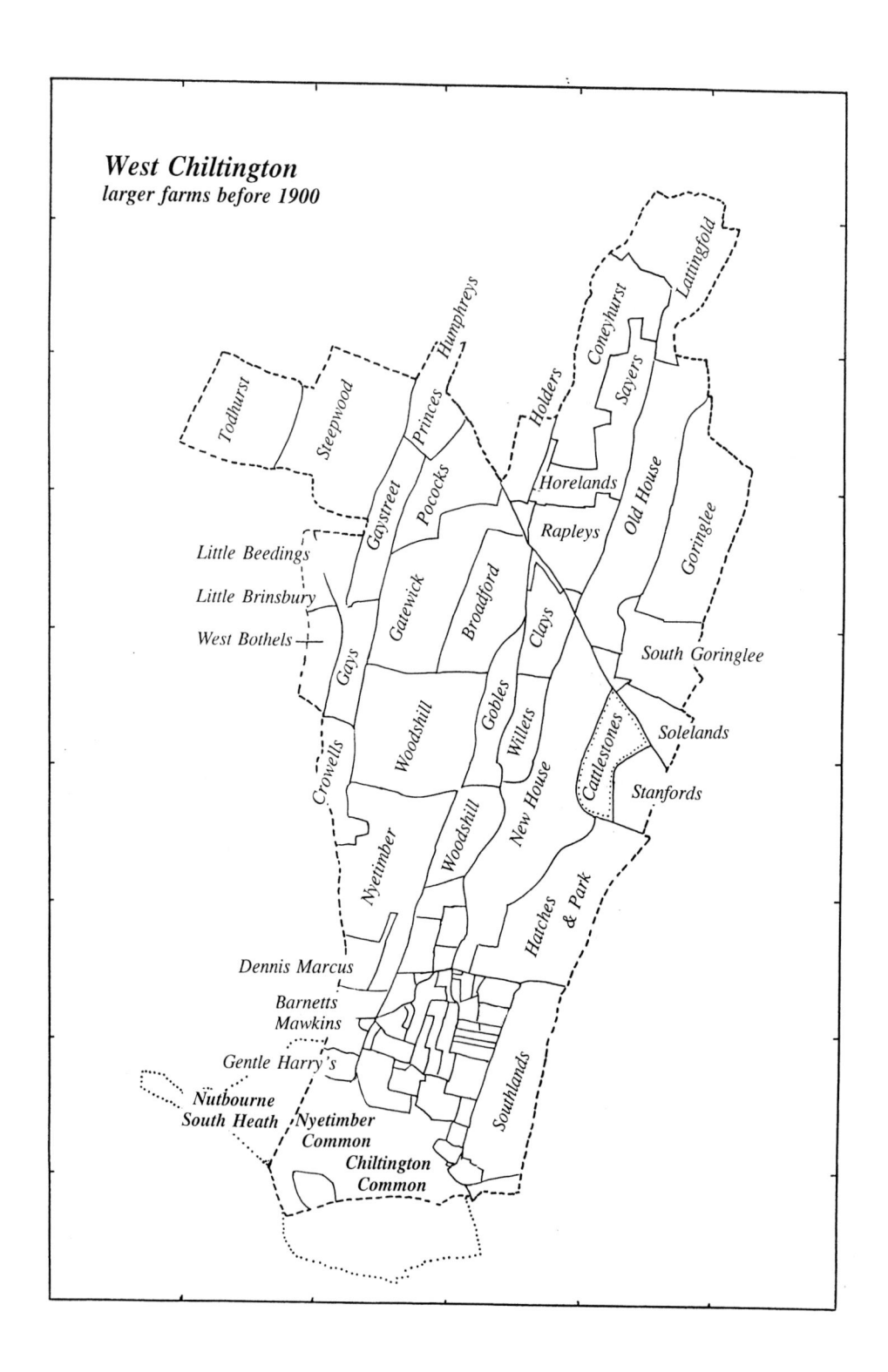

supervised by a three way consortium of Clive Coulson, Brian Barnes whose brainchild it was, and his father-in-law Max Faulkner from Gay Street. These two men were both Ryder Cup players, and Max Faulkner had won The Open in 1951. In June 1988 the course was opened, and over the following couple of years over two thousand trees were planted to enhance the site. The edges of the course follow exactly the old field boundaries: Sparrows Farm buildings were on the left: stables, cart house, and food stores, and there was a walled-in yard. There was also a barn. There was Sparrows Field, and Birds Field was where the practice area is now; the Clubhouse is in the corner of Birds Field and Mast (pronounced mars) Field. The first tee is in a dip called Piney Hills, and the big field called Twenty Acres is where the vines are now. To the north below Sparrows in the valley is Puckermead. In June 1995 the three controlling interests were sold to Geoffrey Cotton who now runs the Club. It is interesting that West Sussex Golf Club which draws its membership from those in West Chiltington, as well as being used by dog walkers and horse riders from the parish, is not, in fact, in West Chiltington at all.

James and Christine Steele came down from Scotland in 1921 where they had been farming, because James suffered from chest problems and was advised that the warmth in the south might be better for him. They and their three sons Archie, Andrew and John and two daughters Margaret known as Daisy, and Agnes known as Nan, lived in Findon where a further son, Mac was born in 1921, with Winnie and Ewen following later. In about 1924 they rented a farm from West Sussex County Council, naming the place Knowetop (Knowe means a hill, or hillock) and were there until about 1948. In those days the access to Knowetop was on a private right of way through Hatches, in East Street, which was owned by Mr and Mrs Ritchie, but in 1970 the access was changed and is now off the Broadford Bridge Road opposite the golf course.

When the family grew up, Archie worked at Kings and Princes in the late 1920s to early 1930s and later at Gatewick Farm; Andrew went to Surrey but returned in the mid 1930s to work with his father and John, until John married Jean McGarva in 1943 moving to a house on the Woodshill estate in the March of that year as the tenancy became available; Daisy worked at home until she got married in 1936; when Mac left school he also worked at home until the war intervened and Archie and he joined the Air Force; Ewen was still at school during the war, being about ten years younger than Mac, but he too stayed in the village to work on the family farms .

The Steele Family – 1953. James and Christina's Golden Wedding, and Archie and Florrie's Silver Wedding
Front Row from left: Harvey Steele, Ramsey Steele, Elizabeth Steele
Seated Row: Archie Steele*, Florrie Steele, Christina Steele, James Steele, Peggy McKnight
Middle Row: Daisy Grey*, Agnes Miller, Andrew Steele*, Annie Watson, Chrissy Sturdement, Ewen Steele*
Back Row: Bill McKnight, Jean Steele, Robbie Steele, John Steele*, George Gray, Alma Steele, Mac Steele*, Bern Sturdement, Jimmy Steele
Those names with an * are the sons and daughters of James and Christina

Alma Abplanalp met Mac Steele at a swimming party on the River Arun at Pulborough while she was training for the Land Army at Brinsbury (Alma says that although she was born and bred in London, she had this unusual surname which was so long that it was sometimes shortened to Miss Ap which of course became Mishap!). They married in 1950 and went to live at Gobles Farm in Broadford Bridge Road, a 60 acre farm rented from Woodshill. They worked the farm in conjunction with Knowetop, rearing the young stock of followers, growing hay and corn and keeping a few chickens. As there was still food rationing Alma remembers "Two of you didn't get very much so we used to go out shooting rabbits, pheasants and the foxes with Les and Fred Pavey our neighbours. We had lights on the guns which mesmerised the pheasants so

Daisy feeding the turkeys at Knowetop

we could get them off the trees; we drove round in Mac's '50 bob and a broody hen car' which by then had no roof so one of us would drive and the other would shoot out of the roof - it was a lot of fun. The car was so called because Mac had bought it from Mrs Ridpath for fifty bob (£2.10s.0d) and a broody hen years before!

Gobles is now two cottages but had been the Parish workhouse; workhouses were provided by each parish; later, larger workhouses were provided by the Unions. Gobles had been either a workhouse or an almshouse, but I don't know which, although an almshouse seems more likely. The workhouse was for those who were evicted from where they were living and had nowhere else to go and were destitute, but the almshouse was for people too old to work. It was provided and financed either by the village or the Church, sometimes by some charitable person, and was meant to provide a caring environment, whereas the workhouse was a government institution with much stricter rules, even separating the men and women although they might have been married to each other for years. In earlier days many of the people who worked on the farms became one of the family and just continued to work to their ability, as a man got older his duties would be easier. To me it seemed as if the whole workforce lived on the farm and came in for meals, eating with the family. There were no rules but on the whole it seemed to work, the grown up children worked on the farm and the elderly parents worked as well and lived with them. We eventually sold Gobles to Mr Bentall of Willetts."

In 1948 New House Farm had become vacant, Captain Thomas having left, so James and Christine with Ewen, Mac and Andrew took over the farm and ran it with Knowetop which they retained from the March to September, making one much larger concern. However, the Council landlords required them to relinquish Knowetop as they could not rent two Council holdings (it was subsequently rented to Bill Stone) so in 1956 Mac and Alma took over New House Farm and built it up to 200 acres serving a pedigree Friesian herd of 80 cattle. Interestingly, the Council rules must have changed later as farming became increasingly intensive and holdings had to amalgamate to be viable, because when the Knowetop tenancy came up again, it was once again tied in with New House Farm under Mac and Alma's supervision.

For over forty years Mac and Alma reared turkeys for the Christmas trade, only giving them up a few years ago. They had had to cut down before this because of the farming regulations that were coming in but until this time they had reared 2,000 turkeys, geese and capons each year. As Alma says "It was a lot of work once a year that had to be fitted in between milking. The houses out the back weren't there until the early 1980s, there were barns there before and that was where we used to keep the turkeys. Our casual labour was about 35 pluckers, from all walks of life, most came during the evenings and weekends, but others would come during the day as well and start after their breakfast. We used to feed them sausage rolls, mince pies, hot dogs and beer, so I used to have to start by making 500 mince pies and 500 of everything else and the kitchen looked like a baker's shop! It was a good atmosphere and part of a typical country Christmas, and I'm sorry it's gone. So are the pluckers, because they would come in from the surrounding area and the money they earned helped towards the costs of their presents and extras, because many of them weren't well paid.

Our turkey chicks would arrive in cardboard boxes by train, and when the railway stopped carrying them, they used to come by truck. The ones we wanted to be really heavy would arrive in May, then some in June and some in July; the later ones would make weights of between 9 -12 lbs, the middle weights would be 12-18 lbs and the heavy ones would go up to 36 lbs. Of course not all of them grow at the same rate, so we never got it completely right. We used to keep them on deep litter with a lot of fresh air so the barns were open sided but with netting to keep them in and the foxes out. We had to be careful they didn't get black head, a disease like a cold which caused them to stagger and fall, and we had such fun and games with the remedies: chopped up eggs and shallot tops I remember having to force down them, but later the feed companies started introducing antibiotics into the feed which solved the problem. We sold a lot privately, and even sent finished turkeys all over the country by rail but we also sold to butchers in Storrington, Pulborough, Billingshurst and Worthing.

In due course Mac started having health problems so in the 1980s the dairy herd was dispersed but the farm continued to rear cattle, turkeys and hens and to grow corn and potatoes.

An old house such as this one is needs to be used or it begins to deteriorate, and, since Mac died and the family has moved away, I am here on my own, so decided to go in for bed and breakfast. It keeps the rooms aired and used, and it brings in some extra income to offset the ongoing maintenance costs; it's hard work but also fun because I meet such interesting people. Many of those who come, arrive at Gatwick; we are far enough away to be quiet, but near enough to get to without exhaustion; others just want a weekend break to walk or see the countryside. Many come in from Belgium now that there is the inter-continental Shuttle train service, and we are a useful jumping-off place to see the rest of the country, then they come back to us for a day or two before they go home, and unload all the extra luggage they 'simply haven't any room for!' I am on the Internet, on the Accommodation Guide web site, and I do get bookings, particularly from America, from that."

Ewen Steele remembers the early days at Knowetop after he left school, and describes his typical farming day: "I got up at 6 o'clock and milked the cows by hand; that was down in the dip. There was an old track we walked to the farm, milked, back to a big breakfast cooked on an old Valor stove. We came in at dinner time for our big meal, and tea time was scones or pancakes. We worked until four-ish, fitting in the haying between milking. We did everything ourselves. In 1949 when we were working at New House, we bought a steam-driven threshing machine and went round the other farms threshing, but when the combine came in we weren't needed any more. Everyone in the village would know when the thresher was going to a farm as you could hear it puffing along, moving slowly and with the baler that ties the straw. They called it a trusser in those days, it made a big sheaf where the straw came out of the thresher." When John Steele married Jean and went to live at Woodshill, the original Knowetop 'partnership' was dissolved and Ewen went to work at Woodshill with John, living in the farm cottage. He and his wife Pat stayed there for many years, before moving on to Willetts Farm when Jean and John's children grew up to take an active part in the farm. Ewen damaged the discs in his upper spine while working with the tractor (in those days there were few springs to support the tractor seat, little protection and less Health and Safety awareness) so he left the heavy farm work and went to work for Ross Poultry in Cootham in 1970 which was taken over by Buxted, before moving on to Cheswood, and retiring in 1990.

Woodshill Farm sits on the crest of the hill that unofficially divides the old village from Broadford Bridge, and is the watershed from where the River Adur flows north, the River Arun flows south and where the soils also change. To the south of Woodshill the soil is predominantly sandy to the pure strip of Thakeham greensand, and to the north it turns into Sussex clay. James Greenfield occupied the 390 acre farm in 1851, farming with three labourers and a boy for the Parham Estate, although by about 1915 Mr and Mrs J Coles owned it and its farmland which continued up the west side of Broadford Bridge Road. Over the years Mr Coles sold off the land until all he was left with was Woodshill itself, Gobles and 90 acres of forestry; this woodland is remembered by many because of the hundreds of daffodils he planted there.

A group of girls born in the 1930s recently had a get-together to reminisce over old times, and recalled meeting on the corner by the Queens Head with their dolls' prams on spring Saturdays and going up to London Copse through the fields. They would take a ball of wool to tie the daffodils and primroses into bunches for decorating the Church on Sunday. London Copse is opposite Woodshill.

Bill Hampton first came to the village aged 2½ in 1909 when his father worked at Woodshill for Mr and Mrs Coles before Mr Hampton volunteered for the First World War. The family lived in a cottage which had a bit of garden with an oak tree, a plum tree and a gooseberry bush, and they grew vegetables and fruit there. Bill says "My earliest recollections of life were at Woodshill where, shortly after we arrived, I got inflammation of the lungs and pneumonia. The remedy for that was a

Woodshill

hot bread poultice in flannel bags on the chest - I remember it, and that nurse! Mrs Coles very kindly got a trained nurse in to look after me and I can see that nurse coming in every morning with that bag. My screaming was so bad that Mother had to get away from it by going for a walk round the fields! The Doctor from Billingshurst said that if I got over that, I'd get over anything, and here I am now in my 90s! After Father volunteered, and left, Mother was expected to do work in the big house to make up for his not being there, for his wage of £1 a week and a cottage. There was no power in those days, my dear, and she got no help. There was a well about 100' deep that the water came from. Woodshill is the second highest point in the village, Highbarn is the highest, and every time Mother wanted water it had to come from the well. If we ever lost a bucket down the well we used to have a grabber, a thing with three hooks on, on the end of a long rope, which we lowered into the well to retrieve the bucket - I can see it now, just a little white reflection. It was terrifying; there was nothing to stop you falling in, only your hands hanging on to the side. Eventually Mother moved to Gentle Harry's Cottage where she worked in the house in lieu of rent.

Before Father volunteered he'd done three years chauffeuring; the Armstrong Siddley at Woodshill was the only car in the village at the time, so he was immediately put onto the army lorries, but the officers could soon see that he was experienced and promoted him to working with the staff cars. There were so few cars in 1914 that there weren't many experienced drivers. So he survived the war and came back, labouring at Nyetimber; he could have had the chauffeur's job if he'd wanted but his heart was with horses; he had been an apprentice at Fontwell Racecourse, and he couldn't really settle. We stayed at Gentle Harry's and he biked to Amberley and all the other places where he worked.

From my bedroom window up at Woodshill I could see the gypsy's camp down Broadford Bridge. They would put up the bent poles with a sheet over them and there they'd be making pegs to take round. They'd come round the houses to buy rabbit skins at twopence a time, and rags, bottles and bones. We were reared on rabbits, that was our chief food and I loved them - stewed, and rabbit pie with some nice pork fat put in it, roasted, any way. I've been catching rabbits all my life, on one farm just the other side of Broadford Bridge a friend and I caught 1,100 one winter; there was always a market for them. Ted Carver and I used to do seven days a week for seven months catching rabbits throughout the winter, in all weathers, and the butchers used to come out from Brighton for them. One Brighton butcher had a brother who was gardening for Colonel Kensington at Voakes, Ted Carpenter was his name, and he used to come out on Sundays to pick up what we had got over three days, and the other three days we used to put the rabbits on the bus down to Brighton, sometimes as many as 50 or 60. We didn't skin them, just sent them as they were, but the gypsies always wanted the skins.

Mr Coles was a hunting man, spent most of his time down in his wood with his birds or the timber; he'd spend no end of time collecting wood. Father had to go down with the pony and buggy and bring it back up and then Mr Coles would be sawing it all up to keep all the rooms warm in the winter because the big house was all flagstones and cold. Some forty years later when I went back to Woodshill to work for Mr Landon, gardening, there it was, the old buggy; been laid there all those years, I recognised it straight away.

Dad used to have to cut the lawn with a big pony drawn mower, but as the pony was only about twelve hands it was small and light enough for its hooves not to cut up the turf. The Coles had two daughters, Doris and Enid, and on tennis garden party days I was roped in as ball boy on the promise of strawberries and cream!

Mondays was washing and drying day at Woodshill; I had to chop the wood to get the copper going and draw the water. Tuesdays was a full day's ironing, for all of us had to help. Mother died in 1960 and had never lived in a house with electricity, always paraffin lamps and candles. It was tough, but we could go anywhere we wanted, play in the woods and fields and never have our parents worry about us."

Dr Ford lived on the Common and knew Mr and Mrs Coles in the late 1950s when they were into their eighties. He explained that he was called in when one of the Horsham stone slabs that roofed the house became dislodged and fell on Mrs Kitty Coles as she was gardening in one of the flower beds that ran along the house walls. Although the slab did not fracture her skull, it did knock her senseless and she was never the same again. Dr Ford had got to know the family, and explained "Mr Coles had been the standard bearer for Cecil Rhodes in the Matabele campaign of the Boer War. Even in his eighties, Mr Coles used to climb a ladder to clean the gutters, and Woodshill is a three storey house. There is an oak post that the stairs wind round, running the full height of the house, from the floor up to the apex of this high roof. It is an interesting property in other ways too, it has a cradle stone in the kitchen, and the drawing room panelled. Another intriguing thing is that they used to have acetylene lighting; the acetylene was generated from their own plant housed in a hut in the garden. You make acetylene by putting water on calcium carbide and they used to use it for batteries and old bicycle lamps."

After Mr Coles died in the late 1950s, the property was sold to a Mr Longhurst, a timber merchant from Epsom. It is said that he felled all the oaks in the woodland, and any oaks in the hedgerows, only sparing those he had pre-marked with white paint. When he had extracted what he could, he sold the remains of the woods to the Forestry Commission, and put the rest of the farm on the market, too; it hung fire for some time until John and Jean Steele bought it in 1960. Included in the price of £5,000 was 8 acres of woodland in the middle of the farm, originally planted by Mr Coles in 1908 and containing a plaque to this effect. Unfortunately even this wood had been cut; mostly firs, it had been felled and sold for pit props during the war; it is Harvie Steele who has replanted it with oak, ash and wild cherry following the two storms of 1987 and spring 1988 which toppled many of the remaining trees, and he now maintains it as an asset. The present occupants of Woodshill are Simon Gray and Minnette LeStrange.

There is a horror story here: Woodshill was once owned by a family there called McArdle. Mr McArdle was a naval commander on the

Hermes and away from home for long periods, and his wife, a South African, was bright and gay and happy; they had two daughters. One day as Ewen Steele was finishing milking, Mr McArdle, who had been washing the car, rushed out and asked him to run for the doctor as his wife had had an accident. It was no accident, though, as she had shot herself through the head with a .22 rifle, in the bathroom leading from the main bedroom. Almost as unfortunate was the fact that, it being 9am, the younger daughter went up and found her. The bloodstains remained for some time, although the next owners (the Landons) did not seem to mind the sudden demise of the previous owner.

Woodshill farm is now quite separate from the main house and is run by John Steele's family. John was the third son of James and Christina; John and Jean had two sons, Harvie and Ramsey who now manage the farm between them, and two daughters who moved away to where their husbands worked, as was traditional at that time. Jean remembers the early days: "When we took over here at Woodshill we had about twenty cows and the dairy was the building on the right as you came in through the entrance. It was convenient for the milk lorries which would come through the forenoon to collect the full churns and leave the empty ones. In those days we were hand milking and cooling the milk in a cooler. The water had only recently been put on and the dairy still only had a tap so the water would flow through the cooler and be collected in a depression in the ground, and be bucketed back to the top again. It wasn't long before we got that changed!"

The family all laugh as Harvie tells the story of the water: "Mr Coles had paid for the water to come up here from Broadford Bridge and was very surprised when he found the men digging out a trench in the village. He told them they were digging in the wrong place, but was assured that they knew what they were doing. When the bill for the work finally arrived he discovered that he had been landed with paying for water to be piped all the way over the hill and down to the village. He had been had and was not amused! Afraid that he would be had again, we never got electricity! It wasn't until 1956/7 that Mr Longhurst had electricity supplied, over from the back of Willetts. Because we didn't have electricity, we didn't have a television, and I can remember scanning the chimneys for aerials. After school on a Friday we used to call in to Granny's at New House Farm to watch Children's Television, the cowboy film! Mr Penfold was the electrician that installed our electricity and I remember coming home from school each day and switching the light switches to see if it was on yet. I also got into trouble about the water because when it was connected, I wanted to be the first to flush the brand new inside toilet - the only problem was that the other end hadn't been connected to the septic tank, and the cistern was full! We still aren't on mains drainage, like quite a lot of the village."

When Willetts Farm was sold up, some of the land returned to the Steele family because Harvie and Ramsey bought it back and incorporated it into Woodshill. At present the farm carries about 280 head of cattle, with 70 being milkers and 25 being dry, the rest are heifers and bullocks, and the two bulls, a Hereford and a Friesian. Harvie and Ramsey use a mixture of their own bulls and AI (Artificial Insemination) for breeding, keeping the dairy calves. In March 1971 a new electrically operated milking parlour was built for five cows each side; they can milk about sixty cows an hour. They milk twice a day, and Harvie explains "We'd get more milk if we milked three times a day as it stimulates the cow to produce more, but it's better this way. When the milk quotas came in, I know of one or two farmers who were milking three times a day and didn't want to get rid of any cows so, to reduce their milk to within the quota, simply milked twice a day instead. The milk quota system came in on 1 April 1984, and we all had to produce 10% less than we had in that month in the year before; they seemed to make the rules up as they went along, because we were then allowed to adjust the figure over three months, then six months, then a year. However, by January, February and March 1985 we were looking back to before the quota system came in for our base figure, that is, to those months in 1983. The record keeping was a nightmare. Initially the milk quota itself had no value, each dairy farmer was just issued with this figure, but if the farmer went out of milk, he could sell his quota to the highest bidder. Then, facing a butter mountain in the EEC, they brought in a butter fat base of 3.72%; we had spent years building a herd that produced rich milk and then discovered that the cows were too good, so were penalised by having the high butter fat content count against our quota. It's a far cry from the way my parents used to farm, but even then there were regulations; there were Ministry checks for hygiene, cleanliness and milk quality - they could tell if you'd watered the milk down, or skimmed off the cream. They used paper strips then, like Litmus paper.

Now we're having a problem with the beef calves because of the BSE situation. The BSE crisis hasn't hit the farm too badly directly, but we have suffered the indirect effects. Normally we wouldn't fatten our beef calves, selling them on at about 15 to 24 months old, but as we can't sell them and the prices are rock bottom anyway, we have to hold on to them. One of the problems with the BSE business was that it was an unknown factor, no-one would come out and say directly what was causing the disease. There was even one stage when they thought it was caused by the warble fly dressing of organophosphate that we used to use because the chemical was put on the cows' backs and was allowed to work itself in; it wasn't compulsory to dress cattle for warble fly but a lot of people did as it was recommended. We couldn't believe that it was the meat and bonemeal feed at first because we've used that for donkey's years and it's never done any harm, but it does have to be sterilised properly and how were we to know if that was happening? We used to mix our own cattle feed years ago, and we used a little bonemeal then, but we'd prepared it so we knew it was good. Now we use a cereal feed based on soya, wheat and maize."

The Steele family and the Pavey family histories meet at Gobles; Grandfather Charles Pavey and his wife Emma farmed Gobles Farm for some thirty years and bore and brought up fifteen children. When their combined ages totalled 1,000 years there was an enormous party to celebrate, which was held at Gracefield Farm in West Chiltington Lane where Fred Pavey Senior farmed. All eight sisters and seven brothers, with succeeding generations, were able to attend.

Alma Steele continues "I'll tell you a story about those cottages at Gobles: long ago when Grandfather Pavey lived there he used to walk his dog across the fields to the Broadford Bridge Road. Some years ago two young lads in the village went off on the new motorbike that one of them had been given for his recent 16th birthday, and didn't come back. A thorough search found the bike in a ditch on the Broadford Bridge Road, one boy dead and the other in a coma, and no apparent reason for the crash. Some years later, which now brings it to quite recently, a WI member was coming to the meeting in the village; she didn't drive so her husband used to drive her, and on this occasion he arrived to collect her, very shaken. It appeared that on his way back home up Broadford Bridge Road he had had to brake very sharply to avoid an old man, and his car nearly went into the ditch. It was at the same time that it had been calculated that the boys had crashed, and in the same place. An old man, walking his dog, had materialised through the hedge onto the road, dressed in farm worker's garb with his trousers tied with string, and had vanished through the hedge on the other side, causing the driver to swerve, almost into the ditch. The driver didn't know the story of the two boys, and it is quite possible that they too had had to swerve to avoid the apparition, and, being inexperienced, had crashed. And the old man looked just like Grandfather Pavey."

Fred Pavey was born at Hillside, Harbolets Road, in 1926, when his father, also Fred, was employed on Danhill Farm. The family moved to Dorking in 1936, where Fred Senior managed a farm for a Colonel Barclay, returning to Willetts Farm as manager for Mr A S Crum in 1939.

When Rowan Bentall purchased the farm in 1959 Fred, who had married Pam Church, bought the new bungalow at Willetts which was known as Willetts Bungalow, before moving on five years later to Coombers, Broadford Bridge. There they grew soft fruit, growing up to 100,000 strawberry plants for fruit production. They would deliver daily, a contractor taking the fruit to London and Fred taking their own van to Brighton, leaving at 3am. The fruit was sold through wholesalers. The plants were grown under cover - cloches, polythene tunnels and mobile glasshouses, which were towed by tractor and winch to cover succeeding crops when necessary. By using the mobile glasshouses, three crops were obtained: first and second crop strawberries followed by autumn cropping raspberries which usually lasted into November and December. The rest of the season was used for cleaning and preparing for the beginning of the strawberry crop in early May. New stock plants were bought in each year and Fred would take runners from these new plants to ensure that there was no build up of disease. It was a successful system and very little spraying of insecticide was necessary.

Coombers, diagonally opposite the corner of the general store, used to be a poultry farm and was owned by Mr and Mrs Greenfield until Fred bought it in 1960. Fred and his brother Les built the bungalow on their land at Coombers and built and opened the kiosk on the main road from Adversane to sell his produce to local people. They did a good trade from there, but closed the shop when they sold Coombers and moved to Gracefield.

Fred recalls "My grandfather on my mother's side (Henry Peirce) built Hillside around 1920. During that period he owned both shops in the little hamlet centred on the cross roads, as well as other property up at Broadford Bridge. The shops were still open while we lived at Willetts; Mrs Mansbridge's general store (she subsequently owned it) on the Broadford Bridge Road sold just about everything, an inner tube for the

Broadford Bridge Post Office – probably 1930s
These roads had grass in the middle until the late 1920s

Brook House with the Store in the background

Broadford Bridge Cross Roads – late 1930s
The telegraph did not arrive until the 1930s; the poles were made of old railway lines stood on end, with wooden cross pieces added

bike, paraffin, groceries, sweets, anything; and there was a Post Office and paper shop on Harbolets Road, which was subsequently owned by Mr Young. The Post Office was a room at the front of the house and when it went back to being a house that front bit was taken down. It was the advent of the supermarket that killed them, I think."

The general store is now a house called Old Store Cottage, and the present owners, Dave and Terri Carpenter explain that the old path and gateway to the shop can still be identified by a line in the front lawn, and a section of stonework in the front wall different from the rest. The old blue and white advertisement sign for Fryco aerated waters is still on the chimney and they have dug up another sign from the garden. Unfortunately the sign for Pratts petrol has gone. Next door to Old Store Cottage stands Little Croft, the home of Mr and Mrs Taylor who believe that their house was once used as a forge or blacksmith's. Although they have not been able to find any documentary evidence to back this up there is anecdotal evidence and they have unearthed from the garden old buckles, parts of wheels and machinery which a blacksmith would have worked on, and, at one end of the house there was a great deal of clinker and ash which could have come from a forge.

Willetts Farm's history is perhaps typical of many farms in the parish. Joyce Gibney (née Tuck), now living in Horsham, recalls her time at Willetts Farm during and after the First World War when, as a small child she went to stay with Aunty Alice and Uncle Tom Evershed to avoid the privations of wartime in London. When the war ended she used to visit during school holidays to enjoy the fresh air and good food, "It was a general farm of about sixty to eighty acres, a reasonable sized farm with cows and bullocks, grazing, corn and oats. In those days you only needed ten cows to get started and you could make a living, but these days you would need over sixty to make the sort of living that would provide everything that people seem to want now. Tom Evershed used to have sheep up from the Romney marshes for the winter grazing as it was too wet there in the winter and they would have got foot rot. We children used to help on the farm, earn our keep as it were, but it didn't feel like work; we felt we were real country children. There were always the animals, we had to feed the chickens, there were calves to be fed, milking to do, buckets to be taken about. It wasn't considered work, it had to be done and we helped. We would go up in the granary and the calf shed. They used to buy linseed cake in sheets and it had to be put in a machine to be ground up. Mangels were cut up in slices for the cattle, which were milked by hand. There were girls there, working on the farms in the First World War, or it may have been a bit later, like the Land Army of the Second World War. Aunty Alice had a girl working with her and she came from the Falklands to help with the chickens.

The daily routine started when Uncle had something to eat early before going out to milking, then came back for a proper breakfast. Dinner was a cooked meal at mid-day and supper was about 6 o'clock, a good meal of bread and cheese, perhaps, but not cooked. There was proper butter from the farm and lashings of cream on the fruit and puddings. The skimmed milk was given to the pigs and chickens; if you had young chicks it was mixed with the cereal. The waste from the house was also used, leftovers for the pigs. You didn't have washing-up liquid so the water from the washing-up was mixed with the chicken meal. You used soda, which you would buy from the corn merchants not the grocers, to get the grease off the plates.

I don't remember the milk being cooled, but it was separated. The milk is poured in at the top, underneath there are two bits of the separator, one took out the cream and one took out the skimmed milk. We children always took a turn of the handle. We also turned the churn handle to make the butter and that was sent to Steyning market. The cream would be put aside in a crock and the butter would be made once or twice a week from the cream that was left over. You put the cream in the churn, sealed it down turned the handle and it would slop about inside; it was quite hard work and would take about an hour to do. We also had to use a hand pump for the water for the house. There was a kitchen range to cook on and to heat the water, and the other job was to chop the wood for fuel; the fires only ever burned wood although there was coal for the range. The wood came in from the clearing in faggots, and you had to go and get a faggot from the woodshed, cut the tie around it and chop the faggot to pieces. We children were about ten when we started work like this, but we grew up sensible enough to be careful and know the danger.

I wore a thin pleated skirt and a knitted jumper, long socks and wellingtons. Aunty Alice wore khaki dungarees! This was on the farm, normally girls did not wear trousers. Normally the ladies wore skirts, blouses and cardigans, and corsets so there were no gaps. My mother never wore a bra. There were suspenders to hold up the stockings, big suspenders that came down over the bottom. The stockings were lisle, quite thick and woolly but we didn't wear stockings until we were about fourteen and I fought against them for as long as I could as the suspenders were such a business. We wore liberty bodices with the buttons on and vests; we wore a lot of clothes. And they all had to be washed and ironed, ironed with a flat iron. You heated the iron on the fire and covered it with a slipper, a shiny metal thing held on with a wire, to stop the dirty iron getting on the clothes. Sometimes the irons were put directly onto the coals when the fire was getting low. Otherwise there was a trivet which held the iron against the fire bars to get hot. There was a kettle on the side and also a teapot; it was real tea, with leaves, not in a teabag, like today. I was reading in a book somewhere that some people used to dry the leaves to use again in some kitchens! Even during the war years I can't remember being short of food, and there was always potatoes, and fruit.

The old farmhouse had wide window sills and we used to have a jigsaw of Britain out on it; we all used to have a go at it, it was a good geography lesson. I can't remember what we used to do, or play, when it was wet. There was a big parlour with a big table, two easy chairs with leather covers and a collection of dining chairs, an open fire and lino on the floor with a rug. We were four adults and six or seven children. The room was lit by paraffin lamps, there was one heavy one, green with brass corners and a globe. We took candles to bed, in candlesticks. It could be cold upstairs, there were no fireplaces up there. One bedroom was divided by curtains into two or three for the girls that helped on the farm at one time. Uncle Tom rented the farm; although it was offered on the market he would not buy it, he didn't want to get into debt, which is so different from today."

The farm passed into the hands of Mr A S Crum who, when he died left it to his son, Colonel J S Crum, eventually being sold to Mr Grace of Herongate, with Fred Pavey Senior the farm manager. After the death of Mr Grace, Mr Bentall bought it in 1959 and continued to run it as a mixed farm until he sold it in 1980 following a tragically fatal accident to one of his men. It was at this time that the first break-up of the estate began with the sale of Willetts End, two bungalows and Gobles as seven lots. What was left of the farm was bought by John and Sally Row who gradually moved over from a mixed farm to beef. In 1987 the rest of the farm was sold in lots: East Cottage Farm which had been the Farm Manager's house was extended and sold with about 21 acres and is now a livery stables; the Willetts Farm House was sold with about five outbuildings and some 10 acres as a private house, and Wealden Grain, which has its main headquarters at Coneyhurst, has renamed its section Willetts Farm and utilised the grain dryers, some of which were there in Mr Bentall's time.

Anthony Archer-Wills moved to Gay Street, West Chiltington, in the spring of 1963 when he was sixteen years old, just after the hard winter when Gay Street was choked with snow from hedge to hedge. His grandmother had bought the house, and his water garden business began in her garden. He landscaped the garden with ponds and interesting trees and shrubs, and it gradually developed so that in the 1970s it was opened to the public under the National Gardens Scheme. Morning coffee and cream teas were served and people came from far and wide to choose plants and fish for their gardens, and to sample the home made cakes.

The business continued to grow and in 1988 he purchased some land in Broadford Bridge Road from Mr John Row at Willetts; the land had been known to him for years as Mr Bentall had been a customer of his.

At one stage they employed fifteen local people who worked in the Broadford Bridge nursery or on outside pond maintenance and construction projects. The construction work is now carried out by outside contractors and they have only a small staff, mainly drawn from West Chiltington. The north end of the lane is quiet and the only passing traffic is on the way to and from the golf course or the village.

Next door to Anthony Archer-Wills nursery is the timber yard of Storrington Sawmills, owned by Paul à Barrow who came to Sussex as a boy from Wiltshire with his mother. After a year at Plumpton agricultural college, with the aid of a helpful bank manager he started his own business in 1987 based at Parham Sawmill. There was a silver lining to the hurricane of that year in that it gave Paul plenty of work and made his name well known; he has now moved to the yard in Broadford Bridge Road and employs two full-time men and at least one part-timer.

Continuing north from Willetts on the east side of Broadford Bridge Road is Clayes Farm, but again the original farmland has been subdivided.

How different from Willetts is Cattlestone Farm, the farm of Frank and Madeleine Dougharty on Harbolets Road. The first problem is to find out how to pronounce their name. Frank explained that centuries ago his family had been on the wrong side at the battle of Culloden and to escape the terrible slaughter that took place afterwards their family hastily assumed an Irish sounding name. They pronounce it dock-erty, although doh-arty is also used. The second problem is that Cattlestone was not actually in West Chiltington Parish, but was an island of Thakeham Parish of great antiquity surrounded by West Chiltington. In 1279 the rector of West Chiltington and several of his helpers came into a field called Rushfield to collect tithes, and found the rector of Thakeham also there to collect tithes. The Thakeham rector was shot with an arrow and attacked with a hatchet; the attacker was then killed by one of the Thakeham rector's men who was later outlawed. The field is still called Rushfield and is part of Cattlestone and for many years tithes were paid annually to Thakeham. The Doughartys' allegiance now is partly to Billingshurst because their children went to school and made friends there, and that is where they go to Church, and partly to West Chiltington because of their interest in the flower show (of which Frank's grandfather was one of the founder members) and because Frank himself went to school in the village, walking across the fields.

Frank explains his recent family history: "My grandfather came here in 1896 and my father was born here in 1901. The farm house used to be two houses and was part of the Shelley holding; we farm here, and we have a son who is interested in farming so we hope to pass it on. We have beef cattle, mostly Simmental/Aberdeen Angus cross, and we breed our own, keeping them until they're fully grown. We also have free range chickens and we grow cereals, and grass for hay; we try to be self-sufficient but it doesn't always happen! The beef cattle go to market in Guildford or Hailsham as all the local markets have closed down. We used to do veal, pigs, sheep and turkeys but as the markets closed we had to turn to other things. Now that more people are keeping recreational horses I grow more hay; with our flower meadows it's good hay and we never seem to have enough. We are environmentally friendly, but unfortunately we're outside the special areas such as Downlands or wetlands or whatever, so we miss out on the extra funding. We have a hill, and during the war we were made to plough it up because it was considered to be good soil. It faces north and has numerous springs coming out of it so it was the first field back into grass after the war. We used to grow mangolds and kale and turnips, then it was silage; farming is all about changing and adapting to circumstances.

I'm a great diarist so have kept records of how things have changed over the generations: the water was laid on in 1948 and electricity the following year; we had a little generator but we mostly only used it at night. We were, still are, very 'Olde Worlde' up here, Madeleine used to do the washing in a copper". Madeleine takes up the story: "We had a metal one and lit a fire under it like a witch's cauldron with a chimney out the back. You brought the water up to the boil, dunked your clothes in it and you had your wringer next to it. We had oil lamps when we were first married; they gave a warm light and warmth!

When the children were little we had a goose and our eldest daughter used to 'dare' it when she was riding her tricycle; one day the goose flew at her and bit her bottom - she still has the scars to prove it!

I recall some of the stories my father used to tell: As the landowner he was responsible for the upkeep of his stretch of road. He used to go to Findon for flints to repair the road, which was actually a track then. Broadford Bridge Road was made up with winklestone which was quarried at Holders Farm up Coneyhurst Lane; not quarried so much as dug out, you can still see where there are dips in the land. Our clay land was fertilised with quicklime which was brought home on dry days - if it had got wet it would have burned the cart. Father used to go to Steyning market on a Wednesday and Pulborough market on a Monday with the pony and cart (before he had his Austin Seven car just before the war); if he needed any shopping he got it at Wiston Post Office which he went right past; the horse was just tied up to a post or a fence, the horses were well behaved and didn't run off. He also remembered that, in his father's day, the sheep used to come from Romney Marsh to Billingshurst Station by cattle wagon for the winter. They were walked from the station to their fields, probably across other fields, and then do the return journey in the spring. Father would still recognise this place as we try to keep it the old way: things are mostly as they used to be, we don't fill in ditches or pull out hedges. As our neighbour's hedges got smaller ours got bigger and wider and busier! We have dormice and harvest mice, lots of flowers, some of them rare, for example the Scandix or Shepherd's Needle was a very common plant but was nearly wiped out by spraying the corn, and there was a time when we were the only farm in Sussex to have it. I think it's beginning to recover a bit now. We still have our skylarks and song thrushes and yellowhammers. It reminds me of my walks to school, past badger setts and through London Copse where all the flowers are. The bluebells there are lovely now as are the wild daffodils, but when the evacuees came down from London they didn't always pick the flowers, they often uprooted the bulbs and broke the flowers off later - I suppose they didn't know any better. We replanted lots of these bulbs but it took a long time to recover. Madeleine came down as one of the evacuees, but says 'I didn't do it, honest!'

I know that farming can be very difficult, Father said that during the Depression they sold a cow for about £2 as the prices for eggs, pigs and cattle had fallen so low. Otherwise I don't think we were all that affected in the country. But in farming times often seem to be hard, we have to be constantly changing as markets for our produce close and rules and regulations from home and Europe demand different standards, we're now farming our 76 acres as permanent pasture and arable."

For centuries the land north and south of Harbolets Road, and east of the Broadford Bridge junction had been owned by the various gentry families of Sussex: Parham Estate included Oldhouse Farm and some of the land at Coneyhurst. Near the present Harbolets house the estate had made over strips of land to be allotments for the cottage holders. On the eastern boundary the heirs of the West Dean Estate had owned Goringlee; by 1895 it was owned by Colonel Boxall while by 1964 South Goringlee was part of the Hungerhill (now called Coolham Manor) Estate. Miss Cordelia Shelley, succeeded by her nephews WW and EAR Dalbiac, at one time owned Brook Farm and Cattlestone Farm, several cottages at Broadford Bridge including the general stores and also eight acres of Coneyhurst Common. As the estates were sold off and the land parcelled into lots, more cottages and smallholdings could be established along the roads.

Ann Salisbury (see Chapter 6) moved to Harbolets in 1966 from her family home Southcroft in Monkmead Lane. Although the location was ideal she recalls that there was not the feeling of 'village community' that there had been in Roundabout; it was more a group of properties whose occupants acted independently. "The only time we really felt part of a community" she says "was after the hurricane when everyone really did pull together. Perhaps it had not always been like that and it was the speed of traffic on an increasingly busy road, coupled with the loss of the corner shops that finally destroyed any community spirit which was difficult enough to generate with the houses so far apart. It was such a contrast to the Roundabout area. Over the years the horses went and I had donkeys, then cattle and finally sheep grazed the land to keep the grass down, but in 1987 I finally sold up and came back into the village with its closer amenities. The house, which had been built in 1904 on the site of another dwelling, still has its seven acres; as it is in a 'green belt' area the land cannot be built on."

Following Harbolets Road (B2133) to the west of Broadford Bridge the parish boundary runs first on one side and then the other, and the bank and ditch that mark it can be seen in the undergrowth. Highfure House in Billingshurst parish can be seen across the fields; the Ireland family who lived there also farmed Wood Barn and Pocock's Barn farms in the last century, and Brook Farm which used to be known as Irelands. There were more cottages along the road then, as well; Mr Humphrey occupied one next to Marringdean Road where the ecclesiastical parish boundary still includes a little rectangular area. There were two cottages where the house, Oakleigh, which has 1898 picked out in contrasting brick on its gable end, stands near Adversane; Jimmy Sands who built and owned it was a blacksmith, wheelwright, carpenter and builder, a Jack-of-all-trades who also built Glendale across the road. He had a smithy in the garden; the brick building with a chimney and the bellows (slightly chewed by mice) is still there and a child of the time can remember playing with the old tools. There are two stories told about Jimmy: he had a man trap fixed to the outside of the smithy until it was stolen, and when visited by Rev Caldecott who chastised him for not attending church he replied that 'if he wanted the church pulled down, then he'd be there to do it!'

Opposite the end of Marringdean Road (the road to Billingshurst) is the drive to Steepwood Farm which is joined to Gay Street by bridleways. Steepwood Farm was farmed by Robert Myram from 1885 and was a typical mixed farm of about 250 acres including woodland. In the 1930s his newly-married son Robert Eustace Myram was offered a chance to buy the property when it came up for sale, but in those days there were no preferential agricultural mortgages (from organisations such as the Agricultural Mortgage Company) so the offer was not taken up. The present Robert Myram (Robert's grandson) continues: "We were very involved with the hunt as father hunted and rode in point-to-points and had successful horses, such as Flashlight II and Churchill III. Mother used to walk foxhound puppies, a tradition carried on by my wife Jane, who would also have bitches to whelp. The hounds have to be about nine months old before they can return to kennels, and so that they have a broader understanding of life outside the kennels they are sent out to puppy-walkers to learn about people, machinery, our cats and dogs and other animals on the farm. This prevents them getting frightened, and therefore misbehaving, when confronted with something they might not have met before.

The land was hunted originally by Lord Leconfield who, at that time owned a large wood called Goatchers Furze, and he sent a team of men in each year to clear the rides and manage the fox covers. When the railway line was electrified and could not be hunted from Petworth the land was loaned to the Crawley and Horsham. We used to have a meet at Steepwood, pony club events and rallies, as well as continuing to run it as a commercial mixed family farm. In 1981 the dairy herd was dispersed and corn growing ceased, to concentrate on sheep and cattle, and turkeys for the Christmas trade.

There used to be a lot of corn grown on the Weald, and during the war Father had one of the reaper-binders from Brinsbury for the war effort; it was a two-man outfit pulled by a Standard Fordson tractor, with, very often, my mother on the binder, cutting the neighbours' corn.

I remember that there used to be a pond on the Marringdean corner where the gypsies would camp, and Smith and Wood had the builders yard next to the shop on the Broadford Bridge Road. Although we were officially in the parish of West Chiltington, our postal address was Billingshurst; I went to school at Highfure and then Summers Place before going on to Horsham and don't really feel part of the parish at all. When Father died the farm was sold and in 1990 we had to leave, buying a small farm in the Wye Valley." Steepwood is now owned by Mr and Mrs Michael Stock who do not farm the land commercially but use the place as a retreat; Michael is a songwriter and record producer who is working to turn his land into a conservation area. Already the ponds have been cleared and added to, the woodland has been extended and a huge coppiced oak has been discovered. Michael has given over much of his land to a fallow deer sanctuary which is managed on his behalf.

The most westerly farm in West Chiltington Parish is Todhurst, part of Brinsbury Agricultural College; between 1840 when it was mapped for the tithe apportionment, and 1864 when it was mapped for Sales Particulars, the farm underwent radical alterations because the London-Portsmouth railway went through many of the small fields. The old field layout was completely bulldozed by steam engine, land drainage was put in throughout, and after the 1864 sale the field fencing ran at right angles to the railway. The final choice of route for the railway had only been reached after several proposals had been rejected. In the West Sussex Record Office is a series of maps with the proposed routes including one that had a 600' tunnel under the hill at Crowell Farm!

'Diversification' is the current vogue word for farmers and it is in this north part of the parish that the changes in land use can be most clearly seen: the water garden specialist, a sawmill, a grain company, a deer sanctuary and an alpaca farm on land that used to support mixed farming - nowadays it is mixed indeed! Bubbles is probably the only alpaca-herding border collie in the county, if not the country, for at the end of Gay Street in the north-western corner of the parish is Gay Street Farm, managed since September 1998 by Nick Harrington-Smith for Arunvale Alpaca, assisted by Bubbles who came with the farm. Arunvale had bought the farm in December 1995, it is said following the Lloyds finance collapse, showing what repercussions a city crisis can have on a rural farm. Before this Gay Street Farm had reared sheep and beef on its 140 acres, and had probably been a traditional mixed farm since the turn of the century. It is now a leading alpaca farm, having a herd of nearly 500 animals. Alpaca come from South America and are modified ruminants being related to the llama; the handful of alpaca already in this country came from predominantly inbred stock and were kept either in zoos or as hobby-animals.

Arunvale is owned by an Australian farming family which has many businesses world-wide and a great interest in farming alpaca commercially; animals had been imported into Australia from South America and done well, so the company decided to expand into this country. They looked for a compact farm, tucked away in the countryside to avoid the high-profile publicity that befell the ostrich industry, and bought Gay Street Farm; they installed a series of managers before they found Nick who had been in farming in Wiltshire all his life. The industry is in its infancy; the first priority of the company is to improve the stock quality by careful selective breeding for a good frame to carry the maximum fleece. When the Spanish Conquistadors arrived in South America they killed many alpaca for their meat and the survivors fled into the mountains - they are called Vicuna and have the best fleece, but they are protected animals so selective breeding has to be done in this country as Peruvian domestic animals face an eighteen-month quarantine if imported. AI is wholly impractical as there are too many problems, but it is possible that embryo transplant may be used, in spite of its expense, for the very best selections. Good breeding is difficult with limited knowledge of the genetic background of each animal; there are shocks, surprises and delight along the way.

One baby, called a cria, is born each year at the end of an $11^{1}/_{2}$ month gestation period; the animals live outdoors on grass with a winter supplement of hay when necessary and live for about 15-20 years. They are shorn once a year for their fleece, which since a Customs dictate in the late 1800s is called fibre not wool; alpaca fleece was so popular at that time, having the feel of cashmere but being stronger, that the Government of the day thought it might threaten our sheep wool industry and brought in restrictive regulations. Arunvale has invested heavily in a mill for processing the fibre in Australia; over here farmers have combined in a co-operative to process their fleeces which are made into high-quality scarves and woollens, the enhanced value being passed back to the primary producers. (There are about 140 members of the breed society although some only have as few as three or four animals, and there are between 1,600 and 1,700 animals in the country.) By slowly building up the market, and gentling the public's awareness, it is hoped that the business will grow organically as the quality of the stock improves and the amount of fleece per animal increases. At present there is no meat market as there is little meat on the frame.

Nick has been delighted that his quality stock has won convincingly at the breed show; he goes to Ardingly South of England Show and holds Open Days at the farm, so people can go and see some of the only three million alpaca in the world.

The parish continues north to Coneyhurst, even across the A272; part of the Blue Idol property is in the parish of West Chiltington, but only the graveyard of the dead, not the house of the living! Joyce Gibney who was at Willetts later owned Leacroft, the house in the triangle field called

Coneyhurst Common right at the top of the parish and she remembers that in the corner of that field there used to be a beer house; there was a path joining it to the main A272. The beer house eventually lost its licence as it was said to be rowdy, and is now a private residence; the triangle field was leased to feed young stock, and at one time ponies. Gillian and Roger Dougherty moved into Little Farm Studio, in West Chiltington Lane, Coneyhurst, seven years ago; the house was given its name by a previous owner who used the barn as his photographic studio. Roger is a company manager who spends time abroad and Gillian needed an interest while he was away, so, on their return from Spain they discovered Little Farm Studio which she runs as a cattery for 26 domestic cats. Gillian explains that the house has a 17th century core, half of which burned down, a Victorian addition and a 1950s extension, and that the property may have been a coaching inn; it is possible that it was even the beer house called The Cricketers that Joyce Gibney remembers. (This is not on the Deeds but was advertised as such by the house agents, and is remembered by a few old residents.) Gillian echoes Fred Pavey's thoughts "Without the local shops, with the children going to school in Billingshurst, and with a bus to Billingshurst and not any public transport to West Chiltington, we almost feel as if we have dual parish allegiance."

Broadford Bridge Village Stores – about 1910
Pratts is a petrol fuel, the sign on the end of the house says
Fryco – Aerated Waters and Beverages

Chapter 5

The Common

We often refer to "The Old Village" and to "The Common" when talking about West Chiltington. Originally the Common was former waste land, that is to say "The Lord's Waste" where the villagers had common rights of pasture, collecting firewood and so on. When the land was enclosed in 1857 each copyhold property received an allotment in respect of their former rights. These allotments differed in size perhaps reflecting the size of the copyhold messuage (the house and its grounds) and lands. There is a geological basis for this land being the old waste land; the Common is on Lower Greensand Folkestone beds (sands, rock and clay) which would naturally support light woodland with little understorey; the soils are easily impoverished and once early attempts at cultivation, or rainfall, have leached the nutrients the soil becomes acid and supports a limited plant community such as heather. Fire, over-grazing and the collecting of wood and furze for fuel would have maintained the open heathland that we know existed in the 1930's, but when those factors are removed the woodland attempts to colonise again.

It is generally, although unofficially, recognised that the boundary between The Common and The Village is near Daux pond, east of the Mill. Children of the 1920s and 30s remember that the land adjacent to Daux Farm was a pond filled by natural springs (the site is now the grass area in front of Mill Field and Whisperwood). Herbert Short (see next section) used to have a large tank on two wheels which he would fill at this pond and take up the hill to the farm for the horses. Watercress also grew around the pond and people would come and pick it, and take it home for sandwich fillings. Now that the area has been filled in, it is prone to flooding.

The built-up area now known as West Chiltington Common comprises five historic areas of common land belonging to different manorial holdings and in some cases, different parishes.

Many roads have changed their names over the years: Gypsy Hill, so

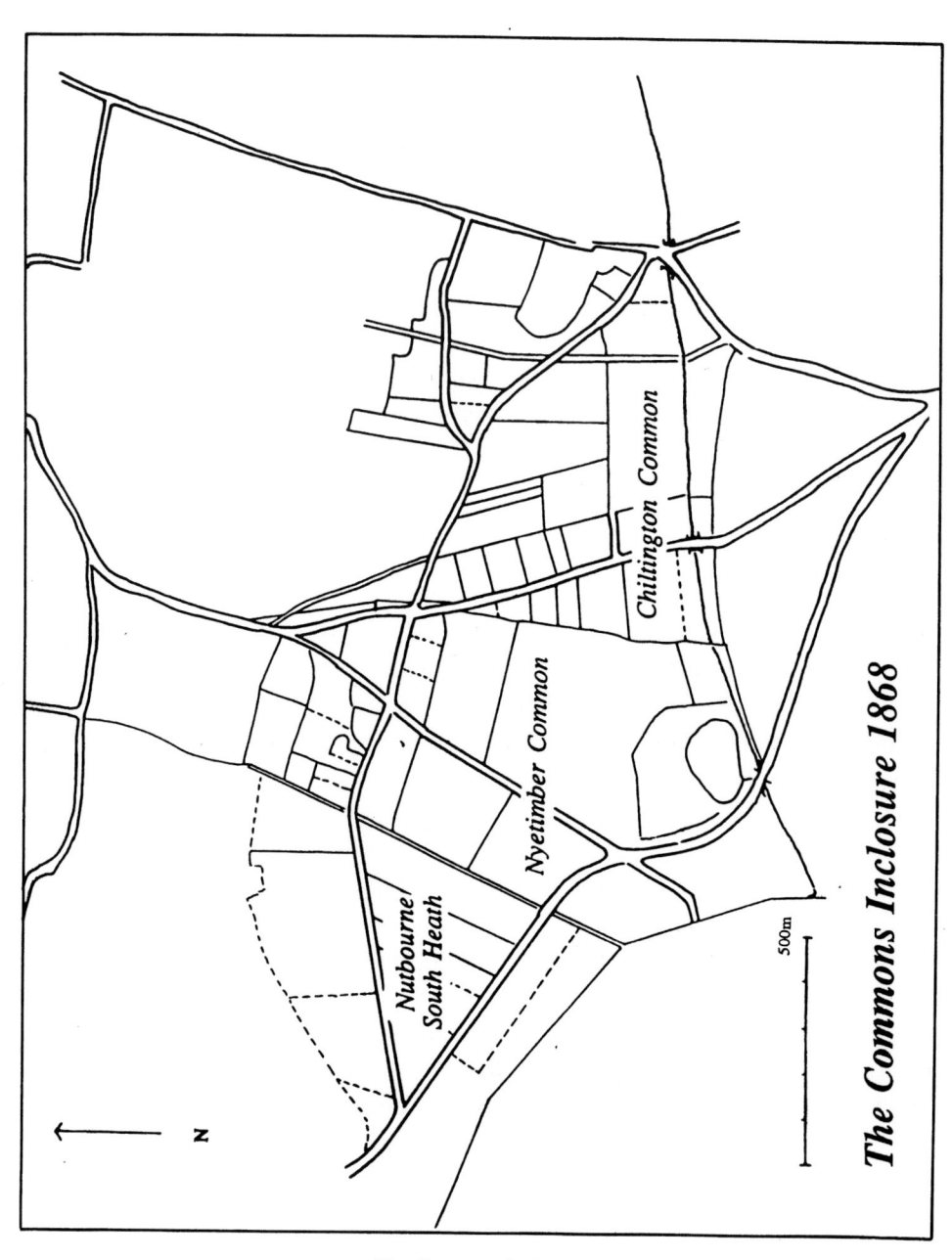

The Common Inclosure

called because of the gypsy caravans there, has become Common Hill; Big Hill has been renamed Mill Road, but Little Hill has retained its name. Harborough Hill used to continue right up to the junction with Nyetimber Lane, but it now stops at Harborough Drive from whence it becomes The Common. This sudden change caused a certain amount of confusion to the residents! In its very early days The Birches was called Council Cottages which was later changed to The Brow.

Elsie Cattell wrote about her first memories of The Common which give a good picture of life in the early part of the century. "I was the ninth child born to Philip and Kate Slater in 1913, we were all born in a cottage on West Chiltington Common called Whales Cottage. Opposite us lived the Barkworths who were gentry and owned much of the surrounding land, otherwise there were fields and common land all around us and just a few odd houses. The muffin man came every Friday with his tray of muffins on his head, swinging his bell to announce his arrival as he walked down through the village. My grandfather, who was called Old Ned, was the local builder, and my father was his only son, so naturally carried on the business. They travelled around by horse and cart as at this time there were very few cars. There were several families of gypsies in what is now Fir Tree Lane living either in caravans, or one or two had more permanent shelters. They were nice people and in the winter you could see the smoke from their fires. They made wooden pegs and sold them from door to door, along with combs and pieces of lace. Many of them could not read or write so Granny Slater used to read their letters for them, and write them too, if necessary."

The sandy Common of heather, bracken and gorse, stretched down from the crossroads to Fir Tree Lane in one direction, and down Mill Road in another, along Lordings Lane, and down the hill towards Pulborough; Martlets was built on Commonland Farm land, and Nightingales was also built on fields. No one used the common land for agriculture, but someone did have a donkey there. The stovold (or area of common/waste land) which stretched from Hindle Close down Lordings Lane and back towards Crossways, is an area fondly remembered by the children of the time who used the space "like our own garden" to build dens in, to climb the trees and to use for hide and seek; they played in its gorse and bracken, gathered wild raspberries, strawberries and blackberries, and watched the rabbits. The area was also used as a recreation field for football and cricket, and with no public transport in those days, Harry Short, who had been born at Holdens (a smallholding in Mill Lane) in 1894, used to drive the teams to away matches in the farm lorry.

Common Hill – early or pre-1920s

Smell can be an evocative sense, and many children remember the pervading smell of the wood fires from the gypsy caravans; they might have been a bit afraid of the gypsies but the smell from their fires was a wonderful, welcoming smell.

The modern Common is centred around the cross roads and the various shops there; long, long before the cross roads was built, the main lane to Common Land Farm was down what is now the footpath to The Martlets, the original cross roads being there while Mill Road did not exist on its present site at all. It is also interesting to think that Mill Road and The Hollows may be so winding because they follow the drove roads that the cattle used to use, and cattle never walk in a straight line!

The Shorts were one of the three biggest market gardeners in West Chiltington, farming Haglands, Commonland and Holden's Farms. Herbert Short had acquired about 120 acres of land; he farmed Old Haglands, his brother lived in Little Haglands, and his sons worked the other farms: arable, vegetables and fruit were grown.

Connie Slater explains that she was one of Herbert's grand-daughters and was born Connie Short in 1921 at Old Haglands Farm where her parents were living after their marriage; they had had to move in there with father's parents as there was no other property vacant at the time.

Grandfather Herbert Short paid his sons a small wage, and with such a large family (there were twelve children) there was no need to hire labour, except at harvest when a threshing machine would come up from Amberley. The boys all helped each other, and their wives worked on the farm; work which included picking the fruit ready for transport to market, as well as running the house and family. The farms were almost self-supporting in fruit and vegetables, and there were ducks on the big pond at Haglands, as well as the ubiquitous rabbits. Grandfather kept a pig for family use, and with the larder full, times were good.

Herbert, the true patriarch, built Melrose Stores in 1928 for his youngest daughter Gertrude who married Leonard Faires, and the garage for another daughter Daisy who had married a mechanic, Billy Ellis. The third daughter Amy, had Downsview built for her with a big wooden garage, a very modern property; she married Bert Andrews who ran the butcher's shop in Melrose Stores. Old Haglands Farm house with its two staircases, stables and the pond was sold in the late 1920s or early 1930s, and during improvements when mains sanitation came in, the three-seater privy was demolished. This privy was unusual in that there were three holes of different sizes, described as father bear, mother bear and baby bear, which caused great amusement during the war to some local children who used to sit in there and giggle about it!

Even as far back as the 1920s there seems to have been a general shortage of accommodation, a problem solved by Herbert Short's family who bought six railway carriages which came up from Arundel by horse and cart, and later by steam traction engine. These Herbert turned into houses. Cousins Ted Faires, Phyllis Rogers and Connie Slater, explain that these were parked in pairs. There were two on what is now the corner of The Martlets and Big Hill, called one and two The Gables, occupied by Connie's family and by her Uncle Sidney and Aunt Annie and their three children. Two were parallel to Mill Road and were occupied by Herbert and his wife Charlotte in No 1 Gorse View; No 2 was rented by Rose and Ernie Stephenson and their daughter Phyllis from the war years until the early 1950s. Rose was Herbert and Charlotte's granddaughter. The rent was 7/6d rising to 10/- per week. Both 1 and 2 were later occupied by Herbert's daughter Ina (who was universally known as Doll) and her husband. Barwell now stands on the site, the old buildings having been demolished. The last two, called one and two Melrose were further up the hill just above Gorse View, and are still in existence.

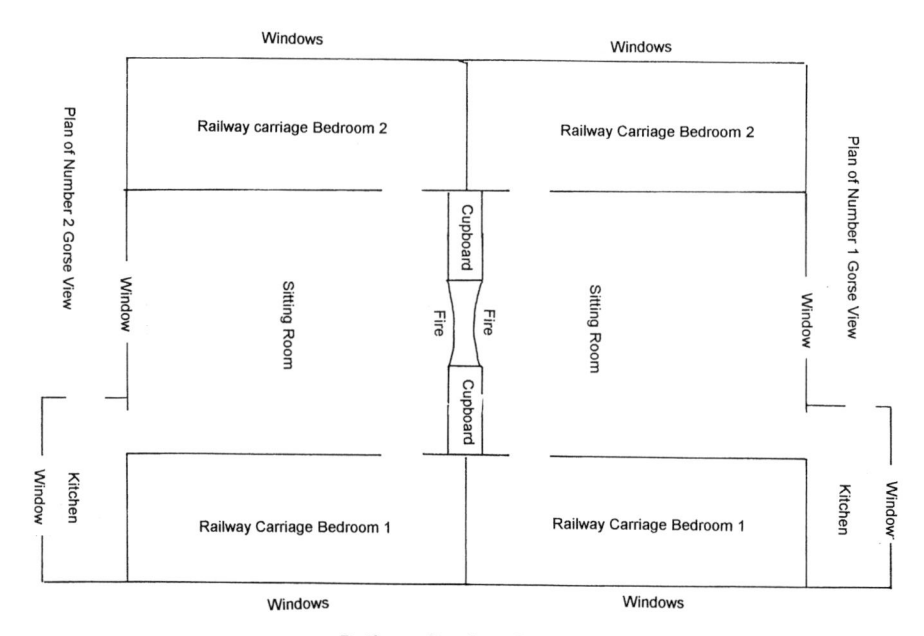

Railway Carriage Interior

    The internal arrangements of these three pairs was the same, the two carriages were parked beside each other with a central space in between which was divided crossways so that the carriages became the four bedrooms, the central space was the living room divided in half for each family with a lean-to kitchen. There was a fire, back to back in each half, in the middle with cupboards beside it, and a pitched corrugated iron roof. The fire in its orange tiled fireplace heated the whole place up so it was very cosy, this fire replaced the original Kitchener stove which had been used both for heating and cooking; cooking was now done on an electric cooker. The central floor was raised to make it level with the carriages, which were standing on wooden railway sleepers; the space underneath was a wonderful retreat for Phyllis and the young Colin Knight to play games. The windows had the old sash openings with leather straps for lifting and lowering them, and 'Smoking' signs, and the doors were a little lower than traditional house doors. The carriages were in their original brown railway livery. These were snug houses, little different from the other dwellings around, none of which had, at this time, running water, electricity or mains drainage. As expectations rose, and money became available, these houses were modernised so that the carriage doors were replaced by traditional timber frames, and the windows were improved as well; however, the traditional central glass oil lights could not be converted to electricity when that modern convenience arrived in the village. From the back door there was a path through the garden, past the privy.

When Herbert Short retired from Haglands he moved up to one of the railway carriages and had a series of greenhouses built on the land that Old Nursery Cottage stands on now. There were three long heated greenhouses, with the coal or coke boiler underground, and two smaller houses. He had a log to sit on, about chair height and three feet across, covered with sacking where he used to sit to prick out the plants. The produce, mainly lettuce, tomatoes and asparagus, with both cut flowers and plants was sold at the front of the plot.

Rosebank, the house diagonally opposite the garage at the cross roads, was the first shop on The Common, and was run by Mr and Mrs H Cozens at the end of the First World War. It housed the post office, and sold general groceries such as tea, sugar, cocoa and flour. Sweets and a penny bar of chocolate are remembered, and drinks were added later when the wooden extension that jutted out from the cottage was constructed. There was also a little library in the back room with its two rows of shelves. The shop had another function, too: just after the bus service started to The Common, round about 1930, the buses were sometimes used as a carter service,

H Cozens Stores – early 1930s
There is a chocolate vending machine by the door, this wooden extension was added for Mrs Manvell. There is a bus timetable on the right with a notice in the corner of the chimney advertising the public telephone, and a cigarette vending machine in the middle with the letters De Reszke at the top.

dropping things off at parcel offices at Central Stores in the village and Rosebank on the Common; the butcher, Mr Seldon from Storrington used Mrs Cozens' shop to deliver his meat to, and paid her a small fee. It reduced his delivery charges and saved him time. Other things were delivered this way from Storrington: accumulators for the radio, fabrics, or anything one had to order; Slaters could get paint or ironmongery up from Worthing within the hour.

The Electoral Roll of 1949 shows that the shop had passed to Lillian and Rosalie Manvell; it was then sold to a Mr and Mrs Betts. Soon after Mr Betts retired he died and the property was sold off; the purchaser took down the wooden structure in the front and the shop closed for ever.

The story of the creation and development of the other shops on The Common is somewhat complicated, and inextricably linked to the Short family, see above. The original Garage was on the site of the showroom that is there now. Billy Ellis married Daisy Short, and they and their two daughters lived beside the Garage in a little wooden bungalow with a galvanised roof, a lawn and a revolving wooden summerhouse, which

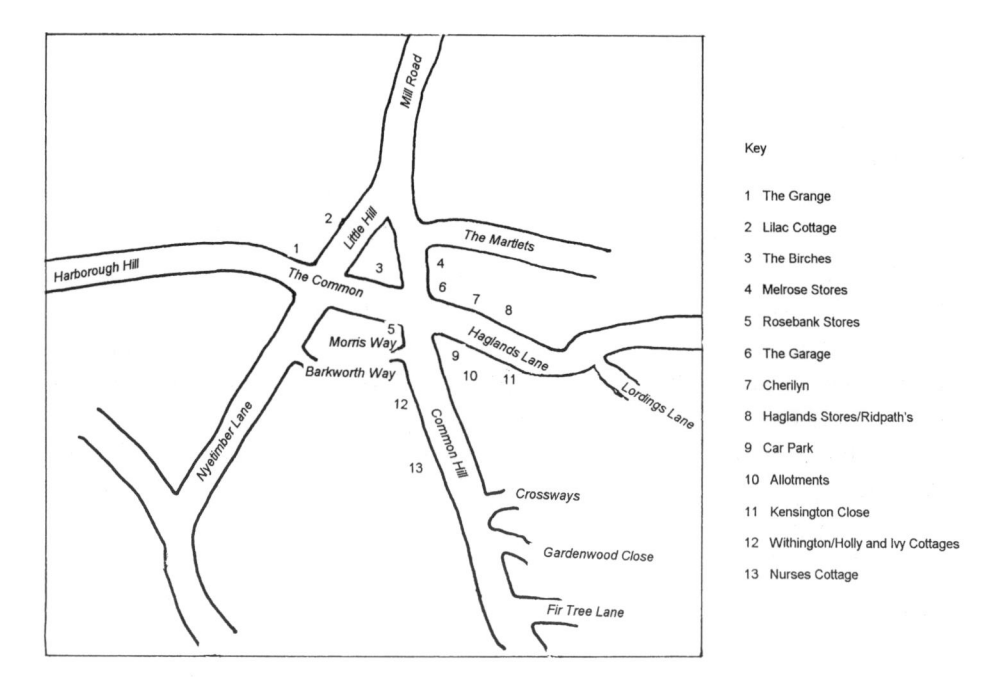

Plan of some houses and the shops at The Common

could be turned to face the sun. Gwen Smith who lived in The Birches in 1926, continues the story "The Ellises lived there for donkey's years; they started off in a railway carriage but it didn't look like one because they built a mock bungalow front for it with two extra bedrooms added, each with a window. On the side was the old huge galvanised place that was the garage, and then they decided to build this new place; upstairs sliding doors separated the dining room from the sitting room and it opened up to make a great big ballroom - it was lovely up there." During the war Herbert and Charlotte Short celebrated their diamond wedding with a party in a room in the garage which had been used as a furniture store.

At first Billy just mended farm carts and the odd car, and hand pumped the petrol, but he was a good mechanic whose skills were much in demand for everything from mending garden mowers to mending cars and charging up the accumulators for the wireless. His father drove the first Southdown bus between Storrington and Worthing. Daisy was a nurse and in the 1930s she allowed the doctor from the surgery in Pulborough to use her house for consultations three mornings a week. The patients would wait in the sitting room and the consultations took place in her bedroom. During the war the Canadians took over the petrol pumps because petrol was rationed to civilians, but they did not take over the garage as such. The petrol was dyed pink so that it could not be used in private cars, but at the very start of the war Ted Faires remembers that he and his Uncle Billy buried cans and cans of petrol in the garden to be their supply before the troops came! Building of the new garage was only permitted if the flat above it had a flat roof, which, coincidentally afforded a wonderful view of the surrounding countryside.

After Mr Ellis left Jack Gardner came and he stayed for many years. Gwen continues "He was a big name on the Parish and District Councils and on lots of committees, in fact my son Ralph ended up working for him because we were in the ridiculous situation of Ralph being paid £1 per week for a job in Worthing when the fares to get there were 18/6d a week. Mr Gardner needed a boy so that he didn't have to leave the office to run errands, and Ralph worked his way up until he ended by managing the place. Eventually Mr Gardner sold out to a London man, it changed hands a few times, and now in 1998 Mr Marino has just bought it."

In front of the pair of railway carriages called Melrose, Herbert Short built a small shop for Gertrude which she called Melrose Stores. (It is curious

Herbert Short's Golden Wedding – 2 Sept. 1932
Front Row from left: Connie Short, Nellie Short, Joyce Short, Ted Faires, Herbert Short (seated),
Jean and Evelyn Ellis, Charlotte Short (seated), Joan Clarke, Dora and
Catherine Short, Nellie Streeter (nee Short)
Middle Row: Sidney Ellis, Ernest Figg, Thomas Short, Daisy Ellis (nee Short), Ronald Streeter,
Gertrude Faires, Doll (Ina) Clarke (nee Short), Amy Andrews (nee Short),
Francis Figg, Thomas Streeter
Back Row: Len Short, Stanley Figg, William Short, Len Faires, Jack (Leslie) Figg,
Sidney Short, Frederick Clarke

that at least three of the families that ran Melrose Stores ended up by running other shops on the Common as well, so this history is rather confusing.) It was a flourishing little shop which she shared with her brother-in-law Albert Andrews whose butcher's shop was entered through the grocery, and his butchers' hooks in the ceiling of Melrose Stores can still be seen. His pork sausages were famous and won certificates in the area, but no-one would disclose the secret recipe! Meat came from the market in Pulborough and was presumably slaughtered there as there were no facilities behind the shop. Unfortunately there were family differences and, as Albert was getting older, he retired from the business. Gertrude's husband Leonard Faires worked for Mr Jupp the builder, as a bricklayer and carpenter, and in the early 1930s Leonard bought the next plot up the road beyond the greenhouses and designed and built Sunbeam Cottage, with a rose garden in front of it; so Gertrude gave up Melrose Stores and they and their son Teddy, moved in to the new cottage.

Stan and Lily Ridpath came to the Common with their three children, David, Muriel and Brenda, and rented Melrose Stores from the Shorts round about 1934. Later in 1936 they also bought a plot of land adjacent to Sunbeam Cottage and over the next couple of years built another shop which they called Ridpath's, later to become Hagland Stores; there is a stone in the wall at the back of the shop commemorating the building. They therefore gave up Melrose Stores to concentrate on the new enterprise.

About 1938 Renee and Bill Knight heard that Melrose Stores was to be let, the Ridpaths having left to run their own shop. They were well qualified for the job following Bill's earlier experience in the trade; he had been apprenticed to a grocery store in Coolham, and at Forest Stores in Ashington and already had a van which he used as a mobile grocer's. Mrs Cozens at Rosebank was most insistent that they did not sell sweets or 'poach' her customers, which they never did, so the two shops ran harmoniously together. One night the girl from Rosebank came across and said that Mrs Cozens, who could be very difficult if crossed, wanted to see them at 7pm; they were terrified and wondered whatever they could have done! It turned out that she was selling Rosebank and had offered the house, shop and land to Renee and Bill for £700. Needless to say, they bought it and installed Renee's mother, Mrs Manvell, and her two sisters there; while Mrs Manvell ran Rosebank, Elsie the elder sister worked in the ammunition factory at Roundabout, and Rosalie (known as Rollie) the younger one, helped Renee in Melrose Stores; help that was much needed as, after they had got the grocery side going, they began selling newspapers. On the first day they sold twenty newspapers, but eventually they ended up with seven rounds to deliver all over the area. Charlie Parsons used to deliver the papers, and would also take a notebook with him for the orders so trade built up fast; many of the customers came from the Roundabout houses which were used more as permanent homes and less as weekend cottages during the war when West Chiltington was thought to be safer than London. During the war the delivery service had to be suspended because of petrol rationing, but after the war there were three or four employees preparing the orders that Mr Knight would deliver in the old Hillman car.

When the Knights had arrived at Melrose Stores there was nothing in the shop but they stocked up through a Horsham wholesaler who allowed them credit for the stock; trade was so good that it did not take long to pay off the loan and to get on an even keel. Phyllis recalls that the shop was dominated by a big brown counter behind which was a door leading down into the railway carriage home. They sold groceries and greengroceries through the years even when the war came and life became very difficult for shopkeepers. The packet of lard had to be cut into 2oz pieces, as that was the ration, as did the cheese. The sugar was in packets, but everything else had to be cut specially, and not a scrap wasted. Biscuits and cakes were sold loose, and were measured out into paper bags from big square storage tins, and the tea, from wooden chests. The hot bread was delivered early in the morning from Steyning. The first thing they bought was a bacon slicer, the bacon came from an old contact in London and the eggs from their own chickens and ducks, while a wholesaler from Worthing supplied things that could not be produced locally. Marmite, Bovril, Bisto and Custard powder came in their own packets and jars as did mustard, HP sauce, and Lifeboy and Pears soaps, although there was not the selection that there is now. Even the newspapers were rationed, so two paper rounds had *The Times* one week, and one other round had it the next week but this could be even further complicated because the papers would come at 6am unless there was a bomb alert in which case they often would not arrive until the children had gone to school so no deliveries could be made at all. At Rosebank Mrs Manvell used to have to shut the customers out when the chocolate was delivered, so that she had time to sort it all out into the tiny allowances. The customers paid for their goods with money and ration coupons, these coupons had to be counted and filed in separate envelopes by Renee (who was solely responsible for the shop as Bill had joined the Forces): butter, cheese, flour etc, and taken once a month to the Council offices in Storrington in order to get a permit to buy some more stock.

Unfortunately Mr Knight started having heart attacks and, after 16 or 17 years there, the shop had to be sold. They took over The Queens Head as the landlord was leaving at that time, leaving Mrs Manvell and Renee's two sisters at Rosebank.

After the war the shop was sold to Mr Llewellyn who decided that the newspapers would be too much for him so in 1960 gave up that side to Ted Faires at Cherilyn who accepted the suggestion with alacrity. Mr Llewellyn in turn sold Melrose Stores on to Mr and Mrs Lancaster and Mrs Lancaster's sister. The shop continued to thrive with the increase in the houses being built in the 1950s and 1960s. They retained it much as it had been, until Mr Lancaster died and his wife and sister-in-law ran it together for some years. By 1964 George Kempster, the owner at that time, had been awarded an alcohol licence, but in spite of this the business started to go downhill; the papers had been necessary to draw people into the shop. With The Post Office in Haglands Stores there was even less reason for people to visit Melrose Stores.

In June 1972 the shop was bought by Don Davis who had been taught the trade by Connie Slater as he had been in the wine trade before and was not used to general grocery. He owned it until 1991 when he sold to Steve and Wendy Holloway. In all those years since the ending of war-time petrol rationing there has been a delivery service. Steve has had experience in the grocery trade, having worked at Tesco, and he and Wendy are the only people left in the village who are living in one of the railway carriage houses. Even the windows here have been left in their original state and it is our last remaining link with the past.

When Stan and Lily Ridpath opened their new shop it was quite small; where the post office area is now was Mrs Ridpath's sitting room with Crittal windows, and beyond that was the shop, with a garage for the van on the end, separated from the main building by a path to the back of the property. During the war Mrs Ridpath turned her sitting room into a café

Ridpath's Stores on Coronation Day – 2.6.1953

selling tea and cakes to the Canadian servicemen; her cakes were very popular, so popular that she was eventually put out of bounds to the servicemen. Undeterred they, who liked her tea and toast so much, crept through a hole in the hedge at the bottom of the garden to get in! It must have been a real occasion for them because they dressed up for tea, and sat at the little tables she set out for them, creating a homely atmosphere. 'Penny's Cakes' made by Mrs Penfold were justly famous, and one of her assistants had a 'war wound' which was a permanent callous on her hand, gained from cutting so much bread for toast! A special licence had to be obtained for the extra rations that she was serving. She would also invite three different servicemen to the house for lunch every Wednesday and Sunday so that they would feel welcome in the village. When Mrs Cozens gave up Rosebank the Post Office was moved to Ridpath's but at the opposite end to where it is at present. Stan Ridpath went to be trained by the Post Office but this extra responsibility, while good for trade, did mean that the family only once went away for a holiday together when cover could be arranged. Mrs Soffe, whose husband worked at the garage, came and managed the shop and the post office for that memorable holiday. Apart from this, Brenda remembers that every Christmas they 'lost' their sitting room for a couple of weeks as Stan turned it into a bazaar selling all the goodies for Christmas; it was such a good idea that he would pick people up from the outlying villages and bring them to the shop to buy. The family had a frantic clearing up operation on Christmas Eve! This pattern was repeated to a lesser extent at Easter when the room was filled with eggs.

Lily Ridpath was a sociable woman who enjoyed the company in the shop, and enjoyed her catering. It is said that she used to serve the teas for the cricket club, under the May tree by the shop, and she used to help Connie Short run the socials and dances during the war. The arrival of home-made ice cream at Ridpath's was also remembered as a coup after the war, (a twopenny round was favourite), because they had a freezer and the Knights at Melrose Stores did not even have a refrigerator.

A slightly unusual aspect of war-time was the 'Wings for Victory' bowling (skittles) competition in which Stan won a pig, a placid beast who liked to have his ears tickled by the children who also collected acorns for it. It was kept in the garden behind the shop along with the chickens. When the Ridpaths gave up the shop and moved to The Haven in Harborough Hill, the pig, or its successor, went too! The Haven, which had quite a bit of land adjoining it, was bought with a view to developing the site for housing. They built Belmont, a bungalow which was eventually occupied by their daughter Muriel and her husband Eric Cadwallader, but the land was actually developed by someone else.

David, Muriel and Brenda took over Ridpath's for two or three years after their parents retired, before they, too, sold it on, this time to Charles W Bell, and went into other jobs in the late 1940s. When Mr Bell died, Will and Lily Carver bought the shop in 1961, enlarging it by turning the sitting room on the east side into the Post Office (its present position); the original post office being on the other end in what was a garage; the vacant space was used to enlarge the shop.

Between Ridpath's and Sunbeam Cottage was a silver birch tree, which was felled by John Taylor who bought the shop in 1965 and who used the space created to build a lean-to butcher's shop which was leased to Richard Haycock (who had another butcher's shop in Pulborough) and his son Kevin. John Hobbs had worked for Dick Haycock when he left school, so after serving in the Royal Navy until 1964 (during which time he married Mr and Mrs Carver's daughter Eileen) and a spell with Carver's builders he returned to the butchery business in 1974 and rented the butcher's shop, selling it to Mr R Woods in 1978. John Taylor also altered the upstairs accommodation to create two flats: one for his mother-in-law and the other for himself and his wife.

The shop has passed through the hands of the Greenfields and the Paveys until in 1998 it was sold by Nick Mustchin to Geof Beattie.

About 1938 Leonard and Gertrude Faires built a flat roofed extension to Sunbeam Cottage consisting of two rooms, one back, one front, each with a french window, which Mrs Faires used to house the lodgers she used to take in to supplement the income. The advent of the war meant that this space was used by, first, the evacuees' teacher from Peckham Mrs Babs Wallace, then by a land army girl, and finally by Mr George Plowden, who was the local policeman during the war. One of the evacuee girls remembers him as a big, fat, jolly man that everyone loved. It appears that soon after he came to the village he got married in London from Sunbeam Cottage where he was lodging with Mrs Faires and then rented a little bungalow down Harborough Drive, being sufficiently well off not to need the police house in The Hatches. To avoid confusion, the house is called Sunbeam Cottage, but when Mrs Faires' son Ted took over the shop he called it Cherilyn after his son Leonard and his daughter Cherie - it was about the closest to the two names they could get that made sense. From

Haglands Lane – 1938

1960 he ran the shop from what had been his mother's extension, as a sweet shop and newsagents. There was little competition with Melrose Stores, they had the grocery and the off-licence and did the deliveries, while Cherilyn had newspapers and cigarettes and tobacco, sweets and crisps. Phyllis Rogers (Ted Faires' cousin) says that it started as a small haberdashery selling knitting wool, needles and patterns and a few pharmaceuticals such as Aspirin. Ted also took over the local car hire service from Mr Todman. This business became so popular that eventually he had a fleet of four cars and a taxi kiosk at Pulborough railway station. As well as business trips, people were now going abroad for their holidays from the expanding Gatwick and Heathrow airports or would require transport to Southampton to catch the ferry. Eventually the business was sold to Nutbourne Garage.

From 1985 the Faires family ran two shops; Ted and his daughter Cherie ran the grocers at Haglands Stores, and Ted and his wife Lily ran Cherilyn. Lily had previously worked in the Post Office at Ridpath's. It was a hard life, Ted got up at 4.30am for the papers and when they were out of the way his wife would come down to open up Cherilyn while he went into Haglands Stores to trim the vegetables and prepare that shop. All the vegetables were laid outside in the front, while the sacks of carrots and potatoes were kept in the stock room. Milk from local farms was sold, and three cartons of 30 dozen boxes of eggs from a farm near Coolham were sold per fortnight. A dozen trays of bread were delivered daily, and huge cheeses came from the wholesalers, as did the bacon. Sadly they were not allowed to cook their own gammon because of the health regulations. In the five years that they owned Haglands Stores they trebled the turnover and were sad to go. Cherilyn was also sold on 13 March 1989 to Steven and Lynda Denham, who had previously worked for WH Smith and were looking through advertisements in the papers for a suitable store to buy.

Since their arrival Cherilyn has continued to develop; the traditional tobacconist's stock has been extended to include some groceries, fresh bread, dairy produce and, recently an off-licence in a new extension. In November 1998 they won the top retail Excellence Award from the National Federation of Retail Newsagents, which recognised their professional approach. Steven puts their success down to old fashioned listening to the customers combined with the latest supermarket technology for stock analysis.

In 1928 a Saturday market was held on the site that is now occupied by the Electricity Board's transformer, between The Garage and Old Nursery Cottage. Mrs Kensington had got the idea off the ground by arranging with Herbert Short who owned the land, to use the large wooden shed from 8am to 1pm every Saturday to sell local produce such as home made cakes, vegetables and fruit, poultry, eggs and jam. A newspaper report of 1936 said that £300 worth of goods had been sold the previous year in this enterprise run by the WI but open to anyone in the village who could bring produce to sell. Two people served inside, and there were tables outside; Tom Downer who delivered milk twice a day for the Greenfields from Kings and Princes came with a churn of milk to sell to those who brought their jugs to fill. A penny in the shilling was retained for the WI funds from the profits. The opening ceremony was performed by the rector Rev Hall, who read a letter of encouragement from Mr W Lawson who was the Director of Agriculture for West Sussex: 'It is a public enterprise and all the profits will go direct to the producers.' The market ran until 1949.

It was not only the Short family who lived in the railway carriages; Mr Reeves, the plumber and his wife lived in a railway carriage in their garden in Lordings Lane while, it is said, their house Firlands was being built by Symonds of Storrington who also built other houses in the area. There are stories of the house being unfinished for some time.

Peter Clark and Sheina Foulkes at the Bluebell Railway explain that in 1887 the London South Western Railway had improved its royal train by the inclusion of coaches with up-to-date facilities. The vehicles that were used were not new but were extensively modified for their royal role; Saloon No 17 had started life in 1885 as an ordinary first and second class carriage with a luggage compartment. During the rebuilding this became the attendant's compartment, while the second class part accommodated a boudoir complete with couch, wash basin, lavatory and dressing table. The first class section was converted into two saloons with luxurious toilet facilities between them; these saloons were of light walnut and birds eye maple panelling, and were designated the 'Gentlemen's' and 'Queen's' Saloons. These saloons also had a clearstory in which the long centre section of the roof was raised - possibly to clear the smoke from the royal gentlemen's cigars! This saloon was used on the LSWR until it was replaced in 1913, but continued in service. In 1923 the LSWR was amalgamated with neighbouring Railways to form the Southern Railway; Saloon 17 was renumbered 4107 and repainted olive green, continuing in use serving the racecourses of the south. In 1931 it was withdrawn from service.

Along with other withdrawn stock gathered at Selhurst she was inspected and bought by Ted Strudwick; the coach was moved to West Chiltington by horse and cart and off-loaded with the aid of planks and oil drums. The large oak tree is still in situ where Ted and his father arranged a pulley system to haul the carriage off the trailer. When Ted came home

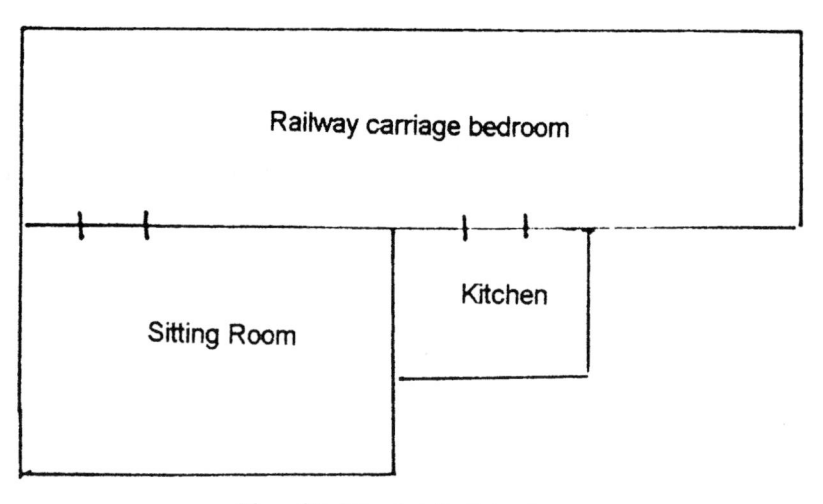

Plan of Ted Strudwick's Extension

after the Second World War he built a road up to the railway carriage from the lane and added a brick extension to the property to create a home for himself and his wife Dora; the railway carriage was the bedroom and the extension provided a sitting room and kitchen, accessed through the carriage doors.

People called him The Bird Man as he was on the RSPCA register of those who could manage the injured birds which he took in. Children of the village, as well as others from further afield used to take him their birds to cure; the garden was full of cages for a wide variety of birds including golden pheasants and little owls. When his father died, his breeding quail took up residence in the old man's railway carriage which was also used as a hospital for the most seriously ill birds. The quails' eggs were taken to market for sale. At the age of 74, having cared for the RSPCA's birds for more than twenty years, he retired and was awarded a Certificate of Merit by them for his work. In an interview with a local paper, he said that his greatest pleasure was to nurse the hawks in his care to sufficient fitness to release back into the wild.

In the 1980s when Dora became ill they had to move out and the original buildings were demolished; two houses were built on the site: Avalon and Wykeham. Another story that concerns Ted Strudwick is told: "while Ted and I were working for Carver's builders at Castlegate, he would set the rabbit snares, and would catch anything from 5-15 rabbits in a day. Ted would put his hand to his ear and say 'There's another one calling me' and off he'd go down the path and come back with another rabbit. It was all scrub land round there so there were rabbits everywhere."

Ted's railway carriage was offered to the Bluebell Railway for restoration; unfortunately the day before it was due to go it is said all the brass lamps and handles were stolen. It was therefore moved to Essex for preservation and safe-keeping.

A second carriage, LBSCR (London Brighton and South Coast Railway) Coach No 142 had also been on Ted Strudwick's site. This London-Brighton compartment coach had also been withdrawn from service in 1931, and was used by Ted's father. This coach was offered to the Bluebell Railway at the same time as 4107 and was accepted, arriving in a very poor condition but with a sound sub-structure. After ten years it has now been fully restored and can be seen running with the number 7598. Money for its restoration was raised by sales from the station bookstall, gifts and donations.

Departure of the Railway Carriage

Most of the true Romany people who used to live in the caravans in the area have settled into static houses now, and are integrated into local society. Jim Smith of Ashington describes his early life: "I was bred and born in a Romany wagon, and before the war, when we were on the Parham Estate, we had three wagons: my Dad's which was a Reading, our girls' wagon that my three sisters had which was a Burton Wagon, and my Granny's Faversham Wagon. Each of these places has a different style which is why they've got different names; the Faversham has the wheels outside the main frame, while the Burton has its wheels more centrally underneath. And then there's the Bowtop Wagon as well.

Dad's Reading was all timber framed, except for the iron round the wheels. He had a curved steps up to the footboard with brass rails bolted onto the side, and beyond the footboard was the stable door which with the top divided vertically and glazed. Inside on the left was a stove about 28″ long; it had a little oven above a grate with a brass fender, and two rings which you could take off to put your kettle or pot on. The old pots were cast iron but there were also steel ones, and all painted of course, just like the enamel of the stove - our stove was covered in flowers. The chimney from the stove went up through the top of the wagon and was encased in a fireproof jacket so it didn't set fire to the roof. Next to the stove was a seat with storage underneath for clothes. On the right of the door as you come in is the table, with a leaf you can let out, and another seat with storage drawers. At the end of the van are glass shutters all engraved with flowers to create a separate bedroom where you can sleep two people, with space under the bed. Over the wagon is a skylight, about a yard wide, which can open for fresh air, and a window down each side with brackets beside them. Dad had a gypsy fair painted on the wood all round the skylight, and the whole wagon was painted with birds, flowers and scenes, both inside and out.

My Grandfather, James Pannell, lived in West Chiltington from the late 1890s; he built a bungalow at the end of what became Carver's Yard in Harborough Hill in 1910. There were stables at the back of it because he was a horse dealer; its been pulled down now and there's three new bungalows in its place. Bill Carver used it as an office. At that time of day you could buy a bit of ground for £6 an acre, there was so much 'hand taking', and Grandfather got $11^1/_2$ acres which went right down to the corner with Monkmead Lane. He just got a bit of land and stopped on it, there weren't so many rules and regulations then. Grandfather was a clever man and his parents had taught him to read and write and he made a lot of money, which he kept as gold. He had a bag of gold. There were people who would try and thieve, but they weren't in our clan of people. There were some that would thieve horses, because we just used to tether them and these people would come down from London with a float sort of thing, look around then drop the tailboard down, in went the horse, never saw it again.

My mother and father couldn't read or write. As they were always on the move they didn't get the chance for schooling, and there was prejudice against our creed of people, a prejudice that's made worse because we get mixed up in people's minds with the tinkers, the 1960s hippies, and new-age travellers. They aren't travellers; they couldn't speak my language, or read it out of a book. We are a proud and ancient people, came from the east with our own traditions; now my father was almost black when the sun was on him, not a bit like these new-age people. You've got to have Romany blood to be able to speak the language, and we don't discuss our traditions and ideals. I'll tell you one problem: I was in the Air Force and did my bit, but no-one knew I was a Romany, I was afraid to tell them for the problems it would cause. But we've always been known as Christians, my wife lies down in West Chiltington churchyard and there's some of us in Storrington churchyard.

Until my father was called up to the Great War, he and my mother and her brothers used to serve refreshments to the troops on the march. They had milk churns full of boiling water for tea and coffee, and mugs of lemonade, all that sort of thing. They went all over the country, right up as far as Kirby Lonsdale in Cumbria, because, that time of day, the soldiers, some could ride but some had to heel-and-toe it and they needed feeding. My parents were given a licence from the Medical Officer at the War Office and with ten to twelve thousand men marching they could take some money. It was called fizzer hawking but you people wouldn't know the meaning of that, 'though fizzer's grubstakes.

By the 1930s Dad was also a heavy horse dealer; he'd go on the train to London to the horse repository at Elephant and Castle and buy about half a dozen horses - Shires, Suffolk Punches, Clydesdales. The train fare was £1 return for my father, 10/- for me, and £1 per head for the horses, one way. We'd take head collars and halters and lead the horses to the station and they would come to Pulborough station in the cattle conveyance the same day. He'd buy them as two year olds, break them in and sell them as three or four year olds to do the milk rounds or farm work in the days before the tractor and the combine harvester. My father would make pegs, but he spent more time with his horses. Now Mother, she'd sell everything from a roll of lino to curtains, door mats, rugs; crockery, enamel-ware and tin, a thimble or a reel of cotton. Her father and mother had taught her the factory contacts; the goods would come to Pulborough Station, and she'd wire the money off from the post office. It didn't cost anything for the service. She had an excise licence, that's like a licence to sell manufactured goods, and after the war I used to go with her driving round the villages selling, there weren't no shops like you've got today, supermarkets that sold everything, you just had the village shops. We were brought up to sell swag, and the swag was your stock, and we could stand anywhere to sell as long as we don't cause an obstruction. Now a peddler's licence was different, it was a licence to sell something that you had made, pegs or birch brooms say. My uncle and aunt had a Romany wagon in Smock Alley Lane and they sold pegs.

Those days are gone. Our traditions and stories, music and culture are in my head, darling, and when we go a lot of it will go too, but the language still lives on. See, the Newlands were also travelling people from this area, but although we've all got houses now, a lot of us can't settle; my niece keeps buying and selling houses, moving on. I've got those canaries - every wagon had a good lurcher dog and birds - they sing against each other and it reminds me of the old times."

Jim Smith's nephew Maurice Peacock, now living in Storrington, adds: "Even when all the family were on the Parham Estate just after the Second

World War, they would go, and come back, so even having a regular stop didn't mean you were settled. They used to go hop picking in September to Yalding in Kent. Uncle's place is decorated like a wagon inside, and so is my place, but I still get itchy feet and can't settle; it's sort of in your blood. Mum's mum lived in Carver's Yard, and Mum and Dad lived in The Birches, so did my sister, but when Dad died we just couldn't live there no more; she moved first and then I went next. It was Dad's wish to be buried in West Chiltington churchyard as he had been brought up in the village. When Gran died I know all her clothes and her belongings were burned, they do that, it's tradition, and her jewellery was split amongst the family. I think the people in and around The Birches were a bit surprised by Dad's funeral but we'd got on well with village people. Now my Grandad, he used to get his living off the local people so we had to get along with them, and we never had any problems. There aren't many true travelling Romany people left."

Council houses were being built in villages all round the country in the early 1920s, and at this time West Chiltington definitely seemed to have a housing problem as indicated by the extract from the Council Minutes of February 1923 when the Clerk was asked to convey the following resolution to the West Sussex County Council 'that in view of the acute housing shortage in West Chiltington, the West Chiltington Parish Council appeals to the County Council to reconsider the question of the vacant cottages on Hatches Estate in the endeavour to alleviate, if only temporarily, the existing hardship in this matter, in the village.'

The Birches development was built in 1926 (the second row being built in 1936.) Even when completed there were problems as in March 1928 the Parish Council had to ask the Rural District Council to supply a good and sufficient supply of drinking water, fit for use, to the Council Cottages, and that the drainage system be put into good order as 'the state of things to be very unsatisfactory and a menace to public health.' For years the Parish Council complained to the RDC until in 1943 something appears to have been done because by October conditions were much better, but a letter was written to the Sanitary Authority regarding the fact that the effluent was being discharged into a ditch by the side of a public highway, thus apparently contravening the building bye-laws.

Two children of the time remember their houses in The Birches, but as children the above problems did not concern them. "Our parents moved into The Birches when they were first built. There was a cold water tap in the scullery, a bath with a cold tap and a copper which was brick built and coal fired. The copper was like a deep bowl of water with a fire whose chimney flue spiralled round it. Because it was so near the fire, if you took the lid off the copper, little black bits of soot fell into the water and when you had a bath there would be little bits of soot in the bath with you. Equally on Mondays, wash day, mother boiled everything in the copper, pulled out with tongs, through the mangle. The water was bailed out when it was finished with. Bath night was once a week as we all had to share the water as you couldn't keep heating all this water and then keep bailing it out. The bathroom was downstairs as you couldn't have carried all this hot water upstairs. Father always had the first bath and mother was always last. Water and electricity were brought to the village in the mid 1930s, prior to that father had emptied the buckets from the privy in the garden. He would dig a huge hole at the top of the garden and bury the waste. The privy was a brick built structure with a wooden seat, and the village women were proud of the clean whiteness of the scrubbed wood. Although life was hard, a great pride was taken in the cleanliness of wooden draining boards, the blackness of leaded grates, the crisp look of washed clothes and curtains and a sparkling front step. This must have been a considerable task with mud everywhere from unmade roads, longer skirts that brought in the dirt and time-consuming washing practices of demanding fabrics, and yet it was accepted as part of life. Mother cooked on a range, supplemented with a little oil stove; the kettle went on that. The grocer brought the paraffin with the groceries. The coalman came once a week; the working class couldn't afford to have it every month. I didn't realise how poor my parents were until mother died and I heard how my brothers and sisters chipped in when they had started work to buy her a coat, as all her money went on us."

One family for whom housing was not a problem were the Barkworths who lived in the house now called Withington, one of the first houses built on The Common. In October 1919 W T Barkworth bought a pair of cottages, Holly (on the south side) and Ivy (on the north) from a Mrs Woolgar, and preferring the name Holly to Ivy, used that name for the single house that resulted from the extensive alterations that he carried out so as to convert them into one. These included replacing the two staircases by one new one, and adding a bath to one of the bedrooms. Mr Barkworth, an artist of independent means, with his wife (who was a cousin of Dr Ralph Vaughan Williams the composer) and five children, three boys and two girls, were

Holly Cottage

Mr and Mrs W T Barkworth at Holly Cottage – early 1930s

considered one of the main 'gentry' families in the village. They are kindly remembered by village children of the 1920s: "Mrs Barkworth was a fascination in her pony and trap, she wore a heavy tweed skirt to her ankles with a jacket and tie. In the summer, the family used to give a party for the village children, with trails winding through the bracken and heather of their land, where there was treasure hung on the trees and furze bushes, and finders was keepers, ending up with a lovely tea. When it was time for us to go home, they would give each of us an apple and an orange and a bag of sweets. They were very good to the village, and we used to look forward to those parties. They were also good in that in the 1960s and 70s their two boys, Edmund and Terence used to walk all the village footpaths to keep them open, wielding a sickle or shears".

Terence Barkworth adds "While in the 1920s our usual method of transport was in a pony and trap we did have a 1912 Wolseley car which was used occasionally; this was rather like a taxi with a small engine in front and a driver's seat, and a high enclosed part behind to take the passengers; it also had wheels with wooden spokes. This was normally driven by Mr Farrell. In the 1930s we used an Austin and my brother Ian had a three-wheel Morgan."

Mr Barkworth died in 1936, but his wife survived him until 1958 living in the house whenever it was possible for her to do so. However, towards the end of the war, when the maid Rosy could no longer work, Mrs Barkworth had to find somewhere else to live; the Rev Hall and his wife kindly allowed her to lodge with them. The Barkworth's eldest son Ian had died tragically in 1934, Terence had married and moved away in 1961, Nora had bought herself a cottage in Yapton so brother and sister Edmund and Sylvia continued to live in Holly Cottage until 1966. In the autumn of 1970 the house and the garden area to the north of it was sold to Dr Ford, but the rest of the land was retained until in about 1985 it was sold to Bovis Homes for development. The houses in Morris Way and Barkworth Way are built on Barkworth's land and the Parish Council suggested that Morris Way be chosen for the road name as Nora, while

The Three-Wheeled Morgan – 1920s

Mrs Sybil Helen Barkworth
There is a railway carriage adjacent to the shed in the background

studying violin and viola at the Royal College of Music, had encouraged her brothers to become interested in Morris and Sword dancing.

Dr Ford (whose wife's long cigarette holder used to fascinate the village children) changed the house name to Withington, the name of the family home in Herefordshire, and carried out some internal alterations to accommodate his surgery. He had his main surgery in Pulborough, but saw patients at Withington on Tuesday and Friday evenings each week.

The name of Holly Cottage lives on in the pair of semi-detached houses between Mole Cottage and Rosebank. The houses are recognisable by the swinging sign outside, which is said to be a relic of the days when Barclays Bank had a branch on the Common.

On 3 July 1967 Barclays Bank opened a small branch more or less on the site now occupied by the garages adjacent to Holly Cottages. It was a small wooden building, open two or three times a week, but was not there long as there were insufficient customers to make it viable, and it closed on 3 December 1971. The bank manager, a Mr Fuller from Mill Road, is remembered as a bespectacled, dapper little man, who had a glass fronted office at the right-hand end of the room where he waited for his customers before serving them from behind the counter. His relationship with his customers was good, and many people were sorry to see the bank close.

By an Inclosure Award dated 7 May 1868 a two-acre parcel of land on the crossroads at the Common was allotted to the Church Wardens and Parish Overseers of the Poor to be held in trust as an allotment for the labouring poor of the parish, at a rent of £1 per annum payable to the Lord of the Manor, the Earl of Abergavenny. Any industrious cottager or poor person could apply to rent a piece of allotment each year. The Parish Council took over the management of the allotment on 31 March 1912, but they had no authority to dispose of the land or to allow it to be used for any other purpose, and they continued to pay the £1 per year rent.

The allotments have been put to various uses over the years some of which were not always in accordance with the Rules. In 1915 the Parish Council's notice was drawn to the fact that one allotment was not cultivated and that the allotment holder simply used it to feed his cow; he was given one week's notice to terminate his tenancy. In 1939 the Parish Council was informed of a request to keep two pigs on the allotments; the applicant had tried to get permission to keep pigs in his garden at The Birches but the Rural District Council had not approved of this, stating that the garden was too near the houses, and suggesting that the Parish Council allotments would be more suitable. In view of the call to produce more food, permission was given providing the building for housing the pigs was properly constructed with a concrete floor and a pit to take the drainage. (There was a precedent as Mr Hampshire had been given permission to keep pigs on the allotments during the First World War.)

In February 1968 the Trustees offered to sell the allotments to the Parish Council for £20 plus their legal fees and surveyor's commission; the Council accepted the offer and the sale was completed in May 1969.

In 1958 the problem of 'dirty' vacant allotments had been raised at a Parish Council meeting but the Council had a statutory duty to provide allotments even though less than a quarter of the original two acres was then being used as such. As this had been the case for at least the previous five years, the Parish Council began to investigate the legal possibilities of disposing of half the ground to the Rural District Council for the purpose of erecting dwellings for older people. By November 1960 the necessary permissions had been sought and the land was sold to Chanctonbury RDC. The first properties were occupied in August 1962, the two blocks eventually containing a total of sixteen bed-sitting room flatlets and twelve one-bedroom flatlets. In July 1962 the Parish Council decided that the new block of old people's housing should be named Kensington Close in recognition of the great services which Colonel Kensington had rendered the parish and district during his 37 years (at that time) on the Council.

The idea was that the tenants of the bigger houses in The Birches could move into the smaller bed-sitters in Kensington Close when their families had grown up and left home and they had become unable to manage their house and garden. They would thus vacate properties which could be let to new couples with young families who needed the space. There were two bonuses to this scheme: the older people were kept in the village close to their families and friends who looked after them, and provided social contact; and they released property for others with children. Nowadays they are 'kept an eye on' by the warden, who acts in the capacity of a good neighbour. Every morning she calls in or contacts the residents to see that they are all right, and she is there to arrange outings and ensure the smooth running of the place. Each flat is self-contained and centrally heated, and the Social Services help to keep the residents living at home for as long as possible; where necessary there are Meals on Wheels, and Care Assistants to help with shopping and other small domestic chores.

The rules state that no one under sixty can live there; they are built for the less-well-off retired of the village, and they can never be sold although some are let to people outside the village but in the HDC area. Extensive refurbishment work was carried out by Horsham District Council in July 1993.

Remaining in the area of the crossroads, the car park has also been built on allotment land. In 1972 at a Parish Council meeting it was suggested that, owing to the number of cars visiting the Common shopping area, a car park should be constructed; by 1984 the matter of car parking was still being raised, and as there were several empty allotments at the Haglands Lane end of the ground at that time, the Parish Council finally decided to go ahead with the project, raising the rate in 1985 to pay for it. The work was completed in the summer of 1985 producing space for 14 cars, and in 1998 a couple of glass recycling bins were installed.

Other memories of life at The Common come from Ivan Pullen who was born in 1928 and his older sister of a couple of years Joy, now Joy Adams: "Great grandfather who was a wheelwright had had a workshop in the woodland in Threals Lane where they used to cut all the timbers, and stack and dry it. It was oak and ash; you needed the hardwood to use on wagons and carts. Grandfather carried on the work of his father, but up on the Common, in the cottage called The Haven (now called Kithurst Cottage) where he had a big workshop even after the war, because he was still making carts for horses when the war started. Our grandparents owned The Haven, which they lived in, and the bungalow next door called Sunnyside which they rented out. Next door to that was the shop, Rosebank. Eventually our parents moved from The Birches into Sunnyside and, after they died, it was decided to sell it. I was sorry that it had to be sold, but there were five of us, six if you count our sister in Canada, and it was easier to sell than to argue who was to have it, although it had been in the family for so many years. After it was sold, the new owners let me go in and see how they had altered it and said 'we've kept your dad's very old door, and some of the low doorways, but can you explain why, when we took the floor up, we found a load of coins underneath that were dated about 1940?' There had been wet rot in that ground floor bedroom floor, so the boards had had to be replaced, and Dad had put the coins and a glass bottle with the family names in under the new boards to commemorate the year he had done the work, hoping that the treasure would remain there for a couple of hundred years! Father was a chauffeur for Mrs Sherrif of Spinney Lane, but we never got a lift in his car and we weren't allowed to acknowledge Dad if he went past with Mrs Sherrif in the back "

Further down Common Hill at White Cottage, now renamed Chiltington Place, lived Sir Robert Davis. He was an inventor of many devices relating to submarine escape, deep-sea diving and breathing apparatus. According to a newspaper article of January 1932 he invented the life-saving apparatus which was used when the 'Poseidon' sank in the North China Sea in June 1931.

Elizabeth Anderson of The Grange, The Common, points out that it is a shame to destroy some of the myths of the village, but her house never was used as a pub, which is a current village belief. The story goes that Henry Cooper, who was a tenant of the house at the time in the mid 1860s, wanted The Grange to be an ale house. Various alterations were made to the house such as altering the front door and gate to allow easier access, but when the work was done and he set off for Chichester to obtain his licence he arrived so drunk that the authorities there refused to give him one and the ale house never came into being. That is all in the past now, and well before the remit of this book, but the story was validated by the late Hector Hornsby who used to live at Lilac Cottage and shows well how stories can appear to turn into facts. However, to bring us into this century The Grange is said to be haunted to such an extent that two local women remembered that, as children, they were scared to pass it, and would certainly not have gone in. Someone who telephoned the house actually heard the moaning over the phone, so it was not all imagination, but during the 1987 hurricane part of the roof was blown off, and 'the ghost' has been a lot quieter since, but is still not silenced! However even this story is contested by Joy Adams who had been asked as a teenager to go and spend nights at The Grange with her Aunt Elsie who had been evacuated to the house during the war; she also remembers as a child being sent by her mother to Miss Duke who lived at The Grange, for two pennyworth of apples. She is fairly confident that there were no stories of ghosts at that time, or she would have been less willing to visit the house. Mr and Mrs Anderson moved into the village when Mr Anderson retired; they came for the nature, the Downs and the countryside.

Dennis and Rosemary Mustchin are probably best known nowadays because Rosemary helped her son and daughter-in-law in Haglands Stores before it was sold to Geoff Beattie in 1998, but Dennis' family has long roots in the village, going back generations. His mother, Irene Lee was brought up at Little Haglands Farm in Haglands Lane, where her father managed the land: dairy and arable. There was also a duck pond on the east side of the house. Irene went to work for Bentalls store in Kingston; in those days the shop assistants did not travel to work but were housed in a dormitory provided by the store. She married Albert Mustchin in 1930. The family have marriage certificates for four generations where the marriage took place in the village Church, and the place of residence is West Chiltington. Uncle Edward Lee managed Whales Farm, an agricultural holding of about 30-40 acres in

Edward Lee in Little Haglands Farm – 1930s
How different is the open farmland behind

Hugh Lee at Little Haglands – 1930s
Little Haglands with its neatly clipped hedges along both sides of the road

the 1920s, and the Mustchins also came from farming stock having managed Southlands Farm. Dennis was born at Fairholme, Mill Road, and brought up at Lakerscroft.

Rosemary considers herself a relative newcomer as her father William Hemsley only came here about fifty years ago to work as a gamekeeper for Charles Haslam at Dan Hill Farm.

Along Monkmead Lane is Monkmead, built in 1911 as 'Munckmead' by Holt and Sons to a design by P Morley Horder, the architect who had set up his practice in 1890 and had also designed Congregational churches, The London School of Tropical Medicine, a house for David Lloyd George and various University buildings. The photograph was taken by Horder before the house had been furnished, and it is interesting to see the landscape before the trees were planted. The materials used are almost entirely from an old brew house building which was purchased by the owner, Edward King who used to own Fryern Park in Storrington. The whole Munckmead estate covered about fifty acres.

Peter Penfold was born on the Common in 1921 and returned to the parish later in the 1920s because his father got a job as a gamekeeper for Mr King. Peter continues "After Mr King, who looked like George V, became old and ill they took him away, to Graylingwell Hospital I think,

Munkmead

and he was never seen again. His sister took over and kept my father on, and we inherited two of the King's dogs, a Cocker Spaniel and a Golden Retriever. We lived in a cottage by the pond and the land all round was rough shooting. I don't remember shooting parties as such, but I do remember the pond being kept clean for fishing parties; this pond was fed by the River Chilt which rises in Perretts Wood, Roundabout, and continues on to the Pulborough Brooks. In the winter when there was skating, Father would make sure that the snow didn't freeze on the ice by knocking it off with a long cane."

The lake is remembered by many war-time school children who skated on it, some being taught by the Canadians who were superb skaters, but it was not as deep in those days as it is today. Then, it was more a field that was grazed in the summer and deliberately flooded in the winter to improve the grassland and to act as a flood plain; being only shallow the water would freeze safely so that a pony and trap could be driven across the ice, and children could skate. Some children remember the pond as 'Kerr's Pond'. Mr Kerr, who lived there just before the Second World War, was well known in the village as he was Commander of the Home Guard which had its parade on Sunday mornings.

Tenants Mr and Mrs Kerr rented the estate for £400 a year which included the house and the woodland known as Nye Timber Copse and also the woodland on the other side of Monkmead Lane leading to the golf course. After Mr Kerr gave up his lease the administrators of the estate sold the property to Dan and Eleanor Williams towards the end of 1957; the woodland on the opposite side of the road leading to the golf course had already been given to Chanctonbury Rural District Council as a permanent open space. The land known as Nye Timber Copse was held back and sold to the Williams family at a later date. The land they owned therefore, stretched along Monkmead Lane as far as a property called Dunfold, and up Nyetimber Lane as far as the new development of Nyetimber Copse; it backed onto the estate known as Ramble Down which had previously been owned by Dr Brooks who lived in Rambledown House.

Michael Williams lived at the house with his parents until in 1959 he left to get married, eventually moving to Heathfield House, Nyetimber Lane, until in 1970 he and his wife purchased Monkmead from his father, Dan. Michael was already in the family building development company whose offices were mainly in Storrington; the Williams Group being the main development company, with Storrington Contractors the contracting company. The development company used to buy pieces of land in the district and the first two developments they were involved in were Crossways Park and Orchard Dell, both of which had originally been started by another developer. They subsequently went on to buy the land which is now known as Rambledown, and followed that with the Nyetimber Copse development. They had their own in-house designer who used mainly brick with a little stone; he designed to the purchaser's requirements so the houses are all different but sympathetic to each other. The woodland of Nyetimber consisting of pine, rhododendron and silver birch was very wet and when Michael came to develop the area the land had to be drained by wide open ditches for almost two years before work could commence.

Heathfield Copse was another development that was carried out by the Williams family, during the time that Michael and his wife Sally lived there. This was in the early 1960s when Martlets was also being built by Maurice Eames. Eames' properties were well built at a very inexpensive price, and pressure was put on other local companies to stay competitive, but eventually he failed to stay afloat on such narrow margins.

Monkmead now stands on between six and eight acres including the lake which covers about four acres, much of the rest having been used for building. Michael believes that West Chiltington will not see such major development again, although there will be limited infilling.

View from the junction of The Birches and Mill Road – 1920s
The house in the centre foreground used to be two cottages, now called Brayvale. On the extreme left is No 1 Hillside, centre left is Sandyridge and Juniper Cottage. The house on the extreme right was pulled down, Shepherds Cottage is there now.

Chapter 6

Roundabout

Prior to the 1920s or 30s the Roundabout area did not exist at all, it was simply part of the common, known as Chiltington Common, Roundabout Warren and Hurston Street Warren. In 1924 Capt H E Denys Elliott bought Roundabout from the Fryern Estate. At that time it comprised what is now known as Roundabout Farm, being some 50 acres, and The Grove, being the parcel of woodland now bounded by Threals Lane, Roundabout Lane and Grove Lane. He bought the land for fruit farming and, having no use for The Grove, immediately sold that on to Reginald Fairfax Wells. He put restrictions into the contract: that every house had to have no less than half an acre of ground; that sand or gravel could not be dug out; that pigs could not be kept; that there was a building line towards the road beyond which he could not build. All this was to keep the area a pleasant place to live but in spite of this Mr Wells was accused by Denys Elliott of building the houses too close together and turning an unspoiled woodland into a garden city. As Denys' son Teddy explained "Father did not approve. If you actually lived here before they were built you would not approve, just as people anywhere don't like new building, but in due course the buildings become accepted." It was only after The Roundabout Hotel was built, followed by a couple of properties with Roundabout in the name, that it was decided to rename Roundabout 'Roundabout Farm' to avoid confusion and make life easier for the General Post Office. The headed notepaper of many of the residents of the Wells cottages used to say Housename, Roadname, Roundabout, Pulborough, with no mention of West Chiltington at all, as if Roundabout was a completely separate hamlet.

Teddy Elliott is the second generation to farm the land, and he recounts a story that his father liked to tell about Mr Wells "He said that he used to sail very close to the wind sometimes; he was Reginald Fairfax Wells, his wife was Mrs R F Wells and one company was called R F Wells Limited so you were never quite sure who you were dealing with, and inevitably the problem was with the other one! One of the last times Father met Wells was about 1938 while driving back from Storrington on a filthy night, raining cats and dogs, and he stopped to give this man a lift - the man turned out to be Wells. 'I'm surprised you'd give me a lift Captain Elliott' he said, to which Father replied 'I would give a dog a lift on a day like this!' Such was the feeling between them, but it's hardly surprising because there was some disagreement about money that I can't fully remember, and then there was the business of the boundaries: Father would put up markers along the boundary of the land he was selling Wells, and Wells would come along and move the markers over in the night, to get a bit more land. A few nights later Father would move them back again, and so it went on until eventually Father used big concrete blocks which couldn't be moved! I came across some of these blocks some years ago."

The area known as The Grove had been quite wooded, mostly with pines, although there might have been heathland beyond. However, most of the trees were cut down during the First World War to make such things as pit props, and what was left was cut down in the Second War for packing cases. The hurricane of 1987 took out a lot more, so what is left now is either very old or replanted. Some of the trees the hurricane took had only been planted as a screen between the Elliotts and the new development so were comparatively recent; larch, Scots Pine and Norway Spruce all came down, but replanting was undertaken although in a different area. The original trees in The Grove had been a hundred years old.

Roundabout Farm is not in West Chiltington Parish, but in Sullington, as were all the properties in the Grove Lane area. In about the 1970s the parish boundaries were going to be changed but Teddy Elliott objected and took his case to the Boundaries Commission in London. As he says "When they asked what my objection was, I said that we had been in Sullington for 400 years and wanted to stay there, so they did a survey of the residents of Grove Lane who opted to be in West Chiltington. Then they decided to put the boundary through the middle of my lawn which seemed ridiculous as there was a croquet lawn there and I wasn't going to play in two parishes! So the boundary is now the private farm track that goes up by the post box in Roundabout Lane." There was more to his objection than a croquet lawn, though; there was talk of extending West Chiltington Parish Church to accommodate the growing population while the charming church at Sullington was finding it difficult to fill its pews, and it seemed illogical to move yet more people into an expanding parish simply to make a straighter line on a map, further denuding an already small parish.

The Roundabout area development was conceived by Reginald Fairfax Wells, who was born in 1877. In the 1890s he studied sculpture at the Royal College of Art, South Kensington, and then at Camberwell, selling his sculpture and bronzes at exhibitions at prominent London venues. He then moved to Coldrum, near Wrotham in Kent where he set up a pottery around 1900 producing slip ware and studio pottery, but some time in 1909 he moved to Keppel Street in Chelsea.

During the First World War the Keppel Street pottery was turned into an aviation factory; Wells had been an enthusiastic model aircraft builder so it was a natural progression for him to make first aircraft parts, then the fuselages and finally whole aircraft. He designed and built the Reo, a single seater bi-plane, and managed to acquire the sales agency and manufacturing rights for the Benoist flying boats, but there is doubt whether he ever built or flew one. During 1916 the factory was expanded and it was reported "some hundreds of workmen are engaged in the production of aeroplanes and seaplanes and building additional workshops" and by March 1917 there were 1,600 workers and a design office had been established. Wells Aviation also had a factory at Chichester; the workers there were paid a penny an hour more than at the nearby works, who had a strike to protest about it! Fifty Vickers FB9 two-seater, fighter aircraft are credited to the Wells company, as are one hundred Sopwith two-seater, fighter-reconnaissance machines. Wells-built planes served with both the Royal Flying Corps and the RNAS. He started The Wells Flying School at Cobnor in early 1917, thought to be one of the first, if not the first flying school.

Wells Aviation Company Limited went into voluntary liquidation in September 1917 and he began another pottery on the Kings Road, London, when the war ended. In 1927 he wrote an article in 'Arts and Crafts' magazine entitled 'The Lure of Making Pottery' and it is written in an easy and friendly style opening with 'Most things start with an idea.....having made your shapes - good, bad and very bad ...' His pottery still comes up for sale occasionally; a Bonhams catalogue of 21-22 June 1995 shows an 8" blue and grey stoneware vase with a catalogue price of between £250 and £350 which it exceeded, although much of his work sells for less; there is a 4" pot for £50-70. There is a note that the name SOON on his ware has no intention of suggesting the old Sung ware of China but was

Reginald Fairfax Wells
Reginald Fairfax Wells, seated. From left behind: his son Harold, his brother Noel, his son Reginald, born 1931

chosen purely for personal reasons, in the hope that he would 'soon be in production again'. He was a member of the International Society of Sculptors, Painters and Gravers, and there are at least twenty three examples of his work in the Liverpool Museum, and some in Worthing. His son, Harold, gave the Victoria and Albert Museum many of his father's pots, nine of which were exhibited at what is thought to be the first retrospective exhibition of his work, at Luton Museum in 1998.

In 1925 he moved down to Hampers Lane in Storrington where he built at least 5 houses; he lived in one called The Spinney (now called The Barton Spinney) at the bottom of Hampers Lane - this is the house that is shown in *The House Desirable* by P A Barron and in the magazine article in *Town and Country Homes* published in 1927. In 1930 he moved, to a house called Terraced Cottage, now known as Old Oaks, Spinney Lane (which was not in West Chiltington parish at that time), with the aid of a mortgage from the Lewes Co-Operative Society. A few years later this house was signed over to his wife, Resca Fronnett Ospovat Wells, and another house was built right next to the original dwelling; rumour has it that the two could not live under the same roof but did not want to be too far from each other! In 1943 Wells moved to East Preston where he built a few more houses, along with others at Angmering and some in Kent.

Until March 1933 West Chiltington came under Thakeham Rural District Council. The Council's building bye-laws were approved in 1928 from which date its first building plans deposited for planning approval survive; unfortunately the original registers of plans do not. The Council minutes list Tiles and Potteries Limited as the builders/owners of many properties built during 1928-30. In the 1934 and 1935 Kelly's Directories the Wells house names have a period charm: Ye Sylva Lyning, Journey's End, Wy Wurrie, See-Saw and Roamers' Roost to name but a few. This latter name illustrates the fact that later this became predominantly a retirement area; Coaster's Cottage was so called because its owner had just retired from The Gold Coast, and many ex-colonials could be found here.

His idea was to build rural retreats for the retired and the artistes of London; he would have had connections with the artistic set being an early follower of the Arts and Crafts Movement and a Studio Potter (one who designs and creates individual pieces rather than having a production line). He tried to create houses that looked as if they had grown out of the land many years before, and to this end he used green timber, and seconds, or even thirds, quality bricks that were irregular, to produce a warped and weathered look. His trademarks were predominantly thatched roofs over eyebrow windows, many tiny windows, an ornamental dentil course of brickwork between the floors, and in many cases the brickwork covered with a whitewashed slurry known locally as Sussex Dinging. Many houses had a loggia, often with storage space beneath, and all had large gardens. His factory at the end of Spinney Lane made all the standardised doors and window frames from the wood he cut in the Roundabout area; apart from the restricted area in The Grove his sand came from the locale, often from the land near which the houses were built and his bricks were made locally. It is said that he had a foreman whose son built Sandwell, on one of his sand pits; these sandpits made a wonderful playground for the local children who remember sand martins nesting in the banks. Wells was also a wood craftsman and the photographs of the house interiors show his furniture, particularly gate-legged and dining tables. It is doubtful that he made all the furniture himself, probably having created the shape and design initially, he left the reproduction work to his carpenters. It is also interesting that many of the original fireplaces contained niches of a size suitable for taking one of his pots.

Because some were designed as weekend retreats there were huge problems encountered by owners who purchased them as permanent residences later; they had tiny kitchens and bathrooms and some were rather cramped. The Nutshell was the smallest of his designs selling for £561; he would produce a basic design and create variations on it so that no two cottages are exactly the same. There are four or five main other designs including the Bungalow type, The Butts type, Scammell type and the largest Speakman type which was priced at £1,350 and had four bedrooms but still only had the 'new L-shaped living room with dining recess'. Most of the cottages had somewhere to put the car, and, unusual for the period, many of these garages were built in sympathy with the house. Some even had outbuildings to be used as studios. They only had wells for water, and cess pits and there was no electricity. He would build one property, and having sold it, invested that money in the next plot of land on which to build his next house; he employed men right from the beginning looking upon the entire concept as a business exercise. A demand was created, and fuelled through advertising articles in home magazines such as *Good Housekeeping, Woman's Life, The Autocar*, and *The London Magazine;* individual commissions were also taken, such as an office for a Captain Clark, or a proposed alteration to a barn for a Mr Jenkinson.

There are almost as many stories about Reginald Wells as there are people to tell them: that he went to live in South America where he loved the farmhouses and incorporated the random stonework idea into his West Chiltington houses, that he went to Nova Scotia to paint, that Rosa was a fiery-tempered Russian who terrified the workmen, a princess, a Pole, that he had a bronze in the foyer of the Savoy Hotel in London....Facts are harder to come by but it is known that he was born in Rio de Janeiro, Brazil where his father, an engineer, was working, and that in 1899 he married Clarissa Rawlings. 'Rosa' was actually 'Resca' and was Russian, an aviator and not a princess. She had wanted to learn how to fly and had lost some of her fingers while cranking the propeller. They met through their common interest in flying and her arrival on the scene, his subsequent divorce at a time when divorce was less accepted than it is now, and her presence in West Chiltington caused much family unhappiness. There certainly is a bronze in the Savoy, a statue of Count Peter but it was designed and cast by Frank Lynn Jenkins (1870-1927).

A life sized bronze Hercules was ordered by the Kaiser based on the small model of 'The Shot Put' which he had seen in a gallery in Berlin before the Great War; this was in the making when war broke out in 1914 so the contract was cancelled and the clay Hercules was smashed up. Her Royal Highness Princess Mary bought a small Wells' bowl for three guineas at an exhibition at the Beaux Arts Gallery, Bruton Place, London, in May 1927. Wells must have been a good business man, and a good potter, because in the last two months of 1926 he sold £737.2.0d worth of pottery, £47.5.0d worth of sculpture and £13.6.6d worth of wooden stands for displaying the above which adds up to almost £800, the cost of one of his smaller cottages.

At first Wells' office was the first house on the right up Spinney Lane now called Spinney Corner; later his office moved and this site was used as his yard. His later office was in Monkmead Lane (on the right of Red Wyn Byn nearly opposite the Sunset Lane junction); this building was burned down about twenty five years ago whilst it was being converted into a house.

This was a fate which befell many of his houses; it was a source of constant comment for the older people in the village, and delight to the youngsters when "there's another Wells house going up!" This will explain why many of the houses are now tiled rather than thatched. Teddy Elliott remembers that as a boy he always used to wear gumboots when walking through the sandy lanes of West Chiltington Common to see a fire because of the many snakes there were there, and some of the children of the time called the area Snakey Woods. The children were fascinated by

R Wells' Tiles and Potteries Office
The frame appears to be made of whole rounded timbers

the fire engines, as children everywhere are, without realising the personal tragedies that these thatch fires caused. One house, Tregennys, one of the earlier houses built, was owned by a brother and a sister. When it caught fire and was quite severely damaged, Mr Wells came back to rebuild it and the couple asked him to add an extra storey so that the bedrooms were upstairs.

During the Second World War Wells was again involved in design and manufacturing of aircraft and boats; he designed a hydrofoil speedboat which apparently was unsuccessful and then went on to make parts for Mosquitoes. This interest in boats persisted because after the war he began a boat building business in Littlehampton in a desire to break the speed record. It is recalled that "his passion became boats which he kept in his yard at Spinney Corner; it did look strange, a forest of masts from his boats. He also had very futuristic ones: one was just like a flying boat, and it had tail fins which were in the water when moving slowly and out when moving fast - it went up like a flying boat which was steered by air pressure as there was less drag than in the water. With its 25 horse-power engine it went at 60 miles per hour."

He died on 19 June 1951 at The Spires, Angmering Lane, East Preston, aged 74, leaving his first wife, two sons and a daughter, and his second wife, Resca; his obituary was published in The Times. During his life he had built a thatched bus shelter on Common Hill, with glass fronted panels at the back to display photographs of his cottages for sale. Over the years the bus shelter had first one, and then other glass panes broken and it fell into disrepair but during the mid 1950s Storrington Council tiled and repaired the shelter as a memorial to him.

One of the key houses he built is now the Roundabout Hotel. Jean Maile who works there has compiled most of this history of the place: R F Wells acquired 60 acres of land from John Kittow in 1927 for £1,600.00. He in turn sold part of this to Resca, and Cupressus Cottage was built on this land in 1932. Rumour has it that Ronald Coleman, the actor, was interested in buying Cupressus Cottage, but Reginald Wells would not approve certain alterations to his specifications, so Coleman did not buy.

As demand for Wells cottages grew, a hotel to house the weekend guests of those cottages was needed, and in 1935 Cupressus Cottage became The Roundabout Hotel, having been bought by Aimee Kathleen Kempster,

The Bus Shelter

who was reputed to have been an opera singer, for £4,500. She had bought it primarily for her son Andre, but the Second World War changed many things and Andre was tragically killed. One day, so the story goes, Mrs Kempster decided that her bedroom needed painting, got in a painter Freddy Hyde, who with his brother ran a painting and decorating business, and married him soon thereafter. Later the hotel was bought by Lawrence and Betty Berg. They were builders, and after Lawrence died Mrs Berg built quite a few houses in the area, having a penchant for pink and stamping her individuality on each house. The houses below Pansala, Spinney Lane were her development, as was Silverwood (though not Silverwood Copse), and some properties in Harborough Hill. The hotel changed hands many times until Richard Begley bought it in 1968; he still owns it in 1999, and has built it up to a thriving three star hotel.

It was a quaint place of nine bedrooms, with servant bells in the rooms, no en-suite bathrooms as is essential today, and with the feel of a large family house rather than of a commercial hotel. The Wells style included an open garage at the front from which one could drive through an arch to the rear garden, which also contained a delightful loggia. The building at the front of the hotel, now Woodland Cottage was the old stable block; although cars were on the scene by this time, horses were still used quite frequently. By the 1970s this wing was altered for staff accommodation. As time went on and demand for more rooms grew, the Billiard Room was altered to house a luxury four-poster suite, the garage was converted into bedrooms while the coal yard was made into two further rooms for staff.

In 1969 a regular event was a disco, a fairly new invention then, which was held in the Cellar Bar downstairs. With no drinking-and-driving restrictions, it attracted people from miles around, and many of the over 40s who visit the hotel today remember coming to this popular venue in their youth. They had either a live band, or records, and it was packed. In the Christmas of 1969 it cost a princely £36.15s to stay for three nights, to include bed, breakfast and dinner.

There are two distinct areas of Wells' cottages: one centred on Sunset, Spinney, Heather and Westward Lanes and the other on Grove, Threals, Fir and Birch Tree Lanes. When Wells was building in Grove Lane in the 1920s, it is thought that he approached the site off Roundabout Lane, as Smock Alley was not made up along its length at that time. It was just a path which has gradually got wider. When Ivan Pullen used to do a paper round in the mid 1930s, Dr Langmead and her husband lived at Quilters

Wells' Cottages – 1930s
The Grove is in the background, there is bracken in the foreground

in Grove Lane and Ivan had to deliver to them; when it rained the rain used to wash all the sand out of the lane which was left as a deep furrow with all the tree roots exposed making the going very difficult. Mr Wells built houses but not roads so people used to put their ashes down to build up the lanes; a resident of Grove Lane recalls that, the lane being steep, a neighbour of his used to go out every so often and shovel the stones that had been washed down the lane, into his wheelbarrow and take them back up the hill - a case of road recycling! All the roads of Wells' houses are unadopted by the Council and privately maintained. There is a continuation of Spinney Lane crossing Monkmead Lane to Common Hill which used to be part of the old lane to Storrington. Although it does not appear to go anywhere, efforts to block it off have been fiercely opposed.

Heather Lane is remembered as just a sandy track through the heather, hence its name. The bottom of Sunset Lane was a mass of sand which the children used to try and ride their bicycles through without falling off - a great game. Another game of the local children was to go to the back of the Roundabout Hotel in winter and sledge down the steep slope of the sand pit; Mr Wells used to chase them off but as soon as his back was turned they returned. Another area much favoured by children was from

Threals Copse to High Bar in Thakeham, which used to be a glorious beech wood with trees for climbing, and bluebells. Various people remember how dense, how thick the stems, how plentiful were the bluebells there, a pleasure only spoiled by the very big red ants nests! The wood also had a wonderful hill for rolling down, and beautiful wild daffodils.

Wells' developments must have been one of the first 'housing estates' in the country but unlike Letchworth (the first Garden City) or Port Sunlight or Bournville (paternalist conurbations for factory workers), there are no shops, infrastructure or central recreational areas, it was simply devised as a collection of cottages.

When asked what the village people thought of the Wells development there were a variety of answers but the general consensus was that he provided work; he employed not only local people but others; it was the time of the Depression and men came from all over the country looking for work. It is remembered that a plumber from Portsmouth had heard that there were houses under construction; he just stood outside the house that was being built and waited to see if he could be employed; the houses only had cold water so the plumbing was relatively uncomplicated but the iron pipes were hard to work with. Wells hired and fired on the spot as one could in those days; he had a strict no-smoking rule and if he thought the condensation on people's breath was smoke, they'd be fired, just like that. Local builders say that he built on the cheap; if he dug a lump of ironstone out of the ground it went into the walls, he would not make bricks unnecessarily, but they have stood the test of time. No-one has yet found the secret of recreating Wells cottages - perhaps because of the advent of sterner Building Regulations!

Many of these weekend houses needed a caretaker to clean and service them during the week, and Mrs Madgewick worked in this capacity for Mary Clare the London actress who used a house in Fir Tree Lane. While Gwen Smith was still at school aged thirteen, Mrs Madgewick enlisted her help for the weekend cooking and washing up that the dinner parties would create. Gwen was also the caretaker for the artist Fred Spurgeon, and his wife who lived at Little Hayden, Bower Lane; she describes Mrs Spurgeon as "'a real Band Box Betty', a tiny woman, very pretty and very particular. She was the daughter of Rothman's, the cigarette family. They were glamorous, the Roundabout people." Bill Pertwee, made famous by his television appearances in Dad's Army, was evacuated to the area; Mary Law, who was the leading lady in The Mousetrap for many years, lived at

Woodlands Cottage, Spinney Lane, during the war years. Her parents owned the house which, early in its life, had had a bedroom with balcony built in the garden for the owner's son who suffered with tuberculosis; the only cure in those days being plenty of good food and fresh air, the balcony enabled him to sleep outside. Early in the 1950s this was extended to form a granny bungalow called Owl Becks. Anthea Askey, the daughter of Arthur Askey the comedian, also used to live in the parish, at Abbotswood, which was built in the late 1950s next to the Roundabout Hotel. These residents emphasise the view that Roundabout was considered the part of the parish catering for the 'rich and famous' but the residents were accepted because although initially they brought their weekend provisions with them, they did shop at the local shops, and did employ the local people, contributing towards the financial stability of the village.

Mrs Margaret Sanson bought her Wells Cottage, Heather Nook, Monkmead Lane, in 1954, the house having been empty for three years. It had been a weekend cottage owned by A L Mond DSc, (Kelly's Directory 1934) who came down to West Chiltington to stay with a friend, and asked Reginald Wells to build him a house; they worked on the design together but he only used the cottage as a permanent residence towards the end of

Westward and Monkmead Lanes 1938
The hills west of Pulborough can be seen in the distance, Thrums is in the foreground

his life. Dr Mond is remembered as being a colourful character: it is possible that he was related to the wealthy Sir Alfred Moritz Mond, the first chairman of ICI, but it is more likely that he came from a family called Mond who lived at Grayfriars, Storington.

Mrs Sanson thinks it was possibly one of the first houses that Wells built in Monkmead Lane, having been built in 1926, and it still retains its original $4\frac{1}{2}$ acres which contain, close to the road, remnants of a Roman road. Much of the inside of the cottage has been left as it was, although the hurricane of 1987 felled 100 trees in the drive and a further 300 across the gardens. The enormous supply of chemicals that Dr Mond had left in his shed was disposed of; it was obvious that he worked and experimented at home. In spite of the dilapidation of the house, the Sansons bought it because of its proximity to the golf course; Wells also advertised thus in *Fairway & Hazard*: 'You found a treasure when you found this place' I said appreciatively, as with cigarettes alight we snuggled into the inglenook. "Thousands of people would give their eyes for a cottage like this". (Extract from article on ideal homes for golfers, referring to Wells cottages.)" Mrs Sanson continues "It was dreadfully neglected; I had daffodils growing out of the straw thatch, and the kitchen was in a ghastly mess with a black coke boiler that was meant to heat the house and the water. The whole was surrounded by rabbit-netting at a distance of only about 9′ from the house, and the swimming pool had netting round it too, to keep out the leaves. George Hampshire had previously been keeping an eye on the garden, and he single-handedly dug out the swimming pool." Sir Edgar and Lady Jones who lived at Codale Cottage, across the road, were friends of Dr Mond and their daughter remembers that it was very special to have a swimming pool in those days; it was heated by two coke boilers which also heated the changing room. It was a well-thought-out system. (Sir Edgar Jones had been the MP for Merthyr in Wales about 1910 and had retired to Codale Cottage.)

A less conventional resident was called Annie; she was quite a character and would walk down to Storrington to do her shopping and then sit on the bonnet of a police car that was parked nearby until the police drove her home. She is thought to have lived in Bower Lane in a very ramshackle house, and she used to ring the St John's Ambulance every so often for help, but the ambulance people were slightly apprehensive of this formidable woman marching about with a shotgun over her shoulder! For all her eccentricity she was kindly thought of by the people who knew her.

A less happy story shows that West Chiltington has not escaped the notoriety of a 'crime of passion'. On a calm but very humid evening in the late 1980s Grove Lane reverberated to the sound of two loud blasts from a shotgun. Nearby neighbours were shocked to find a woman lying in the lane, dying from the wounds she had received from the shotgun blasts. Her partner had already returned to the house and notified the police, but the neighbours were not to know this and naturally felt somewhat anxious. Most people in the vicinity were horrified that such a thing could happen in such quiet and picturesque surroundings. However the full force of the law was demonstrated when a man was convicted of murder in 1990 at Lewes Crown Court and sentenced to life imprisonment.

There are many people who remember their childhood in the Roundabout area and the stories below will give an indication of the atmosphere that prevailed between the 1930s and the beginning of the 1960s. It was a special time in the century for those with financial security and self confidence, life was merry and gay (to use the terminology of the time) and there is a great similarity in the memories recorded below, of space, freedom and enjoyment.

Common Hill – late 1920s
The Cottage is in the foreground, Green Shadows behind

When war broke out, John Ascoli went, with his mother, to live in his grandparents' Wells cottage, Roslin in Westward Lane. His family was all involved in the fashion business in London, and his mother used to go up by train every day in spite of the dangers; often the bombs nearby used to hold up the train which would stop in the tunnel at Merstham to hide. Because she travelled regularly on business, his mother was allowed petrol coupons so she could drive to Pulborough station. Sometimes John would accompany her on her visits to Harrods and the other stores to get orders for the business of which she was a director, just in order to be with her, and would watch her pack the frocks in tissue paper in plain cardboard boxes. The highlight of his journey was when he was lucky enough to have an egg which he took with him from a local farm asking for it to be cooked for him on the train; there was no restaurant car in those days.

His overwhelming memory of those days is of the freedom; the countryside offered such space to a ten year old boy from Surbiton. He would cycle to Storrington, or to Pulborough to shop for his grandparents, or along Broadford Bridge Road to the farm to get a rabbit, or the very occasional chicken as a great treat, and eggs. Shopping was mostly done in Pulborough, at Pictons the grocers for a blue bag of sugar from the big drum, or Corderys the ironmongers to charge up the accumulator for the wireless. There was little traffic on the road, and he remembers his decision one day to collect car registration number plates, but in a whole day only seeing two cars! Unfortunately one of those two cars was later seen to have had a crash outside the garage on the Common, which rather dampened his enthusiasm. During the war cars had metal cones on the headlamps with slits in them to diffuse the light and allow just enough to see by for night driving without the light being seen from above by the enemy aircraft, and it may have been this lack of light that caused the accident.

There was freedom and fun in the atmosphere as well; the Canadian soldiers from the camp in Monkmead woods were friendly and would invite him to share their marvellous

Roslin Cottage, Westward Lane – 1938

cocoa and huge slabs of fruit cake; he would see the army radio lorries hidden in the Roundabout area and was allowed to sit up on them and chatter away before cycling home to tell his grandmother all about it. He watched the army steam rollers building the roads, and in the evenings and at weekends the officers would come to one of the Roundabout houses for a cocktail party. In spite of there being a war on, there always seemed lots to drink, lots of cigarettes, and enough food, although culinary expectations were not as high as they are now. There was a feeling of community in the Roundabout area, a separate entity from the village, a little hamlet on its own.

The houses in Roundabout were a revelation to him after a year in Gay Street in an old, unmodernised cottage; by now there was mains water, a septic tank and mains electricity. In one house there was also a water softener, an enormous upright cylindrical tank that one put salt into.

Carol Fisher (née Cox) says of her time in Sunset Lane in 1952: "My memory of those 1930s, 40s and 50s days in Roundabouts was not of fear, bombing and rationing, but of freedom, space and parties. Everyone remembers the parties. We met everyone on a daily basis, I could tell you now the names of everybody who lived in Sunset Lane because we met so often and always for cocktails on Sundays. I remember an enormous punchbowl, Pimms on the front lawn, colonial types eating canapés, residents in the houses not weekenders, riding a neighbour's pony down their huge garden, space, sunshine and family. I was lucky that when I came down at six weeks old, I came with my parents, my grandparents lived down the lane, and my great grandmother lived at Romanys in Sunset Lane. Mummy shopped either in the village or at Greenfields where she had a little hardback book with her orders entered in, and paid at the end of the month. Neither I, nor Jeremy my husband who also spent a childhood in Roundabouts, noticed a barrier with the village children, we were just all children together". Jeremy adds: "Although there was a difference in what our parents and the village children's parents did for a living, there wasn't the materialism about that there is now, and we all had so much less. Perhaps it was a result of the war, rationing meant we all had the same allowance, and we all co-operated together, too. Carol and her parents grew vegetables in the garden, and had a pig fed on scraps, just as everyone else did. When I first came down here I lived at Winterfold in Birch Tree Lane with my parents and nanny, and Father took the train to London to work. We lived in the house exactly as Wells had built it, complete with thatched garage and, unusually, didn't need to do any alterations at all even though we were living there full time and not using it as a weekend cottage. When we returned to the village some years later, we lived at Dalebanks in Monkmead Lane and you might be interested to know, it's possible that the Wells family still has access across the garden of Dalebanks. From the Roundabout Hotel Mr Wells' lorries couldn't make the turn into Common Hill so he retained the right to go through Dalebanks' garden; at the back is a lane which is still fenced apart and comes out at Ragman's Castle. Father tried to break this contract, but never succeeded."

Michael Fitzgerald's parents moved into Westward Lane in 1947 from Surrey; his father knew about Wells' houses and determined to have one although the dream was not realised until a couple of years before he retired. Michael was away at boarding school when his parents moved, and he remembers being rather shocked to discover that he had to leave all his old friends from Surrey behind; as he says: "I was a bit lonely at first because there weren't many younger children around at that time. It was only in the 1950s that young families started to move in, before that it was very much an area for retired or older people, partly I suppose because the houses were relatively expensive and partly because it was rather remote and it wasn't practical to have to go everywhere by bus. I ended up by joining the cricket club to find friends, otherwise the people I met were the tradesmen and the daily help. In the '50s there was still a sort of them-and-us system, but we met as equals at the cricket club, although even in those days it didn't have a large proportion of local village people, which was a shame. It seems that the 'real village' used the band as their social focal point, and the cricket club was mostly incomers. I wonder now whether it wasn't more a physical gulf between groups as we were so far away geographically from the village and the common and people didn't move around like they do today; the Martlets hadn't been built and so there were fields there - it was like separate areas.

My mother, like many other people, had a daily help, a local girl who arrived on her bicycle, and a gardener for a couple of days a week. My parents-in-law had a full time gardener because their garden was very big and wooded in those days; they had moved into Little Warren which included all the land that was sold for building Wyndham Lea in 1966, plus a little land that was incorporated into the Rambledown estate. My mother and mother-in-law did their own cooking, but if they entertained they were helped out by their daily helps' daughters who came in for the occasion."

After living in Dorking, Michael and his wife Judith came to live in Grove Lane in about 1964 because they both still had friends in the area and the rail journey from Pulborough to London was better than the Dorking line. He continues "When I first knew Pulborough station the steam trains were running from there to Petworth and Guildford; the line was closed before Dr Beeching axed the other lines from 1963 onwards. Quite a lot of people commuted using that London line, arriving at the station by the hourly bus from West Chiltington to Pulborough or coming in their own cars which they could park, free, on the old market site beside the station on any day other than market day. There was a weekly cattle market there up to about the late 1960s but only some of the pens were a permanent fixture so there was usually space to weave in and park, otherwise we used the area alongside the railway line. The station had flowers growing in tubs on the platforms and looked well tended and cared for; there was a sense of pride amongst the staff but it was much busier then; all the school children used the trains."

Little Thatch is generally thought to have been the first house that Reginald Wells built, which would be logical as it occupies a prominent site, good for sales, on the road from Storrington to West Chiltington, but there are other claimants.

While staying in Shoreham with her parents and children, Eileen Van Tromp had bought a weekend cottage, La Chaumiere, from Mr Wells in 1933. Her daughter Elizabeth says that her mother went for a drive in her little Austin Seven and saw 'this enchanting little cottage.' She drove on and found the estate office, and saw Mr King who was the agent at that time. Reginald Wells happened to be in the office and she said 'I've simply got to have one of your cottages' so he took her to see La Chaumiere which was available. Having discovered the price, she asked him to keep it for her because she did not have enough money to buy it, so he arranged a private mortgage for her, for the £400 asking price, to be repaid at ten shillings per month. At that time there was in Spinney Lane only La Chaumiere, Nutshell (now Squirrels), Tregennys; Little Barmoor in Sunset Lane, and one other, all built to the same basic design. Then he would change designs and built a few more like that, before going on to a third design for a few more houses again.

When the blitz hit London Eileen moved from Purley permanently to La Chaumiere with her children Elizabeth (Liz) and Bill and extended the property. Bill spent his childhood there and became a farm pupil at Hurston Farm, with Peter Cellier (later to be known on television as the actor from the programme 'Personal Services'.) Peter's parents were an interesting couple, living at Furzefield, Crossways; his father was in black and white films, 'How Green was my Valley' was the most remembered; and his mother, Phyllis, who liked sporty cars used to dash around in an SS, an early Jaguar. She also gave time to the community, and during the war was allowed petrol coupons because she used to drive for voluntary work.

Eileen was a dancing teacher; she would have liked to have been a dancer but had grown too tall. As she and her husband had separated she earned her living writing ballets and dances, or re-choreographing existing ballets for use by schools, or companies with smaller corps de ballet, and advertised in *The Dancing Times*. Enquiries came from dancing mistresses all over the world, and as ballet has no notation as music has, she would laboriously type her instructions with one finger on a huge and ancient typewriter.

Miss E Leighton owned Romany in Sunset Lane, then a property with a substantial plot including over five acres across the road. Eileen's father bought this land for his grandaughter Liz, who kept ponies. Liz recalls a childhood event: "Janet Bateman, who lived down the road in a house called Stovold, Peter Cellier and I built a brushwood house on this land which was very overgrown and tussocky. One day we decided that we were going to cook dinner in the house; Peter brought the matches, and the embers which we finally blew into flames started a major fire. We all scattered in different directions, but the gardener from Perretts had seen the flames, and fearful of the thatch on the roof of Miss Maud Heath's house, Broom Cottage, had already raised the alarm. It was quite a good thing in a way, though, because the fire had burned years of dead grass off, and the new grass that came was good for the ponies." (With the thatched roofs, heather and dried grass, fire was a constant threat.) In 1945 Eileen had a little house built on some of this land because the family had outgrown La Chaumiere, which was sold to General Green from Blue Cedar for his daughter-in-law. Eileen called the new house Meadowbrook, which was built by Mr Field who, before the war, had been Wells' foreman. When Field came back from the war Wells had stopped building, but still retained much of his stock of door and window frames, assorted timbers, and other building materials in his store. As Field would otherwise be out of a job, Wells suggested that he take over the stock, and start up on his own; having worked for Wells all those years before the war the designs and skills were well learned. Meadowbrook was built as a three bedroom house with a downstairs cloakroom (the wartime restrictions only allowed one toilet per new house and Eileen decided that if the house was to be filled with the children's friends it was more sensible to have the toilet downstairs) and a kitchen and living room. Later Bill's first tractor was kept in the field with the ponies, and it was from here that his business began.

Eileen then asked Field to build a mirror-image of Meadowbrook in the substantial garden, for her mother. After her mother died, Eileen moved into the cottage, called Meadow Cottage, and Meadowbrook went into the ownership of her daughter. Meadowbrook is an interesting cottage, being built in the mid 1940s, and differing from the earlier Wells style by being plastered inside instead of the more usual dinged rough brickwork, and by having a fully tiled roof and substantial bedroom accommodation. Eventually Meadowbrook was sold to Robin Douglas-Home who was a popular society pianist, wrote for the *Daily Express* and was a photographer. He was perhaps better known for the people he associated with: his wife was the model Sandra Paul; his brother Charles became editor of *The Times;* one uncle was Sir Alec Douglas-Home the Prime Minister; another was William Douglas-Home the playwright. He bought the house following his divorce in 1965, and either he or Mr Hamilton from whom he purchased the house added an extension for a housekeeper, and he added an aviary for his birds. He came to the house with his two dogs for weekends, and he and his set would have parties before going back to London for the Monday morning. One of his guests was HRH Princess Margaret, and there are amusing memories of her visits: the people of Roundabout knew when she had arrived because of the policeman posted at the end of the Lane. Fairy Fuss who lived opposite in Romanys would know when she was coming because she would be visited by Robin Douglas-Home's housekeeper who wanted to borrow the silver fish knives and forks as Robin had none of his own. Robin Douglas-Home and Princess Margaret were often seen walking in the lanes and woods with the dogs. The house achieved publicity when an article in the *Daily Express* showed an old photograph of the Princess and a group of Robin's family in the garden of Meadowbrook, and another of her in the dining room of the house. The interior of the house was featured again when Alan

Whicker interviewed Robin for the BBC2 programme *Whicker's World* in April 1967. Sadly, Robin Douglas-Home suffered from depression, and aged only 36 he took an overdose of sleeping pills while at Meadowbrook. It was some eighteen months before his affairs were sorted out and the house sold again.

Obsessed with ballet, Eileen Van Tromp determined that her daughter Elizabeth should dance, but she, like her mother, grew too tall, and, having left Mr Freeman's school finally started The Roundabout Riding School in Sunset Lane. Before Eileen had started building she had sited the footpath into the field at the bottom on the Broom Cottage side of the plot, but she later moved the path to where Welby now stands. This path had a gate at the Sunset Lane end upon which was proudly displayed the riding school board.

Eileen Van Tromp was an interesting character as an article in a January 1959 newspaper shows. While she was training to be a ballet dancer she took a supplementary course at the Chelsea School of Art in textiles. After she came to Meadowbrook she took up spinning and weaving, using the wool from the hedgerows, and collected enough to make her children's socks. By 1952 she was supplying a friend who had a shop in Pulborough with her hand woven scarves, tweeds and cushion covers, which she also dyed herself using natural dyes from onion skins, privet berries, dandelions, marigolds, lichen, and woad which she grew at the bottom of her garden; by 1959 she had four agents for her wares. As well as this she managed to find time to try her hand at pottery and to become very involved with the costumes for the village pantomimes. She was also a friend of Resca Wells, having a common interest in painting.

There were some other colourful characters in Roundabouts; Bill remembers General Green from Blue Cedar who became the CO of the local Home Guard and whose car was camouflaged, but was still conspicuous being such an individual; his front garden was a miniature golf course with bunkers. He and Mrs Green were shooting people and very generous. Then there was John Hatt who lived at Heatherland, Sunset Lane; when he came back from the war he had a little car that was called The Hat Box. One night, when he had not put the brake on properly, this car had run down his drive and across the lane, coming to rest against the fence at Meadowbrook. There was a timid knock on the door the next morning: 'please can I have my car back!'

The Australian mannequin Fairy was internationally recognised before the war, and had come over to England with two friends to model; she married Heine Fuss, for whom she modelled, and they came to live in Sunset Lane. Sadly Heine died of a stroke when they were on holiday in Australia. She had a son called Adam, an angelic looking child with blue eyes and blond curly hair, who is principally remembered for the mischief he got up to, including floating his gumboots down the stream by Tiddletags. Tiddletags, meaning 'small toads' was the original name for the little two-up and two-down stone cottage in Heather Lane, which had a tiny pond where the children remember going to collect toads. (The house has been extended and is now called Pond Cottage.) The children often used to go and play in the mud beside the little pond and when his boots sank, or got stuck, Adam was too small to rescue them so had to enlist help, usually from Eileen Van Tromp. He is also remembered as removing the lanterns that the contractors left in the lane at night while they were installing mains drainage, and putting them into the ditch that had been dug.

Although Millie Collet had been born and brought up in Worthing, she came to live in April Cottage, Sunset Lane, with her uncle and aunt Mr and Mrs Bill Moore-Alpine. She remembers having her seventeenth birthday there, and 'coming out' as girls did in those days, with dinner at the Roundabout Hotel and on to the Hunt Ball in Horsham. From the early 1950s the Roundabout Hotel was a focal meeting place and many of the residents of Roundabout would congregate there by walking up Sunset Lane, through the sandpit and into the back of the hotel, for a half of bitter, or cocktails. The bar was downstairs with a little cubby-hole for the drinks, and was very well patronised. During the war when there was little petrol, the Roundabout Hotel was the only place to go as frequenting pubs was rather frowned upon for young people and the ladies.

Having left April Cottage Millie lived in Pansala, Spinney Lane, with her friend Joy Saville, from the 1960s and says "This could have been one of the earlier houses that Wells built as he used to sit his prospective customers in what used to be Joy's and my dining room before we built on, and then he would take them round the area so that they could choose a plot. The house had originally been owned by Joy's father who had left it to her; nobody really knows why it's called Pansala except that one day my cousins came home from Ceylon and said that it meant 'a temple' in Sinhalese, but I don't know if that's true. When Joy died in 1980 it didn't take long for the developers to arrive; I remember Mrs Berg had asked Joy whether she would be prepared to sell the wood adjacent to the house for development years before, and her reply had been 'over my dead body!' How sadly prophetic, because within a couple of years, after I sold up and moved, new houses were built by Mrs Berg, between Pansala and Perretts, in the water-meadows that used to be so full of orchids."

April Cottage was sold to Mrs Doreen Hugaerts, an English woman who spent most of her time in Belgium only coming back to the cottage for a couple of weeks a year. At some stage in her life it appears that she became a prison visitor and met William Vassall, the Admiralty clerk who was jailed for eighteen years on 22 October 1962 for spying for the Soviet Union. Vassall was described as a quietly-spoken vicar's son, who fell into the clutches of the Russians having been lured to a homosexual party while posted to the British Embassy in Moscow, and blackmailed. The Vassall scandal rocked the Conservative government of Harold Macmillan and rumbled on for months: Deputy First Lord of the Admiralty Thomas Galbraith resigned from the government although he was later cleared of any impropriety in his relationship with Vassall; a *Daily Sketch* journalist was jailed for refusing to reveal his sources to the Vassall tribunal, followed by two other journalists also being jailed, creating very bad divisions between the press and the government. It was shortly thereafter that the Profumo affair finally brought down the Macmillan government. It is easy to imagine the consternation locally, particularly among the retired military personnel, when it was discovered that Mrs Hugaerts had offered Vassall her house in Sunset Lane, to avoid the attention of the news media, following his release from prison in October 1972. The present owners of the house, Jenneth and Aidan Moore say "Mrs Hugaerts' cousin was Joy Saville from Pansala, and she and her friend Millie Collet used to keep an eye on April Cottage while her cousin was abroad. Vassell thought April Cottage was idyllic; so peaceful after prison. He later wrote an autobiography as John Vassall, *Vassall, the Autobiography of a Spy*, and there is a description of this cottage; when the cottage had been built there was also a round house in the garden, the Rondavel, built to accommodate the piano of the first buyer as the house was so small, and Vassall describes the carpet and the floral curtains in there, which were still there when we bought it. We could recognise so much from this book! After he left here he went to a monastery in Storrington. When his book came out we were pestered by the press who wanted to see the house; I even found reporters in the back garden.

Bringing the Roundabout story right up to date, there is an annual meeting at the Roundabout Hotel of the Roundabout Road Fund at which we discuss the subscription for the road fund, and use the rest of the time as an excuse for a social occasion. When Wells conceived this development it was unique and we owe it to the new people buying these cottages to explain to them the ethos of the place. There have been other houses built among the Wells cottages which has changed the area somewhat but the lanes are still a very special place in which to live."

Sometimes, as in the Van Tromp's case, the houses were handed down within families; Air Marshall Sir Maurice Heath had inherited his house, Broom Cottage, from his aunt. He had had an illustrious career, having directed SAS operations in Oman in 1957 and been thanked by Sultan Said bin Taimur, he continued to work in the Middle East; in 1955 he joined the Air Ministry. He retired and joined a London firm of estate agents, was a Gentleman Usher to the Queen from 1966 to 1979; in 1977 he was appointed Deputy Lieutenant for West Sussex and for many years was president of the Storrington branch of the Royal Air Force Association. He died in 1998.

Ann Salisbury moved into Southcroft, Monkmead Lane, with her parents in 1938 and it is noteworthy in that neither the house name, nor the house boundaries have changed in all the years. Her parents lived in Wimbledon, in a house called The Croft, so, as the new weekend cottage was south of the old one, the new place became Southcroft. They purchased the house from Mr Wells and Ann loved coming to the cottage during the school holidays when the family used it. She remembers a cricket pitch for her brother, a swing and sand pit, and eventually a swimming pool. There was a huge vegetable patch which, during the war, more than fed the family and was managed superbly by the gardener, George Hampshire Sr, referred to in those days simply as Hampshire. During the war the family would spend longer periods in West Chiltington to avoid London's blitz. After her parents gave the house to her, she built stables in 1950 for her beloved 'Mitzi and friends', but these were pulled down by the next people to own the property. The house was thatched with straw which was cheap and plentiful, but her parents, tired of the endless repairs that a straw thatch required, finally had the roof replaced with Norfolk reed thatch which was a great deal more expensive but much more durable. The expense was somewhat offset by the reduction in the repair bills, the roof only needing the sparrow hedging on the ridge repairing once to Ann's knowledge. The garden at Southcroft was not large enough for pasture for the horses so Ann rented the fields owned by Eileen Van Tromp behind her house. She remembers that as a teenager she would walk through the twitten at the side of Southcroft, turn left into Westward Lane and right into Sunset Lane to Meadowbrook where the horses were.

In 1966 she moved to Harbolets (which is the east-west road joining Ashington to Adversane) as she needed the extra land for her horses.

Grove Lane has a ghost as Jeremy Fisher relates: "about 1971 Firwood Cottage was bought by a friend of mine, Theo, a commercial artist who had previously been living in Surrey. As the house needed a lot doing to it he decided to come down in the evenings to work on the place with the builders, but after a few days they started to notice strange happenings: the unplugged kettle would be full of hot water; they would light a fire to warm the house up and suddenly this fire would go out and the grate and fireplace would be stone cold; tools would disappear - they would put a hammer down and when they reached out for it again, it had gone. One day one of the builders came down by himself in his old van, and as he turned into the drive he saw an old man in the garden. He jumped out of the van and ran across the undergrowth to find him and see what he was up to, getting very scratched in the process. When Theo turned up a bit later on he remarked on the builder's scratches and cuts and asked him how he'd done it: he replied that he had been chasing an intruder through the brambles, to which Theo said 'but there aren't any brambles'. On

Roundabout Lane – 1930s
The Hollies in the foreground with the entrance to Grove Lane on the left centre

going back outside, there were no brambles. A few days later they came down again and this old man was inside the house this time, looking at them through the window, but on going indoors there was no-one to be found. Either that day, or a few days later, one of the builders goes upstairs to the bathroom. On the left of the toilet in this long thin bathroom is the bathroom cabinet with a mirror, on the right of the toilet is the bath against the wall. As the builder looks into the mirror he sees reflected, not the wall above the bath, but a long passageway, and worse, superimposed on his shoulders is not his head, but the head of the old man, which says 'Go away!' The builder fled, never to come back. These happenings were not a figment of a fevered imagination because other men on the site had seen many of the manifestations though not this final one. Theo was alarmed when he heard the story because he was planning to move into the house with his family and wondered what on earth he was bringing them to, so he went up to the church to enlist the help of the rector who happened to know of someone who was very interested in the paranormal. He met Theo back at the cottage and realised that there was a very disturbed soul there who needed putting to rest. He blessed the whole cottage and garden, and there have never been any problems since. This story appeared in *The News of the World* at the time, and John and Louise Hodge, the present owners of the house, had a phone call only a few months ago from someone who was researching ghost stories for a book. I believe there used to be an old manor house on that site which might have been where the old man came from." This story has also been independently told by Peter Penfold who was the electrician on site at the time; he adds that the builders were from Horsham and would not go back to work at the cottage.

Meg Judd's experiences of the paranormal are more productive. Meg and Gerry and their two sons Jeremy and Michael moved to Birch Tree Lane in 1951 when they came home from South Africa; they knew the area because Jerry's parents had retired to Heath Common. His mother, whose maiden name was Knowles, used to stay at the Queen's Head when she was a child as her uncle was the landlord there and she still had relatives living in Thakeham. Meg became very involved in West Chiltington affairs and was, amongst other things, a school governor and the youngest ever President of the WI.

After the death of her younger son from an asthma attack in 1968 she took up painting as a therapy. It was then that she discovered she was able to create spontaneous and beautiful images from what is described as 'a force outside herself'. Those who have seen her paintings are struck by the apparent religious or period content though Meg herself is not particularly religious, nor does she have any special knowledge of history. She believes that she is merely a conduit through which this force passes and is most fortunate to have been given such a gift. In 1986, apart from articles in newspapers, the paintings were featured in the magazine *Beyond Science*, and she was also interviewed by BBC Radio Sussex on the subject.

Gerry Judd was a keen but frustrated gardener, working in London and having only the weekends to devote to his garden. Soon after moving to Birch Tree Lane he bought a camellia at the Chelsea Flower Show knowing that it would be happy in the local acid soil; this was the beginning of what was to become an obsession. Being a Member of the International Camellia Society he received 'cuttings' by air mail from other members in Italy, China and New Zealand; these he struck and are now the mature and beautiful trees to be seen and enjoyed not only in his garden but in many other gardens in the district.

Meg wryly adds "we had a well for the water with a hand pump in the kitchen (with a side-to-side pumping action) and of course no main drains…..the 'State of the Cesspools' was a constant source of interest and could be relied on as a subject of conversation at any local social gathering!"

Guy and Jean Peace who arrived at their house in Fir Tree Lane along a similar route escaping London bombing and having family in the area, add that when they bought their Wells house an electric pump for the water had been installed, but when electricity was brought to the house the cables all ran down the walls not through the cavities, which made it very unsightly. They also elaborate on the difference between a septic tank which they had where the waste is biologically degraded naturally in two tanks until it is clean enough to filter itself back into a stream or drain, and a cesspit which has to be pumped out and emptied regularly.

(As some of the Roundabout houses have changed hands, their names have also been changed by the new owners; this may have led to a certain confusion in this chapter. I have tried to catch up on the new names, but apologise where I have failed - AS)

The wooded area of Roundabout seems an unlikely place for the war effort but Elsie Hampshire (née Manvell) knows differently. Reginald Wells' building career was coming to an end as the Second World War began, he was thinking of demolishing his workshop in Spinney Lane and moving on to something else; somehow Eustace and Partners in London heard about this and arranged that they should set up a factory on the site for the manufacture of waterproof ammunition crates. (It is said that Eustace had been bombed out of their London premises.) These were substantial boxes, a good six feet square, made of wood and lined with a tarred black paper, so that if the ships carrying the ammunition were sunk the ammunition itself, if salvaged, would still be serviceable. At least twenty people were employed in the factory, the young men were eventually called up and replaced by others, perhaps those who had failed a medical for example, and overseen by Mr Moore, Eustace's manager, who lived at Thakeham. All sorts of people were employed: a French woman; the rector of Storrington's daughter Miss Faithfull; many local girls and even one girl who suffered from epilepsy and who might not otherwise have been able to participate in the war effort. Everyone was given initial training, except one or two of the men who were already carpenters and glad of the work as the house building industry had all but stopped. It is strange to think that these crates all had hand-made dovetailed joints, and yet were used simply to transport ammunition. The factory worked set hours every day with a short break for lunch when the staff stopped for their sandwiches.

Once a week a van would come from London bringing the timber and materials, and taking away the finished crates. The girls were reluctant to discuss what they were making with others in the village; if the enemy got to know what they were doing their factory would become a target for bombers. In spite of this apprehension there was a happy atmosphere in the factory; people just got on and did what they had to do with a wonderfully philosophical air.

Miss Furlong had bought her cottage in the belief that Wells' workshop would be demolished and that she would have a view! Living so near the factory she had the key and acted as caretaker. The women all wore the typical 1940's overalls, crossed over at the front and tied at the back, but they had had to supply these themselves. Elsie still has a mark on her hand where the chisel slipped, and Bernard Crabb cut his finger badly on one of the machines, but injuries were not considered important - part of the war effort. The factory was decommissioned very quickly at the end of the war. Contrary to what might have been written elsewhere, this was the only munitions factory in the village.

Eustace Munitions Factory
Back Row from left: Mr Lee Sr, Douglas Lee his son
Middle Row: Miss Faithfull, Miss Furlong, Elsie Streeter, Kathy Short, Dorothy Manvell, Mr Crockford, Elsie Hampshire, Mr Windeath, —, Joan White from Nutbourne
Front Row: Florrie Pullen, Daisy Ashby, Dora Short, —, —, Connie Short, Brenda Pullen

Chapter 7

The Outskirts

On the north-eastern edge of the village this 'outskirts road' is a long one that nowadays has four names: going southwards it is The Sinnocks from the junction with East Street to the Juggs Lane corner, then it becomes Southlands Lane, past Southlands Farm to the junction with Haglands Lane from where it becomes Smock Alley. The final section is called Roundabout Lane and goes from the Threals Lane junction beyond the Five Bells to Roundabout Farm on the junction with the road to Storrington.

The name 'The Sinnocks' applied (and still does) to the field where Fly Farm is now situated. Up to 1930 when the last strip was sold this field was divided into five or six strips allocated to several farms in the village. The name may be derived from 'Innocks' a middle English word meaning 'intakes' or 'bringing into cultivation', suggesting a 13th century date for its cultivation as arable land. Or it could come from 'Inhooks' which was 'land that was enclosed for a period during its fallow year'.

Smock Alley may also have an ancient meaning: Kenneth Neale in 1974 interpreted the name as meaning a lover's lane. Before farm labourers wore smocks, he wrote, smocks were ladies' underwear (knickers) and he quoted various literary references to roving 'down petticoat lane and up smock alley'! Similar activities may have occurred along the bridleway from the Sinnocks to Thakeham; in 1836 when the path was called a wapple-way, a certain gate on the parish boundary was called Maid Robbing Gate - of what was the maiden robbed, one wonders?

Much of the land was owned by Naldretts or the Green brothers, on one side of the road south to Juggs Lane, and by the Hatches Estate on the other side to Haglands Lane.

An amusing story is told concerning Marigolds, the house on the corner of East Street and The Sinnocks. During the war an evacuee went out with one of the soldiers from the camp and when he offered to escort her home she used to tell him to drop her off at Marigolds, with "I'm going in now". When he had gone on down the lane and was well out of sight, she used to walk to her own less exalted home which certainly wasn't Marigolds! A reflection on human pride.

The Greenfield family used to live in what is now the Rectory; Marigolds was built about 1930 as a retirement house for Percy Greenfield and his four unmarried sisters, having purchased the land from Naldretts. Unfortunately he died a year or two after its completion and before he had disposed of his business at Ingatestone, Essex. Like his four sisters, Percy never married. On retirement, Stanley, Percy's brother, moved to Marigolds with his two sons, John and Alan, their mother having tragically died, to live with the four spinsters. With the passing of the years, Stanley and his four sisters passed away and, to pay death duties, Marigolds had to be sold. Stanley's elder son John bought a plot of land and built Charbury, East Street, while Alan, the younger son, moved away.

When the Greenfields left Marigolds, it was bought by the Murrells; Roger Murrell like his neighbours, was also working in horticulture and when he was unsuccessful in acquiring the tenancy to Sinnock Nursery his father helped him buy land at Mare Hill, and today Murrells is another successful nursery. The Nolan family were the next occupants; Mr Nolan was a retired greengrocer from Brighton. After a brutal burglary when the family was tied up and stabbed they did not feel they could stay and the property was sold to Miss Bagot who bred fox terriers.

In November 1965 Mervyn and Pauline Webb came to the village via the Land Settlement Association. (The LSA had been formed after the First World War, in about the 1930s, to benefit a group of out-of-work Welsh miners: they gave the miners a piece of land and a few pigs and chickens and the miners then built their bungalows and got started as smallholders. Obviously there were initial problems with the scheme, but by the end of the Second World War one paid in a stake for the land, the initial stock, and advice on everything from greenhouses to pig breeding and chicken farming, and the produce was sold through the LSA which acted like a co-operative.) Trained in Kent, they worked in Cambridge because the place in Sussex where they would have liked to go had no vacancies. After a few years they realised that Cambridge was not for them and, still wanting to get into Sussex, they applied to the County Council for a Council Holding. This was a fairly complicated business including an interview simply to go on the waiting list for a place, and as they had applied to several County

Councils they had no idea where they would end up. After much interviewing, they were granted the tenancy of what is now called Weathertop, in the Sinnocks, but used to be Sinnocks Nurseries, a smallholding of three acres which they took over from Tom Howard, whose parents had been the original tenants in the 1930s when the house was built. Tom and his unmarried sister Ena who acted as his housekeeper, grew vegetables and a few raspberries and strawberries, but there were no glasshouses.

Mervyn and Pauline describe what happened "We only had £500 when we came from Cambridge, so there were fairly tense negotiations for the tenancy, which ended up with their accepting our figure and throwing in an ancient mower! It was all a bit hand-to-mouth in the early days; we carried on with the crops that we inherited but added the chickens, pigs and goats we'd brought with us. The goats were our milk supply and any surplus went to the pigs, it was a bit like that television programme *The Good Life*.

We had to leave our glass behind in Cambridge where we had been growing tomatoes and things under glass, so in 1966 we bought some second-hand glass from a local nursery sale. Mac Steele lent us his tractor and trailer to bring these Dutch Lights back, and soon the Howard's immaculate garden and drive had been churned up and spoiled, but things had to change. The more glass we put up, the less space there was for the pigs we had, so Bill Hampton who lived in a caravan at the bottom of the field opposite, which had been his market garden, allowed us to keep them on his land. In the end we had 16 sows and a boar, and sold the weaners to a farmer at Goose Green. Bill was kind enough to let the girls keep their ponies on his land, too. There are a couple of interesting facts about Bill's accommodation; originally he had lived in a woodcutter's hut which had been towed down from Slindon on rubber tyres which were nearly off by the time it got here, so they just left it in the field and that was where it stayed. When he moved into the caravan he left the hut and it's now slowly collapsing. Next to it was his huge hut of about 50' by 30' where he kept his tools and machinery; it used to be a First World War prisoner of war hut, and had previously been the living accommodation for two families, on the site now occupied by Little Naldretts in East Street. It was only one of many in the area and was beautifully lined in pine; such good wood that it has been reused in our daughter's kitchen!

Apart from the pigs we were acting as the village greengrocer with a stall out in front selling all sorts of fruit and vegetables, and our eggs, as well as flowers.

In 1980 the 10½ acre field opposite, part of Naldretts Farm, came on the market and we decided to buy it, after all it had been our ambition to own our own land. When leaving The Sinnocks Nurseries, we were also leaving the house behind, so we had to have planning permission to build a house on the new site. We could only get this by proving that we were a viable business so we had to put up glass and polythene tunnels first, and ran the two sites for a couple of years which was a bit of a gamble. The fact that we had made a go of the council holding didn't seem to count, but eventually we got the permission and moved over, living in a caravan while the house was being built. We had rather hoped that the incoming tenant would buy our glass from us so we could start again with everything new, but he didn't have the money, so we brought it with us. Bill Hampton had previously rented the land from the Carvers who had owned Naldretts Farm, (Ted Carver was a market gardener, the brother of Bill Carver the builder, and used to live at Gentle Harry's) and when we bought we said he could stay. Bill used to work for the Paveys, annually strawing their strawberries; they were strawberry specialists and made good money at it. We couldn't believe that in Cambridge when we had grown strawberries we would pick into pound punnets which sold for a shilling, and here, they were selling for half a crown a quarter! We would see Bill driving his old 1930s Morris with its yellowed windscreen up the ruts in the field every day, through the permanently open gate, and back in the evening; parking the car in the small garage beside his big shed. He did gardening jobs around the village; he really loved the gardening job at Marigolds on the corner, but when Miss Bagot bought Marigolds, Bill announced that he didn't take kindly to being given orders by a woman so was coming to work for us full time, whether we could afford it or not! We had employed him when we could afford it and needed extra labour, but this was his, more permanent arrangement.

By 1987 we were doing all right, growing under polytunnels and glass, but the hurricane of that year finished us. We weren't insured, no-one was, partly because you can't insure the polythene of a tunnel, only the metal frame that holds it and even then, only if it comes up to a certain specification, and partly because no-one would insure old glass; the premiums were prohibitive as you had to insure each pane. In one night we were wiped out; we were awake all night but there was nothing we could do. Funnily enough, Bill slept right through it all! Some years before, when we were still on the Weathertop site, he had twice had his hut broken into and on the first occasion they had stolen his gun so he was a bit apprehensive. We had given him a caravan to live in instead of the hut and had put it near our house, but when we moved across the road Bill and the van had come with us, back home really, and the van was parked up here. There was a polythene sheet over the top of it to make it a bit warmer, and although the van had rocked a bit in the wind, it was still there, and Bill fast asleep. Before this, though, that polythene sheet had had a slit cut in it for a pipe to take the rainwater into an old tin bath because Bill wouldn't drink tap water. I used to worry sometimes that he would poison himself, or our grandchildren, with all the loopy things that wriggled about in it. He adores children and was so good with them; when the grandchildren used to come over they would go to his caravan and sit on boxes having lunch with him, Bovril made with rainwater and bread and dripping - they all loved it. I will never forget the picture of Bill in his straw hat with a hole in it and his trousers tied up with string, and Ellie our grandaughter at about 2 years old in her dungarees, dancing down the rows of runner beans and taking hands and dancing and singing at the end of the row. Those are really fond memories of a wonderful old man, and a little girl.

For a year after the hurricane we cleared up and tried to decide what to do. Meanwhile we were selling to Tesco in Horsham, mostly vegetables such as runner beans, courgettes, marrows and aubergines, and lettuces. The manager there thought our produce was so good he asked us to supply other Tesco stores in the locality with vegetables and with lettuces but we weren't big enough, so we bought lettuces in from another grower and sold it on; in the end we were acting as a wholesaler to about eight Tesco stores! We finally agreed to take out a loan and buy some new glasshouses because we were asked to supply bedding plants to another Tesco and to a garden centre in Worthing and the polythene tunnels just weren't suitable; that was when the local managers could source their own material, nowadays it all comes from a central supplier. Almost as soon as the order for the glass was placed, the Tesco manager rang us up and said that he would not be allowed to continue with the order as this central supply arrangement had come in so we had no alternative but to open to the public again, concentrating on bedding plants to pay off the loan. We were victims of our own success in the end because we were very busy, and our daughter who helped as much as she could had two children by then, and we were looking after an elderly mother. We tried to get permission for accommodation for a manager so we could let up a bit, but were turned down on the grounds that the business wouldn't support two families, and in the end it was just too much for us.

We decided to sell, just the nursery not the house, and one day, looking through the local newspaper discovered that a Peter Manfield had a permanent advertisement in the paper because he was looking for a nursery - and his parents already had a house in the area. So we sold up and nearly retired, just selling through the WI market in Storrington which we had done for years. We also retained our links with the hotels because some time before, we had made friends with a London chef called Dennis O'Sullivan (who used to live in Heathfield House on the Common) and we would grow specially for him. He would take our produce up to London in his car and knew how good it was. Word spread among the chefs, most of whom were from France, or abroad anyway, and soon we were getting old envelopes and cigarette packets with seed from home in them - 'please can you grow this for Monsieur This or That'. We were ahead of our time because in those days no-one had heard of baby turnips, mange tout, coloured lettuce or sugarsnap peas. By the 1980s though, Dennis had retired, the financial squeeze was hitting the hotel trade and the unusual was becoming more commonly available.

But now we have retired and face another difficulty: only in the UK is there tied accommodation, in the rest of Europe there is no such thing. Strictly speaking we can only sell this house, as it is tied to the land, to someone who is or was in the horticultural or agricultural business, so at the moment I can't see us retiring to a bungalow on the beach. However, with neighbours as good as the Manfields, we really don't mind staying here!"

Mervyn and Pauline sold three acres to Peter Manfield in 1994, who called his plot The Village Nurseries. Peter's father Roy had taken early retirement from his job as a bank manager in Caterham and he and his wife Sheila, who had had many years working in garden centres, had started a tropical plant display business for offices. They decided to move to Sussex and came upon West Chiltington quite by chance. At that time Peter, who had worked in garden centres in Epsom and Kent, was also looking to start his own business. Apart from the convenience of the locality, it was the beautiful glasshouse, erected after the great storm, that was the main attraction. Peter continues "The first year was hard. We all sank a lot into this venture; I sold my house to raise extra money, and now live locally. For the first month or so I was still working out my notice at the garden centre so the bulk of the work was in Sheila's hands, propagating the bedding plants and getting started. We took Mervyn's advice about advertising though; because we don't get any passing trade it was most important to let everyone know we were here. That's one reason why you will see us in the parish magazine and at village functions, although we do enjoy them as well!

By the second year we had increased the range of plants and moved into hardy nursery stock as well, and the area under glass and polythene began to grow, too. We put up the building that is the shop and now we have about one acre of polythene tunnel, and glasshouses, the latter having a computer controlled system to regulate the blinds, the air vents and the humidity which works well until there is a power cut! In theory we can go home to bed and let it look after itself, but we will have to think about a back up system, in the future. We also have a netting shade house, and have improved the outside plant area as well. We still do much of our own propagating, the rest we buy in as small plants or plugs and grow on. We have been well supported by the village, and are very grateful, and the vandalism is limited to attacking the signs for the nursery rather than the place itself. We do have problems with animal vandals though, and have recently put up yards of rabbit netting, and got a couple of cats; the mice only ate a few seeds but prevention is better than a mouse problem and the cats also catch rabbits! We have seen both roe and muntjac deer in the next field, they're very pretty when they're not eating my plants! It's still hard work, but I hope we've been accepted and we look forward to a stable future."

Down the road from Mervyn and Pauline Webb was another smallholding, owned by the Bicknells. After the Second World War Vivienne Bicknell and her husband Alan had also become involved with the Land Settlement Association, in Andover, but Vivienne was from Sussex and after eight years away she wanted to come home. However, they did not want the co-operative approach of the LSA as they felt their produce would be good enough to stand alone, so they came to West Chiltington in 1969 and got a Council smallholding of four acres in Sinnocks. The houses, built in the 1930s had some land; the tenancy was purchased as a going concern, to include greenhouses and everything on the plot, from the previous tenant, while the Council was paid for the land and the house.

They mainly concentrated on sweet peas with chrysanthemums, catch crops, bedding plants and salad crops including about 4,500 tomato plants. There were also chickens and one or two pigs. Fargro was the local horticultural sundries supplier with a depot in Worthing of everything that the business needed, seeds, fertilisers, packing boxes, and the delivery lorry; most of the produce was sold at Covent Garden and Fargro's lorry would come every night except Saturdays so that the produce could be at the market by two or three in the morning. The Bicknells sold under their own name, to specific traders, creating a reputation for themselves. There were only a few growers of sweet peas and their produce was good enough to go to the big hotels in London; they made good money but worked hard for it. In the summer when they were busiest Vivienne would be out on the smallholding by 6am, and still be bunching the flowers at midnight; they were bunched in separate colours which were then boxed. When the sweet peas were over some time in July, they put the chrysanthemums in so the greenhouses were always in use, except for a short time in the winter when the sterilising was done.

It was a friendly atmosphere on the smallholdings, with everyone knowing everyone else and helping each other. The other smallholders grew tomatoes, courgettes and peppers, strawberries, a variety of fruit and vegetables. Vivienne remembers that when they decided to grow sweet peas, because Alan loved them so much, they went for advice to a man who lived at the windmill who was very enthusiastic about his sweet peas. However his wife told them not to touch them as it was such a demanding job; if the plants were left even for one day they would just grow away and it was very difficult to get back in control. So they grew cucumbers once, but Alan's love was for sweet peas, which was just as well because Vivienne's ginger cat's love was for cucumbers; he would go into the tunnel and nibble bits out of the whole row. After blocking up all the entrances to the tunnel, the cat went up on top and made a hole in the polythene to get in, and continued nibbling! He must have been addicted as he ate the cucumbers from up the road as well.

It is another sign of the changing times that, when Alan had to retire in the mid 1980s there was no incoming tenant to purchase the going concern, and the Council sold the land and the house to a private purchaser who called the house Ploughboys Rest. Sheep graze where Alan and Vivienne had had their polytunnels although the shell of one glass house still stands. Of the eleven smallholders only two now remain, and it is assumed that when these give up their land will be sold also.

Margaret Baker was born in 1918 in Reading, and after school she enrolled at King's College, London for a journalistic course. By September 1946 she and her parents had left their home in Brighton and moved to a furnished bungalow near Pulborough while waiting to move to a cottage that was being built for them on the corner of Juggs Lane and Sinnocks. This site had been purchased from the Greenfield family, who had bought it in one of the Abergavenny Estate sales. They eventually called the new cottage Farthings after the farmhouse in *Four Farthings and a Thimble,* a book that she had written in 1948. The cottage was set in a three acre field edged with hazel hedges, the land was planted with apple trees and they kept ducks and chickens because a smallholding was planned for after her father's retirement. Unfortunately her father died only a few years after his retirement and, the property being too big for her to manage on her own, she and her mother moved on to Somerset in 1952 and the house was bought by Sir Armigel de Vere Wade.

In 1941 she had written her first children's book *The Singing Butterfly* which she sold for £6.10.0d but said that it had never, to her knowledge, been published; war-time paper rationing making markets difficult in England. However, after the war many of her children's books and short stories were published, and in 1954 *A Castle and Sixpence* was made into a serialised drama by BBC Children's Television, who the following year also serialised *Benbow and the Angels*. By 1987 she had written nearly forty books many of which were published by Brockhampton Press.

Sir Armigel de Vere Wade had been Chief Secretary to the Government of Kenya 1934-39 and acting Governor and Commander-in-Chief for two brief periods in 1935 and 1936/7 and he lived in Farthings until his death in 1966, survived by his widow Monica. Lady Wade was his second wife (his first wife, Constance, having died in Kenya in 1938), who had been Constance's companion. She sold the house in 1975 when it was bought by Jim Court, who, in 1990, bought the adjoining field of almost six acres, primarily to prevent the possibility of a housing development in this rural area.

A little further south, on the same side of Southlands Lane, is Smugglers. The Sales Particulars show that it was part of the Abergavenny Estate Sale on 28 October 1930 and was bought by Charles Greenfield; it was called The Cloche Gardens and was run by a Mr Campbell helped by Tom and Bert Gumbrell. In April 1953 it was sold it when it comprised a market garden and pig farm of $7\frac{1}{2}$ acres. There were pig styes and a farrowing pen, tractor shed and greenhouse, a garage, a workshop and a three bedroom house built by Slaters for the new owners Mr and Mrs G W Dixon, the headmaster. (Mr Dixon was also Clerk to the Parish Council from 1934 to 1973, and died in 1980.) He farmed it, appearing to have more interest in it than in his school charges. Mrs Dixon kept dogs and perhaps ran some sort of kennels from there, before they moved to Commonland Farm.

Bernard Daughtrey came to West Chiltington as a boy of ten at Michaelmas 1927 when his father took over one of the County Council smallholdings at Southlands Farm, a bit further down Sinnocks. Mr Daughtrey Sr had to apply through Chichester for the rental, but as he had come from a farming family there were no difficulties; however one of his neighbours who had been a tailor had to have farming tuition first. Bernard remembers life in those early days when milk produced at Southlands had to be taken down to the gate for delivery to Worthing in the days before the Milk Marketing Board. He says "In the spring when there was plenty of grass you got more milk and the dairymen wouldn't take it all; the small dairy people who delivered it round the town only had a certain number of customers and they only wanted a certain quota. So we had to make butter with what wasn't taken; there wasn't much money in it but it was a good product and did help to get rid of the surplus stock. It was churned by hand in a big wooden barrel, an up-and-over churn they used to call it, and on some days in sultry weather you could churn for half a day and it still wouldn't turn, with luck on a good day it would go in ten minutes if it was a cool early morning. When it had turned, we had to work it and squeeze all the buttermilk out by putting it on the table and patting and turning it over until it was dry enough, then we made it up into small pats with those wooden paddles like ping-pong bats, put our own marker or stamp on it and wrapped it. I think margarine was about at that time but most people used butter, or dripping from the meat, you see. In fact my aunt had a boarding house in Eastbourne and she used to send us a shoebox full of dripping once a month from the meat they used. The buttermilk would be sold very cheaply, or given to the pigs, most farms had a pig or two. Before I left school I was milking three or four cows every morning, they were selected as being gentle and not likely to knock me out of the door! Some had to be tied up because they were temperamental, but most were gentle. There is a story which I heard of the milk from Amberley Castle: they had Jersey cows so the milk was very rich and creamy, but if the cows had been fed on kale or turnips in winter it tainted the milk which then tasted 'funny'; it never did anyone any harm but it just tasted odd.

There weren't the modern fabrics then that we have now to keep the weather out, there were oilskins but many of the men used to go to work with just a sack tied over their backs to keep the rain off.

We grew big cabbages for feed for the cows in those days and bought in gluten, which is maize meal, and linseed cake which is made out of linseed oil, and cotton cake. We used to have to break this up in a cake cracker, a hand turned thing with a hopper and a rack with cogs on which broke the cake up into little pieces. We'd have half hay and half oats chaff and make a big pile of it, and then spread cut up mangel (or mangold, which is a large coarse yellow-orange kind of beet cultivated as cattle food) on the top with a measure of this gluten and perhaps a bit of bran or a bit of oat meal, and then it was all mixed up and put into the mangers. We also had to chop the chaff with a cutter that was hand turned until we got one of those little stationary engines to do the work. This was petrol or paraffin driven, I expect you've seen them at the local shows, my father's was a little Amanco but there were loads of different makes. However, there was a milling machine to process the oats. You went to every cow with a bucket of water and gave the young stock calves their milk. For the horses we would grow a strip of rye grass which we'd cut with a scythe, which helped when the grass hadn't come in, and when that was eaten we went on to trefolium and a bit of vetch or tares. They would also have clover hay, but you daren't give that to the cows because it was too rich and would blow them, you see, so they had mangels and stem kale. The mangels were stored in a clamp; some of the farms had huge ones, which were built like this: you put down bundles of faggots or hedge trimmings first to keep the mangels off the ground, making a sort of floor, and then you piled the mangels up into an inverted V shape, it could be as much as 40 yards long, and then you would put a layer of straw all over it and finally dig a trench each side, throwing the earth up to cover the whole clamp in with just a row of little holes packed with straw at intervals in the top for breathing; this would make the whole thing weatherproof. The horses would have a mangel a day just to keep them going.

Everything had to be stored; when we cut the corn we would bring the sheaves from the fields with the ears on, and make a corn rick, where once again there were faggots for the floor to keep the bottom dry. A corn rick was made in a circle, and there was an art in getting it right, and thatched to keep the weather out; you might see half a dozen corn ricks in the bottom of a field near the road and in the winter a thrashing machine would come along, draw in and do the whole lot. This machine was a steam traction engine with a drum and an elevator, or perhaps a bailing machine on, some farmers had two or even three and hired themselves out, like a modern contractor. Sometimes the sheaves would be put in the big barns and a thrashing drum put in the middle and they would just use it directly from the big barns. When my father, and all the small farmers in West Chiltington were harvesting, one would have a binder, and they'd borrow a horse off you because it took three horses on the binder and you might only have two, we all mucked in together which is how we managed to get along, and not have to employ extra men which we couldn't afford. We needed three horses if we used the binder for a whole day, or if the land was a bit hilly, they would work three abreast. The carter would arrive at 5 or 5.30 in the morning and feed and water his horses, and probably have them ready to go out into the field at about 6.30 when we would start. We worked until about 9.30 when we would stop for twenty minutes or so, and the carter would have his lunch and the horses would have a nosebag, and then we'd go on until 1 o'clock, when we'd break for an hour. The horses were taken out of the traces and put in the shade, and then we'd carry on until we decided to finish, it could be as late as 5 or 6 o'clock. But normally we wouldn't work them too many hours, and if there was a spare horse, because, say a farmer wasn't using his that day, we'd use that one to spread the load. You relied on your horses and you had to look after them. I've seen carters cry if they lost a horse; they were devoted to them. Last thing at night, about 10pm, we'd go down to the stable and give them a bucket of water and just check that they were all right, and that was the end of our day, unless there was a calving or something like that, and then we could be up all night. And then back up the next morning for milking, to get the milk to the gate for 8 o'clock. My father remembered cutting the hay at Rackham, where I was born, and sending it on the train from Amberley to London for the London horses.

The horses were bought in broken, there were specialist farmers that would do that because there just wasn't time on a working farm; there were always horses for sale from farm sales. One of ours came from Mr Mustchin the coalman when he bought a lorry for his deliveries and was getting rid of his horse, quite a lot of the farmers got hold of horses that way at that time.

When I left school in 1931 the village had four or five cars, that was all, Mr Morgan from Nyetimber had one, Colonel Kensington from Voakes had one, so did Mrs Coles at Woods Hill, and Mr Mills the schoolmaster had a Morris Oxford even while I was still at school. There were no buses in the village when we came, so we used to walk to Storrington, but the road from Smock Alley up to Roundabout was full of ruts and holes, and down by the hotel the sand was so deep you couldn't ride a bike down there.

Father's health failed so we came out of farming in 1930, just before I left school, and I then went to work at Linfield's."

Southlands Farm is still a West Sussex County Council farm, unlike many of the others which have been sold off. Marie and Bernard Armstrong came to live there in 1956 with their four children, because Bernard, who had worked first for his father and then on a farm at Hangleton, wanted a place of his own. Southlands Farm had been divided into two farms, one farm owned by a family called Wakeley, being 40 acres and a cottage; and 60 acres of land with the farmhouse belonging to a family called Snook who had had it as a dairy farm. The Snooks and Wakeleys had lived there at least ten years until the sale in 1956. It is remembered that Mr Snook used to deliver the milk: "he had a big churn which shone and you used to take your jug out and they measured it for you with a ladle, then you would cover your jug with a muslin cover weighted down with beads round the edge. They used to charge a penny a pint. Mr Wakeley had succeeded Mr Scott who also used to deliver milk; he would walk round with his cart with his two-gallon brass pails with their measures hanging inside on a little ledge. It was fresh milk, they milked in the mornings, cooled it and came round, it wasn't pasteurised or anything. They didn't have any tests on cattle until years later. Some places delivered the milk twice a day." At least two other farms also delivered milk in the 1930s: Alex Lawson used to deliver from his farm in Nyetimber Lane and Captain Thomas who lived in New House Farm also had a few customers - Harry Horlock who worked for him used to deliver the milk. At first he walked the round, then later he would come round on a bicycle with the churn on the handlebars and ladle out what you wanted.
   Mr Armstrong, who used the Snook's cowshed to begin with, slowly built up a good dairy herd from his own cows, selling the bull calves. It was Marie's job to rear the calves by, at first she had to put her hand in the bucket of milk and get them to suck her finger, unlike nowadays when there are large covered sheds with automatic calf feeders. She enjoyed her work except when the calves inadvertently bit her! The farm prospered: a modern milking parlour was installed, with water and electricity, where ten cows at a time would go in one end to be milked and leave at the other end; the cattle feed going straight to the cows while they were being milked. The redundant cowshed was used for other purposes. In June 1961 her son David, who had been helping his father, married a local girl called Betty, and they rented accommodation for a few years until, when Mr

Wakeley eventually retired, his two sons each got a smallholding at Sinnocks, and the Armstrongs were offered the whole one hundred acres. The young people moved into the farm cottage, and the future of the farm seemed secure. It is not an automatic right for sons to be offered their father's tenancies by the County Council, but after Marie's husband died of a stroke in 1983 the tenancy was eventually offered to David. This caused a slight domestic upheaval as the tenant had to live in the farmhouse and the farmworker in the cottage, so Marie and her son had to swap houses! Marie continued to help out on the farm, but the BSE crisis was beginning. She explains "David lost about forty cows; if a cow staggered and looked ill your own vet wasn't allowed to see her, you had to get a Ministry vet in and he destroyed her by injection. You can't imagine how heartbreaking it was to see these lovely cows just going down onto this great bed of straw, and then being taken away in a big van to be incinerated. It had to be done, I suppose, but it was always the best milkers that went - strange when all you heard about was the beef cattle. There was so much hysteria and confusion at the time that I would like to emphasise here that dairy as well as beef herds were affected, and that the carcasses did not go for meat. If only we had known what was being put into that feed we would never have given it to the cows.

I'm sure that the stress of this BSE business was one of the contributory factors that led to my son's fatal heart attack in September 1996 at the age of 55. My daughter-in-law is continuing with the farm, ably helped by Trevor, her son-in-law who was David's right hand man, and by Andrew Steele who is so good with the cows. She employs casual labour to help with the harvest, ploughing and planting, and there is still a dairy herd. I try to keep going by remembering the good times; you know, when we moved in in 1956 we had no electricity although the pole nearby was a promise that it would come soon, and we had a little petrol engine in a shed which powered the milking machine. We used lamps in the house, it's strange to think how we managed."

Nowadays, travelling by road, Whales Cottages on Common Hill seem a long way from Whales Farm in Southlands Lane, but when they were built there were no houses in between across the fields. The cottages were built (presumably by Mr Comper, or by his niece and heir Mrs Annie Bearman) on the plot of land on the Common allotted to Whales Farm in 1868 at the Common Inclosure. Caroline Wells has reconstructed the probable ownership of every plot of land on the Common up to the beginning of this century, using the Abergavenny Surveys of 1800 and 1898, and maps of the common.

Whales Farm is also a good example of how farms and smallholdings have been broken up over the years. Originally a farm of 30-40 acres, the house was sold off and the land bought by someone else who, in their turn, built a house. The pattern has repeated itself over the years until the land holding is very diminished in size.

A cottage called Buffens or Ruffens in Smock Alley is said to have provided ale for the sheep and cattle drovers who were taking their stock to market or fresh pastures via the Common where they would camp for the night. Some think that the old Five Bells pub was originally built on Puffins' land, and Buffens is the old name for Puffins. The old pub had been small, consisting of a tap room with store room for the casks, a parlour or second bar, and a living room for the tenant with a couple of bedrooms upstairs. Henry Mustchin was the first-remembered landlord of The Five Bells in 1925. In 1929 when Tom Hopkins was landlord he had a thirsty customer, Charlie Winton; one day Charlie called in for a quiet drink when all of a sudden there was an explosion and a room full of smoke. Charlie had put his gun across his knees forgetting that it was still loaded; the gun had gone off

The Five Bells – Postcard received in June 1933
Billy Shaw, the Carrier, outside the pub. He carried on in his father's footsteps

blowing a hole through the front door! The hole remained, blocked with hardboard until the pub was sold.

The modern Five Bells was built in 1935 on the site of the old pub, next door to Puffins. Jim King, of King and Barnes Brewery who used to own the pub, had said that out of all the public house stock that the company owned, there was not one purpose-built pub, so he decided to rectify this by building two, the Hornbrook in Horsham, and The Five Bells. The new pub was much bigger, having five bedrooms and three rooms downstairs; the sites overlapped slightly so that a small corner of the old flagstone floor was incorporated into the new building. The old pub was taken down as the new one was put up; some of the old tiles were used to give a more mellow appearance by the men who worked from boards supported by tapered wooden scaffolding poles. The area now used as the top car park used to be a pond, which had to be drained, and the pub sign also changed at that time.

Joan Gould had been the tenant from about 1964; Bill Edwards took over from her on Thursday 3 September 1983. Bill says "It was Joan who

Building the New Five Bells

opened up the downstairs of the place; now you see one long bar which serves what had been the two bars and if you stand outside, there are the two doors. The small area to the left of the bar is what used to be called the tea room. Joan also provided accommodation occasionally because there were enough bedrooms, but I found that because this was a country house design, although there are five bedrooms upstairs there was no provision made for a sitting room for the tenant, and the kitchen is not ideal for a pub that serves food. Food has been served here for a long time. There is a charming idiosyncrasy on the plans: what the rest of the country calls stillage, here in Sussex it is called stollage, and is written so.

I took over on a Thursday because licensing day is a Thursday: first I had to go to Petworth Court, later to 'Petworth Court at Chichester', before licensing moved again to Horsham Magistrates Court. I am entitled to open as many hours as I wish within the Permitted Hours which are 11am to 11pm during the week, and from 12 midday to 10.30pm on Sunday. Beer is sold in $^1/_2$ or $^1/_3$ pint or multiples thereof, for example the very strong barley wine beer comes in one third of a pint bottles although they're not as usual as half pints. I think the pub got its wine licence in about 1938.

In 1989 the brewery sold up, and I bought the freehold. This gave me the freedom to sell whatever beers I wanted, and as I believe in real ales I stock a range of guest beers each week. I have had a couple of Beer Festivals which have gone very well; we are bucking the national trend of selling lager beers, and are in CAMRA's (the Campaign for Real Ales) recommended book. In 1990 I myself built the conservatory which serves as a restaurant and is managed by my wife and daughter. This is called 'keeping it in the family', something the Edwards have done for years as my father was born in his father's pub, the Crabtree at Lower Beeding, and ran the Punchbowl at Ockley, and my grandfather was also born in his father's pub.

An acre of what had been the pub garden was also sold in 1989 by the brewery for building the two houses next door called Oakdale and Hollybrook; they had already sold the land across the road many years before to the Water Board."

In 1895 Lordings Farm in Lordings Lane had been called Frogs Hole and was only a cottage where Phil and Kate Slater started their married life and gave birth to Albert and Sabina (Cis). In this century it is remembered as having had a sandy track up to it and was where Billy Shaw lived. He was

Lordings Farm

Frank Dougharty's maternal uncle and a great character. Frank and Madeleine describe him "He lived in Lordings Farm and his father or grandfather had had the Five Bells pub; my mother came from that side of the family and was brought up at Lordings Farm. Billy was a general trader who kept chickens and pigs and a wicked goat called Toby who used to lie in wait for everyone - if you turned your back he'd have you! We used to have Uncle Billy over for Christmas Day and he would come in, straight from the pigs, stick his feet on the fender and his boots would steam! He did remove his cap, but kept his scarf on although we would build up the fire so he was nice and warm. People used to take pity on him and give him money but he was a fairly wealthy man even though he looked like a tramp; Huntleys used to belong to him and before we were married there was a thought that we might live there. Instead of doing his washing in the copper he used it to boil up the pig swill; the house was full of chickens and gradually after years of neglect it fell down around him. The chickens used to be on the furniture, there were tin cans everywhere, and feathers! Yet he must have had something because he had ladies round him although he never married; they took him dinner or had him round to their homes for meals. Perhaps it was his money! He had inherited the farm from his father, William, who used to go down to Brighton trading, and one time when his father didn't come back they sent out a search party to look for him and found him dead and the horse still standing waiting for him. We suspect he was murdered because all his money had been taken. Strange family because Emma, Billy's sister, was a character too, she had been a nurse at Netherne mental hospital in Surrey. Every week she would ride her sit-up-and-beg bike down from the village to see our mother and us even though she was quite ancient; she was very prim and proper and very unlike Billy. She was busy with the Church and Uncle Bill would have nothing to do with it."

As with any unusual character there are many stories told about him by the children of that time: they remember walking across the fields to Haglands Farm, crossing Haglands Lane, climbing the stile and heading towards Sandy Lane (now called Lordings Lane) and peering into his windowless cottage while he was selling his eggs in Worthing. The boys would also sell him the skins of rabbits they had snared, for 2d, and he would sell these on for 6d at the market. He would also take his eggs and produce to the market at Pulborough every Monday, leaving at 8.30am with his flat, four-wheeled cart pulled by his horse. As they came home from school the children would hear the cart returning, but there was no sign of Billy, he was flat on his back on the floor of the cart. The well-trained horse would have made his own way home, even turning into the entrance! It is said that he was drunk, but Frank Dougharty maintains that he never drank, having heard too many of the problems from the family's pub days. Joan Gould (qv) adds that on the day she and her husband took over the Five Bells, Billy Shaw arrived at the back door with a welcome-present of a cabbage and a dozen eggs. The gifts continued to arrive every week so she reciprocated by cooking Billy a steak and kidney pie each week in thanks.

At the village show one year he had tar and feathers all over his back with a sign 'Stuck Up But Not Proud!' as he was always covered with feathers from his chickens, so he must have had a sense of humour. He also owned the field that is now Gardenwood Close, and he allowed the girls to play stoolball on his land. One of them remembers the wonderful smell of the grass and the smoke coming from the chimneys of the gypsy encampment in Fir Tree Lane.

Just beyond the junction of Lordings Lane and Haglands Lane is Haglands Copse which was built on Col and Mrs Drabble's land at New Barn Farm. His son, Timothy, takes up the story "When my father retired at the age of

New Barn Farm

45 from the regular army in 1947 on a full pension, having done his 22 years service, he and my mother lived at my grandfather's place in the New Forest. My father, who had been born at Cowfold, decided to 'come back to Sussex' to farm pigs and chickens, just in a small way, to give his retirement some interest. I remember those pigs; we had three sows who were called Anne, Betty and Meg. They never made my father a fortune, but he enjoyed them; they were good fun and at least he broke even! When my parents bought New Barn Farm in 1950 he had just over 14 acres, but they added to that another 2½ acres, making a total of about 17 acres. They owned the land where Larch End, The Martlets, now is, and James Mursell's barn conversion called Oakfield Barn used to be our barn which stood on what we called 'The Eight Acre'; this was the field where the gymkhana used to be held. Our neighbours were the Leveys whose house, Haglands Farm was, I think, built by the Chesman family who owned Old Haglands. I may be wrong, but I believe the Chesmans built the house for themselves to retire to, sometime in the 1950s. Anyway, our boundary with the Levey's six acres or so was a beech hedge; it may still be there.

After about ten years my father realised that carrying heavy buckets of pig feed about was too much for his arthritic back and hips, so he gave that up and rented the land out for grazing first to Mrs Champ of Churchfield Farm, and then to Mac Steele who had it for about thirty years. We retained the chickens which were housed in the redundant pig styes in the barn.

The house itself had been built as a two-up and two-down white rendered cottage with a tiled roof in 1831; there was a plaque with the date on it over the front door. The first extension was added on the side of the house in the early 1920s I believe; you could always tell which part of the house you were in by the door handles: the original cottage had the metal stable latch type of handle while the new part had brass round door knobs.

David Drabble and one of the pigs

The second extension of kitchen and breakfast room was added at the back of the house in the mid 1930s and this part had bakelite turn-down handles. It ended up as an ideal family home. There were lots of rooms but they weren't big; we had a drawing room, sitting room and dining room downstairs and seven bedrooms upstairs, although my parents turned the small room my brother David had had into a second bathroom, and one of the other bedrooms into my father's dressing room. We had a good sized garden and a tennis court. I was fifteen when we moved there, and David was not quite three so he had a nanny whom my mother brought with us from the New Forest; she was called Muriel and I realised later that being about eighteen, was like a big sister to me. She married and went to Canada eventually.

In 1969 at the age of 67, my father had a stroke, from which he recovered enough to be able to drive around locally and holiday abroad, but he died in 1974 after suffering two further strokes. My father had had an idea that, in due course, he would design and build his own house on his lower fields, the area that is the bottom of Haglands Copse. The house would be all on the ground floor, with a 'penthouse' suite for guests, but it never materialised. The Village Plan had been brought out in the late 1960s scheduling the areas for future development, and my parents and the Leveys decided to employ a local architect/developer who had been recommended to them, called Mr Booth, to design a small development of bungalows to be built on their lands at a future date scheduled in the Plan. The idea was that when my parents got older and needed to be in a closer community, they would try and bring the neighbours to them rather than move to an area with neighbours. In 1976 the date arrived and Mr Booth exercised his option to buy and develop, and Haglands Copse came into being. The first job of the builders was to create a new access drive to both New Barn and Haglands Farms and to Haglands Copse itself, because the previous drive had been through what are now the back gardens of numbers 2 and 4. My mother was protected from the disruption by a close-boarded fence and hedge, and the entire development was built quite quickly: the two bungalows at the top on the right as you enter the Close, the bungalows on the left as you go down the hill, and some along the bottom.

It worked very well for a few years until in about 1982 my mother had a minor stroke and was admitted to hospital and then to a nursing home. She came back home, but finally decided that she would be happier and more secure back in the nursing home; so she returned, and died there in

1984. New Barn Farm house had to be sold and a couple with young children bought it and lived there for about five years. The house had looked a bit sad when it was sold, like houses do that are too big for the single elderly occupant who lives there. Later the purchasers obtained planning permission to demolish it and build four more bungalows on the site, Numbers 6,8,10 and 10a. Needless to say I was so upset at this, that I've hardly been back since.

My parents were both public spirited people and were gradually absorbed into the village and the church, becoming instrumental in getting the Village Hall built. Father was a good organiser; it was often a case of 'ask a busy man and he will find time'. Their main commitments in the village, as commemorated on the Church notice board which I gave in their memory a few years ago, were to the British Legion and to the church itself; my mother was secretary to the PCC for about thirty years, and my father was both treasurer and Churchwarden. But it is their work for the Village Hall for which they are most remembered. They organised and ran the gymkhana for some years, and we were all roped in to help when we had it on our land; both on the Larch End field and on the Eight Acre. They were helped in this venture by Colonel Stuart Walter who was living in the mill at the time with his family. The Hall was built before all the money to fund it had been raised, an act of faith I suppose you'd call it. They organised what were called Snob Dances to help raise the shortfall. These dances were black tie affairs, held in the brand new village hall with music supplied by the pianist Bob Harvey who used to play at the Berkeley Hotel in London, and were by invitation only. Snacks were served, and unusually at this type of event beer was available, and we danced to what I will call 'hunt ball music'. One or two noses were put out of joint inevitably by the invitation-only format, but we held certainly two and possibly three, and raised a lot of money."

Going back to East Street and continuing eastwards towards Picketty Corner, Ewen Steele remembers that in 1936 the army from Aldershot had a summer camp in Danhill Big Field below Voakes. He remembers standing at the Queens Head and watching them arrive in the village, and it took all Saturday to move in with their gun carriages, the horses and all their belongings and equipment. They all came up through the village, including a regiment of Scots Greys with their horses, all of which were grey. It is said that there were a thousand horses, and at the camp they were all tied up at long poles, like the cowboys' horses in films. They came for a few weeks, during which time he took his Shetland pony up there and the soldiers plaited its mane for him.

When Lt-Colonel Guy Belfield Kensington retired from the army he decided to settle in the village, round about 1924, because he had so enjoyed his visits here with his wife Lillian Mary, who was the daughter of the Clarkes who had owned Hatches in East Street. Col Kensington became the 'squire' of the village, living at Voakes in East Street, with a staff of kitchen-maid, chauffeur, live-in cook, another maid and an odd-job man, some of whom lived in tied cottages on the estate. It is a typical gentleman's property of the period, having been sold from the Sandgate Estate in 1887, and containing such things as servants' bells for the rooms. Curiously it sits astride the parish boundary of Thakeham and West Chiltington.

There are many stories of the Kensingtons' commitment to this village, and of their charity. They set up organisations, drove ideas forward, persuaded with their enthusiasm without undermining the values of the village. Some of the girls of that time remember dressing up in nurses' uniforms and, led by the band, collecting from house to house in the villages for the West Chiltington Bed in Worthing Hospital, which was one of Mrs Kensington's cherished charities. The girls, aged from about 13-16, were excited by the romance of dressing up as nurses, and raised a great deal of money; Mrs Kensington was delighted and used to give them tea at Voakes. On a quieter and more self effacing note Gwen Smith tells how her sister fell gravely ill at the beginning of the war.

Lt-Col Guy Belfield Kensington – in The Juggs 1959

Collecting for the West Chiltington Bed – 1935

"Eventually it became evident that my sister would have to be moved from Chichester to Stanmore where she spent three years in hospital, but nowhere could an ambulance be found to transport her. In despair, Father approached Colonel Kensington who said 'leave it to me, Mr Humphrey'. Sure enough, a couple of hours later he arrived at the house in his car to report that there was no news yet, but that he was awaiting a telephone call, and would keep in touch. Back he came again in the evening to say 'have her ready at 9 o'clock tomorrow morning, there's an army ambulance coming for her with a nurse as escort'. He worked a real miracle as you couldn't raise an ambulance anywhere, not a civilian one, not a Red Cross one, nothing, and yet he did that for us. They also started a Hospital Scheme where you paid 2d a week for adults and 1d a week for children as an insurance to offset the 5/- cost of a doctor's visit and the 2/6 cost of a prescription."

Lt-Colonel Kensington was first elected to the Parish Council in April 1925 and remained a Parish Councillor for 40 years until 1965 when he died in office. He was Chairman of the Council for 9 years, and the

Rector's Warden for thirty-two years, through four incumbencies, until failing health prevented him continuing in 1961. He was an Overseer from April 1925 until that office ceased in 1927, and served on the County Council for 31 years having been elected in 1931; he also became a JP for West Sussex in 1934. Although he was a newcomer, he devoted his life here to the good of the village, and no-one has anything but praise for him and what he accomplished with such empathy.

At various times he owned property in the village, most of which has now been bought by the tenants. He was predeceased by his wife on 13 February 1951 at the age of 74 in whose memory the altar rail in the Church was given, and died himself on 26 August 1965 aged 89. The family name has died out as Lt-Col and Mrs Kensington only had one child, Enid, who married a Captain Wall in 1924.

Gay Street is another 'Outskirts' road, on the western side of the parish, running from Stream Lane out towards the A29 and being the parish boundary between West Chiltington and the village of Nutbourne in the parish of Pulborough. Elsie Pullen was born into the Willmer family in 1925 and lived at Lower Jordans, Gay Street. There were twelve children born there, but one was stillborn, and Jimmy died aged eighteen months from whooping cough. Although she was only about five at the time, Elsie can remember not being allowed to go to the funeral and watching from under the plum tree as the little white coffin was taken up the road. Her grandparents were in Dennis Marcus Farm, just down the lane. When Mr Morgan lived in Nyetimber she remembers that he had the drive down to Lower Jordans sprayed with tar which was then covered with white gravel which made travel a little cleaner. This long drive was then brushed clean before he arrived home. She would always know when he had returned from business in London where he would often spend the night, because his peacock would shout to welcome him home; this bird would strut down the driveway after him just like a pet although it had the free run of the property. She also remembers that one Christmas when the Silver Band did not go up to the house as they traditionally had, she and her family were asked by Miss Reed, the housekeeper, to go instead and sing carols to her. Every year a big hamper of goodies would arrive for the family from Nyetimber and her memories of Johnny Morgan are of his kindness and generosity.

She also remembers that Mr and Mrs Tipper used to bring their fish van right out to Lower Jordans, and fillet the fish in the van, while surrounded by the farm cats who used to get the left-over bits. Growing, storage and preparation of food features large in many people's memories of those days; Elsie says that they grew everything they needed at Lower Jordans and they had enough potatoes to last right through the year, storing them wherever was dark and dry, under the stairs and in a big dark cupboard. They had enough to last until the earlies were ready to start the cycle again. They used to keep chickens and pigs as well.

Her father had an old Trojan car that he used to take her and the other children round the cornfields in after the corn was harvested. Because the car had solid tyres there was no danger of puncture from the sharp corn stubble, and the children enjoyed the treat. As well as the corn, her father used to keep pigs, and was recognised as a vet; he would neuter cats for a shilling, but primarily he knew about pigs. It seems he picked the knowledge up as he went along because he had had no formal training in a college, but he was registered with the local government department who would come and look over his books. He used to write all his calls down and keep proper records; Elsie remembers him coming home and saying 'Get the book out, gal' and transferring his notes into the book, so many Saddlebacks and so many Old English Whites delivered or treated. These were the two main breeds kept in the village. He would visit the Steele family, and the Greens, and was frequently called out to the many families who kept a pig or two, charging them a shilling for the visit. The Willmers themselves had two styes, with a sow and piglets in one and perhaps one pig in the adjacent one. Then when the piglets went, the second pig would have her litter, so they always had stock. Mr Willmer used to bring a boar in, and having interested it in the feed bucket, the boar would follow the bucket round the house and up the garden to where the sow was. Two pigs were killed each year for the family. Someone used to come in to slaughter them and cut them up, and then the business of preserving them began: first the skins were shaved in a huge iron bath with a cut-throat razor, then the pig was jointed and cured by rubbing with salt in a vast grey crock, square like an oversized butler's sink, and then her mother used to hang the joints in the chimney to smoke for bacon. The hooks are still there in the house. Once the meat was in the chimney the family could only burn wood, day and night, until the meat was smoked. The joints were not sooty because they were hung in muslin bags; those got very dark with the smoke, as did the rind, but the joint underneath was quite clean. As well as bacon there was pork, pickled pork and brawn (made from the pig's head); some joints had to be eaten before others, but nothing was wasted. Bread was also kept in a crock, a big one with a lid.

Her father's friend Jim Bacon used to work the thrasher which was parked in Dennis Marcus Farm. It was a Marshall steam engine, registration number BP5819 (the children used to think that the letters stood for Bacon and Pullen as it was Mr Bacon who owned it and Mr Pullen who helped with working it!) which ran on coal, and was built in 1906; the engine was sold and after many adventures came to the hands of restorers J H Sharman and T H Winslade who displayed it recently at Othery, near Bridgwater in Somerset. The engine was used all year round, because temporary ricks had to be made first as the corn could not all be threshed straight away, and a wooden caravan was often towed behind the threshing tackle for the men to live in when away from home. (She remembers the fun the children had climbing up the ladder to the top of the ricks and playing hide and seek.) This thrasher was the last one left in the village and it became redundant with the advent of the combine harvester. The steam engine was also used for hauling trees, and the timber used to go to Storrington sawmills, which used to be on the site of Timberlands.

Fred Pullen lived with Jim Bacon and his wife at Dennis Marcus Farm for many years and later married Elsie who had been looking after them.

The Steam Threshing Machine

Threshing – 1930s
From left: Bert Ruff, —, —, Jim Bacon, Fred Pullen. This vehicle succeeded the steam engine

Working on the farm – 1930s
Fred Pullen with the sack of grain

Every parish has tales of tunnels, ghosts and smuggling and there is supposed to be a tunnel from Crowell in Gay Street down to Nyetimber Manor. Like the tunnel at Fryars (see chapter 3), there is said to be no evidence now of its existence, although Jamie Mill, who lived at Crowell Farm as a child, remembers crawling along a brick construction under the yard. Roger and Bertha Smither who live at Crowell remember that Mrs Minnie Draycott who used to live at Crowell Cottage, would recall giving Jamie and his brother Christopher up to nine torches to enable them to play in the extensive tunnel network which ran from Crowell to Collerys Farm. They were well-built monastic tunnels lined with brick which had alcoves along their length. Unfortunately the area has now got buildings and drainage pipes above the tunnels, so no further exploration will be possible. Collerys Farm used to have a malthouse, and was owned by Dennett Allen who, with his brother Alfred ran a very successful malting business. In 1857 a raid by Customs and Excise men exposed an undeclared amount of malt for which tax had not been paid, hidden behind a false wall in a large arched vault at the brothers' Worthing malthouse, and raids on their other properties followed. The men were convicted on 16 June 1857 and it is possible that the tunnels in this area were used for concealing some of their undeclared malt.

The Manor of Nyetimber was given by William the Conqueror to Earl Roger, and is recorded in Domesday Book. It passed to The Cluniac Priory of Lewes until the dissolution of the Monasteries when Henry VIII gave it to Thomas Cromwell, and when he fell from favour it was given to Anne of Cleves. Later it came to the Goring family who owned it for several hundred years. Carp were kept in one of the two stew ponds (a naturally spring-fed pond in which fish were kept alive for food during the winter) and the fry were bred in a similar pond in front of Crowell Farm down the road. This pond is also interesting in that, no matter what the weather, the water level remains constant.

In June 1919 John Junius Morgan fell in love with the place while he was searching around for antiques, bought it and restored it. The story goes that while he was in Italy during the Great War he met two sisters from Storrington. After the war they invited him to their home village to use as a base for antique hunting, which is how he found this corner of the country in the first place. John Junius was the cousin of John Pierpoint Morgan of the American banking family, and his mother retained the Pierpoint in her name even after her marriage. Johnny Morgan was a self

Nyetimber Manor before the restoration in 1919

contained man, a man who was happy to walk across his woods, through what used to be called The Gallops, to a simple lunch with his friend Mr Coles at Woodshill. He spent a lot of his time in London and the property was looked after by two or three gardeners, the housekeeper who was one of the Storrington sisters, and a chauffeur who drove the Humber or the Rolls. There was also a lorry, a low vehicle which could be covered in or open, and could even have seats put in it; it is said that at one stage there were ten servants. Johnny Morgan was a millionaire, one of the six richest men in America, but was very generous. As well as sponsoring the village's silver band, he invited painting groups to the estate as he was, himself, a painter. This tradition is still carried on today as the Chanctonbury Art Group is still welcomed to paint in the grounds twice a year. Elsie Pullen (née Willmer, see above) remembers the time her mother was in Brighton hospital: on the way to Pulborough Station to catch the train for London, Mr Morgan asked Mr Ralph his chauffeur how Mrs Willmer was and when was she coming home from hospital? When he learned that Mrs Willmer was due out that day, he immediately said 'don't bother to collect me from the station tonight, I'll get a taxi home, you go to Brighton and bring Mrs Willmer home'. As Elsie says "he put mother first, he was a real Christian gentleman."

John Junius Morgan

He is more painfully remembered by Bill Hampton who was the delivery-boy for the Village Stores in the early 1920s. "He didn't want a telephone although there were one or two about, so sometimes I had to deliver telegrams at night, after dark, and twice I was bitten by his dogs. Same place each time they got me; they were bad bites and I had to go to Pulborough to have them cauterised. I was a big country boy and didn't take a scrap of notice of dogs or anything, but By Jove they broke my nerve before I'd been in the job six months. He had all sorts of dogs, a Great Dane and two or three Terriers; it was a terrier called Pluggy that bit me - he loved the taste of humans!"

Johnny Morgan had had tragedy in his life; his only son died aged four and his wife was so distraught that she never recovered from the shock and had to be nursed in an institution. He himself died in 1949, and is buried in the village churchyard facing his beloved house and the Downs; it is the only gravestone that is 'the wrong way round'.

After his death the house was sold and it is interesting to see that the estate had been added to, rather than depleted, in the thirty years of his ownership; this was quite against the trend at the time when properties were being broken up. The Sales Particulars of 1951 show that the Nyetimber estate then included, as well as the original 1919 purchase of the house and garden and the land: Lower Jordans Farm which had been bought in 1920 from Edward Comper; a field beside Gay Street bought in 1924 from Reginald Blunt; some further land at Lower Jordans Farm bought from Baron Leconfield; and Crowell Cottage and adjacent land around Crowell Farm both bought in 1925. By the 1951 sale the property, of 174 acres 3 roods 9 poles, which was all sold together not as separate lots, had been developed to include a garage for 5 cars, a squash court and a description of Nyetimber's own private electricity supply 'Power House containing 10-hp Ruston Hornsby petrol paraffin engine driving a 110 volt Newton dynamo with switchboard in glazed cupboard and main switches. This engine also has belting connected to overhead shafting, driving a pump connected to a well from which water was obtained before the main was installed. Also… a battery room containing 54 cells in excellent order.' Mains water was installed, and electricity was on the way as leave for its installation had been negotiated. Included in the sale a massive Gothic brass door knocker was noted, and the entire contents of the house were to be auctioned twenty days later.

The property was later bought by Ken Nicholas, a builder who split it up. The old house had been called Nyetimber Farm, but after the sale he gave Clive Coulson the name Nyetimber Farm for his house and 17 acres, and the old house became simply Nyetimber or Nyetimber Manor. It was Clive Coulson who used his land to build the golf course, and sold the house which became Badgers Wood. It is now known as Ravens Wood, and is over 100 acres as the new owners have added woodland to it.

Colin and Maureen Sims bought Nyetimber from Ken Nicholas in 1983 when it had been run as a dairy farm, as it had been for many years. Colin decided to discontinue the dairy side, because, as he says: "that was the time of the introduction of the EEC milk quotas and you had to obtain a dairy licence, these licences were not transferable with the property. The profits made from milk wouldn't cover our restocking with cows and buying a licence so we decided to go for sheep although I didn't know anything about sheep! Mr Nicholas had semi-retired, the place was running down so we could make a new start which we did with 300 sheep; 100 Welsh at first and then 160 or so mules later. We also had pigs and chickens, and a couple of cows which came with the place; the pigs were commercial but the chickens were more like pets because my daughter bred and showed them although she did sell the eggs at school.

I said to both of the children when we moved that they should each have their own enterprise and Benna chose the chickens, while Robin wanted to keep pigs. We bought a sow, but she really was a nasty beast and frightened the life out of us all, although we wouldn't give up on her and she had lots of piglets. Eventually we took her to The Horsham Bacon Factory. Actually one of our pigs did fly; right through the window in the piggery. We can't work out why she decided to jump, but unbeknownst to her there's a big drop on the other side, so she crashed through the window and rolled down the slope breaking only the glass and no bones! I don't know what it was about our pigs because a boar got out one day and chased Maureen all the way down to the house, and then wandered off and wrecked a neighbour's beautiful garden! Then the cows got the idea and one night we had a call to say they were in West Chiltington village so we had to go and pick them up! The cows were Guernseys which we kept for our own milk, butter and cream, with the left-over skim milk going to the pigs with bread, as that was a good way of fattening them. We used to make our own butter and cream; I suppose we tried to run the place a bit like they used to do, keeping the old dairy and being self-sufficient also in meat, vegetables and fruit, and selling the surplus. So it was the pigs and sheep that had to make the money; we sold to Fred the butcher in West Chiltington who loved our pork because it wasn't too fatty.

We kept three boars to service the herd of sows we had; by this time it was getting quite intensive with the sows in a crush, so the piglets were quite large before we weaned them off. I had a farm manager and a lad, and in order to make ends meet put the sheep out on rented land to ensure we could keep maximum numbers without depleting our grass. In the end the farm was trying to support not only our family, but the upkeep of an expensive house and outbuildings, and as is often the case with intensive farming when something goes wrong it goes wrong seriously. First we had potato blight, but worse was what happened to the mange-tout - they were actually for a Royal Garden Party and the night before we were going to pick there had been a torrential downpour and the whole lot blew. Finally we got serious dog attacks which interrupted the lambing so that there was no income from the sheep that year, and that forced us to sell. Added to which, the overseas farmers were getting subsidies for their crops and the British farmers weren't, so lamb and beef prices were tumbling.

When we sold it was the time that land prices were falling quite dramatically so we were advised to market the property in America. When the Moss family first made contact they were interested in the soil content and type; they were looking very specifically for something that fell within narrow criteria, for wine making. When we bought the property it came with all the furniture; we all had four-poster beds! We lived with the alterations that Nicholas had had done; he had tried to modernise it, for example he had reduced the main bedroom size to incorporate a dressing room and bathroom, but it wasn't totally successful and I think the Mosses have restored it. It's funny to think that things like the old bell in the tower are still used; visitors ring the bell and Stuart knows that he's wanted, no matter where on the estate he is." This is the largest bell in Sussex that is not attached to a clock, and even in the Lewes Priory days it is probable that the workers were summoned from the hillsides by a bell, although a plaque on it says that this bell was cast for Mr Morgan.

So in 1986 Stuart and Sandra Moss from Chicago bought Nyetimber having seen it advertised in Country Life, and not in America after all. They picked it out only because they remembered having seen that the orchard across the road had been for sale the year before and had been advertised as suitable for vines, and it was on the same slope. They tell an amusing story of so many estate agents being unable to accept that they were not interested in the number of bedrooms, but in the soil, because their idea was to find a site suitable for creating a world class sparkling wine. It had taken about five years to locate the correct spot; armed with geological maps and meteorology charts they approached Brinsbury agricultural college which had been a recording station for the Met Office for thirty years and had exact weather data, which they then combined with Ordnance Survey data to find the correct greensand soil. Only 0.03% of land in Britain has the sort of greensand soil Stuart and Sandy wanted; Nyetimber sits on the Thakeham Cut, a very narrow strip of 100% greensand, and is near enough to the Sussex/Hampshire border, which is the area that gets the most sunshine in England. It has its own microclimate, for, standing in the vineyard one can see the rain clouds come in from the south-west over the Downs and part, to shed their rain on Billingshurst or Storrington, leaving West Chiltington dry. Although the Romans, and the Priory had made wine, English wine had fallen from favour and was not well thought of, something the Mosses were determined to change in spite of knowing nothing about wine at that stage. Stuart was a manufacturer of x-ray equipment and Sandra was an antiques expert when they used to come over here on business but were too busy to look at the country, so they decided they would like to retire to England one day and start visiting National Trust and other properties, and have time to look around. Their plans got brought forward however as their interest in making wine developed; a good school had to be found for their daughter and they had set about looking seriously for the ideal site.

The couple faced expense, disbelief in their ability, questioning of their sanity, general opposition from the so-called experts who said that English wine could only be made from German grape varieties and these would not grow on the greensand that Nyetimber stood on. Chardonnay and Pinot Noir are classic French varieties and cannot be grown here. However 100,000 vines of three classic varieties (Chardonnay, Pinot Noir and Pinot Meunier) were planted in 1988, 1990 and 1991, and a purpose-built winery was created with computerised equipment and advice from an expert oenologist from Champagne whose instructions are diligently followed. When, in 1992 they harvested their first crop of 52 tons of Chardonnay grapes, the opposition was finally silenced, and when they won a blind tasting against the wines from Champagne itself the opposition was convinced. Other honours followed; they won the gold award and trophy at the International Wine and Spirit Competition in 1997 beating the field of sparkling wines from 43 different countries, and won again in 1998. In 1999 they won again, an unprecedented achievement, and won the Gold Medal for the highest points in sparkling wine, the trophy for the Best English/Welsh Wine, and the trophy for the most impressive wine presentation. When the Queen and Prince Philip celebrated their golden wedding anniversary with a lunch, Nyetimber was selected in another blind tasting as the wine to serve to the honoured guests. The highest accolade probably came from Jancis Robinson, a Master of Wine with one of the most discerning palates in the country, who said that she had been deceived into thinking it was a good French Champagne.

It is the attention to detail that is partly responsible for the success of the venture; careful soil surveys to assess the potential of the site; the purchase of grafted vines from Champagne; the hiring once a year of the bottling plant which has to come over from France (Stuart will not let the wine out of his sight until it is sold); top of the range machinery; hours of thought for the label design; alignment of label, wire twist and logo; a final check with the x-ray viewer before polishing the bottles and packing. All this, plus an unquenchable enthusiasm and endless learning has led to a prize winning product. The added bonus is that Stuart and Sandy have reinvented English viticulture, proving that it can be done successfully.

Stuart and Sandy had a stormy reception to England as they arrived only a fortnight before the hurricane of 1987 when 700 trees came down. This was followed by more gales early the following year and they really thought they had come to the wrong place. The power was out for three weeks with seven breaks on the cable between them and the next house, and all the neighbours seemed to have gone to stay with family elsewhere. As Sandy says: "there we were with two cans of beans in the larder, and nothing. No heat in the house, and sleeping on an airbed on the floor, but we did have a solid fuel Aga and lots of wood, so we had hot showers and tea! Our possessions had not arrived from the States so we didn't have a chain saw, and you couldn't buy candles, so we had to have them sent down from Yorkshire. An interesting introduction to country life! Over the next two years we planted 5,500 replacement trees, mostly hardwoods that we'll not see in their prime in our lifetime, and we planted them more or less in the gaps that the fallen trees had left. This did not suit the government grant committee who wanted them planted in blocks and everything else levelled, so we got no grant. What we did get was piles of brushwood that we used for game cover, coppicing of some of the fallen trunks and because we'd left trees standing, we have wood of varying ages." The timber was left to season in the barns and is now used for all estate work. The top road was created by the logging trucks that came in to clear away the fallen timber, but was retained to minimise the traffic past the farms in Lower Jordans Lane, and for the combine harvester that was used in the first year when Stuart planted wheat.

At first they were a bit of a curiosity, and rumours circulated that they were going to take all the barns down and ship them to the States, but when neighbours realised that there were calluses on the hands, that Sandy's finger nails were dirty, and that they both worked long hours themselves in the vineyard and on the house, they were happily accepted. Sandy has even climbed the chimneys to sweep them in true Dickensian fashion. They explain what they have done: "We have met people over the years who have supplied us with background information for the house as they can remember it. One woman, whose aunt had been Mr Morgan's housekeeper, arrived clutching a book of photos; she told us a lot about what the house had been like, and gave us boxes of photographs because she said they meant nothing to her children who would probably get rid of them when she died, and she wanted them to come back to the house where they belonged. This is a problem with many people, they retire to smaller houses as they get older, and the next generation put in the bin 'all that old rubbish of Mum's' which is then lost forever. A man whose father had been farm manager to Mr Morgan also came with information and then, when the first publicity of the wine came out in the *Financial Times*, it was repeated in the *Australian Financial Times* which prompted a call from a man in Australia who was Morgan's godson. His father had been at Oxford with Morgan and a firm friendship had developed between the two men; Morgan had taken his ten year old godson under his wing when his mother had died, and invited him to spend holidays and weekends with him which was how the godson came to spend so much time here. With all this history coming in as well as the documents we've managed to research, we were in a better position to restore and repair the house sympathetically. A house of this age and history needs a once-over every fifty to a hundred years. Nothing had really been upgraded since Morgan's time, and we felt that the plumbing and electrics needed bringing up to date, and a few mistakes rectified. For example, we learned that The Gun Room had, at one stage, had linenfold panelling but it had all gone, and a doorway had been cut through to the outside. It just so happened that we managed to track down some linenfold panelling and it fitted the room exactly, including the bit under the new window which had replaced the doorway. We've had the window frame copied from the other one in the room, and a place in London is finding us some old glass to fit into it. We will then have an original sixteenth century dining room with original sixteenth century furniture. Obviously you have to decide how far back you're going to go, we do have a telephone, a computer and a washing machine, but we've also repaired the servants' bells in each room so that they all now work. We have electric light, but we also have candles and an assortment of rush lights.

The furniture is all English oak; I ran an antiques business in America concentrating on 15th-17th century oak furniture and used to come over here to buy pieces. It's funny to think that they've all now come back to England, and are so right in this house. Morgan also collected oak of this period, this is one reason why he bought the house: two Americans in the same house, in the same century, with the same passion!

We learned that during the Second World War Morgan had been a plane spotter for the army and we even found his plane-spotting chart in the house. He had had to survey this section of the sky and report on aeroplane movements. That chart, and a bread peel (the long handled utensil for putting the loaves into the oven) were the only things left in the house when we moved in. But we did find what we think is a priest's hole, it is a hole the height and width of a standing man narrowing to a space only

J J Morgan in plane-spotting kit

big enough for a pair of feet to stand in, with access from the top, and if it isn't a priest's hole we have no idea what else it could be. In Parham there are a couple of items which we think might have come from here when Morgan's executors sold the house and contents, but that's hardly surprising when you think that people must have come from all over to the Estate sale. The remains of the Power House generator, quoted in the 1951 Sales Particulars, we gave to the museum at Amberley, only to discover that they had already been given the first part of it, so it is all hooked up now and working again, which is nice.

According to his godson, he owned a yacht and an apartment in Paris. Every Wednesday, come Hell, high water or war, he would call for the Rolls and be driven up to London for half a lobster and a bottle of champagne! We have unearthed a number of pieces of stone from the garden, one flower border was edged with carved stones, and we've found what look like Norman arch keystones, all of which we've kept, so our life is made up of days of discovery.

Our daughter, Jennifer's initials are JJM, and scratched in one end of the fireplace beam Morgan had had his initials etched - JJM, so we knew the house was right for us and her. She did very well at her school ending up as Head Girl, and winning a Gold Duke of Edinburgh's Award, then going on to study astro-physics at University. That is not a good training for running either a vineyard or a medieval house, but she came home from her job in Colorado to be married from here, and has a great love of the place, thinking of England as home. She has, in fact a better palate than mine, but prefers to take corks out of bottles rather than put them in! I developed my palate and learned a lot at Plumpton where they ran year's courses on viticulture or winemaking, and both Stuart and I worked a harvest in Champagne, learning all we could. The French were very helpful, thinking that anyone as foolish as we were needed all the help we could get, but we aren't really a threat to them economically as we only produce 50,000 bottles a year while they produce 300 million. One of the wine writers summed it up nicely: 'American inspiration, French equipment and British soil and climate', and I think if we'd been born here we wouldn't have attempted to make a vintage sparkling wine because we would have grown up knowing you couldn't. It was a hard ten years until the first bottles came off, but then we knew we were right.

We came here for peace and a private life which is why the place isn't open to the public, but we do do some after-dinner speaking, to help put the village on the map a bit. We only sell through special outlets, such as

Fortnum and Mason's, and Hennings, and hotels and restaurants such as Gravetye Manor, Amberley Castle and The Old Forge, and to local shops where it means something. Lots of people in Nyetimber Copse have bought our wine, for the name, as have people called Nye, and it's lovely for a celebration. It's lovely any time!"

Chapter 8

Parish Matters

The Elizabethan Poor Laws of 1601, an early provision of social assistance, placed a clear obligation on parishes to levy local taxes and to be responsible for the relief of its poor. They appointed parish officials called Overseers of the Poor to administer the laws and provide relief to the aged, sick, and infant poor who could not work, as well as work for the able bodied. The increase in expenditures on public relief was so great that the new Poor Law Amendment Act of 1834 was enacted whereby groups of parishes were combined into Poor Law Unions that became established on a nation-wide basis. They built and were responsible for workhouses, and they employed paupers and the poor at profitable work.

Social welfare services and the social security system supplanted workhouses altogether in the first half of the 20th century, but the Poor Laws were maintained, with various changes, until after World War II. The Local Government Act of 1894 transferred the administration of all parishes to new civil institutions including parish councils; property held for non-ecclesiastical purpose was also transferred away from Church officials. The Act created institutions having a civil origin, status and affiliations: the Parish Meeting and the Parish Council. The Act took a year to pass and excited much controversy for Mr Gladstone's Government; it was the proposal to create parish councils that caused the uproar. For the first time the traditional functions of the parish were to be administered by laymen. Until 1914 Parish Councils were locally opposed, often derided, and poor.

> *The first Parish Meeting, under the Local Government Act of 1894 having been duly convened by the Overseers, for the purpose of Electing a Parish Council, was held in the School Room this 4th day of December 1894 at 6 o'clock in the evening.*

So begins the first entry in the first Minute book for the first West Chiltington Parish Meeting.

At the new Parish Council meeting the nine councillors elected William

Knight Rowland to be their Chairman. For the first 67 years the Parish Council held its meetings mainly in the School Room and occasionally in the Comrades' Hall, then in the Reading Room and since 1996 in the Village Hall Annexe.

In its 106 years the Parish Council has had a total of 101 Councillors of which there have been only 10 Chairmen. In the early years a councillor served for one year. The Parish Council continued to have 9 councillors until the May 1976 elections when the number was increased to 11. In 1987, following boundary changes, the number was increased to 13.

The West Chiltington Parish Council continued to appoint annually, two Overseers and an Assistant Overseer until 1927. Often, but not always, the Overseers were also parish councillors. From 1 April 1927, as a result of the new Rating and Valuation Act 1925, the Overseers of the Poor (together with the Poor Rate) were abolished and their functions and interests were transferred to other bodies. From that date the post of Rate Collector was created. The social legislation of the 1930s and 1940s gradually replaced the Poor Laws but the Poor Law system was not abolished until 1947.

The old minute books of the Parish reveal that in the early years the meetings were mainly concerned with administrative matters as shown by the following extracts from the minutes. Often there was not even a quorum. The language used has been left untouched. This was, after all, the form originally written and as such it sheds light on the era.

February 1895 - 'As the Council have no furniture or other necessaries wherewith to carry on the business of the Meetings, it was unanimously resolved that a table, 8 chairs, a lamp and an ink stand be provided for the use of the Council Meetings'.

January 1897 - 'An informal discussion took place on the question of lighting the Parish with oil lamps'.

April 1899 - The Clerk was directed to obtain candles, etc. for use during the meetings and necessary stationery……. 'the documents of the Parish, and the Tithe map, held by Mr Thomas Greenfield be handed over to the Parish Council and that the Clerk be instructed to obtain a box in which to keep them'.

Until April 1937, the West Chiltington Parish Council was composed entirely of men but in that year a change took place, as reported in the local press: 'Although in many respects West Chiltington is a go-ahead parish it is extremely anti-feminist, but at the third attempt Mrs Naomi R Lawson, a champion of the rights of women, by the narrow margin of one vote secured a seat on the Parish Council at the Annual Parish Meeting. Most of those who voted for her were men. Voting was by a show of hands and there were ten candidates for the nine seats'.

In November 1942 much discussion took place on the question of the position of the Parish Council after the War and the vital part it could play during the post-war period of reconstruction. The opinion was strongly held that the Rural District Council had robbed parish councils of all or most of its power. The following resolution was agreed: 'that this Parish Council considers that most of the powers of Parish Councils have been abrogated by the District Councils and trusts that amending legislation will be passed reinstating and increasing the statutory powers of Parish Councils, in order that they may play a full part in post-war reconstruction, and that they may assist to the full in promoting the general welfare of their Parish and Village. It is also suggested that the Parish Council should be the determining power over any other body in regard to any legislation affecting the Parish alone'.

It was felt that the RDC and the other authorities had overlooked the fact that a parish council was representative of its parish and would have been of great help in the event of invasion. The Parish Council had no direct representative on the Invasion Committee set up by the RDC; the ordinary public had very little idea of what was expected of them in the event of invasion. Other points raised in this connection dealt with dances, air raid dangers due to carelessness at the Hall, the security of the parish, and the co-operation of the civil population with members of the Civil Defence Services.

The Parish Council Minutes have provided a great deal of information for this book. Inevitably they concern many different aspects of life in West Chiltington over the past hundred years and have therefore played a part in helping to convey that life onto the printed page. It was necessary to be selective about what was included and the mundane minutiae of the meetings have been avoided. Though interesting snippets and facts emerge one always craves more information, which is not always available.

Although the Parish Council is responsible for the parish much of its work goes unrecognised by its people. A subject which is recognised, and had been a concern for many years, was the provision and maintenance of a Recreation Ground. This matter was first raised at Parish Council meetings at the end of 1928 and in 1934 the Parish Council called a Public Meeting to obtain the views of parishioners as to the desirability, or otherwise, of a scheme to acquire a public Recreation Ground and a Village Hall. A Committee was appointed which looked at several possible locations and at a second Public Meeting held in December 1934 it recommended the one which seemed most suitable for a Recreation Ground with a site for a Village Hall adjoining, which is the present location. The Committee felt that 'the important matter now is to secure a Recreation Ground while land for it is still available, and the Committee are strongly of the opinion that no time should be lost in acquiring for West Chiltington those facilities that are being so rapidly obtained by other villages'. The crowded meeting decided without a single dissenting voice to acquire by subscriptions and public efforts, a Recreation Ground and a site for a Village Hall.

As a result the 'Jubilee Recreation Ground and the Village Hall Site Fund' was opened in 1935 as a permanent memorial to commemorate the Silver Jubilee of King George V. No part of the cost was to be allowed to fall on the rates and the Committee was instructed to vest the land in the National Playing Fields' Association, to ensure that it be held in perpetuity.

The land acquired was a level field at a central position on the road between West Chiltington Village and the Common. In October 1935 the land was bought from Raymond Gocher of Gentle Harry's Farm, and sold to the NPFA who are the freeholders, while a Committee of Management consisting of representatives of all the village organisations, the Parish Council and some co-opted members, was set up to administer the ground.

The main seven acre field had been used as a market garden but in a short space of time it was transformed into a Recreation Ground and in August 1936 glorious weather favoured the official opening by Lt-Col Ravenscroft, JP, of Storrington, the local representative of the NPFA. The first event to take place on the Ground was a cricket match specially arranged for the occasion between a local team and the 38th Field Company of the Royal Engineers, then in camp at Danhill. One of the Engineers was Norman (Jack) Cattell who later married Elsie Slater and lived in Mill Road. The Ground was much used by troops and others during the War.

In March 1946 Mrs Kensington gave a further 2.5 acres of land to the immediate north of the Ground which was again vested in the NPFA, making a total area of approximately 12.5 acres which included the playing field proper, the large car park and the marshy land beyond which was used as a refuse tip for many years. Reg Slater the builder says "when grandfather was building Bancroft, opposite the village hall, there was a rotatiller churning up the field to a depth of two feet; the drainage has been a problem ever since. The marshy area, which is now the car park, was filled with soil from the entrance of the Orchard Dell site, followed by the soil from when the main drains were brought to the village. We were also doing up the barn opposite the Queens Head, and another contractor was building a road next to it and didn't know what to do with his rubbish, so we all tipped onto the marsh. In fact it became a regular tip for some years until it got out of hand and we had to stop it and get it levelled. There's a little green Austin Ruby under the children's play area somewhere, BYY 58 if someone wants to dig it up!"

The pavilion, completed in April 1937, was the gift of Colonel Norman Clarke (Mrs Kensington's brother) and had a covered veranda added in 1938; electricity was connected in the summer of 1954. Before that the only form of lighting for use on dark evenings in the pavilion was by the two wall oil lamps and an Aladdin Storm Lamp provided by the Football Club. The pavilion was connected to main drains in 1963/64 and a minimum supply of hot water was available from 1967.

In 1946 a fully fitted mobile wooden canteen was installed at the Recreation Ground. It was given by the WVS, and was brought down from the docks in London by Lt-Col and Mrs Kensington and apparently made a spectacular entrance during a cricket match. The old tea hut was moved and became a scoring hut, but by 1952 the canteen had started to deteriorate badly as its construction was quite flimsy and only intended to last for a short time, so permission was given for a new hut to be obtained. By 1958 a car park been constructed to the south of the ground and a bridge was built across the stream. The car park was given a tarmac surface for the first time in November 1997.

Plans to improve and extend the pavilion have caused many problems over the years. It was not until 1975 that showers and toilets were installed, and no progress was made on an extension until 1991. This was a joint project, with the Parish Council paying for the full cost of the building work and the Football Club paying for the internal fixtures and fittings; the extension was completed in the summer of 1992.

In January 1977 the management committee, wishing to make the recreation ground self-supporting, asked the Parish Council to take over as management trustees while the NPFA would remain owners; this came to pass on 1 April 1977. One of the first items that had to be dealt with was the drainage; a number of the pipes laid some years earlier had become blocked, particularly in front of the pavilion. Most of the money from the

Village Fayre of 1977 was spent on improving the drainage, and during the 1980s various other improvements were made to the ground such as further drainage work and installing floodlights for the Football Club.

There have been a total of five groundsmen at the recreation ground since 1935. Alfred Crabb was the first groundsman; he worked for a very small wage for 26 years and died suddenly in June 1961 aged 62. John Hampshire took over on 1st March 1964, and worked for 25 years before his sudden death on 13 October 1990. Ernest Gumbrell took up the post from October 1992 and resigned at the end of February 1998. He says "my duties included mowing and maintaining the recreation ground with its football and croquet pitches, digging out the ditches, and having the responsibility for Church Meadow, the Hayling Pond area, and roadside edges in Roundabout. A year or so ago, Horsham District Council gave the Parish Council thousands of daffodil bulbs to plant and I planted them round the children's play area, in front of the Reading Room and around the village." The bane of his life is the mindless vandalism that he sees, broken fencing in the recreation ground, boys in his tractor shed, damage to the village hall, for the money that is spent repairing the damage cannot be spent on new projects or good maintenance.

In 1964 Col Drabble had allowed his old Ferguson tractor to be used with the gang mowers; prior to this an old car had been purchased specifically for pulling the gang mowers but this had been vandalised in 1963. A Ransomes gang mower was ordered which initially was stored in Col Drabble's garage. A tractor/mower shed was completed by July 1964 but due to mistaken measurements it was not quite wide enough; the plan was for a hut built of blocks with double doors at each end so that the tractor mowers could drive in and out without unhitching. The necessary alterations to the mower shed were carried out by March 1965 and it was agreed that the Dennis motor-mower should be kept for the moment.

In May 1980 it became apparent that at the end of the season it would no longer be possible to obtain TVO fuel for the tractor so a new tractor would need to be purchased. The Parish Council did manage to buy 175 gallons of TVO from Selsey Parish Council. This represented about two years' supply but by September 1983 there was no further supply of TVO. Consequently, the Groundsman tried the tractor on Esso blue paraffin and on domestic heating oil and it ran well on the latter so 100 gallons of heating oil was purchased. By March 1986 the time had come to buy a 'new' tractor; a second-hand one was purchased and an approach made to

The Fair – held on what is now the car park 1960s
The building top right is the new tractor shed that was too small; foreground the old barn

the Chalk Pits Museum to see if they would be interested in having the old tractor and a Dennis Mower which was used in the 1930s. The Museum however was not interested so the old tractor was sold for £150. In March 1998 the Parish Council made the decision to appoint a contractor who would use his own equipment and they could mothball their own.

A 'lengthman' or a 'sidesman' (or scythesman) was the name for the hedger and ditcher, and two or three are remembered as wonderful men who used to plod round with their wheelbarrow, spades, swaphooks and brooms, tidying the hedges, clearing the leaves and digging out the ditches. These were often filled with water, but that is what ditches are for! The men, two of whom were nicknamed Quicksilver and Lightning, were very slow and old, and would sit on their wheelbarrow for an hour or two to catch their breath, but they were good and the hedges and ditches were well kept. Charles Adams was one village lengthman for twenty five years; at his retirement the *West Sussex Gazette* noted that West

Chiltington was twice judged the Best Kept Village during his time, although he replied that the villagers themselves helped to keep the village tidy. These men were employed by West Sussex Council, with George Curtis, the roads' surveyor who lived in Lordings Lane, as their boss. When they retired they were never replaced as the responsibility had passed from the District Council to various other authorities.

Having decided upon the provision of a Recreation Ground, the next question was of a hall for the village. The parish has had a number of halls during the century, the first being The British Legion's Old Comrades' Memorial Hall. This had been an old Army hut of the First World War and was erected during 1921-22 as a memorial to those who had fallen during that 'War to End all Wars' by The Comrades of the Great War, an organisation which later merged with the British Legion. In 1925 the freehold had been bought thereby securing the future of the Hall which has been described in other chapters with fond memories of its failings, but it served the village well for over 36 years.

Because by 1958 the new Village Hall had been built, Brigadier Saunders-Jacobs, the Legion's Branch President, told those present at a decisive Legion's branch meeting that there was no longer a demand to hire their hall, and they could not retain it without revenue from lettings.

The Old Comrades Hall
The blocked windows of the Elephant & Castle behind – possibly blocked because of the 1697 window tax

Therefore it was decided to sell it for £150 to the village's Boys' Club as its headquarters. The Legion would have as its headquarters in future one of the committee rooms in the new Village Hall, and Lt-Colonel Walter offered to donate a Legion badge for the new headquarters.

As the village grew between the wars it had become obvious that a larger and more modern building than the Old Comrades' Hall was needed, so in November 1935, the site of the current Village Hall was acquired from Clara Todd together with an area to provide the road access to the Ground. The site was under the immediate control of a Council of Management until the Charity Commissioners took over in March 1936. In October 1938 discussions began concerning the building work, but the war intervened so it was 1945 before preliminary steps were taken. However it was felt doubtful whether building could begin for a considerable while in view of the acute need for houses at that time. A fair sum towards the project had already been raised, and in 1950 the Parish Council agreed to assist the Recreation Ground Committee to raise funds to build the village hall in Festival Of Britain Year 1951, to which end a fete was held in June 1950. It was agreed that money should not be spent on the hall from rates, either in building or maintenance; it should be financed by grants from various quarters and voluntary donations. By 1955 when the first public meeting in the village pledged support, and a committee was formed, the funds had reached £1,300.

A representative from Reema described the prefabricated concrete building that his company was recommending, at a public meeting in December 1955, detailing the cost as £2,287 to include site clearance and drainage. All queries from the public being answered satisfactorily, it was decided to go ahead. Plans were passed, and when the building was well under way the Committee discussed details of furnishings, fire precautions, hire charges, a licence for amateur dramatics and the acquisition of a piano. A gymkhana was held in the summer of 1957 which raised over £400 for the funds; fund-raising was still going on into January 1958 when the latest in a series of dances raised £73 from 200 people. It was also noted in a newspaper report of that time that in order to reduce the bank charges of the overdraft, four people had each lent £100 free of interest. The main sources of regular revenue were the Dramatic Society, the WI and the Badminton Club, but major fund-raising schemes were still needed.

The hall was opened on 2 November 1957 by Colonel Drabble, chairman of the building committee, who said that if sufficient money could be raised to maintain the hall and its running costs, by an event such as the gymkhana, it ought to be possible to let the hall to village organisations free of charge. At the opening there was a tea at which the Silver Band played. Col Drabble had been supported in the venture by Col Kensington who had been chairman of the Village Hall Committee, and treasurer Col Walter.

1958 brought the start of a Derby and Joan Club, badminton, a weekly doctor's clinic, and fund raising activities, mainly dances. A regular baby clinic was organised by the District Nurse, and a public library started in one of the side rooms. By January 1963 the hall was registered as a charity and Reema was being consulted about an extension.

In 1965 a memorial seat to Sir Winston Churchill was erected, and when Colonel Walter died, the St George's Club in London presented a number of rose bushes to be planted in his memory. In 1966 the Women's Section of the British Legion presented the identification board on the outside wall to celebrate their 25th anniversary. In 1970 new oil-fired central heating was installed, and in 1974 the Parish Council handed over Dick Green's interesting collection of old postcards of the village which were framed and hung in the hall for all to enjoy. In 1978 a fund-raising Friends of the Village Hall was organised which has continued successfully with an annual draw. In 1981 Stan Gooch, who had served for many years as Secretary, Treasurer and booking secretary (mostly at the same time!) died, and a seat was placed near the hall, in his memory.

The library finally closed in September 1973, the County providing a mobile one instead. Through the years 'hardy annual' subjects were brought up at committee meetings: an extension to the hall, toilets near the stage, the installation of a telephone, and the state of the floor (the requirements of dancers and badminton players differing). Most of these problems were eventually resolved.

There was nothing behind the stage, not even toilets, and the main dressing room for the Dramatic Society was used as a chair storeroom, so in 1992 application was approved for a rear extension, and grants were applied for. By 1994 the work was finished; the extension having a floor level with the stage, two toilets, a kitchen and a small storeroom. The huge task of organising and overseeing the work was undertaken by Frank Warriner, who had sold his building business on his retirement, and the interior decoration was undertaken by the Dramatic Society.

The 1995 Committee then turned its attention to the front of the hall;

Village Hall – 1960s

again grants were applied for and received, and work began, closing the hall for a month. In September 1997 the front extension was opened, having added an extra six feet to the overall length of the building, and includes new toilet facilities, including one for the disabled, a new kitchen and storage, and a new foyer. At the same time the opportunity was taken to renew the maple floor to the whole of the main hall. It is a lovely building and very well used, giving a centre to the social life of the village.

West of the old forge, down The Hollows, there used to be another hall for the village, called New Hall. This hall was built by Slaters in the late 1920s or early 1930s for Mrs Tyrell, the landlady at the Queens Head. She was a woman who liked dancing and socials, and the Old Comrades' Hall having really been built as a recreational hall for the ex-servicemen, many of whom had been crippled, she felt that another hall, for another purpose, was needed. There was a slope up to it along a narrow pathway and at the back of the hall there was a cine machine to give film shows, manned by Sid Ellis, a very keen cinema projectionist. He was assisted by a Mr Vine from Storrington and the two men used to run weekly film shows as well as going round to other village halls. Dances to live music were held in the hall (the disco did not come until later) and there were pantomimes. There were also square dances, and hops were organised by someone who had an interest; 'The Swinging Sixties' did not appear to have a great impact on the village. There was also a youth club which met there and a story is told of old 'Widler' Ayling from Nutbourne, who owned a really old canvas-hood Austin Seven. He left the car there while he went to the pub, and one night a group of local boys lifted the back of the car up and put a chair under the spare wheel on the back so the wheels of the car were just clear of the ground. When 'Widler' came back from the pub, pickled as usual, he wound the engine with the crank handle, got in, put it in reverse, and nothing happened. "Bloody half shaft's gone" he stormed, and walked home, leaving the car where it was! There is a now a house on the site of New Hall, called Charta House.

Before the Great War a travelling fair would come to the village two, or sometimes three, times a year when there would be races and games on the Saturday. There is a delightful story of one pastime called Churchwarden's Pipe in which the older men lit their long clay pipes and smoked them, but the purpose of this exercise is unclear. What is remembered though, is that the pipes, being made of clay were very fragile and their stems broke, so when they became really short they were smoked upside down to protect the nose!

From about 1924 Harris's Fair used to come to the village at the same time as the Flower Show and children of that time remember sitting on the bank at Kings and Princes watching the engines go through the coalyard and into the Rectory Field behind. Then they would watch the roundabouts and swing boats being set up, and help the men push back up the hill the big water tanks which had been taken to the pond to be filled for the steam engines. All the schoolchildren had a ticket for a free tea, run by the Women's Institute, and in the evening there was a fancy dress dance in the village hall. Everyone would dress up, the adults as well as the children. The Flower Show was very well supported and looked forward to from year to year, with cups and prizes awarded; the tent was not cleared until

Flower Show Day – 12 August 1921
On the way to the Show

Flower Show Day – 12 August 1922
The spire is still on the school in the background

7pm so that those who had been working all day could go up and see the winners. Entries were taken down on the Friday night, and 'Old Callaway' used to be on guard the whole of Friday night until the judging on Saturday. As some 'true villagers' sadly remarked: "In those days we were nearly all working-class people, everyone went to the Show, and everyone knew everyone who went. It was a real focal point in the year; those who had left the village, perhaps to find work or get married, came back, the races and games were enjoyed by both adults and children and went on well into the evening. Because the teachers were local they and the children were much more involved than now, and the tent had poems, paintings, writing exercises and crafts that the children had done. There's a different sort of person in the village since the building of the new estates in the 1960s and we've lost our closeness." It became less of a feature when more people had cars and could visit families, not only at Flower Show time but at any time, when teachers were not local and when the school had its own open days.

Guy Peace, who became secretary of the Gymkhana when Col Drabble had to give up, explains how the modern Village Fayre has evolved "The first gymkhana, held in 1951 in Mr Snook's field and organised by Col

Walter, was a fund-raising exercise; money was needed to reshingle the Church spire with cedar wood shingles. The gymkhana was also held in 1952 and '53 but in 1954 it was decided that a Fair including a dog show be held in June to raise funds for the Recreation Ground alone. In 1955 Joy Adamson the television personality opened the Fair. The gymkhana restarted in 1957 run by a sub-committee of the Village Hall committee, with a view to raising funds again but this time for the proposed new village hall. It was quite a big gymkhana with two rings for horses, and two rings for the dog show that ran in tandem with it; the cricket club organised the car park, the football club provided the strong men to put up the jumps, the WI did the teas and Mac Steele lent his land at New House Farm for the event. The event has also been held at Southlands Farm, and at New Barn Farm, latterly it moved to the recreation ground.

Cicily Friar of Woolvens Farm near Ashington organised the gymkhana, and we ran hunter classes, most of the usual things but not Grade A. It was very successful for many years, but it was its success that contributed to its eventual closure. People came from far and wide; because the show was registered with the British Show Jumping Board competitors could gain points by winning here which counted towards their entitlement to take part in higher competitions. The Duke of Norfolk's daughters used to come over, and we once had the Prince Philip Cup here, but the problem was that if we hadn't registered our show with the BSJ and had their certified judges and their specified jumps, anyone who entered a horse would be banned from further BSJ competition, so we were registered and that led to further difficulties. All the officials wanted paying, and it just got too big with the locals being pushed out. It was silly because there were enough people round here with jumps, and enough ex-cavalry men who would have judged to have been able to have kept it as a local competition for the village.

We raised a lot of money; one year Norman Wisdom came and sold his autograph, or you could have your photograph taken with him for a shilling; he was good at raising money like that. Initially we used him for his name, but after that he just used to turn up in his 10th Hussar's blazer; he was a cavalry man.

In 1968 we had our last gymkhana and on 6 June 1970 the first Village Fayre and Dog Show was held, which continued the tradition of fund-raising for the Village."

The dog show displayed the many facets of working dogs, and was a popular and well supported event. A programme for the 1988 West

Chiltington Village Fayre and Dog Show (plus terrier and lurcher) informs that the show commenced at 1.30pm and tickets could be bought for a hot air balloon tethered lift off, there was a children's fancy dress competition and a fun run on two courses. There was a tug-of-war between four local pubs and an Indian Club Swinging Display as well as the Exemption Dog Show of 25 classes plus extra trophies for best in Show, Puppy, Veteran and a Scurry. There were many people who were very disappointed when the village dog show stopped. It ran until about 1994 and was latterly organised by Angela Field who lives in The Birches. She continues: "The Flower Show is always in August, but the Dog Show and the Fayre is in June. The Dog Show was quite tiny when it started and had pedigree, novelty and obedience classes, but we had to drop the obedience because it wasn't worth getting a judge in for only a dozen dogs. Added to which it took up half the arena and cost us money what with a present for the judge and entrance of only 50p. I took it over from Mrs Stone (whose Red Setters did very well at Crufts,) because she wanted to retire. They advertised in the Parish Magazine for someone to take it on, and with the support of the family I decided to have a go. I had had a dog at Crufts, too, but that was my only qualification! It was a bit of a scramble, but we managed. When Brian Walter took over the running of the Fayre from Frank Warriner we worked very well together, and decided to reintroduce maypole dancing, 'olde worlde' stalls and fancy dress on the Fayre side, and I would reintroduce the terriers and lurcher classes, on the dog side. We used to have four rings, pedigrees in one, crossbred and novelty in the second where we always started off with a border collie class (and I put up a whopping great trophy for the best border collie), terriers in the third and lurchers in the fourth. In January I would start looking for the stewards and booking the judges; I had very good judges from quite a long way away, so that they didn't know the dogs, or the handlers.

By the end I had nearly 700 dogs, some were coming from as far away as Wales. The lurcher classes attracted lots of entries because it allowed them to qualify for the South of England; you see we had both an Open and an Exemption ring at the Dog Show so it could be both serious and fun. I've never seen so many lorries in my life, bringing up to five or six dogs to qualify for the South of England. And for six years the Best in Show dog went on to qualify at Crufts; it was well known that if you won at West Chiltington you could go on to win quite a lot.

Rosettes are very expensive so I got sponsors for the classes, and bought some of the cups at car boot sales then had our own motif put on; I wanted people to have something to take away so we had fifty specials, for every child that entered. The idea was that the family would come and enjoy themselves, stay for longer than they had anticipated, and have drinks, sandwiches, refreshments, and decide to come the next year. The money didn't appear in our books, but we drew so many people in that we really boosted the profits for the day. We started at 11am but there would be people arriving from 9am, so for the last couple of years my friend from down the road did the food, just charging for what she spent and we made as much as £300, or £400 sometimes. There were a couple of girls that ran a waitress service, and it's surprising how much people will spend if the tea is brought out to them. Also, the people sitting next to them would think 'that looks nice' and order tea as well; the Fayre opened at 2pm although some of the dog people had been in the beer tent for some time before that!

I gave up after I'd done it for six years, partly because Brian gave up the Fayre and partly because it was such hard work. We used to set up in the Rec about 4pm on Friday, marking out the rings and that, and then be there from 8am on the Saturday, and have to do the clearing up. You know how it is, a lot of people think they want to be associated with it, but it's usually you and the family that ends up doing all the work. As nobody else could be found to run it, it stopped. It was a shame as we were pulling in between two and three thousand pounds, but the dog people did get a bit alienated when, within three weeks of handing the money over a notice went up about exercising dogs in the Rec, I mean, notices are expensive and we weren't raising money for notices! The money was supposed to be divided half for the upkeep of the Village Hall, heating, lighting and so on, and half was to go towards the groundsman's costs. When we first came here we used to walk the dogs in fields that have now been built on; it was lovely with the bluebells and all the squirrels running about, and the freedom for the children to build camps and play."

Brian Walter began his task to involve all of West Chiltington in the activities of the Fayre - the Village and the Common, around 1989. His widow, Angela continues the story: "The Fayre used to be held in what is now the Recreation Ground car park and can be seen to be very different from what it was when we ran it. Brian organised the Fayre extremely well and put in a lot of effort; if you look at this programme for 1991 there were thirty seven stalls round the edge of the field, including seven Society and Organisation stalls, and side shows and refreshments. The Youth Club ran six side shows including wellie throwing, face painting and doughnut eating, and the Floral Club ran Egg Citing where blown eggs were placed on a tray, a child lifted an egg and a note inside revealed whether he could win a prize from the bran tub. The Grand Draw was a good money raiser; many villagers took part and I wish I could mention them all. Brian began to build up the equipment for the Fayre, making stilts, the Catch-a-Rat, and he made the Unrideable Horse which caused a lot of amusement with Dr King running it on one occasion. Those things, and many others that he made such as the uprights for the ring ropes, are still stored in the shed for future use. There was a very big Fancy Dress Competition with over fifty entries; one year I can remember the Saturday having a very wet start and Rev Gerald Evans and his wife Sheila who were judging the Fancy Dress were brought into the arena in an Avon dinghy on a trailer, under an umbrella, to perform the opening ceremony! The Worthing Town Crier came as Master of Ceremonies. The arena in the recreation field had displays all afternoon; one year Brian obtained an old car from the breaker's yard, and we had a demonstration by the Fire Brigade (flares and all) on how to cut off the roof and rescue the people trapped inside. In 1994 the Press Review leaflet listed a circus skills workshop, two bouncy castles, birds of prey, classic and vintage cars, a glider display, a fiercely competitive tug-of-war (clubs and pubs raising teams including all-women teams); this was taken very seriously to win the trophies.

The lovely teas were always a treat in the Village Hall provided by the ladies of the Women's Institute.

We attracted so many people that we had to have 'a police presence'! Brian worked with the surrounding villages and Parham to make sure the dates didn't clash, and we got a terrific number of people. The village was big enough, and enthusiastic enough to be able to support both the Fayre and the Fete and Flower Show; The Fete and Flower Show produces its money by selling programmes all round the district and this income goes to put up the tent; it's purely a pleasure afternoon and now it has become a pleasure weekend. But the Fayre was always a fund-raising exercise so it had to be good to persuade people to come. We bridge both because my daughter is Chairman of the Floral Club whose displays are a focal point of the Fete and Flower Show!

We used to live next to the Recreation Ground in a house called Bearwood, (but now that I've moved it has reverted to its original name of Chase House,) and we had a huge old barn of about 40' long. Brian was also on the committee of the Village Hall and our barn came in very handy being alongside the Village Hall car park. Mr Figg, who was born in 1907 and lived in Mill Road, told me that the children from the village school used to meet in the barn on firework night with flaming torches and participate with games and apple bobbing. I believe the barn was built in Tudor times and has a lean-to at one end very similar to the one in Daux Farm; the timbers are very interesting. It now has a free standing upstairs to make an office and workshop beneath.

Brian was very keen to see the Village Hall improve and enlarge. Fundraising under the guidance of Mrs Hilda Andrews the then Chairman produced the required amount of money; Brian drew up the original drawings on our dining-room table which were approved by the Committee and Wilmers of Pulborough were appointed to get Horsham's planning approval. At this time Brian became increasingly ill and had to hand over and take a back seat, sadly never seeing its completion. Brian loved to get involved with the village and its people, and to see them enjoying themselves - his ability and gift to use his hands enabled him to be very proud of restoring the Village Stocks outside the Church."

In 1919 The West Chiltington Fete and Flower Show was founded as part of the Peace Celebrations, and has been held every year, on the first Saturday after the first Monday in August, apart from a break of six years

The WI Stall at the Flower Show – 1934
Mrs Kensington, the WI President is on the extreme right, with Mrs Hall (the Rector's wife and vice-president) next to her

The Flower Show 1939
William Dixon the Headmaster presenting prizes to David Dixon (his son),
Edith Green and Elva Johnson (aged 4)

during the Second World War. Largely inspired by the enthusiasm of its first President and Chairman, the Reverend Andrew Caldecott, it rapidly established itself as a popular feature in the village calendar, and subsequent Presidents have carried the torch on: in 1928 Lt-Col Kensington, succeeded by Lt-Col Drabble in 1966, who was himself succeeded by General Sir Victor Balfour in 1974.

At the heart of the event was a programme of horticultural interest and competition supported by side shows and sports, which was held on Gadds Meadow, known locally as the Flower Show Field. The Show opened with a procession starting from the Church, up Little Hill, around the Common and back down Big Hill to the Show; this was led by Mr E Pullen and the Silver Band, behind which came decorated vehicles, perambulators and bicycles, the Girl Guides and Scouts, followed by the rest of the village. The programme was spiced by traditional events such as the Egg and Spoon Race, Wheelbarrow and Sack races, a tug-of-war between the single and the married, and some very intriguing events such as the Lovers Race for Mixed Adults, the Catch-a-Train Race, and the Bun and Whistle Race for Ladies! The village garden competition was open 'to those working for a weekly wage and not employed as whole time gardeners', and the village marathon was a prestige event. Starting from Gadds Meadow the competitors pounded round 2½ miles via the Sinnocks, Haglands Lane, Big Hill and Rectory Hollow, to the finish.

A certain amount of disorderly informality was tolerated as part of the flavour of the occasion, but the Committee seems to have been mildly anxious when in 1925 they resolved 'to endeavour to arrange the procession in better order, at any rate whilst moving through the village'. But a greater disorder, of the world, came in 1939 bringing social life in England to an abrupt end.

The 'Peace Celebration' Show of 1919 was revived as 'The Victory Celebration' Show in 1946; the same, but different. After the 1950s the processions ceased, but for many years the Silver Band continued to make its unique contribution to the Show which was supported by the village. Some of the old events survived, the village garden competition was re-instated in 1974 and the funfair continued to enliven the proceedings at the Recreation Ground where the Show is now held; there are special displays by the Floral Art Club, local nurseries and enthusiasts. Once the tea tent collapsed in a storm, the WI tent enveloped officials and judges, and in 1974 the Show ended with The Great Sheep Chase where the fugitive sheep ended up literally bogged down at the bottom of Harborough Hill allowing recapture by two stalwarts of the Show Committee.

The five words 'The WI did the refreshments' can in no way give any indication of the baking, preparing and overall commitment of the two WIs to the village Fete and Flower Show, and to the Fayre.

During the 1920s there was a baby show in conjunction with the fair which an obliging Colonel Kensington was persuaded to judge. Elsie Pullen remembers that one year her younger brother Percy won the Best Baby, and was awarded a Bible, and Reg Slater was one of the bonny babies in 1929.

Sue Overton-Smith remembers the anticipation for the Annual Flower Show in the 1950s: "We children always entered the races, did paintings, made miniature gardens and arranged vases of wild flowers. It was a chance to meet everyone, to listen to the band and to have a ride in the swing boats and on the roundabouts at the fair afterwards. Dr Ford's three children, William, Charles and Penny won a prize in the fancy dress competition as Annie Get Your Gun (the title of a musical film) with the boys as the horse!"

pony out of the shafts and rub him down and settle him in his stable. Without the pony, the trap tilted up and shed its load, but the wife would leave her husband lying on the ground until morning!

The building now known as the Elephant and Castle was built in 1665 as a dwelling house for Jesse Moulding who combined the duties of sexton and parish clerk with his work as a coffin maker. It is said that the windows were bricked in so that the occupiers did not have to pay the window tax. It continued to be occupied by the sexton (whose job description included care of church and churchyard, ringing the church bell, attending upon the rector and acting as grave digger) until eventually in 1804 it was sold as a private house to a wheelwright called Richard Girling. When his son Jacob inherited it in 1830 he obtained a beer licence, and it has continued as an ale house, (known as the Elephant and Castle since 1842) until in 1952, King and Barnes brewery who had bought it in 1920, got a full licence to sell wines and spirits as well as beer. It used not to have the bar as it is now; there was only one bar with a hatch through which the beer was sold. There was no proper cellar, the beer barrels stood in the area that is now the saloon bar and dining room.

Bert Whitfield the Publican in The Elephant & Castle Garden

Renee Manvell came to the village with her parents George and Kate who were landlords at The Queens Head. She particularly remembers 2 February every year, licensing day, when her father used to pick up the local landlords from around, Mr Cook from the Five Bells, and those from The Half Moon and The Anchor at Storrington. There was no drink/driving in those days and when they had been granted their licences for the following year her father and friends partied home. She also remembers the man who used to come into the Queens with half a dozen rabbits and a pack of cards; a dozen customers were asked to pay a penny and then the cards were shuffled and drawn; the person with the highest card won the rabbit. This was repeated until he had sold all six and made six shillings.

She was married from there in 1935, to Bill Knight. Sometime during the war Mr Manvell died and his wife, who suffered with leg ulcers, decided to give up the pub and move over to Rosebank on The Common to be near her daughter and to work at a job which required less standing. Strangely, about the mid 1950s Renee and her husband moved back to the pub leaving mother at Rosebank. They bought one of The Hatches cottages for Bill Knight's parents, for £800. Mr Knight senior was a good gardener who managed the garden at The Queens Head; the area that is now a car park grew fruit and vegetables, and there were the usual ducks, chickens, rabbits and even ponies in the stable because Renee's daughter rode.

Renee served basic pub food, steak and kidney pies, sausage in a roll for 8d or in bread for 6d, but that was all, for, with a sick husband and three children she had no time for fancy catering. Licensing hours were 10.30am to 2.30pm and 6pm to 10pm with an extension for bank holidays, but extensions were hard to get. There was a situation which the landlords did not like, whereby different areas had different licensing hours, so that Storrington, licensed under Steyning, closed half an hour earlier than West Chiltington, licensed under Petworth, so the drinkers would rush over from Storrington for an extra half hour. The pub was tied first to Rock Brewery at Brighton, then to United Brewery and finally to Whitbread, where it still is. Eventually the pub was sold to Norman and Freda Nash and was sold again after Norman died.

There are many stories of inebriates being taken home by their ponies; here is one: It is said that someone who lived in West Chiltington Lane was a real drunkard and used to come up to the Queens Head in his pony and trap and get 'absolutely stoned'. At the end of the session, he was put in his trap and the pony used to take him home where his wife would take the

The pubs were another of the centres of social life in the village; they provided a communal place to meet and talk and exchange gossip, for both the men and women. Nora Heffer recalls that even the WI darts team used to meet in the Elephant to practice and play their matches.

In the National Library of Wales at Aberystwyth is the diary of William Dillwyn, a Quaker. In it he describes a journey he had to make in 1774 from Portsmouth to London, via West Chiltington. It is a memorable book for this entry about our village: having failed to find the person he wanted in Storrington he entered 'a dirty, straggling village where at a dirty inn I made a tolerable dinner'! The following day he set out again 'on a most miry road through to Coneyhurst and through mud to the turnpike road'. The Inn is presumed to be the Queens Head, which in those days was owned by John Trower, the manor reeve who was married to Ann Jarret, the daughter of the village carpenter.

Times moved on and by the Abergavenny Estate sale of Friday 19 June 1925, Lot 26 is described as 'The well known Fully Licensed Public House known as The Queens Head. The house is brick and Stone built, with tiled roof, and contains:- On the Ground Floor - Entrance Passage; Bar Room and Servery 16' 3" x 12'; Smoking Room with fireplace; Tap Room with fireplace and Small Room at rear divided by movable partitions; Kitchen with range and oven, brick oven and sink; Small back Room with fireplace and fitted cupboard; Large Beer Cellar with stone slab floor and steps to road.' On the first floor there were five bedrooms with one further bedroom on the second floor. Outside there were 'Wash House with two coppers and pump; Small Store over; Coal and Wood Shed with store adjoining (sometimes used as the local mortuary); Three-stall Stable; Large Side Yard; Coach House with double doors; Pigsty; Urinal; Privy. A Large and Well Stocked Kitchen Garden. Water is obtained from a Well on the Premises.

This Lot is let to the Rock Brewery, Brighton, on Lease for 14 years from March 25th 1915, at a Rent of £54 per annum.' The sale of this Lot was subject to a condition that the owner of Lot 28 (Pollards) would continue to be allowed to use the pump in the yard!

The bus used to come and turn just outside the Queens Head, but on hunt days it was often late. There are two main packs of foxhounds: the Leconfield, and the Horsham and Crawley; no longer do they meet in the village, but they do meet in the area. Round the walls in the public bar Bill Knight put in seats from old Southdown buses in 1956 when the pub was renovated, which were described as very comfortable

In 1969 the Fete and Flower Show celebrated its Golden Jubilee, and marked its 50th Show (the discrepancy is due to the wartime break) in 1975 by the production of a history from which these notes are partly taken. In 1983 and perhaps before, there was a Best Kept Garden Competition open to all residents and divided into two sections: for gardens up to $1/4$ acre and for gardens over $1/4$ acre, although the size did not matter as much as the condition of the garden. In 1984 there were 10 entries but due to lack of support this section was discontinued in 1988. The Fete and Flower Show has changed format as times have changed, and at the end of the century it is as vibrant as at its inception; it has turned into a Village Weekend with the show itself on the Saturday, The Tent Service on the Sunday and the Mary How Trust's fund-raising evening on the Monday. For three years this was a Caribbean Evening, with Caribbean weather, but in 1999 the format changed to a spit roast with Celtic folk music. The Tent Service is worship for all the family including the pets; there are horses, dogs, cats, mice and goats, and even some birds, all of which behave remarkably well.

The Queens Head

Shove Halfpenny in the Elephant & Castle – 1938 or 39
From left: Charlie Puttick, Fred Morris the landlord, Dick Green

Freddie Gravett is remembered as one of the landlords, but he had to augment his income from the beer house with chimney sweeping so when he worked behind the bar soon after sweeping he sometimes served the beer with sooty hands! He had to do the serving as his wife, it is said, could not be bothered and he and Mrs Gravett used to quarrel fiercely and loudly, with language that carried for miles! The Silver Band used to play on Sunday evenings, alternating with the Queens Head, under an oak tree which has since been replaced by a copper beech. Everyone used to go with their children and take a drink and crisps, and the Cocozza's ice cream man used to come on his bicycle with the big box in front. Before the First World War the wassail men used to meet there at Christmas time and many of the same men would meet again in the summer for the annual Strawberry Match, the cricket match which took place at the end of strawberry picking. Pat Steele remembers that in the 1930s old Mrs Morris from the pub would come up the pub garden once a week with a tray of tea which she carried over the stile and across to Mrs Hare Winton, Pat's mother who lived in the bungalow in what is now Holly Close. No one can

The Elephant & Castle – 1910 after the Strawberry Match

Wassailing at Christmas 1910 – The Elephant

remember why she did this, but the thought of an elderly lady carrying a tray of tea from the pub has amused Pat ever since. Mr Morris bought Pat her first mackintosh, sou'wester and wellington boots when at the age of four she was told to go over to the pub for her Christmas present from the Morrises; a pleasure that was marred only by her falling over the stile.

The present landlord who took over in 1992 and is a South African, continues the social traditions of the pub; one of his recent ventures being a South African Supper to support St Mary's, raising money for the new vestry. All the pubs now serve excellent food, in complete contrast to even thirty years ago.

Although West Chiltington is a picturesque and pretty parish, sufficiently pretty for Eagle Star Insurance to film the facade of the Church for a television advertisement in 1990, it is not a backwater preserved in aspic but a village subject to external influences. All is not what it seems; it contains human beings just as everywhere else does, and is therefore subject to the same crimes that beset humans everywhere; the village has had its drug problems, its child abuse, its resident 'fence', its arguments, disagreements and fights. The police used to know a lot of what went on because they knew their 'patch', something which modern 'panda car policing' cannot hope to do so well. There used to be a day book kept by the police, detailing what had happened during that particular shift, but this practice was discontinued when it was discovered the potential for opinion being used instead of fact. Steve Leal, the 'village bobby' for many years and now retired in the village, said that the book might contain such things as 'I know him, I've known his character for years, and he *can't* have done it', but these days such opinions are not valued in our fact-orientated society. All records of facts are now kept on computer.

Bert Parsonage is one of the earliest 'village bobbies' to be remembered; he lived at Number 3 Hatches Cottages in East Street and his son, also called Bert, went to the village school eighty years ago. PC George Plowden also lived in Hatches Cottages and is remembered with mixed feeling depending upon which side of the law one happened to be! One resident's mother was very upset when he charged her for not having a licence for her dog, and yet he was known to pay people's criminal fines if they were in financial difficulties; he was a well educated man, and gentle.

Later the Police House was moved to The Juggs. The Police House on the Common was built about the early 1950s; it was purpose-built and doubled as the office, so the family was always on duty. The land had previously been used for football and cricket by the local youngsters whose reaction can be imagined when they discovered what was going to be built on 'their' land!

When Steve Leal retired in the autumn of 1994 the village showed their appreciation of all the good work he had done. The Parish Magazine wrote: 'What an occasion! There cannot be many members of the Police Force that had had such a send off. On Saturday evening, October 15, the Village Hall was packed with that seemed like at least half the village wishing to send Steve and Grace on their way into retirement. A magnificent repast provided by ladies from both WIs and the MU was spread before us, together with wine dispensed by a phalanx of 'policemen' - bar tenders wearing police helmets - a nice touch! The assembled company rose to their feet and applauded the Leal family as they processed down the hall to the centre table. After the refreshments, a hilarious entertainment by some members of the Dramatic Society had us in helpless laughter as they performed various numbers and 'dances' all in the Police vein. Finally after Steve cut the magnificent cake he was presented with a crystal bowl and a substantial cheque; the proceedings ended with the singing of 'For he's a jolly good fellow!'"

This popularity, though, was gained at some cost to himself and his family for it was a twenty four-hours-a-day, seven-days-a-week total commitment. PC Leal moved into the Police House on the Common in July 1972 having worked his way up from being a town policeman, to a Panda car policeman in East Preston, and having decided that a rural posting was what he wanted. He soon discovered that quite a lot of his time was spent on parish problems rather than specifically 'police' matters, and he tells a story to illustrate: "I was telling a lad off and I gave him a real ear-bending. A lady was listening and as I sent him on his way she said 'it's about time someone gave him a telling off. He's my nephew, you know!' I thought 'Oh no, now I've put my foot in it' but I'd done the right thing because he had needed telling by someone in authority, and it worked, so I thought that that was the way I would go on. Set standards, be fair, don't compromise. I remember a domestic problem which concerned the sharing of property when a couple were separating; they were arguing about who should have what and I went to the house and actually ended up deciding who should have the pillowcases, the bath towels. They just needed an unbiased viewpoint. The idea was to prevent a local problem becoming a police matter, and you just can't cost that. We had people coming in the middle of the night sometimes, Grace would make a pot of tea and we'd sort the matter out. Everyone had my phone number, and if the matter was very delicate, people might even speak to Grace rather than me, but it takes years to build up that sort of trust. I stayed long enough to do that, 22 years, but in the end, a combination of the influx of so many new people and a general disregard for others made it very difficult.

I covered Nutbourne, North Heath and this parish, and the Pulborough men kept an eye on things when I was on holiday. It was a big area; I had a motor cycle when I first came and that was funny: I was a police car driver and when we arrived here I went to the garage and inside was a motor bike, an old Velocette, but I couldn't ride a motor bike so had to go away and be taught! In spite of the fact that there was always something going wrong with it I became quite attached to it in the end; the children would see me off down the road just to see how far I got before it broke down! In the end I got another Velocette and it went very well; even when I was given a van I preferred the bike because I could leave it and go walkabout, and that's the way to get talking to people.

I got to know all the children after a while because I got involved with the school. I sat in on lessons and talked to them and built up this trust; when the teachers went home I was still around. I remember once that a group of children were annoying an old lady who lived in The Juggs so I banned them from playing outside her house and they left her alone after that. Often my very presence was a deterrent to bad behaviour; children are naturally naughty and would look for my van so they could go off and be naughty somewhere else, but with the motor bike I could put it in the bushes and the children never knew where I was! They never did anything criminal or too bad, but a ticking off just kept them in line, and there was never any cheek, they accepted what I said. If there was a disco at Pulborough I used to round up the West Chiltington boys to ensure that they left before there was any trouble, but I am concerned that nowadays it is much more difficult to maintain that closeness of people to the police; policing was a vocation and a commitment and I'm afraid that it's now just a job. I cannot stress strongly enough how important it is to catch the children young, while still at school, and demand respect from them; they will never forget it. One lad had epilepsy and Swansea withdrew his driving licence so his friends decided that if he couldn't drive neither would they, and they all walked everywhere - drink at the Queens Head, walk it all off to Pulborough, tank up again and walk it all off home! They had fun and did no harm, I had the support of their parents, it just worked. Of course there is always one you don't win, one bad apple.

Brian Palmer who was here before me started an archery club, it was a thriving team until he left, so he must have been the driving force. I started a football team for the youngsters, too.

Because everybody knew everybody there wasn't much petty crime; outside criminals would be dealt with by CID from Littlehampton who would come up for the day, otherwise I was left much on my own. In those days there was enough manpower for us all to do house-to-house questions just to see if anyone had seen anything and because people were regular in their habits they would notice if there was anything unusual. I once had someone knock on my door and ask directions, the post office had sent him; later that day I went to a burglary and realised that it was him that had knocked on my door; I could describe him and his partner!

There's too much paperwork today so things don't get dealt with quickly enough. This lad hid in the allotments after being caught stealing from the apple orchard by the farm manager, I catch him, tell him off, remove the apples. The farm manager is happy, the lad won't do it again. Dealt with. In contrast when, one November, I caught a boy stealing money from a farm I, in my uniform, marched him home through the village with my hand on his collar to embarrass him, and in my report to the court asked for it to be dealt with before Christmas; it was eventually dealt with in February. I was annoyed that that family had had to spend an anxious Christmas, and I wonder whether I could have dealt with the problem another way. I remember one case of antisocial behaviour that was caused by a man not taking his medication, so I just had a word with his GP and the matter was sorted out but that could only happen in a small closely knit village. I was also able to take direct action when needed: I remember one old chap up on the allotments who often used to have a bonfire, and one day the smoke was blowing right across to the shops so someone asked him to put it out, and he wouldn't, so they called me. Defiantly he challenged me 'Are you going to make me put it out then?' so I just jumped over the fence and kicked his bonfire out and he said 'If you're going to be like that, then' and stumped off home. But he was impressed that I'd dealt with the matter myself and not called in the fire brigade, even though I was off duty and could have done.

When I came, if a dog was roaming in the village we would tie it up and speak to the owner and that would be that. Now we have nothing to do with dogs, the dog warden is part of the Council and the dogs go straight to the pound. I used to know every dog in the village; Dougal the Old English Sheepdog was owned by Fred Slater in the builder's yard and he used to lie in the middle of the road - everyone used to drive round him. When anyone complained I said that if anything happened to him, you would be the one in trouble as he had lived here all his life and was an old villager! Remus was a black Labrador who belonged to Dr Ford at the Common, he used to come out of the house, cross the road and walk up to the butcher's shop every day, collect his bones or whatever, and go back home. When the newcomers to the village complained I said that they must slow down for the dog, life in a village is slower, and Remus has a right to be here; another old villager! With all the new building that went on, so many houses in a short time, we had an influx of newcomers, some of whom complained about the cows in the fields, and there being no street lights, but country is different from town. It's nice to see that people have settled down a bit now.

Because I was so proprietorial and felt so passionately about the village I'm very proud to say that I have been accepted as an old villager but I had to work for it. There is a seat outside Kensington Close and four old boys used to sit there so I used to spend time talking to them, I read up a lot about West Chiltington so I could talk to them; some of them could name every policeman in the village over the years. They had stories about each of them, how they went about their work and what they did. So I thought I must find out about them - every policeman had to write about things that happened in the village in the 'beat book' which had been started when the policeman was in The Juggs: population, acreage, names of roads. I carried on doing it. Then one of the men died, and there was an empty space on the bench and because I had spent so much time talking to them they invited me to sit down with them. That became my seat then and I used to go up in the afternoons to sit there and talk to people that went past; it was a focal point and everyone knew where to find me. One day I went across the road and bought ice creams and when I looked up, Hilda Andrews had taken a photo of the four of us in a row with our ices!"

A few years after Steve's retirement our police presence is PC Karen Annis who was keen to stress that we are not losing our village bobby because we have her! As she says: "What has changed is that the force has reviewed its estate strategy and is selling off the police houses; police officers can buy them if they want to. Nowadays new recruits aren't given either accommodation or rent allowance. On my last beat in Faygate where, like Steve, I was the only officer, even though everyone had telephones I still had people knocking on the door at all hours. If you wanted to be a rural officer you took that on with no extra pay and it was expected; we did know what we were letting ourselves in for. When this 'cluster station' idea came in people were concerned about how they would get hold of a police officer if they didn't live in the village, but what is forgotten is the fact that rural officers cater for more than one village but can only live in one place. By working in cluster stations we are pooling our resources and there should be better communication as we can call on other officers to help in our village if it is needed. We talk to others on the same shift and have a formal meeting about twice a year with the whole sector.

The cluster system works by splitting the division into sectors. West Chiltington comes under Steyning Sector with its two clusters sites, one at Steyning itself and one at Pulborough which West Chiltington comes under. They are also setting up writing offices, the nearest is at Sullington Village Hall, where we can write up our reports without having to go all the way to the main sector office. The paper work has increased despite efforts to reduce it. When the new Crawley Police Station opens, the custody block will have a prisoner process unit where we hand over prisoner, statements and information, leaving us free to get back to our sector that much sooner.

Listening to police officers who have been in the force longer, things have changed, but on the whole the rural officers are still taken to the heart of the community. Being in a small community we can get to know people; there's often more than one way to solve a problem and 'official procedure' is not always the best way. Unfortunately in this day and age it is not realistic to have one officer for every village, but the thing to remember is that even though I do not live in West Chiltington and you cannot come and knock on my door, you still have a dedicated police officer."

District Nurses were recruited on a widening scale from the end of the 1880s and at the beginning of the 20th Century nurses began to organise National Associations. The Sussex County Nursing Association was formed (affiliated to Queen Victoria's Jubilee Institute for Nurses), with the local branch being The West Chiltington & Thakeham District Nursing Association. This became affiliated to The West Sussex County Nursing Association in 1919, with Miss Edith Mary Cotton of Windways, The Common, and Mrs Kensington taking an active interest from the beginning.

WEST SUSSEX COUNTY NURSING ASSOCIATION UNIFORM.

Regulation uniform for all Nurses (except Queen's) is as follows:-

Dresses - blue grey castor cloth (dark side out) with detachable lower sleeves.

Belt - Washing - white- or of same material as dress.

Aprons - White with rounded bibs.

Collars - Stiff linen collars. Turn down collars may be worn if preferred, but must be plain and not low in neck.

Cap -The "West Sussex" storm cap. In Summer a plain navy blue hat with blue band may be worn.

Coat - Navy blue serge or gabardine coat with belt.

Mackintosh - Navy blue or black.

Shoes - black.

Stockings - black or grey.

Uniform must always be worn when on duty and should be neat and in good repair. The West Sussex bronze badge is supplied by the County Superintendent to all nurses and must be given up on leaving the Association.

Nurse Riley was the Nurse for West Chiltington and Thakeham in 1928/29 during which twelve months she made 1,705 visits. She was succeeded by Nurse Wing from 1929/30 whose workload was made heavier by a measles epidemic requiring 41 Epidemic Visits.

RULES FOR DISTRICT NURSES.

1. The Nurse, when on duty must wear the Uniform Dress and no ornaments. She is strictly forbidden to gossip, or to interfere in any way in the religious opinions of her patients or their friends.

2. It is the Nurse's duty to do all that concerns the bed and person of her patients; to remove. or to see removed, all that is offensive from the room; to use disinfectants, and to explain their importance to those in attendance on the patient. The Nurse must see that the room is ventilated and cleaned, and do her best to improve the general surroundings of her patients, and instruct the friends of the patients in the best method of attending to the patient in the intervals between her visits.

3. The Nurse shall be responsible for all appliances, clothing etc lent by their Local Association to her patients, and must see that they are all returned in good condition.

4. The Nurse shall invariably carry out the directions of the Medical Attendant. She must send in a report of the work once a month to the Superintendent, and any case which is beyond her skill she must at once communicate to the Superintendent. Post card must not be used for this purpose.

5. The Nurse must be punctual in starting her work, she must be ready to begin at 9 a.m.

And must always leave at her lodging (on the slate provided) a note of where she may be found in case of any sudden call for her services.
6. The Nurse should not accept presents from the patients, or friends of the patients; no Nurse shall leave her District or have friends to stay in the same house with her without the permission of the Hon. Secretary of the Local Association.
7. The Nurse will have a month's holiday in the year, and she must not leave her District without permission from the Secretary and sending notice of her holiday to the County Superintendent.

The District Nursing Associations dealt with the nurse's accommodation and many of them tried to provide a residence for their nurse. The West Chiltington & Thakeham District Nursing Association was no exception; due to the enthusiasm of Mrs Kensington, Nurses Cottage, designed by her husband Colonel Kensington, was erected in 1930. It was built on a small piece of land which formed part of a much larger plot owned by Mrs Kensington on Common Hill. (The remainder of the plot was sold by Mrs Kensington in October 1935 and the house Haslewood was built on the site.) A plaque on the wall indicates that Nurses Cottage came under the authority of the West Sussex County Nursing Service and many similar nurses houses appeared around the District. The Midwives Act 1936 meant that certain nurses had to be provided with a car, and all nurses had to be provided with a telephone and a pension scheme.

Mrs Daisy Ellis, whose husband owned the garage, is the first nurse that people can remember, in the 1920s, doing general nursing and midwifery duties from her house adjacent to the garage. Nurse Edith Wing was the first occupant of Nurses Cottage when it was completed in 1930. She was succeeded in 1931 by Nurse Gray who in 1932 was joined by Nurse Ballance. They lived there together until 1935; then until her retirement at the end of 1938 Nurse Ballance lived alone in Nurse's Cottage. She is remembered for two things: she gave a Bible to babies she delivered, and quite a few of the villagers still have them, and she was lame, which is unfortunate with a name like Ballance! From 1939 Nurse Stead was our nurse; the outbreak of war brought its problems for the nurses with evacuation doubling their work. Nurse Stead continued after the war and was the District Nurse for a total of 16 years until 1955 when she was succeeded by Nurse Patsy Wright-Warren who remained until 1961. In 1964 Nurse Beasley moved in.

Lorna Beasley did her nursing training in Worthing, followed by a two year Health Visitor course in Leamington Spa. She enjoyed that area and invited her daughter, who was at school in Worthing, to leave her school and start at another near Leamington Spa, but she refused, so Nurse Beasley started to look in The Nursing Times for jobs nearer the Worthing school. In 1963 she followed up an advertisement, was interviewed and offered the job of combined District Nurse, Midwife and Health Visitor to West Chiltington, with accommodation provided at Nurses Cottage, which in those days was a two bedroom cottage with a sitting room and combined scullery/bathroom downstairs. The main disadvantage was that the treatment room could only be approached from outside, with no access from the house. In due course the County Council extended the house for her, providing a further bedroom and upstairs bathroom, with a downstairs cloakroom and a proper kitchen, and a new treatment room on the site of the garage, giving access to it from inside. A new garage was constructed.

When she first arrived she covered not only West Chiltington but Thakeham, up to the Dan Hill cross roads, and along Harbolets Road, although travelling was made easier with her car. Her predecessors had covered two areas, one had covered this West Chiltington area and the other had covered Pulborough. Nurse Beasley continued the duties very much as her predecessors had done until the mid 1970s.

In about 1974/5 the health visiting, midwifery and district nursing duties were removed from the County Council's jurisdiction to that of the District Council. There were many ramifications of this change, one was that the local authority could no longer support the expense of providing accommodation for the nurses and sold off their housing stock, including West Chiltington's Nurses Cottage. As Nurse Beasley was the sitting tenant she got first refusal, and jumped at the opportunity to buy. This alteration to the system was partly brought about because home deliveries of babies was no longer considered acceptable, and the midwifery service was divorced from Nurse Beasley's general duties so that hospital-born babies were looked after for the first ten days of their lives by the midwife, and then discharged to the care of the local health visitor who kept an eye on them at regular clinics. When the children were five and went to school, their care was taken over by the school nurse, a new post created by the change, as before Nurse Beasley herself had run the school clinics. In effect, the job of one nurse was fragmented into separate midwifery and school nurse posts, with the District Nurse losing her autonomy and being tied to a specific doctor's practice. Now, the nurses from Storrington use the new surgery by the library as their base to check case notes and collect their list of calls for the village, and the nurses from Pulborough do the same at a Pulborough surgery.

Nurse Beasley who now works for Worthing Priority Care Trust dispelled any concerns of lack of communication between the different departments by saying "When I was the only one, I did see the babies through from birth to when they left the village school, but as the school nurses are in the adjacent room to us in the central surgery we can discuss any child that is giving cause for concern on a daily basis. In fact, recently a questionnaire came round asking whether we thought we ought to meet the school nurses monthly or two-monthly to discuss cases, and we replied 'neither' as we already saw each other on a daily basis anyway. When a child is four years old there is a form we have to fill in with details of problems he may have had, speech therapy or psychological help for example, and any medical history, or history of accidents, and we give this form and the medical notes to the school nurse so there is discussion and continuity. It's changed a bit from the old days when one of the nurses' duties was to look for scabies and nits by examining the children's hands and hair on her visits to the school; the school nurses now do the medicals and teach such things as hygiene. I don't suppose the general public knows about the way the welfare system follows through: the doctor checks the babies at six weeks and again at six months; the health visitors check general development at eight months, such things as hearing, vision, manipulation and sitting and standing, and again at eighteen months. We see them again at three years, and at four years we see them for the last time and complete the form to hand on to the school nurses; it's very comprehensive.

Cod liver oil and orange juice used to be given to the babies, free and routinely, but now the formula milk incorporates so many vitamins that this is no longer done although the vitamin A and D drops can still be obtained, but for a small price."

From about 1960 until at least 1989, the Village Hall was booked by the Pulborough doctors for $1^1/_2$ hours one weekday morning, so that patients who could not get to the main surgery could be seen. Prescriptions were written and a general surgery was run. The doctors occupied the same little room that was used as the clinic for the babies on another day. Jean Peace adds "Nurse Patsy Wright Warren came to me in 1959 and said that she was thinking of starting a baby clinic in the village and would I go and help her. So the Red Cross used to send a person to do the weighing, I did the books and a doctor was available for advice. We held it every month, the children were weighed and cod liver oil and orange juice were given out."

Dr John Ford came to live in The Gleddings, Common Hill in December 1951 with his wife Barbara. He was a partner in a practice in Pulborough, and at that time Nurse Stead was the District Nurse and Midwife for the village and was living in Nurses Cottage. She would care for any patient in the village whether their doctor practised in Storrington or Pulborough, and is remembered as a wonderful asset to the village, kind and caring. Although latterly she had a car, she is primarily remembered as cycling round the area. At that time it was the custom to deliver babies at home, and Dr Ford remembers "Once I delivered ten babies in twelve days, and was up seven nights out of ten! Nurse Stead would visit the mother and new baby twice a day for the first ten days after which she would leave the mother to cope but would call in regularly to check that she was managing. At that time the nurses had a degree of autonomy and patients would sometimes visit them with cuts and bruises, and minor ailments rather than go into the town surgery to see the doctor. The nurses gave a great personal service and the District Nurse was a power in the village, they were on call all the time, but arranged their times off by standing in for each other so that if you couldn't get one, you rang another one. They did virtually everything from caring for the babies, running the infant welfare clinics, and visiting the schools both to assist the County Medical Officer when he came to the schools, and to give health education lessons to the children. The GPs did most of the inoculations; in West Sussex we had one of the highest immunisation rates in the country. The District Nurse would look after the whole community but their energies were centred on the old and the young, as they still are, with house visits for the less able and special care for the elderly.

The whole system changed in the mid 1970s because the Royal College of Gynaecologists and Obstetricians reckoned that only they should be responsible for delivering babies. This was a bit arrogant really, as the midwives were often a great deal better at it than the doctors were because they had had so much more practice. I believe it was from that time that the domiciliary service started to deteriorate. They argued that more babies survived because of hospital delivery, but I dispute that; if a GP thought that there was going to be a problem he could always ring for an ambulance which would take the mother in to hospital, and hospitals can be a focus for cross-infection which is a problem you wouldn't get with a home delivery. Our local hospital was Worthing, but the obstetric department was later moved to Southlands Hospital which is within a mile of the West Sussex county boundary; it's 17 miles to Southlands and 18 to Chichester, or thereabouts. What would be ideal is a hospital in the middle, and the centre of population is Pulborough, where the A29 and A283 cross! I can't see them building a hospital there, though!"

Strangely enough the Parish Council Minutes show that on 28 October 1914 'It had come to the Parish Council's attention that the County Council had contemplated purchasing some land on the Common on which to build a County Smallpox Isolation Hospital.' It was unanimously agreed that 'The Parish Council of West Chiltington desire to make a most emphatic protest against the proposal of the West Sussex County Council to build a County Smallpox Isolation Hospital on the land between the three roads near West Chiltington Common. Houses are situated near by on each of these three roads, whilst the value of the surrounding property would be largely depreciated, and its development seriously interfered with, if such a proposal were to be carried out'. The Parish Council was then asked to suggest an alternative site, at a suitable price, and in January 1915 put forward two sites, one in Greatham parish, the other at the western end of Hurston Warren.

There is a letter dated 19 April 1945 to the Parish Council from Coolham Parish Council, concerning a proposal to build a Cottage Hospital for the area, as a memorial. General opinion was that such a service was urgently needed. The Clerk was instructed to reply that the suggestion was good and that the matter be further explored. There has been no further news!

It was necessary, even in the early days when the population of West Chiltington was approximately 1,244 in 1921, to have a means of local communication. Roger Harrison, the present editor of the Parish Magazine, has given the following resume of its history: "'The West Chiltington Parochial Church Council is issuing their Quarterly Leaflet in order that those living in outlying homes may, equally with themselves, have the opportunity of knowing something about coming events, and so keep more in touch with the doings of our Church and Village.' So spoke our predecessors in February 1934 and now 66 years later we are saying the same, though perhaps in less stilted writing. They go on in that first issue as follows: 'A member of our Council has kindly undertaken to distribute the leaflet, so will you please do your best to welcome it and her. In these days of stress and strain (1934! Roger added!) we do need to pull together as much as possible and in this way you may get to know some meeting you would like to attend, or find help in some other way. Please wish us God Speed. We shall welcome suggestions from any quarter. Our best wishes to you all. Communications for the next issue should be sent to Voakes by April 19th.'

How history repeats itself; in this first issue there is an acknowledgement of a gift of a 'Breeches Bible' 'because the Church was so lovingly cared for' and we have been acknowledging gifts ever since. Clubs and societies have reported what they have done and advertised what they will be doing, births, marriages and deaths, comings and goings are all included. The Rev Hall was the rector when the magazine was launched, and rectors have come and gone, frequently being the editor until Rev Lucas' retirement in 1983 when the editorship passed to me during the interregnum. I have had it ever since!

The quarterly leaflet was continued into the 1960s although by then the title had become St. Mary's Quarterly Magazine and had grown from eight to eleven pages and gone up from 1/6d to 4/- per annum. By the time Rev Ken Lucas came it was called The Roundabout, and his contribution under the heading of Parson Lucas' Diary was a wonderful comment on village life. In 1935 there were seven advertisements taking up half a page; one of which, S F Gooch at the Post Office had the telephone number West Chiltington 1. By 1998 there were over sixty advertisements from local firms advertising all sorts of domestic, business and professional services; the magazine has over twenty eight pages as well as the ads., and the cost is 25p per monthly issue.

Looking through these early numbers is a fascinating occupation - for instance one issue recalls the raising of the Altar from its 'hiding place' in the floor whence it was put at the time of the Reformation when all stone Altars were forbidden. Another issue records a meeting to decide if we should build a village hall - vote 39 for, 15 against! From time to time we have entered competitions for the best parish magazine and it was in Revd Lucas' time that we actually came second in a National Competition. I was deputed to go to Lambeth Palace to receive the prize of £25 from the Archbishop of Canterbury.

So today (1998) the circulation is 850 with 44 people delivering it round the village; it is also on sale in the shops. A network of Street Contacts has been set up to welcome newcomers to the village and the Church and to introduce them to the Parish Magazine which will tell them what is going on. The magazine is moving into the new century as typewriters and Gestetner have been left behind and it is produced by word processor."

The Reading Room in Church Street dates from 1888. The Marquess of Abergavenny and the Rector at that time, Rev Pickering, were friends, and the Marquess gave the Village a small piece of land on which it built a single room for use as a recreation and reading room for local working men on condition that if no longer required, it was to be given back to the Abergavenny Estate. It was built by Mr H Terry of Storrington and was under the control of the Rector and Churchwardens, as trustees, but it had absolutely nothing to do with the Church.

In 1926 there had been a club using the premises, but in about 1936 the West Chiltington Silver Band took over its management. For a short time it was renamed the West Chiltington Billiards and Social Club and the band also used it as a practice room which it has continued to do to the present day. For years the building deteriorated but in the early 1960s it was proposed to revive the Reading Room as a meeting room for the village and at that time there was also a plan to insert a second storey in the roof to house the Village Museum, which was then without a home. However, in July 1961 the Trustees decided to give up the idea because 'to put in a second floor would make the ceiling too low for the band because it would ruin the room acoustically'. Instead the Committee planned to wall off a third of the room to house the museum collection, and the remaining two thirds of the premises to be used for meetings, as well as storage for the equipment of the Silver Band. Work on the approved alterations was completed in 1962.

In March 1963 the Trustees formally asked if the Parish Council would take over the management and administration of the Reading Room/Museum. In due course it was confirmed that responsibility should have been taken over in 1894 by the Parish Council together with its other statutory civil duties under the Local Government Act of that year. Consequently it was agreed that the Parish Council should assume Managing Trusteeship with effect from 1st March 1964. In 1968, in view of the expenses involved, the Parish Council made enquiries as to whether it was legally possible to dispose of the building and site; correspondence from the Trustees of The Marquess of Abergavenny pointed out that if the Reading Room ceased to be used as a Parish Room, the property would revert to the Trustees as proprietor. Consequently the Parish Council agreed that such work as would make the Reading Room waterproof and prevent further deterioration should be undertaken and these matters have continued to be undertaken by the Council over the years.

The Museum is also now managed by the Parish Council; the collection was started in 1931 by Mrs Kensington, from Voakes. Conscious of the need to record in some practical way links with West Chiltington's past, Mrs Kensington founded the tiny museum. Notes, hand-written by her in 1931 state her aims:- 'This little collection of 'bygones' has been started in the hope that it may assist in keeping together some of the old work implements and handicrafts of our Village and County. During the last Century since machines have taken the place of hand work, many articles of interest are disappearing, and their uses are unknown to the younger generation. These notes are only an attempt to encourage the preservation of our local history'.

Mrs Kensington enlisted the aid of other residents who possessed curios and old things of one sort and another. Initially, local people were able to view the collection in the old bakehouse but about 1935/36 the collection was moved to Step House (opposite the Village Post Office in the village centre), which was owned by Lt-Col Kensington, where it was housed in a small room for many years. It was first put on view to the general public in 1945. Following Mrs Kensington's death early in 1951, Col Kensington continued the good work started by his wife.

At a Parish Council meeting in 1960 Lt-Col Kensington brought up the question of the Museum collection which was still maintained in Step House. Wishing to sell the building, he wanted to see the museum housed

Step House

in the old Reading Room (then used by the band). Initially the trustees felt that there was not enough room for it, so they considered extending the Reading Room. Consideration was also given to the possible alternative of another small building being erected nearby. It was felt that the Museum should be located near the Church so that the many visitors to the Church might also discover the Museum. In 1961 the Trustees applied for planning permission to make alterations to the Reading Room in order to house what had become known as 'The Kensington Collection'.

Step House was sold in March 1961. Consequently, the collection found itself without a home and was packed into suitcases to be stored at Voakes for approximately 12 months. Following the necessary alterations to the building, the collection was finally moved to its present permanent location in the Reading Room, Church Street. The Museum was re-opened to the public on 18 July 1962. In 1974 a suggestion was received from the County Council that they take over the running of the Museum and remove some of its contents. The offer was declined.

West Chiltington Museum may possibly be the smallest in the country, but it contains many items of local historic interest and quite a number not of local association. The collection includes war memorabilia, old farming implements, royal memorabilia and domestic items from times past. Slowly the original 'Kensington Collection' of approximately 200 items has grown over the years and the now contains in the region of 270. One of the oldest items is a pair of ladies' mules or overshoes dating from approximately 1715 and there is an old Prayer Book circa 1768. There is also a watchman's rattle that was used for raising the alarm in the days before there were police officers. This was one of the first articles around which Mrs Kensington began to build her collection. A stonebreaker, of 1834, from the Thakeham Workhouse is a harsh reminder of those days when in return for a night's lodgings and a meagre breakfast a vagrant tramp would thump stones to pieces; it is a solid metal tub with the stonebreaker upright in its middle.

There is a matching set of tea cup, saucer and plate, decorated with drawings of West Chiltington Church which were drawn by a German artist before and during the First World War. It was believed locally that the man in question was a member of a spy organisation and his job was to make pictures of important buildings in order to make use of them during a future German occupation! There is a flintlock pistol, together with powder flask; such a pistol was carried for protection by Colonel Kensington's great-grandfather as he rode across the then barren, unprotected Putney Heath, hideout of highway robbers. On a more peaceful note there is a blue Victorian sun bonnet, from about 1900, known as a 'slat bonnet' which women, anxious not to become sun-tanned always wore whilst out of doors.

In 1980/81 after several years of neglect, Mrs Beryl Phippen and Mrs Mary Eames spent many months cataloguing and displaying the exhibits, a transformation that resulted in the Museum as it is today.

When the century opened Queen Victoria was still on the throne; upon her death on 22 January 1901 the Parish Council unanimously expressed its sorrow and sense of loss.

In one of the earliest memories of Royal events, Bill Hampton recalls that the school children each received a commemorative mug for the coronation of King George V in June 1911, but as he was not yet of school age, he and his mother went to the Green's barn in Church Street to collect his mug. He also remembers that for years his mother used a similarly decorated commemorative jug for the milk.

The King's Silver Jubilee was celebrated in style in 1935 with a decision by the Parish Council to give every child in the Parish a half-pint handled beaker and a 6d medal. There were parades led by the band, and a fancy dress parade in which Ewen Steele, aged six, dressed up as a jockey on a Shetland pony; the highlight amongst many events being the catching of a greasy pig.

The Coronation of King George VI and Queen Elizabeth took place on 12 May 1937. There were day-long celebrations in the village in spite of the weather; in the morning there was a church service conducted by the Rev Hall, and the Westminster Service was broadcast. In the afternoon the British Legion and the Silver Band led a fancy dress procession which was judged outside the Church by Mrs Rawlinson and Miss Blake, followed by a programme of sports on the recreation ground. Each child was given a coronation mug, and there was a children's tea to follow at the Comrades Hall; the adults had tea in two sittings at the school, the catering arrangements were organised by Stanley Ridpath and his wife with a team of helpers. The food was memorable, and so was the beer because Col Kensington gave eighteen gallons of ale to the proceedings! In the evening there was a children's cinema show, followed by an adult's film show, arranged and produced by Mr S Ellis. A large audience gathered at the school to listen to a broadcast of the Homage of the Empire and to the first speech by the new King, but so many attended that the broadcast had to be

Coronation Celebrations – May 1937
Albert Mustchin at the rear of the front group

Coronation Celebrations – May 1937
Mollie Geal is the nurse, front left: Mrs Faires with Evelyn & Jean Faires are in the car

relayed to the crowd in the school playground. Finally the day was rounded off with a firework display on the recreation ground followed by a dance which went on until midnight at the Old Comrades Hall. The Parish Council Minutes show that sanction to spend money on the Coronation celebrations had to be given by the Ministry of Health, and it was agreed to levy a rate of 3d to meet the expenses. It was also hoped that a drinking fountain be provided as a permanent memorial.

Colonel Kensington was the chairman of the general committee which made all the arrangements, and he and Mrs Kensington gave a flagpole and St George's flag to the church to celebrate the coronation. Mrs Kensington designed many of the street decorations and a newspaper cutting exhorts "here is an opportunity for all patriotic ladies! On Friday 30 instant, Mrs Kensington is holding a Garland Party at Voakes. The object is to make garlands, with materials she is kindly providing, to be used in the public decoration of certain places in the parish at the Coronation. All who care to help are asked to be at Voakes by 2.30pm - 17.4.37" Unfortunately Col Kensington was watching the coronation in London so the rector stood in for him.

The Queen's coronation on 2 June 1953 was celebrated throughout the land. In West Chiltington a special projection television set was brought up from Worthing and put in the Church so that the ceremony could be viewed by more people. It was a not entirely successful idea because television projected onto a screen was not a very advanced technique and the picture was rather dim, a problem that was exacerbated by the fact that the windows had not been blacked out very well. However, the reception from the aerial attached to the war memorial was quite good. The Coronation Tea was served in The New Hall. The Parish Accounts showed that there had been a total expenditure of £91.18s.2d on the Coronation celebrations.

The Queen's Silver Jubilee was celebrated in conjunction with the Village Fayre on 11 June 1977; the Silver Band members remember getting rather wet as the weather was not too kind. Mugs were presented to all the children at the school and the village was decorated with bunting and streamers purchased by the Parish Council. A children's street party was held at Broadford Bridge and the WI gave a party for senior citizens. A message of congratulation was sent to the Queen and £600 was raised and sent to the Silver Jubilee Appeal Fund.

On 29 July 1981 the marriage of the Prince of Wales to Lady Diana Spencer was celebrated with street parties countrywide, and West

Royal Wedding Day – 29 July 1981

Chiltington was no exception. Trestle tables were set out in Church Street, Union Jacks were abundant and there was bunting across the road.

As well as these 'official' royal events is a mystery one: Gwen Smith recalls "when I was quite small, about 1933/4, I remember playing cricket one day on the common, we had a wooden box as the wicket, and this limousine came along - you never saw anything like it in your life! There was this car with two motor cycle outriders and the flag on it; we stood as scruffy little kids, little girls in long dresses and some of us had boots up our legs as we were in those days, and the little boys in short trousers. We said 'Oh look at that lovely car! Isn't it big? Doesn't it shine? What's that flag on it for?' and there was this lady in a fawn suit and matching hat with a feather, and another lady. Dad followed it along to see where it had gone; it came up past The Birches and turned left down Big Hill. This car came on two occasions and I believe it carried Queen Mary and her lady-in-waiting but people didn't seem to take much notice; my father would be working on the road and the car would pass by and he'd just doff his cap to the occupant. He didn't make any fuss, it was a sleepy village, it was lovely." There is, however, no record anywhere of Queen Mary visiting the village, so who were the lady and her companion?

Queen Mary was godmother to Diana, daughter of Colonel and Mrs FitzGeorge-Balfour who married in 1943 and lived at The Old Rectory from about 1944. (The Colonel was knighted in 1967 thereafter being known as General Sir Victor FitzGeorge-Balfour). The Queen did not attend Diana's christening in 1946, her place being taken by her proxy, Diana's grandmother Princess Galitzine. (Dr Ford (qv) adds "Colonel Balfour's great grandfather was Queen Victoria's cousin, and in their drawing room in the rectory they had a picture of a very pretty young girl which was a painting of the young Victoria, painted when she was about 18. The Colonel was a charming man and had the look of Victoria about him.") Diana is remembered as having kept her pony in the Old Rectory's field and she and her brother Robin played with the local children. When her father retired from the Army her parents were able to come and live more permanently at The Old Rectory from where they could become more involved in village life.

The Birches had been built in 1926 to begin to alleviate the housing problem but in August 1931 a circular from the Ministry of Health on rural housing was considered by the Parish Council who discussed the probable number of houses required; proposals for additional Council housing were first put forward by the RDC in January 1944.

Between May 1944 and March 1945 there were protracted discussions and site meetings but finally Col Kensington's efforts resulted in getting their proposed site approved. The approved plan called for 28 houses over 2 years, at a density of 6 to the acre. The original site at Pond Land Field suggested by the Parish Council had been adopted although the County Town Planning Officer had objected, preferring the site at Cucumber Field. The development at The Juggs was completed in 1946/47.

In August 1945 the RDC proposed a 'points' system to be used in allocating tenants to the new Council houses at The Juggs; the Parish Council put forward the following suggestions: that points for all children living at home should be equal, irrespective of age; and that there should be 1 point for each member of the family aged 18 and over fully engaged in agricultural or horticultural work. They suggested that the points scored should be regarded only as a guide and that primary consideration should be given to those resident in the Parish. It was also suggested that, where possible, a certain proportion of houses built should be set aside for single and aged people.

As a Parish Councillor for twenty years and Chairman for six, Mac Steele took a great interest in everything that went on in the village.

During the 1980s house prices had risen considerably and in 1988/9 he determined to try and find a way to prevent the young people of the village being forced to move away because of the lack of affordable housing. He negotiated the purchase of the site on which Steele Close now stands; this is a shared equity housing scheme to enable 'young villagers' to stay in the village and was the first scheme of its type in the Horsham District. In conjunction with the English Villages Housing Association and Sanctuary Housing Association, six two-bedroom houses were built to be occupied either on a shared equity or a rental basis, on land that was sold by Mervyn Webb, whose own daughter had had difficulty in finding affordable housing in the area. The Housing Association selects who will be allowed to buy from people who had been born and brought up in the village, or who have close connections here, and when the houses are sold the sale price can only keep pace with inflation, not exceed it.

It was entirely appropriate that the road was named Steele Close when the houses were officially opened in July 1994, less than two years before Mac died.

The Opening of Steele Close – July 1994
Mac Steele hands the keys for the first dwelling to Jason Francis, watched by Margot Bonnett (Clerk to the Parish) and Mervyn Webb who sold the land at a very reduced rate

On the night of 15/16 October 1987 The Hurricane, more correctly known as The Great Storm, hit parts of the South East. Having arisen between Iberia and the Azores, tracking north-east it made landfall at the Solent from where it rose to its peak of 959 millibars and cut a swathe of chaos through Bury Gap, across Wiggonholt to West Chiltington which suffered tremendous damage, until it petered out two days later in the North Sea just beyond the Wash. Roads were blocked by fallen trees, taking power lines and telephone cables with them, and the village was virtually cut-off for two days.

Ernie Gumbrell's photo shows the Green's oak tree which fell across Juggs Lane at 3am. Ernie, a great teller of stories, says that in the old days, if someone died of an infection such as pleurisy they would be buried with a small plaque, and an oak tree would be planted over the body. It is his theory that there was such a plaque underneath this old oak from a death many, many years ago. He also says that this particular oak was nearly 500 years old and could be seen from many miles away.

The local and national newspapers carried graphic reports of the difficulties being endured in the south-east; 100,000 homes were without electricity more than a week after the event, and some homes had no water or telephone. Many families only coped because neighbours rallied round to help each other; using a petrol driven chain saw, or a hand bow-saw, lanes were cleared and access to the main road achieved. The Aga or Rayburn came into its own and fed families who would otherwise have managed as the Gumbrellls managed, on jacket potatoes wrapped in tin foil in the embers of the fire, with a kettle perched on top, until they were able to borrow a camping gas stove. Those with gas for heating and cooking were better off for it was many weeks before electricity was reconnected to all the houses.

Jim Cannell, from The Birches, worked for West Sussex County Council, and he describes how the clearance began: "It just happened that I had got a call about 10.30pm for a tree that was across the road at Adversane cross-roads (there used to be two of us on duty to cover emergencies) so had collected my Alsation and set off in the Land Rover, but couldn't get past the Martlets because of fallen trees; I tried other ways and they were as bad. I radioed my mate at Billingshurst, but he couldn't get to me, so we were both stranded! About midnight we get a call from headquarters telling all County Council vehicles to get off the road because there was a hurricane coming through, although there were already trees falling. After 12.30am it just went berserk; it was cold; the wind stopped and it went completely still; the temperature came back up and it was so hot I took my coat off, and then, just before 1am, *bang*, that's when it came through. What we had had earlier was what the forecasters had predicted - a gale, force 5-6, but what we had then was force 9, sometimes force 10; winds of 100 miles an hour plus. The car was covered in red sand, blown in from the Sahara people say, that's why it was so hot. The radio in the cab went out for four or five days and I couldn't get through to the office, so I used my CB radio; don't know where I'd have been without it.

I started at The Birches and walked down the middle of the road, towards Pulborough first, cutting through the tree trunks, and eventually one of our drivers who lived at Heath Mill on the way to Pulborough and had his JCB there managed to get up to me, and we carried on from there, clearing the main roads first. He pushed the trees I'd sawn to either side of the road, at first it didn't matter if we blocked people's drives as we just had to get the main roads open for the emergency vehicles that might have been needed. But we had problems; the first was petrol for the chain saws; with no electricity the garage couldn't pump the fuel, so I had to drain the tank of my car for fuel for the saws, and then we ran out of chain-saw oil so I just had to use ordinary oil for them. You couldn't buy a chain saw for love nor money, nor the oil to go in one!

The South Wales Electricity Board, and the electricity boards from Devon and Somerset, were asked for help; they came here by helicopter and landed in the cricket field; some of the accents were so strong we couldn't understand them! Then the Ghurkas arrived; they worked barefoot up in the trees, only using their knifes for cutting the branches off the power lines, they did such a good job that the electricians could then come along and just repair the line right the way through. If they had a large branch they would borrow a handsaw but mostly they just used their knives, and one day I was looking at one of their knives, they wouldn't let you touch them, and I said something about throwing it; the sergeant heard me and spoke to the soldier and he just threw it straight across the road into a pole! The Ghurkas were wonderful, but very different: they never took sugar in their drinks, they called it 'the white death' an expression I've used ever since. Also they would cut all the pastry off the meat pies and only eat the meat with bread, they didn't touch pastry or cakes, just bread, butter and cheese. I remember they found a squirrel's drey with a baby squirrel in it which they put in their vehicle and nursed - that was shown on Southern TV. Only their sergeant spoke English which made communication difficult, but I liked them. What really kept us going was Mr and Mrs Knowles and a lady called Linda, who had an Aga and provided us with hot tea, pies and things that they cooked; they belonged to the Red Cross. Mr Williams from Monkmead allowed one of his drivers to help me and for three weeks Mr Williams would bring a Sunday dinner up for me and the family.

Because I'd worked for the County Council for thirty-odd years, they left me to get on with it, but when we'd cleared enough roads for the lorries and the JCBs to get through, which took three or four days and I've never been so tired in my life, we got instructions; we cut up the trees and took them to Yew Tree Farm in Broadford Bridge for a huge bonfire; it burned day and night for about two months. We managed to save some of the good timber which we had to cut into 16' lengths which was stored at Broadford Bridge.

We only had to clear the Council's roads, A roads first, then the B roads and bus routes, so the private lanes were left. And when I say cleared, it was only a single track down the middle of the road, with the debris pushed to the side, until we could get other vehicles in to help. The Royal Engineers came with a tank transporter and helped with a huge tree in

Fallen Oak Tree in Juggs Lane – 15/16 October 1987
Kerry Dumbrill and Kenny Duke

Greenhurst Lane and another in the Juggs which were too big for us. Other problems which you wouldn't think of: the dairy farmers had to milk by hand to relieve the cows, and then throw the milk away as the tankers couldn't get through; the farmers were a great help with their tractors. What was a problem though, were the people at weekends with their cameras, and the fact that some people wouldn't understand that we couldn't clear their drives because we had to clear the roads first. Apart from the Ghurkas' squirrel, we never saw any other squirrels, and there were no birds about, it was eerie. West Chiltington got it worst: it was bad between Melrose Stores and the entrance to Martlets, and from Stream Lane up through the Hollows and out to Voakes most of the trees and shrubs were destroyed, and Roundabout was bad too. It took a good two weeks working flat out to clear, after which I went to Jersey for a holiday, and slept most of the time!"

Even the leaves on the remaining trees were scorched black by the salt laden winds, and the area was covered in red desert sand; many women complained that it was difficult to get the windows clean again!

As the clearance work progressed and many standing trees were found to be unsafe and were removed, the full extent of the damage became apparent, with the loss of many of favourite landmark trees, including the 1937 Coronation Cedar in the recreation ground. So, early in November the Rural Preservation Society decided to replace this tree with a good sized specimen which would not look conspicuously 'new', and to fill some of the other gaps with similar 18′ high trees which would appear reasonably established overnight. A sub-committee under the chairmanship of Frank Warriner was set up and the 'Planting Of Trees after the Tempest' Plan was born. Frank explains that fund-raising efforts began; the public was invited to make donations, and if £70 were given a family could have their own named tree with a polished brass plaque. A raffle was also organised with the prize of a champagne lunch flight on Concorde.

However, in December the Government, rather slower off the mark than Frank Warriner, announced that grants would be made available to Parish Councils (but not to Preservation Societies) for replacement trees, and the West Chiltington Parish Council accordingly set up its own Tree Fund, claiming the grants and asking for public donations for many small 24″ saplings. The public was somewhat confused by these two funds so POTT's fund-raising activities ceased. There was another difficulty, that of suitable sites for mature trees. West Sussex County Council would not allow them in areas adjoining the highways, and POTT was advised against getting permission for private land because of possible problems arising from maintenance, public liability or when the property changed hands; the sites had to be on public property.

Five mature trees had already been purchased by POTT; the most important was the 18' Douglas Fir which was a replacement for the Coronation Tree, and was planted at the entrance to the recreation ground; there was a 12' Holm Oak donated by the Haigh family and planted near the front of the village hall; a 14' Gingko Biloba on Mill Lane; an 18' Tilia Petiolaris Lime in the churchyard and a 20' Field Maple donated by Joyce Pullen who had left the village but asked for the tree to be planted in the recreation ground where she had derived so much pleasure as a girl. The trees were professionally planted on 16 January 1988, exactly three months after the storm.

Two weeks later people were horrified to find that someone had cut through the 4" bole of the Fir and removed the top 12'; it was a deliberate act of vandalism as the top was left lying beside the trunk. When fund-raising ended there was a surplus of £266 which was handed over to the Parish Council's fund, so in the autumn of 1990 the Council invited POTT to select and plant another tree to replace the mutilated Fir, which the Council would pay for. An Acer Negundo was planted on 31 December 1990.

The Parish Council's main planting was along the river banks beside the recreation ground car park where willows, aspens, sorbus and horse chestnuts were planted, with four ornamental trees in Kensington Close, and a further five in the churchyard and church car park. Hayling Pond area had a copper beech as did The Common cross roads, there were three specimen native trees and five smaller ones at the school, and a row of eight oaks were planted along Broadford Bridge Road beside Willetts Farm with a further thirty trees along the road to the north. However, some of these trees also fought a battle against vandalism and many had to be replaced; this became so expensive after repeated replanting that Douglas Andrews, chairman of the Parish Council at the time, ended up by planting seedling saplings from his own garden. Young Samantha Moranne from Daux Farm planted a seedling horse chestnut that she had grown from a conker as the village united against the vandals.

The automatic reaction had been 'to clear everything and replant' but advisors from the arboricultural associations began to recommend a slower approach. They advised against burning the fallen trees and replacing the old, slow-growing hardwoods with quicker growing species just for effect, and explained that the extra light available to woodland floors would change the local ecology but not necessarily for the worse - extra bluebells and spring flowers would provide nectar and pollen early in the season, and organisms which lived on dead or rotting wood would increase and provide extra food higher up the food chain. Bird and mammal populations would change, but the animal kingdom is used to natural events such as flood, drought and severe winters, and would adapt and survive. A storm is a change, not a disaster, to nature, and while urban trees in their artificial environments would need to be replaced as a matter of priority, the countryside must not panic and try to replace everything at once. One reason why the storm took such a toll was that many of the trees that fell were of the same age, having been planted at the same time, and perhaps it would be better if country folk staggered their replanting so that, in a few hundred years, if this happened again, there would not be the same result.

Alastair Grigor wrote a poem to commemorate the work of POTT,

"'Twas when the moon was setting and the dark was over all,
The trees began to whisper, and the wind began to roll" - Tennyson
And in the early morning 'twas the trees that paid the toll - A Grigor

---

The ancient oaks down cross the Weald,
The noble pines all prone,
And silver birch - the Forest Queen -
Lying flat where they were blown
    The hurricane that autumn night
    Quite changed the Sussex scene.
    Will ravished woods e'er wave again
    Their canopies of green?
Replant - a challenge - Sussex folk,
Of hamlet, village, town.
That gauntlet now they all take up,
Their arms they won't lay down.
    West Chiltington, that envied place
    The finest in the Weald
    Here, village Hampden, he stood up
    Said 'treescape must be healed'.

"Come on" said he, "get cracking folk,
I'm going to start a fund
To pay for trees to take the place
Of those down on the ground.
 My fund I call Pee-O-Tee-Tee
 Now that is not a chamber!
 but Planting Trees that Tempest felled
 Just kindly do remember!
My raffle tickets, thirty quid,
I'm only selling fifty,
A trip on Concorde the first prize,
Now with your cheques be nifty.
 What's thirty quid - two pints of malt,
 A lunch for one at Manleys,
 A shopping trip to M & S,
 A kiddies toy from Hamleys."
But Sussex folk it is well known
They simply won't be druv,
With native cunning they can see
Iron fist in velvet glove.
 Howe'er 'nough folk then did subscribe
 To purchase well-grown trees,
 Which planted, local press announced,
 Won't blow down in a breeze.
They won't, they'll grow, but one will not
Twas cut in half by yob,
A cretinous sub-human being,
Who should be cracked on nob!
 To English Water Gardens, Thanks,
 Blue Cedar given free
 Replaces the cut-down Douglas Fir
 As Coronation Tree.
And in the golden years to come
Whatever else it got,
The village will have lovely trees
Thanks to the folk of POTT

Teddy Elliott from Roundabout Farm lost hundreds of trees, many of which should never have been growing on such light sandy soil which may explain why they fell. The oaks that came down had what is called 'the shakes' which is where the trunk has splits running up and down and is caused by the tree rocking in the ground. This timber is not worth much to a merchant, and even less when there is a glut of good wood from the storm.

West Chiltington has never been the hub of a transport network. Its location between the two north-south national Primary Routes, the A29 and the A24 and the east-west routes (A283 and B2133) have ensured its isolation and its attractiveness as a place to live.

The road network has remain unchanged over the period covered by this book, the pattern having been established over the recent centuries as a response to the movement of people and especially rural goods to the larger settlements of Storrington and Pulborough, the major towns of Worthing and Horsham and the ports of Littlehampton and Arundel.

The local roads all reflect some element of the past. Names such as Smock Alley, The Sinnocks, Stream Lane, Mill Road and The Hollows are all reminders of past activities. These roads serve the needs of the local community and provide links between Storrington and Horsham (witness the northbound commuter rush in the morning through the Hollows and The Sinnocks) and links to the Primary Road Network (green backed signs) via Storrington and Pulborough.

The local road network will remain as it is now and, apart from periodic maintenance, will probably look the same in another hundred years.

There is a bus stop on West Chiltington Road called Peacock Tree. Ivan Pullen relates how it got its unusual name: "When the lady came to live in that house she didn't like the name of it, I've forgotten what it was, so she decided to call it Peacock Tree. Father was her chauffeur-gardener at that time and, as he cut the hedges he suggested that he should make this tree look like a peacock. Then in the 1930s she moved away. When Father came back from the war the new owners of Peacock Tree discovered that it was him who had done the work before and asked him to shape it all out again as it had got all overgrown. The name has stuck and now people must wonder why." Sadly the peacock has overgrown again and is now quite unrecognisable.

Bus services have provided the motorised link between the village and the outside world for at least 60 years. The close relationship between the village and the towns and markets of Storrington and Pulborough is reflected in the bus service.

In the days of the familiar green and cream Southdown buses, Service 70 ran between Storrington bus station and Pulborough railway station via a stop at Common Hill. This service ran from 1930 until 1946 when the service was replaced by Service 1 between Worthing and Pulborough. An hourly service in each direction served Common Hill with a diversion every two hours to a stop near The Queens Head. Ivan Pullen recalls that the cost of a trip to Worthing was one shilling but in 1947 they started running double deckers to Worthing and that was half a crown. They would pick you up from your door sometimes; they picked up Jack Parsons from the pub and took him home!

Service 1 was the mainstay of bus services to the village running from 1946 until 1976 when it was replaced by Service 211 which provided an irregular 52 minute journey between Worthing and Pulborough station stopping at Common Hill. Jean Peace recalls: "in those days there was also a bus from Brighton every hour, Route 22 I think it was; it went through Pulborough to Storrington and I imagine it was the same time as the Worthing Number 1 service. We all used to catch the bus from the bottom of Fir Tree Lane into Storrington to do our shopping after which we would go to The Old Forge for a cup of tea or coffee. The bus turned round in the Square and someone would come dashing in saying 'the bus has come' and we'd all hurtle out with our shopping to catch the bus back. I also remember that once during the war when we caught that bus we had to go through the Canadian Camp and they had to open the gates at either end for us; the bus went down Monkmead Lane, not the main road as it usually did."

With the coming of bus deregulation in the early 1980s and opening up to competition, a range of operators appeared. Today the village is served by a number of services, all of which are financially supported by West Sussex County Council using Rural Bus Transport grants. The County Council, as highway authority, recognises the importance of rural bus services and the social role that they play even though their commercial viability is poor.

Horsham can be reached by a daily bus service (except Sundays) calling at Common Hill and the Queens Head. This, Service 70, has recently been introduced by Compass Travel. The same company operates Service 73 from The Queens Head via Common Hill and Storrington to Amberley Railway Station. This runs three times a day and links with current rail services.

An additional east-west service, Stagecoach Service 1, from Midhurst to Worthing calls at Common Hill hourly and links the village to these destinations and Storrington and Pulborough.

The present day sees the village connected to the outside world by a bus service with similar frequencies and destinations to those that have existed for the last 60 years. Unfortunately the old village no longer has a direct service to Worthing and Pulborough but the Compass service is intended to link with it.

The inclusion of rail services in the transport section is simply to indicate that the current vogue for 'integrated transport' has been with the village for many years. The bus operators have long realised the need to connect with mainline rail stations and the bus services above (Services 70, 1, 211 and the current 1, and 73) did and still do just that.

Prior to the swinging of Dr. Beeching's axe in the 1960s it was possible to get a bus to Pulborough Station and connect with the rail services to the south, to London and to Midhurst and Petersfield.

The local stations of Pulborough and Billingshurst have changed little over the years and, apart from the changes in livery over the last decade and the absence of the on-site local station managers, it is quite easy to reflect back to the headier days of steam.

The local minibus service was started as a result of the efforts of the Pulborough and District Community Care Association in October 1973, who recognised the need to provide assistance to those people living in remote areas, off the bus routes, who by reason of old age or infirmity were unable to use public transport and did not have the use of a car.

Mrs Rita Cockburn happened to own an old but serviceable 12 seater minibus which she offered to lend for a six month trial period from November 1974 to assess the need for the service, which ran on Friday mornings and proved a great success. As the service became more widely known it became more popular and fund-raising began, to allow the Association to obtain its own minibus, which it acquired at cost from Harwoods Garage, in December 1975. West Chiltington was included in the scheme, which had previously only run in Pulborough, on 1 January 1976.

The bus should have had a Public Service Vehicle licence, which would have defeated the object of a voluntary service operated by volunteer drivers, but this was circumvented by operating the minibus scheme as a club. Another problem was the Southdown Bus Company's accusation that the Association was 'poaching' its passengers, but the situation was defused by the Minibus Act of 1977.

Today the Community Minibus Association serves local rural communities; West Chiltington having the bus every Thursday when passengers are taken to Storrington, both in the morning and the afternoon, and to the Mothers Union meeting in the Church Hall on the first Thursday of the month. The bus also goes to Worthing every other Tuesday, and there are outings to places of interest. The service relies entirely upon the time and effort of a band of volunteer drivers and escorts, without whom the residents of West Chiltington would not be able to visit the shops, hairdressers or coffee shops.

By the beginning of this century interest in the motor car was increasing, and with the unmade roads splashing mud onto the cars, it was difficult to identify the offenders of the few regulations that existed to protect other road users. So, in 1903 the Motor Car Act was introduced, causing vehicles to be licensed annually and to have, and display prominently, a registration mark for which they were charged £1 for the registration fee and 5/- for the licence. The speed limit was raised to 20 mph but there were heavy fines, which could be levied now the offenders could be identified, for speeding and reckless driving. However, the car grew in popularity and numbers, and in 1920 the Roads Act was passed requiring Councils to register all vehicles at the time of licensing with an individual number on a plate. The first registration marks had been made up of one letter with one number; the first, A 1, being issued by London County Council in 1903, followed later by two letters and four numbers but by the mid 1930s this format was exhausted in some areas and a new system of three letters and three numbers was introduced. West Chiltington came under the Brighton Registration Office which had eleven apparently unrelated pairs of letters, and the system worked by using AOP 1 to AOP 999 and following with BOP 1 to BOP 999 and COP etc right through the eleven pairs of letters prefixing each with A, B, C, through the alphabet, excepting certain letters such as I, Q, Z. By the mid 1950s even this combination was exhausted, so the letters and numbers were reversed to 1 DOP etc. As more and more cars came onto the roads, the numbering system was used up ever faster, so that from 1963 a suffix letter was added, thus HOP 379 A; the registration year running from 1 January, although this was changed to 1 August in 1967. By 1983 they were running out of numbers yet again, and the suffix became a prefix, thus A 475 KOP which should last us through the century!

The early 1930s saw the beginnings of the electrification of West Chiltington. In October attention was drawn to the dangerous state of the pavement in Church Street caused by The Electric Light Company, who after laying their underground cable, had failed to leave the pavement in an even state. Electric light was installed in the school by the end of 1935 and in the Village Post Office and Stores in 1937. Also in 1937 the Steyning Electricity Company was asked by the RDC to lay underground, a length of low tension cable which it had wished to erect overhead along Westward Lane.

A press cutting from August 1938 stated: 'There is a good deal of indignation in West Chiltington at the action of the local electricity supply company in raising its charges. Apparently consumers have been informed that if they do not signify their acceptance of the new charges within a certain time they will cease to be afforded a supply. Some have signed under protest and others have so far refused to sign. It is understood that the Parish Council is to be asked to take up the matter', which must have been resolved because by April 1939 the village had been provided with electricity. There was general agreement that poles should be removed if possible and the Electricity Company be pressed to put cables underground.

At the turn of the Century West Chiltington's water supply came from numerous natural springs and wells around the parish. In December 1907 the Parish Council noted that the North Sussex Gas and Water Company was negotiating for the purchase of the spring rising in the meadow at Naldretts. The following resolution was forwarded to the Thakeham District Council: 'the Parish Council of West Chiltington, in view of the grave risk run by tapping the village water supply, emphatically protests against any proposal or scheme which may be promoted by the North Sussex Gas and Water Company for taking the spring rising in the meadow at Naldretts to supply Pulborough, Billingshurst and district with water, and earnestly hopes that the Rural District Council will support it in its protest'. This protest resulted in the North Sussex Water Company agreeing 'that the wells and springs at West Chiltington are not to be interfered with'.

By 1928 however, the Parish Council had to ask the Rural District Council to supply a good and sufficient supply of drinking water, fit for use, to The Birches. Early in 1929 the RDC had provided details of the new Water Supply Scheme but parishioners felt that the scheme was not required; even today residents will say "Our good supply of water came from a deep underground stream and tasted like tonic water - and sparkled like it, too. The local water was not the hard limey sort that we have now; that's caused by the treatment the water gets nowadays and the fact that half comes from bore holes and half from the rivers. We are not best pleased that we've lost our lovely water which was free, and now have to pay for something which is not as tasty!"

It was decided that a referendum be taken of the whole parish to find out whether they were or were not, in favour of a public water supply for the village and Common, for which the parish must find £4,620 as the West Chiltington contribution towards the initial cost. The results of the referendum were known by April 1929. Votes showed that of the 236 sent out, 200 were returned: 172 were against and 28 for it. It was therefore agreed that the Council's objections be conveyed emphasising that 'the parishioners neither wanted nor could afford the scheme, that it would only serve a small area which was primarily agricultural not residential, that there had been no complaints from the Ministry of Health, and that the Council objects to being brought into the scheme merely to help Pulborough and Storrington.'

At a Parish Meeting held in July 1929 it was also agreed that a petition be sent to the Ministry of Health to express in strongly worded terms that: 'The public of West Chiltington had never asked for a piped supply and has voted 172-28 against it; there has never been a shortage of water in the Parish and the only houses with a deficient supply were the Council Cottages! No one had complained about the state of the wells in the Parish and no samples of well water had been taken except from those on the pipe line.' The final point made was that this was a poor Parish and could not afford the scheme!

In spite of this opposition, in 1934 the RDC was asked to carry the water main around Broadford Bridge, there being a serious shortage there, and in 1936 the Horsham RDC advised the Parish Council that they were laying water mains outside their district to connect with the existing mains in West Chiltington Parish, at Coneyhurst Common. A public inquiry was held in November 1940 on the proposal of the Councils of the Rural Districts of Chanctonbury and Horsham to borrow £186,840 for works of water supply. Apparently in the Horsham area bore holes had silted up, and it had been laid down that areas with water should pass on surplus water and not make a profit; thus the scheme was mainly for the benefit of Horsham. After much discussion the Parish Council stated that the idea should be deferred until after the war, on the grounds that the Government has asked that all possible economies should be taken.

The sewerage system was also of concern to the Parish Council. In 1928 they had to ask the RDC to put the drainage system into good order at The Birches as the state of things were considered to be very unsatisfactory and a menace to public health.

In 1944 the Parish Council discussed a comprehensive questionnaire on post war development that had been received from the RDC; in respect of the question on sewerage the Parish Council replied that 'drainage in the Parish is very unsatisfactory but the Parish Council realises that other areas and problems must be given priority'.

Early in 1946 the question of sewerage was again raised, as it appeared that this was not being absorbed by the soakaway in Church Gardens Meadow, but overflowing onto the ground. In May 1946 the village drainage in general came under discussion and it was conceded that the only real cure was the provision of main drainage. The problems concerning the drainage from the village, the school and the new council houses continued but by November 1948 a comprehensive sewerage scheme for the major part of the district was proposed by the RDC. It was not until March 1963 that the sewerage scheme at the Common was almost completed with the village scheme commencing shortly thereafter; the whole scheme took 18 months to two years to complete.

In the early part of the century the disposal of refuse caused many problems to the Parish Council. In November 1904 the Parish Council found it necessary to ask the Rural District Council to remove the heaps of refuse in front of the houses from the corner of East Street up to Hatches Cottages. In 1921, a circular from the West Sussex County Council entitled 'Rats and Mice (Destruction) Act 1919' was discussed and the Parish Council informed the County Council that 'in the opinion of this Parish Council the main centre of infestation of rats in this parish is in Hatches Estate, now the property of the West Sussex County Council, and this Parish Council is also of the opinion that the old method of paying a certain sum per tail is the most efficacious way of dealing with the matter'.

In October 1932 the matter of refuse dumping and collection was discussed by the Parish Council, and it was decided that the method then in force, whereby each householder was responsible for the destruction of his own refuse, should be unaltered. There should not have been a problem because all organic waste could be composted, and, as everyone had open fires cardboard and paper were burned. There was no plastic or polythene, and empty tins and bottles (such as corned beef, Coleman's mustard, boot polish, evaporated milk and tinned fruit) were buried in the garden. In 1935 however discussions took place concerning a possible refuse collection scheme for the parish, and the Chanctonbury District Council were asked what steps they were considering taking in this matter. In 1936 the District Council provided details of the Comprehensive Refuse Collection Scheme they were considering for the disposal of household refuse, but not all areas were to be included. The Parish Council indicated that it felt that some sort of scheme was essential 'provided that the rate did not exceed 4d, and that the collection of night soil was made a special charge on those who benefited only'.

For a period of time dustbins were collected from the back door, but in 1996 the Parish Council was informed that the Horsham District Council were to introduce wheeled bin collection from the kerbside for every house in the district. All parts of the district were provided with plastic wheeled bins for refuse collection by the Spring of 1998.

Dustbins Old and New

Chapter 9

The Church

In this parish we have a rector rather than a vicar, and the reason for this dates back to medieval times when the parish system was established. That is, our country was divided up into parishes with a 'parson' (the person acting legally on behalf of the Church of England) responsible for the spiritual care of all its inhabitants.

If the parson received the use of a house, church-owned land which he could farm (called glebe land), and tithes (a tithe was one tenth) of the produce of the land within the parish boundary, then he was called a rector. However, if the land was owned, for example, by a monastery then the income from the glebe land and the tithe income were paid to the monastery, which appointed a parson to look after the parish. He was

The Church – about 1910

called a vicar in that he acted vicariously (as a substitute) for the monastery. Both rectors and vicars have the same rights and duties.

Tithe rent charges were abolished in 1936 and all glebe land is now owned by the local diocese. Although the ancient titles are still used, both rector and vicar are now paid centrally by the Church Commissioners.

At the beginning of the century there was more than one church in the parish; The Congregational Union started its Mission in West Chiltington around 1895. Founded by George Scutt from Mare Hill it first met in a room over a carpenter's shop in Church Street, then moved to a disused hay loft near the mill and finally to a cottage and barn at Roundabout. In 1904 the first Chapel was built on land just south of Holly and Ivy Cottages on Common Hill, owned by Mr Hurl who gave the Chapel a 999 year lease. In 1919 when Mr Barkworth bought these cottages he wanted to build a garage where the Chapel was, so he offered to buy the land and another site on the Common, transferring the Chapel to this new site. Not only would he transfer the Chapel at his own expense, but enlarge it, as it was very well attended. Eventually the Chapel was moved in September 1924 and officially reopened in November; during the move services were held in the Laundry, Little Hill, thanks to Mr Hornsby, Secretary to the Chapel.

Before it was moved the Chapel was twice nearly burned down. The first time was January 1923 when two of the lamps that had been left alight from the morning service to keep the place warm for Sunday School at 3pm, flared up and filled the place with black, oily smoke and soot, and some of the interior wood cladding was too hot to touch. The second time was in April the following year when a youth smoking on the Common set fire to the gorse and heather; quick action by passers by and local residents saved both the Chapel and Nurses Cottage.

The Chapel was non-denominational and was originally called the Mission Hall, but became the West Chiltington Congregational Church when it moved, and the Free Church in 1925 as they wanted to attract members from other non-conformist churches. It did not look much like a chapel, being based on a typical Sussex barn structure with a brick base, timber frame, tongue and grooved timber inside and green corrugated iron cladding outside. It was similar in structure to The Comrades' Hall (which was also built in the 1920s), and comprised a very small entrance hall leading to the main hall of 40' by 16' with a vestry on the east side and staging for the minister on the south side. The congregation sat on wooden pews, and the building was heated by a large 'tortoise stove' at first, but this was replaced by radiant electric heaters high up on the walls. It was cold and draughty in the winter, but perhaps people were hardier then!

It was used every Sunday by both the children from The Common as a Sunday School, and by some of the adults for services. Elsie Cattell says that she used to walk from Huntleys to the Sunday School held in the school building where they learned their catechism in the morning, prior to their trooping into Church at 11.00 for the main service, then walk home; to Sunday School on the Common and back in the afternoon, and back to Church with her parents in the evenings. She still sits in the same pew she and her family have occupied since she was a girl!

The Chapel had a thriving Sunday School of about 70 children; but this gradually dwindled when a new Church was built at Mare Hill on the Pulborough boundary, perhaps due to a reliable Southdown bus service and the increased use of motor cars. The old Mare Hill Chapel which was situated next to The White Horse in Pulborough has now been sold and is an antique shop, although in its glory days Jomo Kenyatta was known to have preached there once.

Miss King played the harmonium for the services, which were of an evangelical inclination. Occasionally there were wonderful magic lantern slide shows, the fuzzy images projected onto a sheet entranced the children. These slides were of an uplifting nature, showing such things as Missionaries Converting the Heathen, and on Sunday afternoons the children would sing hymns and have Bible readings. One of the highlights was the annual outing, often to Worthing or Littlehampton in a charabanc. Joy Adams recalls that in the 1930s she used to get a halfpenny a week after Sunday School, which made the weekly lessons more acceptable. When times were hard when her father was out of work, her mother would send up the road for two pennyworth of sweets instead, which were divided up amongst the six children, a saving of one penny. Every Christmas there was a Sunday School party with a tree as tall as the room and presents, which became better the more times you had been to Sunday School; one year Mrs Barkworth gave crackers and handed out the presents. In 1923 there was a Christmas entertainment as well; there was only seating for 90 in the audience, but between 130-140 came so it must have been crowded. George Hornsby helped out, and the children went from the time they started school until they were about fourteen.

Miss Bolwell, who was a teacher at the Council School, became Sunday

School Superintendent following George Scutt. She also played the organ and in 1921 she founded The Snowdrop Band which she ran jointly with Mrs Wharton. By 1922 there were about 30 members and there is a press report of them having an Open Air Fete and Entertainment at the Laundry Meadow on the Common (where Flowerdown, Trees and Woodstock are now). It included a maypole dance and a sale of work to raise funds, the boys contributing raffia work and the girls did 'dainty pieces of fancy work and garments'. Mrs Coles from Woodshill opened the Fete. By the autumn of 1924 The Snowdrop Band had grown to such an extent that it had to be divided into two groups; the Rev Murray, a retired Baptist minister who lived in the village, led the boys while the girls remained with Miss Bolwell and Mrs Wharton. Connie Slater recalls that by the 1930s there was just a group of about six to eight girls aged between about ten and twelve who met once or twice a week at Miss Bolwell's house, Malt Cottage. There were nature walks, poetry readings and discussions, and handicrafts such as embroidery, followed by a glass of squash. Each autumn she would give each girl a flower pot with soil and a snowdrop bulb, and the best one won a prize. Once a year there was a present for each girl. Although she did not have much money, she was a kind-hearted soul who gave a lot to the girls.

Miss Bolwell having retired, it appears that the Snowdrop Band ceased as Miss King, who had taken over as organist, ran a children's organisation called the Sunrise Band every Tuesday evening instead. Miss King resigned in 1941 and ran a Mission from a building in the garden of her house, Viewlands in Nyetimber Lane (see next section).

For many years the Chapel ran a Helping Hand Slate Club which had its annual share-out in December - a way of saving for Christmas.

Services were held until the end of 1967 and the building was still used as a youth club, run by Mr Knox, until in 1970 the Chapel was sold to Peter Knowles who used it as a printing works until his retirement in 1994. Just before the sale in 1970 fire again tried to claim the building; the Rev Desmond Bending and two young people were tidying up the outside and started a bonfire which got out of hand. The water had been cut off prior to the sale so it was fortunate that one of the men working at the Telephone Exchange behind the building had been a member of the London Fire Brigade and used his hose and water supply! The building was finally demolished in 1997 and a house called Chauntry Cottage was built on the site.

In the early 1900s Mr and Mrs King had come from Surrey and had built a weekend cottage called Viewlands in Nyetimber Lane, which was just a sandy lane at that time. The Kings were connected to the Evangelical Church in Worthing (which has since been demolished) and they had a small Chapel built on their land. One of the builders of the cottage and Chapel was a converted ex-seaman called 'Sailor' Compton; he was an evangelical who held open air children's meetings at Washington and West Chiltington. The Viewlands mission was entirely 'faith maintained', there was no income except in answer to prayer, but they kept going. When Mr and Mrs King died prior to the Second World War there was a short gap in the services, during which unfortunately, Miss Nellie King, their daughter, fell out with the main Congregational Church and set up her own Sunday School in opposition, in Viewlands, so Nyetimber Lane was known thereafter by the children as 'Miss King's Lane'.

Sue Overton-Smith recalls: "I was three when I went to Viewlands Mission Sunday School in 1951; Miss King was a wonderful lady. She used to play the harmonium and, in the winter we always had a roaring log fire. We would be joined by old Mr Ford who lived next door; he wore a hat and had a long white flowing beard. Different speakers came each week from the Tabernacle in Worthing, including Mr Newbold who gave us pictures with biblical texts on them when we managed to find the appropriate verses in the Bible, Mr Harris who seemed very elderly, and Mr Windfield. These men often used flannelgraphs (where a board covered with material was used as a background for felt cut-outs which could be moved around, a bit like the modern fuzzy-felt) to help tell Bible stories. There were also two men who came from America, with a tape recorder; they had been missionaries and taught us a song beginning 'God sees the little sparrow fall…' and finishing with …'I know he loves me too.' There were two young men, probably teenagers, who also taught us, as did Miss King herself; she was very good at telling us stories and I remember the way she said 'Amen' several times during visiting speakers' prayers."

Earlier Christmases in her Chapel are fondly remembered by Brian Ruff who says: "Mr Cowdray from Storrington was always Father Christmas; we always knew it was him, but it was great fun. Miss King provided the presents from all the collections during the year. In the summer she organised garden parties, and outings; I remember Swanbourne Lake at Arundel because of the boats that they had there, and our sandwiches for picnic lunch. In the autumn we had apple bobbing and games with the apples hanging from washing lines, which we had to catch with our teeth, and there were treasure hunts at the back of Heathfield Copse." Sue continues "We also used to have Christmas parties with a delicious tea and Father Christmas, who also gave presents to our parents who had come to listen to us recite. Our summer outings were to Bognor, Leith Hill or Chessington Zoo, and we had a bonfire party on 5 November with potatoes baked in the ashes. Before I started school I used to go with my mother to prayer meetings on Wednesday afternoons during which I remember resting my head on Miss King's lap, and we also used to go to Mother's Union meetings at Miss Wright's in Harborough Gorse."

Miss King delighted in her Sunday School children but Elva Lipscomb (née Johnson) says that her father, a strict man, would not allow her to go to the fun and games at Miss King's because he considered them a sort of bribery to encourage children away from the other Chapel.

One of the people who drove the preachers to West Chiltington was David Summers, and when Miss King died in 1967, he and his wife were requested by the trustees to continue the Child Evangelical work from Viewlands. They lived in the house from 1967 to 1988, and, in addition to the continued use of the Chapel, Viewlands became the centre for a county-wide mission for children. The land was sold to developers in 1988 and Mr and Mrs Summers moved to Storrington. Houses were built on the site, one of which is called 'Kingswood'.

The continuing health of the church depends in part on the enthusiasm of its young people so various Sunday Schools have played their parts in the memories of the village. The Parochial Church Council Minutes show in 1934, under the terms of the Trust Deed, a Sunday School was held in West Chiltington School (cost 2/6d when the fire was lit and 1/6d without it) and decisions made about what religious instruction should be taught in the village school. Tim Fooks continues "The Sunday School is next mentioned in 1955 when the then Rector's daughter Felicity Williams used to take afternoon Sunday classes, and the principle of keeping the post in the family carried on in 1959 when 'Tiggy' Jones the rector's wife, took on the responsibility. By the 1960s responsibility was passed to Margaret Jones the local electrician's wife, who brought light of a non-electrical variety to the children! In their various ways every Rector has developed youth work; they have been supported in this by a long list of dedicated and enthusiastic helpers."

The Rev Lucas was greatly helped in his Sunday School work by Duncan Green, a young, qualified youth leader with marked gifts of leadership among teenagers, who, with his wife Janet started a Church youth group for 14-18 year-olds, called the Cygnets, and a Bible study group for 10-12 year-olds called the Admirals. The youngsters also undertook painting and repair works, and in 1980 helped to clear and gravel the church car park. Tim Fooks continues: "Over the subsequent years other villagers, most notably the Knowles, Steele, and Overton-Smith families have run the Sunday School. In 1998 Pam Wells took over and instituted an annual party, most of which involved getting very wet in the Wells' swimming pool!

With the arrival of Gerald Evans as Rector the Sunday School was renamed Junior Church, and an effort was made to make St Mary's a 'child-friendly' place for worship: the Family Service was reformed, he worked closely with the school, and three families arrived on the scene with keen parents and appropriately aged children. Thus the Junior Church flourished with about 25 children, and for the first time was able to run two classes: one for 3-6 year-olds and one for 7-11s, but the problem of larger numbers was that they overflowed the Church Hall into the Youth Hall where, despite the heating system, the only way to stay warm was to exercise the children vigorously for several minutes and at regular intervals!

Musical talent is provided by guitarists Liz and Paul Appleton and music plays an important part in the meetings. Unofficially renamed The Alive and Kicking Group in defiance of the trend for church falling numbers, Junior Church runs projects such as the Easter tea-towel idea and cake making for elderly residents. It is hoped the children's work will continue to provide a dynamic, fun and friendly introduction to the wonders of the Christian faith and its relevance life as effective members of the community, in the new century, under the new management of Rev Kevin O'Donnell." Kevin himself adds: "When I was inducted on 15 April 1999, I became the youngest Rector of St Mary's for some time, reflecting the changing profile of the village; not so long ago this had been largely a retirement village but is so no longer. Younger professional families, commuters to Horsham, Guildford the South Coast and London, people working from home with faxes and the Internet have changed the age profile so that it must be about 50/50 for workers and retired. My brief was to reach out to the new villagers and develop services for young families and young people; I have added a short, lively Family communion service every third Sunday in the month, and a worship group with modern instruments. I also realise that Sunday mornings are lie-in time after all the rushing about during the week and clubs/shopping on Saturdays so the youth services now start at 11.00am."

On the wall in the south aisle of the church is a list of the Rectors of the Church from 1274 to the present time. One can read the list of names, wondering about these men, and the contribution each made to the on-going life of the Church of Christ in the village of West Chiltington. The list is incomplete, for the first name is dated 1274, but the church itself dates from the early 12th century. We have no record of the first rectors of the Norman church, nor of the priests who held office in the earlier church, which we know from its mention in Domesday Book stood at the centre of the tiny village of only about 20 households in Saxon times. Much information pertaining to this earlier period is covered in Sylvia Saunders-Jacobs' books on the village and the church, by archives in the museum and by excellent notes written by Gladys Engledow. This chapter has largely been compiled from Parish Magazine articles and PCC minutes; with the changes in our lives now occurring so fast it has become recognised how important records are. However, in 1926 it was noted that the Church Register for 1638-1711 had been missing for some years. It was not until 1930 that there was talk of purchasing a safe for the storage of records, but that only seems to have been a tin box on the vestry floor! In 1948 the Diocesan Archivist sent a letter to the PCC emphasising the importance and value of old Church Records as a source of information about the village, so the PCC agreed to spend £17 on having them repaired and rebound. They were then given to the Archivist at the Diocesan Registry in Chichester for safe keeping, but the current registers continued to be kept in tin boxes on the vestry floor and it was not until 1979 that new measures were passed to preserve them.

Throughout the life of the Church it has been maintained, improved and embellished by gifts and donations from parishioners, often in memory of a loved or respected friend. It is impossible to list these gifts here, but information may sometimes be obtained from the church office.

Andrew Caldecott (1898-1928) was the first rector of the new century; he was liked and respected by his parishioners. He was said to know every inch of the parish, and it was he who wrote an attractive booklet, a history of this part of West Sussex, which is still a valuable source of information. He also inaugurated the first Parish Magazine, and was influential with the Lord of the Manor in getting permission to build the Comrades' Hall on his land. He carried into the twentieth century the well-founded tradition in West Chiltington of rectors who have cared for their Church and won the loyalty of their parishioners; a girl of that time remembers that he would give her and her friends sweets as they ran home from school.

He chaired the meeting at which the first Parochial Church Council was elected on 16 April 1920, following the Church of England Enabling Act. Mr R W Mills, the headmaster of the school, was appointed secretary at that first meeting, where the only business seems to have been the reading of some letters expressing concern about the delay in erecting the war memorial.

In 1922 Mr Green was appointed sexton at a salary of £10; his main duty was as grave-digger. In 1926 the fee for grave digging was put up from 10/- to 15/- for parishioners, but remained at £1 for non-parishioners. Occasionally the sexton would ring the church bell with one of the ropes that hung by the chancel steps, but when Mr Pullen was employed to do this the wage was 2/6d per Sunday. This contrasts with Robert Gripps who was only paid 1/- to blow the organ bellows in 1928; by 1939 the 'bellows boy' was still only paid 1/- per week.

The Church before restoration in 1882

The appointments of People's Warden and Rector's Warden are made annually by the people and Rector respectively and their job is to handle the secular and legal affairs of the parish. In the case of West Chiltington this includes the rental that the railway has to pay to the Church for allowing passage over its land.

The Parochial Church Council records have one or two amusing insights of the working of the committee; in 1926 Mr Swan, the Rector's Warden who had been the last ambassador to the Tsar of Russia, offered the committee a supply of dry faggots so that the whole PCC could test the

Church Interior with bell ropes – pre-1951

new fire extinguisher! At the start of the century the church was heated with a stove which had to be lit on Fridays in winter to get the building warm enough for Sunday services; lighting was by candles or oil lamps.

In 1924 there is a minute that Mr Mills had suffered a loss in salary of £25 because average attendance at the school had dropped below one hundred. It was pointed out that this was a national problem and that little could be done except to urge employers to employ married men with children where possible!

When Rev Caldecott retired there were 106 people on the Electoral Roll; 88 residents signed a 'Memorial' regretting his going and requesting that the curate, the Rev Hall should be strongly recommended for the living.

So in 1928 after a very brief interregnum George Hall came to the parish where he stayed for twenty years and is remembered as being tall and thin with a nice wife; he also rang the church bells. He had been ordained deacon in 1912 and priest a year later; in 1914 he had gone to Newfoundland where he spent 14 years.

Almost the first thing that needed attention was the purchase of Church Garden Meadow from the Rev Caldecott for future use as a burial ground. It was realised that sometime in the foreseeable future the original churchyard would have filled up; the final spaces in the graveyard were reserved for people such as widows whose husbands were buried in the original part, or elderly couples who had booked their places. The churchyard had been extended just before the First World War; it was extended again after the Second War when a tarmac path was laid from the church door down the slope to the new area to prevent accidents occurring to coffin-bearers slipping on the grass.

Another expensive item was 'to put the frescoes into a fit state of preservation'. It was to be done under the supervision of the Director of the London School of Art, Professor W Tristram, and was completed by July 1929 at a cost of £50. Appeals were set up to fund both these expenses but some money came out of Church funds.

In November 1928 there was a rather unholy row over the Communion service; the Rector had introduced a choral communion which seemed to the organist Mrs Thomas, like a Papist Adoration of the Sacrament and it went against her conscience. After playing for it for several Sundays she asked the Rector to allow her to retire; he refused but brought in another organist to play. Evidently most of the choir sympathised with Mrs

Church Outing – 1920s

Thomas whose appointment had not been terminated, neither had she resigned, so they walked out of the choir stalls and either left, or sat in the body of the church, notably silent when it came to Communion. The tale was reported in both the local and the national press, and a special PCC meeting was called to discuss the matter. Capt Thomas regretted the impasse with his wife and suggested she should have been allowed to state her case, but the Rector was clearly angry at what he considered her interference. Henry Meeten, who also did not like the Rector's Anglo-Catholic practices, said that the petition for Rev Hall to be Rector had come from a small percentage of newer residents in the parish, few of whom attended the Church, so were a minority. A point was made that the Rector should give some heed to the people who paid him - the tithe payers.

In the end it was agreed that Mrs Thomas be asked to play the organ until the end of the year when her resignation would be accepted, but it is not quite clear how the story ends although Capt Thomas left to join the Congregational Mission Chapel. One can only suppose that Mr Mills did not like Choral Communion either as he resigned as choirmaster at the same meeting, but was given a handsome striking clock in appreciation of his work during a difficult period.

A happier note is struck by Elsie Pullen who remembers the annual Summer Fete in July, held in the Rectory Garden; Pulborough church had its Summer Fete the following week so they never clashed. There were little stalls in the garden, and Elsie recalls that one year when the envelope containing the wining number for the Mystery Parcel was opened no-one claimed the number; the Rector's wife was asked to call out the first number that came into her head - 21 - and it was Elsie's ticket. The Mystery Parcel was as full as a hamper and much appreciated.

At the Quinquennial Inspection many repairs were found to be necessary; to the bells; to the headstones in the churchyard; to the roof; and spraying against death watch beetle. In 1933 electricity was installed and the oil lamps were sold for £5.

In 1934 there were discussions on how to improve the young men of the parish 'by inviting them to Church and providing suitable and profitable occupation in the evenings', and how to raise funds for the working party making clothes for distressed areas as this was at the height of the Depression.

The old Rectory in the Hollows had been enlarged and improved in 1873 with finance from a mortgage from Queen Anne's Bounty. (Queen Anne's Bounty was a fund established in 1704 to receive and use ecclesiastical money that had previously been confiscated by Henry VIII and which then became the property of Queen Anne, to supplement the incomes of the poorer clergy. The fund was abolished by the Tithe Act and in 1948 Queen Anne's Bounty and the Ecclesiastical Commission were combined to form the Church Commission.) The present Rectory was purchased in 1937, with a mortgage from Queen Anne's Bounty, and with the proceeds from the sale of the Old Rectory.

The last years of Rev Hall's time in West Chiltington were overshadowed by the problems of the Second World War. PCC records show the difficulty of travel for the committee members and parishioners with the blackout, no buses on Sundays and petrol rationing, air raid precautions, appeals for parishioners to serve as Air Raid Wardens, and of classes of first aid training; even the church had to obey the blackout regulations and only use candles. There was a stirrup pump, a few buckets of water and some sandbags in the church in case of a hit. The population of the village was increased by 20% by official evacuees, and there were many unofficial evacuees also, all to be absorbed into village and congregational life. In 1947 when there were still difficulties and the congregations were dwindling, people with cars were exhorted to give lifts to those without transport, and Mrs Rawlinson (Major Rawlinson was People's Warden at this time) suggested that two evening services per month be held in her house, Harbolets, at Broadford Bridge.

Having led and encouraged his parishioners through the difficult years of the war George Hall left for his next appointment, taking with him gifts and love and exchanging parishes with the Rev WHC Williams, Rector of Great and Little Snoring in Norfolk, who thus became the next Rector of St Mary's, West Chiltington.

William Harold Cecil Williams arrived in 1948 and is remembered as a very popular Rector, who used to cycle round the village, waving and calling a cheerful greeting to everyone whom he met. Fortunately there was little traffic in those days!

From records of the time one gathers that he was very energetic and hardworking, and very successful in maintaining the close link of the Church with village concerns and activities. He restarted the Parish Magazine in 1950 which had had to stop publication during the war because of the paper shortage; his family were instrumental in founding West Chiltington Dramatic Society; and also took a leading part in fundraising for the repair of the Church spire. There was a problem here though, substantial repairs had been needed for some time but a permit was required from Timber Control so the work was delayed until 1950.

The Choir
From left: Stan Gooch, Bernard Crabbe, Taffy Horler, Eric Streeter, Rev Williams

The Rector had a full programme of three, sometimes four, services on Sundays; took the services at Broadford Bridge, and held a Sunday School on Sunday afternoons. The services were all according to the traditional Book of Common Prayer pattern, and there were at first no vestments or altar furnishings in use. During this period various gifts of altar linen and altar frontals were made and in 1950 an oak chest was installed to contain the altar frontals when not in use.

Various changes were made in the Church. In 1949 the brass eagle, which was regarded as not in keeping with other Church furnishings, was replaced by the present oak lectern. New oak altar rails were set in place and dedicated in 1952. Very notably, in 1956 the old harmonium which was pumped by lads from the village was replaced by a Walker organ, which has given excellent service until recently. The wooden pipes at the back were so riddled with woodworm that it was a joke for the boys blowing to watch the worms being blown out, only to crawl back again! This old organ was sold for the value, of £50, of its metal pipes. The Walker organ cost £1,450, a lot of money for the Church to raise in those days.

It is interesting for us today, in 1999, as a new Vestry is being built, to note that it was in 1957 that mention was first made of the need of a new Vestry, as the present one was considered to be too small to accommodate clergy and the Churchwardens, an opinion that must have been echoed repeatedly for 40 years since, until at last the problem is being solved.

Harold Williams was succeeded by the Rev Raymond Morgan Jones in 1958, who had spent most of his ministerial career as a chaplain in the Royal Navy. West Chiltington was his first and only parochial appointment.

This was a period during which the population of the parish increased very rapidly; when he arrived there were 124 on the Electoral Roll but by the time he left there were 287. In particular, Matins, the chief Sunday service, tended to be overcrowded. The sung Eucharist was re-introduced which reflected the general movement in the Church of England at this time: to make a sung Eucharist the chief service of Sunday worship.

Rev Jones also initiated a number of changes in the furnishing and arrangements of the church; he rearranged the seating in the chancel and the number of choir stalls was increased to accommodate a larger choir. The car parking problem was solved in 1963 when part of Church Garden Meadow was covered with hard-core. He also started a street warden scheme to help the church keep in touch with newcomers, and a Hospital Transport Scheme run by Mr Gooch, in conjunction with a Benevolent Fund. The waxing performed in the 1929 restoration of the mural paintings was, by our present standards, incorrect so further restoration became necessary including facing of the outside walls to prevent damp penetration. The Church was redecorated following work on the frescoes during which a coloured medallion on the Lady Chapel arch was discovered. It was thought to be the original Consecration Cross of the Lady Chapel and it was researched by Sylvia Saunders-Jacobs who found its correct name to be a swastika pelta. These could be traced back for twenty centuries but their significance is unknown; the fleur-de-lys above it is the symbol for the Virgin Mary. It is said that at this time the bells were rehung with a chiming instead of a pealing mechanism, and another bell was added. There was a seemingly endless list of repairs and improvements: rewiring, central heating, the battle against the wood beetles, the rectory, the churchyard, the stonework, the car park, the roof and gutters. At this time an increasing number of people were cremated instead of buried, so a Garden of Remembrance on the south side of the Church was started for the interment of ashes.

Another major scheme was the building of the Church Hall which was needed for meetings which had been held in the Rectory. A large fund raising scheme was undertaken; the hall was opened in May 1967 and called the Kensington Memorial Hall after Col Kensington.

In his long incumbency perhaps Rev Jones will be best remembered by the fact that he had read somewhere about hidden altar tables and began to realise that the original altar table (or mensa), which had been dismantled at the time of the Reformation, might be buried in the floor of the sanctuary. In 1959 he obtained permission for it to be excavated and Slaters was employed. After digging down about 18″ Reg Slater (under the eye of his Uncle Albert Slater) found a slab of what he thought was stone, lifted it and rolled the 14cwt block out of the south door on rollers. A London firm of stonemasons removed the unprepossessing block and returned with it as a wonderful winklestone altar table, expertly renovated and repolished, and erected on four new stone pillars. These pillars will be seen to be a slightly different colour from the top, this is because they are, in fact, made of concrete and covered with a thin winklestone 'veneer' which has been dug from the Stonepits Field on Old House Farm and sliced like a piece of glass. Once more the original altar of the ancient church was in its rightful place.

The oak table which had been used for communion services was then placed at the east end of the south aisle, which was used as a Lady Chapel altar until sheer pressure on the accommodation necessitated its removal to give room for more seating. It is now in store at the Rectory and will be reinstated as an altar, when the present Choir Vestry can be refurbished as a Lady Chapel.

The rector's wife, Mamie, was very active in the parish and interested in the young people; after church on a Sunday some of the teenagers used to go back to the Rectory with the family and one day it is remembered that Mamie took them round the garden to collect nuts. The young people helped her run the Sunday School, when it was held in the old school, having sat on pews behind the organ for the first part of the service. She started a Young Wives' Group and was active in visiting the sick and others in distress in the parish. She was also involved in several of the non-church organisations of the village and she and the Rector were both very popular. He retired in 1972, and they went to live in Hampshire although he took many of the services during the interregnum. (A minister is not allowed to retire in his last parish because 'it is no use having a new captain if the old one is still in the team'.)

The Reverend Canon John G R Northridge became the Rector in April 1972 having served as Rector of Egham in Surrey, before working for the Bible Society, in Kenya, and in Chichester. While in Kenya he was also

The Lady Chapel

responsible for a regular programme for Kenya Radio, a programme rather similar to our 'Lift up your Hearts'. Before leaving Kenya he was made an Honorary Canon of Nairobi Cathedral, in recognition of his work for the Church in Kenya. His first visit to St Mary's was in 1972 when he came to the Church as a visiting preacher on behalf of the Bible Society. His sermon on that occasion made a great impression so it was with great pleasure that the parish heard that he was to be the next Rector.

One of his immediate concerns was to encourage younger members of the congregation, relying on them to help in various ways, especially with the monthly Family Services which he initiated. The chief Sunday service at that time was still Matins, but he also introduced a monthly Family communion service. He also introduced the use of the Series 2 Communion Service, one of the experimental services, which led the way to the publication in 1980 of the Alternative Services Book.

The Church had had several Flower Festivals which helped pay the Sussex Church Campaign which was helping to fund the building of the Church Hall, but the payment in June 1973 was to be the final instalment. The Church was decorated with flowers for The Celebration of Beauty, a weekend of recitals of recorded music, leading to the climax of a splendid Evensong on the Sunday evening, with poetry and more music - a memorable weekend of celebratory music in a beautiful setting.

He was interested in art and music, and in a wide variety of social and church problems; his experience in Kenya and in his work for the Bible Society having given him a keen interest in the World Church. He was very anxious to make his first Annual Parish Meeting in April 1973 less formal and stereotyped so, after the conclusion of the formal business, a member of the congregation was invited to 'interview' him, asking any questions which she chose. In this way an informal review was made of a wide range of parish activities, and an insight was gained into his own views and policies as Rector of the parish. One of his policies was to alter the membership of the PCC, asking four members to retire each year and not be eligible for re-election for a year, to keep new people coming onto the Council.

Towards the end of 1973 he became gravely ill and died on February 2nd 1974, after a ministry at St Mary's of only 21 months. During that short period he had served the parish tirelessly and had won the gratitude and affection of his people.

The Reverend Kenneth Ashley Lucas was the next Rector; at this time there was an increasing tendency for candidates for the Ministry to seek

Rev K A Lucas

ordination after an earlier period in some other field of employment. There are obvious advantages in this new approach by which experience is gained in the secular world before ordination. Rev Lucas came to the ministry in later life; after serving in the Army during the Second World War, his career was spent mainly in the textile industry finally becoming Company Director of his own company in Newhaven.

When he became Rector in June 1974 there were 300 people on the Electoral Roll. He established the Parish Communion as the main service and held Healing Services on St Mark's and St Luke's Day, but so many people came that he increased them to four services per year in 1980.

Serving as one of the Governors of the village primary school, he enjoyed the access which this gave him to the children and their parents, seeing this as a doorway into the wider community beyond the church congregation. As part of his outreach in a fast-growing village the Rector held a Cheese and Wine party at the Rectory in September 1977 which was specially intended to welcome newcomers from the newly developed Holly Close and Nyetimber Copse; it was so successful that it became an annual event which was held in the Kensington Memorial Hall in December for many years. He also inaugurated Lenten Lunches in 1973 and a Harvest Supper in 1975; Mrs Paterson offering the use of a marquee at Denis Marcus Farm. Although it was a most enjoyable occasion it was very cold so future Harvest Suppers have been held indoors! In 1976 a Patronal Festival was suggested; the date was to be the Sunday nearest to the nativity of the Virgin Mary which was 8 September.

There was a very special occasion on 12 February 1978 when Lucy Meeten was presented with flowers at Matins to commemorate the day eighty years earlier when she had been brought to Church as a small child for the Induction of the Reverend Caldecott; she had been born in 1895 and was the oldest regular churchgoer.

As a pianist, with a great interest in Church music, Kenneth enjoyed close co-operation with both the organist and choirmaster. On the Christmas morning service in 1979 he delighted in presenting Stan Gooch with the Royal School of Church Music's Medallion and Long Service Certificate commemorating fifty years of faithful service to the Church choir; he had also been choirmaster for many years.

Kenneth also edited the Parish Magazine, making it a useful mirror of all the facets of parochial life. One monthly feature of the magazine was 'Parson Lucas' Diary' which gave a detailed account of his own daily activities as a Rector who involved himself as fully as possible in the life of his parish and the village community. It was under his editorship that one year St Mary's Parish Magazine won a national prize for the best parish magazine.

It was in the autumn of 1979 that the first recorded Church vandalism occurred; children were caught misbehaving in the building. The PCC decided to keep the Church closed until the school bus had left in the morning, and re-lock it before its return in the afternoon. They also arranged a rota of people to be on duty in Church while it was open during the holidays.

The Parochial Church Council agreed to adopt Stewardship as an essential part of parochial policy and commitment. A Stewardship Campaign in 1982 under the leadership of Bob Newman was very successful with considerable benefit to the parish finances, but, more importantly, it also established a greater awareness in the congregation of individual responsibility for the financial commitment needed, not only for maintenance of the church and its services, but also for generous giving to the needs of the world-wide church and the world.

Kenneth was also concerned for the needs of elderly folk who needed sheltered housing. He worked hard to establish an Abbeyfield Home in West Chiltington, but a suitable property could not be found and his efforts were not successful. Another of his interests was the Healing Ministry, and two or three times a year he held healing services to which those in need of healing could come for prayer and the laying on of hands.

1982 was a landmark year for the Church of England; the first new service book for three hundred years was introduced - The Alternative Service Book.

Kenneth's wife, Florence was his very active partner and supporter in all his responsibilities. Her own especial contribution to parochial life was to found and lead the Pins and Needles Group, a group of ladies in the parish who met regularly to knit and sew a wide variety of articles which were sold for charity. Not only were considerable sums of money raised and distributed to good causes, but also the meetings of the group were a focus of friendship and fellowship in the parish. It was Hilda Andrews of this group who made the curtains for the Kensington Memorial Hall.

Kenneth and Florence were both friendly, outgoing people who built steadily on the traditions of the parish as an active, living Christian community. They retired in 1982 to their house in Newhaven.

After an interregnum of just five months, the Rev James Lacey Reeves - Jim to everyone in the parish - was inducted as Rector in 1983. He was also a late entrant to the ordained ministry; working for 19 years in the Port of London Transport Industry specialising in labour relations, then in 1966 with a friend, he set up a firm of insurance brokers. During these years he became increasingly interested in church affairs; in 1955 he had qualified as a lay reader, and then from 1960-63 he trained for the ministry in his spare time, being ordained in Horsham where he became Curate. It is said that he asked to be addressed as Father, but this was quietly ignored!

Jim was a very energetic, forward-looking and innovative parish priest, and a number of changes were made during his time as Rector. The population of the village was still growing rapidly, as new housing developments took place; he was very aware of the opportunities for outreach which this presented. During this period of change and experiment in liturgical matters, the congregation began to know and to enjoy many of the modern hymns which were published at the time, and this resulted in Combined Mission Praise becoming the chief hymn book, although the older hymns were still used and valued. Parish Communion and the Family Service were moved from 9.45am to 9.30am to allow time to prepare for Matins at 11.30am, but following the introduction of a regular monthly Healing Service in place of Matins, the numbers attending this service dropped rapidly and Matins was discontinued in 1994. Evensong, the last link with the Book of Common Prayer services, was also poorly attended, but moving it to 3pm in the winter of 1987/8 had disastrous results and it was moved back to its usual time of 6pm. The Alternative Services Book, which had been introduced by Kenneth Lucas, was now chiefly used. The Peace at Eucharist was exchanged, at first shyly and tentatively, but quite soon very wholeheartedly. Jim himself was in Church by 6am every weekday for a period of silence, followed by a celebration of Holy Communion, at which he was always joined by his wife Elise, and a small group of parishioners.

It is remembered that the readers at his first Christmas service of Nine Lessons and Carols represented the different parts of village life: the shopkeeper, the builder, the churchwarden, the milkman, the headmistress, the policeman, the farmer, so that each facet of the parish felt involved.

Jim made every effort to establish contact with those in the village who did not normally attend church, so once a month the Sunday Eucharist was regarded as a Family Service, to which young parents were encouraged to bring their children, with a crèche provided for the under four-year-olds. As there was no Sunday School during the school holidays these services were also geared more for the children. With the reorganisation of school management in 1988 it came as a blow to him to discover that his services were no longer required as a representative of the Local Education Authority on the Board of Governors of the school.

It was during Jim's incumbency that the idea of Street Contacts was born, expanding the scheme introduced by Rev Jones, whereby new arrivals would be welcomed by a Church member who would give them a copy of the Parish Magazine and invite them to Church.

Jim decided to invite eight fathers to a supper, as he was concerned that so few came to Church; this started a monthly discussion group called the Monday Club. Another important emphasis was on Bible Study and teaching the faith; soon after he arrived he instituted a weekly Bible Study Group which became firmly established and grew in numbers. There are now in 1999 five groups involving about fifty members of the parish.

In November 1983, at the request of Father Cassidy at the Roman Catholic Church in Storrington, a Roman Catholic Mass was celebrated in St Mary's, attended by members of both congregations. This was of ecumenical significance, as it would undoubtedly have been the first celebration of a Mass in St Mary's since the Reformation, but does not seem to have been repeated.

The Rev Bilal Habibi, an Arab priest who ran three parishes in Nablus, Israel, preached at St Mary's on two Sundays in 1989. His interesting talks outlined some of the difficulties he encountered, but money sent out to help him never arrived; eventually a second donation reached him via the Church Missionary Society.

Mr and Mrs Bell who owned Stocks Cottage had their garden open for the Easter weekend of 1984 under the National Gardens Scheme. As the church roof fund was to be a co-beneficiary with the Macmillan Nurses, the Rector suggested a flower festival in the Church to make it a Village Easter Celebration, with their proceeds to go to the Roof Fund and the National Society for the Prevention of Cruelty to Children. It must have been a success as another flower festival was held in 1989 which coincided with the sponsored bicycle ride for the Historic Churches Trust. The weekend ended with a 'Songs of Praise' service and raised nearly £1,000 for the Church Urban Fund.

In 1986, after the publication of the Archbishop of Canterbury's report *Faith in the City* and his subsequent setting up of the Church Urban Fund, it was suggested that St Mary's should be twinned, in fellowship and mutual support, with a deprived inner city parish. Jim gave this suggestion his full support, so the link with the parish of St Anselm in North Lambeth in London was established and is now very firmly part of parochial life and outreach to the Church and society beyond our own parish, although the links between Brownies, Guides, WI and Mothers' Union were slow to get started. This was partly due to frequent staff changes at the North Lambeth school, and the fact that in London people move around more frequently than here, so it was difficult to retain continuity. The support, benefits and exchanges go both ways; prayers are said in each parish every day for the other one and a Link person in each parish co-ordinates activities. There has been financial support for the North Lambeth school, money was raised for the Guides to visit us in the summer of 1987 and the two groups camped together in 1989. St Mary's also helped to finance visits for children and families to Knowles Tooth, our Diocesan House run for those with special needs; other children came to West Chiltington for holidays and in 1990 three children came for a 10-day holiday and stayed three weeks! St Anselm's helps St Mary's run the Yellow Stall at the Village Fayre and we help them run a Produce Stall at the Lambeth Palace Fete each year. We also send our Harvest Festival gifts to their Drop-In Centre for the homeless, which is why our Harvest Festival has changed emphasis from fresh produce to tinned or dry goods and toiletries.

In 1986 there were thirty-six choir members which was sufficient to divide between morning (when the ten child choristers attended) and evening services. Many choristers attended courses run by the Royal School of Church Music, paid for by the adult choir members pooling their wedding and funeral fees into the Choir Fund which also paid for a summer outing and a winter treat. In many churches across the Christian world, worshippers sing their words of prayer to a particular musical setting of the Family Communion; that music has particular significance in St Mary's since it was written by Bob Newman who was choirmaster for the morning choir.

When Bob and his wife Betty were looking for somewhere to retire in 1980, they remembered family outings from Middlesex with their three children which had taken them through the Sussex countryside to South Coast resorts; the happy associations of the area and luck in calling at the right estate agents in Pulborough, brought them to West Chiltington. The following eighteen years provided many of the happiest of their lives with time for gardening, village activities, the church, family, exciting holidays and music.

Bob loved music and had the ability to share his enjoyment of it with others by encouragement, enthusiasm and patience. He was an accomplished pianist with a good tenor voice and could compose and arrange music. On his arrival in the village he immediately joined the church choir and later became its choir master. He founded and led the Chiltingtones barber shop group - close harmony singers who regularly entertained at functions in the area. He was involved as soloist, accompanist and arranger at a variety of concerts, recitals and local entertainment, supported other music groups and gave piano lessons to several youngsters in the village. With others he recruited sixteen children for the choir in 1990; they were called the Skylarks and Thrushes.

His biggest undertaking was the one which meant most to him; he set out to write a musical setting for the whole of the Communion Service. It took many hours, but was finally completed, accepted and approved and has been sung regularly in the church ever since. Many copies have been requested and it is now at various churches throughout the country and as far afield as South America. He had just written the music for the final prayer before he suffered the first of several devastating strokes which eventually caused his death in 1998. His ashes are laid in the churchyard, but his memory will live on in the musical legacy he leaves in the church and village.

On the structural-maintenance side of Jim's ministry, the south slope of the Chancel roof had to be repaired as the rain was damaging the murals; fortunately most of the cost for the murals was covered by insurance, although the work on the roof was not. In January 1984 the list of Rectors was fixed on the wall of the south aisle and dedicated, and the following year the hand rails for the Chancel steps were installed. The Hurricane of 1987 caused considerable damage to the weathervane and the roof and water leaked into the Lady Chapel; temporary repairs were blown away in a further storm the following January. Therefore in May 1988 complete re-roofing began, and the Chancel, part of whose ceiling had fallen down, was re-decorated. A new weathervane was made at Amberley Chalk Pits Museum, gilded, erected on the repaired spire and floodlit for Christmas 1991. The old weathervane was sold to the owners of Forge Cottage, where it had originally been made. An amplification system was installed to solve the acoustic problems of the church building; the narrow chancel arch effectively cuts off the chancel from the nave which was a great handicap, both to clergy conducting the services and to the choir in leading the singing. Finally the car park was resurfaced.

Starting in 1989 there were a series of thefts from the Church necessitating extra security measures and the storage of silver and items of value away from the building. There was also vandalism in the Churchyard and a disclaimer notice had to be put up after a claim for compensation was lodged on behalf of a child who, playing in the Churchyard, had broken a cross which damaged his leg. Although he had completely recovered from the accident which had happened over a year previously, the Diocesan insurers reluctantly thought it best to pay as an appeal would have been too costly.

In all his ministry Jim was supported by his wife, Elise. They were both friendly out-going people who enjoyed their relationships with members of the congregation, and shared fully in the life of the parish and the village community. It was sad that the onset of illness necessitated Jim's early retirement. They left the parish to live in Midhurst at the end of 1992.

The Reverend Gerald Arthur Evans was inducted as Rector of St Mary's in May 1993; a Welshman born in Swansea, his National Service was with the RAF and it was during a posting to Cyprus that he met his wife Sheila, who was also serving with the RAF in the Princess Mary's Nursing Service. Gerald then entered the steel industry, but in 1974 changed course and joined the administrative staff of the Church of England Children's Society. Later he trained as a lay reader and was ordained in 1977, serving for some years at Sussex churches before coming to St Mary's. During much of this time Sheila continued with her nursing, most recently as practice Sister in a Midhurst General Practice.

Gerald's outstanding gifts as a parish priest were in his pastoral ministry. He quickly came to know, and be known by, not only members of the congregation, but also by others in the village who did not regularly attend church; this caring attitude to people was evident in his conduct of the services at such family occasions as baptisms, weddings and funerals. He built constructively on the established pattern of services, which included his emphasis on lay participation; members of the congregation were involved as fully as possible in reading lessons, leading intercessions, administering the Chalice at the Eucharist and in helping to devise and carry out special services. This readiness to share and delegate was an essential element in his ability to draw the congregation into partnership with him in the worship and activities of the church. A Church Youth Group was formed, the members of which helped with the Junior Church, and were also trained to serve at the altar and to sing in the choir. Gerald also maintained a close contact with the village school and was very committed to house visiting, including home communion for those who were sick or frail and unable to attend church; an Aumbry to hold a small reservoir of consecrated Elements for the sick and dying was incorporated and blessed in 1997. Two innovations of his were, first, the introduction of Taizé services, which focused on a special theme, and drew on the Taizé tradition of meditative chants, readings and periods of silence; and second, the annual Tent Service. Gerald comments "In all these developments I received enthusiastic encouragement and invaluable practical help from our licensed Reader, Gladys Engledow. Gladys had visited Taizé in Southern France three times and it was she who devised the services for St Mary's so creatively and with such skill. In addition, Gladys, who had taught divinity for much of her working life, has led two Bible study groups for many years, leads services regularly, sings in the choir, administers the chalice, serves on the PCC - and has just celebrated her 95th Birthday! What a wonderful life of commitment and service."

As is always the case, the Rector had also to attend to the material needs of the Church building; the entrance to the overflow car park was created for his induction service; because about 6,000 visitors come to the Church every year, wooden hand-held guides were made and given; British Gas finally supplied gas to the village so the Hall could have a new, gas-fired boiler in 1994, with new PVC doors and total re-decoration in 1997; the church windows, which had been cleaned in 1990 and found to be billowing, were finally taken out and repaired; the porch and vestry were re-roofed; the murals needed further attention. In 1997 a modern electronic organ was installed to replace the Walker organ, which after forty years excellent service was now in need of major and expensive repair; Peter Knowles the organist played the last hymn at Evensong on the old organ before it was removed - he had been the first to play it when it was new in 1956. In 1994 Sheila, with the help of Olive Gambles, masterminded a scheme to equip the whole church with replacement tapestry kneelers. These, embroidered and made up by ladies in the congregation, have made an attractive addition to the furnishings of the church. Clinton Bothwell, with four volunteers, prepared a detailed record of all the graves and memorials in the church and churchyard, copies of which can be found in the Record Office in Chichester, in Storrington library and in the church office.

The 50th anniversary of D-Day on 6 June 1994 was marked at Evensong; 1995 saw the 50th anniversaries of VE and VJ Day but the PCC decided to focus on the national celebrations.

Back in 1987 Linda Podlasinska had become involved with an Anglican church in the USA whose choir had come over to England to sing, and stayed in the homes of church members to whom a small payment was made. Known as 'Homestay' it was cheaper than hotels and a return visit could be made on a similar basis. In 1997 it was proposed to have a visit from forty adults from Trinity Episcopalian Church, Castine, Maine, who would stay here for four nights of their trip, ending with Evensong, a meal, and a concert in the Village Hall.

The most expensive venture during Gerald's incumbency was the decision to tackle the problem of overcrowding which, after years of steady growth both in the population of the village and of the church congregations, had become acute. Discussions were begun with both the civic and diocesan authorities, and it was finally decided to build a new vestry, outside the south-east door of the church to provide adequate and appropriate accommodation both for the clergy and the choir, and also suitable storage and 'housekeeping' facilities. This would release the south-east corner of the church from its present use as a choir vestry and a storage place to give additional seating, while the Lady Chapel could be reinstated giving greater sanctity and dignity to this area of the church. In 1998 these plans received diocesan approval, and it was decided to proceed and to launch St Mary's Millennium Appeal Fund for £180,000 to finance the project.

Gerald had given himself wholeheartedly to these plans and the lengthy negotiations involved. It was a great disappointment to him, as indeed to the whole parish, when, late in 1998 his health gave cause for anxiety and he was urged to retire. The building plans, however, went ahead under the direction of the Churchwardens. When the new vestry and Lady Chapel are completed they will be a testimony to the inspiration and enthusiasm which Gerald gave to the planning process.

When Gerald left the parish at the end of January 1998, St Mary's Church in West Chiltington lost an exceptionally devoted and hardworking priest who was greatly loved in the parish and in the village.

In April 1999, the Reverend Kevin George O'Donnell and his family arrived in the parish. Thanks to the hard work of the churchwardens he came to a church whose vitality and congregations had not much diminished during the long interregnum. Rev O'Donnell came from a career in school teaching, being ordained Priest in 1989, returning to teaching and becoming School Chaplain in Ascot for three years.

As the Rev Caldecott bridged the beginning of this century, so Rev O'Donnell bridges the end of it and his name will be the next to be inscribed on the list on the wall of the south aisle of the church - but the story of his incumbency as Rector belongs to the future and to the new millennium. Already there is a new beginning: when he came, he and his wife Gill had two boys, in June a third son was born. Kevin says "Gill is already making good relationships among the mother and baby circuit, and is planning to start a morning Mothers and Toddlers group, with a brief Church service beforehand. I am hoping to run a Christian basics course such as 'Alpha' and have just begun to set up a parish bookstall. The regular services will remain more or less as they have been, to make all sections of the village feel included. A priest is a bridge builder moving across social groups and ages; I would like to encourage our mixed population of business people and retired people to have an input in parish and village life, using their skills appropriately. I think we are probably going to see fewer people who want to see out their days here, and this is the nature of the rural suburbia that this whole area is becoming, for better or for worse. Our village can only sustain so much growth in population and facilities though, and this is a cause for concern.

What will the new millennium bring? My prayer is for more stability, integration between age groups, and friendly co-operation; the older and the younger have so much to give to one another."

Looking down Church Street towards the Church – 1999

Chapter 10

Schooldays

The first school was a pair of stone cottages just beside the Church gate, from 1635 to 1875. This first school is said to have been built on the site of a slaughterhouse and pigstyes, and was financed by money from the will of William Smyth of Angmering which provided for a licensed schoolmaster to teach the young people "as well rich as poor, either male, or female, then born or to be born in Chiltington aforesaid for ever". These cottages were demolished in 1874/5 to make room for the new school which has since been sold and turned into a house, as the children outgrew the premises yet again, and another new school had to be built in 1975.

In his will of 1632 William Smyth left a legacy to provide financial assistance to young people resident in the parish to enable them to further their education. The 'Smyth's Educational Foundation at West

The First School

Old School House 1876.

Sketch of Old School House – 1876

Chiltington' - to give it its full title, is now invested in Charity Commission shares, an NSB account and a parcel of 2 hectares of grazing land in North Heath. Together these produce annual income of about £1,000, nearly all of which is available for distribution in the form of grants to individuals or to organisations in the parish. Originally tuition and entrance fees for students attending secondary or technical school; money for books or expenses; tools or equipment; even provision towards a school library, musical instruments or sewing machines was covered, but as times and education changed the Trust now provides assistance in the form of cash grants. These may be made to organisations catering for young people or to individuals; for example to enable them to undertake voluntary work in developing countries in their 'gap year' between leaving school and going to university; to assist with the costs of tuition or materials used in their studies; or to assist with the expenses of following their chosen career.

    There are six trustees: the Rector, one appointed by the County Council (traditionally our local County Councillor) and four appointed by the Parish Council (of which one is often the school headteacher). They meet twice a year and welcome applications for grants from students and young people in employment who live in the parish, or organisations for young people in the parish. More information can be obtained from either the headteacher at the school, or the Clerk to the Parish who is the Trust's treasurer.

In 1880 all children were compelled to attend school up to the age of ten, but in 1893 the school-leaving age was raised to eleven, and to twelve in 1899 except for those employed in agriculture. The educational system was completely reorganised in 1902 when the responsibility for providing elementary, secondary and technical education was given to 330 Local Education Authorities under a central board of Education; these 'board' schools later became 'council' schools. By 1918 the leaving age was raised again, to fourteen, and Mrs Edith Green, now in her 90s, remembers that her husband left the village school at the age of twelve, in order to help his father on the farm. This is one of the earliest memories of the school; another is that there was a school at Little Haglands where, about the 1860s, old Ned Slater had to pay twopence a week to be taught. The single-roomed building, which was about 4' away from the corner of the house, towards the road, is thought to have served about a dozen children, and was later knocked down.

In 1947 the school-leaving age was again raised, to fifteen, with the final rise coming in 1965, when it became sixteen.

Bill Hampton started school at West Chiltington when he was 5 years old, in 1912. He walked to school from Woodshill, meeting the children from nearby farms on the way, and made the point that although there were only a few families, they had enough children to fill the school; on average there were 70-80 children although once it got as high as 100. He lists the families: "There were nine families produced ninety children: the Paveys had fifteen, the Freemans twelve, the Cripps who lived close to the mill and did the trap work to the station had eleven, the Shorts and Slaters had ten each. Geals down at Dennis Marcus Farm had nine, and there were one or two others: the Gumbrells, the Coopers, Bill Green, these nine families kept the school attendance up! The children would walk to school from as far as Willetts and Cattlestone Farms in their hobnailed boots and when the pelts (the bordering of leather at the front of a shoe or boot that attached to the upper sole) came off, John Geal had a little shop close to the Church where he charged 2d for a pelt, sometimes three or four of us would go in and get them tacked on. They were real heavy boots and we wore knee high socks and knickerbockers, and Mother was good with the knitting needles. Not fine clothes as they are today, but serviceable.

I don't think the hours have altered since my time either, 9am start, out again 9.45 for play, 12 noon mid-day meal. We didn't get dinner, we had to take a bit of sandwich or cake and in the winter we took the largest potato we could find, cut our initials in it, and stuck it in the coal fire in the room. When they came out they were black, but we were pleased to eat them. Yes. Yes, that coal fire was all the heating we had, we had to sit indoors in school with our overcoats on, but we were none the worse off for it. We were hardened; my mother came from Bosham and she used to like to go back once a year to see the relatives. Twice, if she'd managed to save any money from selling rabbit skins or bottles or something. There were three of us, the youngest was five, I was six and the eldest sister was eight, and at 6am Mother used to get us all down to Billingshurst station. It was a four mile walk from Woodshill; she would push the little one in what we called a mail cart (I think it came from a town somewhere and the postman had used it to deliver parcels) which was an iron framed thing with four wheels on it and a wicker work basket seat. When we got to Bosham Station there was another mile walk to Old Bosham, half a mile further to see the relatives, another mile back to the station and the final four miles from Billingshurst. I reckon when I was six I walked eleven miles."

Elsie Cattell says that there were four classes in her day (1918-1927), and the children went from the ages of five to fourteen. The old bell rang to signal the start of school. The Headmaster Mr Mills, a tall man with

School Class about 1920
These are the white pinafores and the school dog! The master on the left was Leslie Brown.

silver-white hair who the children looked up to and admired, took the top class, with Miss Walder taking the infants and Miss Cork and another teacher taking the next two classes up. All the children walked to school; there was no uniform but the boys in their shorts often had skinned knees from the gravel playground. The girls wore long dresses and boots and a white pinafore (which showed every mark!) worn over the clothes in the early days, and later skirts and jumpers; as small children they wore ankle socks with black shoes, but by the time they were about eleven they had graduated to black stockings. As all the clothes were made from natural fibres, wool, cotton and linen, washing and drying was quite a performance so skirts were sponged clean where possible. (Elsie recalled Sunday nights when thirteen buckets of water were collected for the big wash day on Monday.) There were no 'indoor' and 'outdoor' shoes so the dirt collected from the dusty or muddy roads which was not wiped off on the coir or coconut matting in the cloakrooms was tramped into the school and the children sat in wet shoes if it had been raining. In the late 1920s there was only a little fire in the corner of the classrooms so if they arrived at school wet or cold six children would go and sit on the form in front of the fire and have a warm, and then another six would go up, but by the 1930s there was a boiler and radiators. Sitting in rows of desks, two to a desk with a lift-up lid and a recessed ink well, they learned reading, writing, history, geography and scripture; the scripture lesson was the first one after morning assembly, which followed the register. There was a religious assembly every morning with hymns and a Bible reading, taken by the headmaster with occasional appearances by the rector, but as there was no big hall for Assembly as it is now known, the partition between the two top classes was pushed back, making a bigger space. This partition was wooden to a height of about 3' with glass above. The children sat still in class and put up their hands when answering or asking a question, kept their pencils, pens and nibs in the desk, with perhaps a sweet for playtime, and hung their coats on pegs in the lobbies - there was a lobby for the boys, another for the girls and a third for the infants, with an entrance round the back. A highlight of the school year was the annual outing, to Bognor one year and Worthing the next. In due course the school numbers must have fallen because the four sizeable classes were reduced to three with the vacant classroom becoming the canteen. In Elsie's day all the children left school at fourteen, there being no 11+ or further education.

Bernard Daughtry who was born in 1917 says: "Once a year the school would put on a concert of sketches, singing, readings and so on to raise

School Holiday to the Isle of Wight – 1934
Waiting to leave from Pulborough Station

School Holiday to the Isle of Wight – 1934
Waiting to leave from Pulborough Station
1. Mr Dixon (Headmaster). 2. Hugh Penfold. 3. Ron Bagley. 4. Joyce Cox. 5. Charlie Parsons. 6. Sylvia Greenfield. 7. Masie Stoner. 8. Doris Lelliott. 9. Florrie Pullen. 10 Joan Sturt. 11. Dick Cook. 12. Miss Willmer (Teacher). 13. Edwin Harris. 14. Ted Tipper. 15. Jim Scott. 16. Maurice Ayling. 17. Bill Tipper. 18. John Mustchin. 19. Ernie Ruff. 20. Eileen Scott. 21. Connie Russell. 22. Michael Greenfield. 23. Brenda Pullen. 24. Fred Horlock.

money for the senior pupils' outing; one year they looked over the liner Olympic in Portsmouth dockyard, in other years they went to London to St Paul's, the Zoo, Pascal's Sweet Factory or Lyons. Mr Morgan from Nyetimber had a covered lorry which he used to take us to the station, from where we would have a saloon coach. There used to be about 30 to 40 children from the school and then various others, older brothers and sisters perhaps, would avail themselves of the coach and pay their way."

A later outing to the Isle of Wight in 1936 is recounted by Michael Greenfield: "We left Pulborough Station and went to Portsmouth where we saw the Victory. All I remember of that day was that the tide was out and there was no water, but filthy black mud in which a couple of kids were standing while people threw them coins. The children were feeling about in the mud up to their knees for the money. When we got to the Isle of Wight we stayed in a boarding house in Ryde which must have been geared up to taking children because there were children from a school in London there, and we had pillow fights at night in the big dormitory. Our parents had to pay for the trip but I can't remember how many of us went. What I can remember was that it was very hot and Mr Dixon took us for long walks! There were day trips to Littlehampton as well, by coach."

Gwen Smith recalls being taken to her first day at school in 1929 by Phoebe Hampshire, the girl next door. It was a mile walk from The Birches, and Phoebe "just took my hand and we went to school and into the classroom. I stood in awe, this great big room with its high ceiling and not a picture on the walls! But the shock was softened by Miss Walder, this lovely lady who I worshipped; she was a beautiful woman with natural wavy hair who never raised her voice to anybody; we would have done anything for her. The school gave us books, rulers, pencils and things and they stayed at school in our desks, we didn't take them home. I remember the first time I wrote with a pen, how grown up I felt! They didn't do dinners at school so although some people would walk home for dinner, the rest of us would take a big potato to school which would cook in the ashes of the fire in the big black range that had to be blackleaded. In the 1930s milk was supplied to the school in one third of a pint bottles, but it cost a halfpenny a bottle. Sometimes in the very cold weather the milk was warmed by all the bottles being stood in this zinc bath, and Miss Walder put a little hot water in the bottom. Later, we were allowed to have cocoa; the cocoa monitor was a good job because it allowed us to leave the classroom a bit earlier. Ink monitor was a good job, too. In the summer we would run all the way home for dinner, stopping for a drink if we got thirsty, from one of the many springs that welled up out of the ground like little spouts."

Cleanliness was obviously next to Godliness as the district nurse, Nurse Balance, would come to the school on Monday mornings and check the children's hair for nits, and to ensure that each child had a clean vest on. On one memorable occasion Elsie Pullen cut her head open at school after slipping and hitting it against a wall in the playground, and Nurse Balance had to take her home after Dr Eames, who was visiting across the road, came and stitched her up in the adjacent school house. If Dr Eames had not been around the district nurse would probably have had to have managed on her own. One had to find one's own way to hospital if possible; hospital costs could be defrayed by the weekly purchase of a stamp, and there was also another scheme of weekly payments to ensure the services of a nursing midwife.

Gwen passed her 11+ but still had to leave school in 1938 at 14; she recounts what happened: "I should have gone to Horsham, the High School for Girls, because I passed the exam. We had all gone to Pulborough to take it in the little old school up Rectory Lane. We had maths and mental arithmetic, composition, history, geography, a wide scope in a two hour exam. This exam was the dividing line, those that passed went on to Horsham, the others stayed in the village school until fourteen. If we went to High School we stayed until we were sixteen, what would have happened to me then I don't know but I wanted to be a teacher and I supposed I would have gone on from there and progressed. I went through the summer holiday after the 11+ thinking 'It's funny I don't hear anything about going to Horsham' and about a week before we went back to school I said to my mother 'what about Horsham then, Mum, I haven't heard anything about it' and she said 'Oh, you're not going. I've written to Mr Dixon and knocked that on the head. We can't afford £12 a year for your fees and uniform.' Two other girls passed and went on, but in those days we just accepted things and it wasn't quite so important to get to the top so I didn't feel terribly put out, in fact I had an advantage as I came top of everything and the challenge to stay top of everything was what kept me going. So I left school on the Friday when I was 14 and started working on the Monday, but I remember that, before this, my mother had asked Mr Dixon if I could have two weeks off school when she was going to be confined with the new baby; I had to run the house and look after her.

Infant Classes 1 and 2 – 1934
Back Row from left: Miss Walder, —, Ken Crowhurst, John Page, Marjorie Slater, —, Maurice Snook, John Gruber, Dorothy Kingshott, Jim Carpenter, Alec Gumbrell, Mr Mills
Middle Row: Chrissie Steele, Ken Humphrey, —, Percy Willmer, Barbara Norman, Joan Norman, Sid Bagley, Rosie Horlock, Irene Scott, Ted Faires, Joan Clark, Reg Slater
Front Row: Ivan Pullen, Pat Hare-Winton, Leonard Geal, —, Pam Thirkettle, Molly Geal, Jean Ellis, Cyril Snook, —

I remember that classroom so well, a huge great room with desks that two people sat at and you had five rows of desks, in fact there were six in some rooms. Now they're saying that 40 children is too many to teach but I counted up and we had 48 in one of our classrooms and one woman looked after that and she managed us all with no bother at all. You had your own desk and you kept that desk and your own things stayed in it, it didn't occur to us to poke around in anyone else's desk. If you brought a few sweets to school to eat at playtime, no one touched them. We did have bother once or twice when I got to the top class in 1935 and all our coats were hanging up in the cloakroom and people would go to get the money to pay for their milk, which was by then a penny a day, and the milk money was missing, but we found out who it was that was light-fingered and helping themselves to our money. Each classroom had its own cloakroom (so it was easy to find out who the culprit was) with pegs round the walls and down both sides of a fixture in the middle."

Joy Adams also remembers the scholarship, which was in two parts; like Gwen having passed the first part, she and a friend went together to Pulborough to sit the second part. She says that she deliberately misunderstood one of the essay questions "It said 'Write one story from the following three titles' so I wrote a small story on all three. So that disqualified me straight out. I knew if I'd got through I couldn't go to High School in Worthing, my parents couldn't afford to send me. Couldn't afford my uniform, or anything like that, so there was no point in my struggling to get through. There was no help in those days, with funding for education. I got a terrible telling off in school when they found out, but what else could I do?" She also makes the point that, because they walked everywhere as children, they made their own games in the countryside. She and friends used to walk back from school across the fields and climb the trees on the way. On the Common she would look for any old pots and pans that people had thrown out and take them to a 'house' made in the shrubs and hedges, a land of make-believe.

When Ray Winton won a scholarship to Worthing High School in the 1930s the whole school was given a day off.

Many people remember that, in the 1930s children would come to the village school for a comparatively short time as their fathers sought seasonal work.

R W Mills had succeeded Mr Chad as headmaster, being succeeded himself by G W Dixon about 1934. The headmaster's house was adjacent to the school with a gate to connect the garden with the school playground; the house is now a private residence called The Stone House. Mr Dixon objected to living in this house which, he said was damp and cold, so about 1933 a new headmaster's house called Mill View was built on the sharp bend where Lordings Lane meets Haglands Lane. The house has been considerably enlarged since and has changed hands; it is now called Tycanol, the kennel name of the two Irish Setters who live there.

Joy Adams remembers that after Mr Dixon left, the Stone House was used only once a year for the dentist (nicknamed Rooks' Nest from the fringe of dark curls that surrounded his bald patch) to come and check the children's teeth; this had been done previously in the Reading Room. On one occasion she can remember sitting in there in front of the big window having her tooth pulled out! Elsie Pullen continues the story by saying that she had to go to Hayling Pond to get buckets of water from the spring for the dentist, and carry them to the reading room in the days before water was laid on. It was a shame that the house was left empty, although the children enjoyed scrumping the apples from the garden!

Ivan Pullen adds that when he was at school from 1933 to 1942 things were much the same as Elsie remembered; but the headmaster Mr Dixon's mind was on other things: "He took the top classes for their last two years, and although interested in English, Poetry and Nature, the other subjects were rather left; he wasn't all that interested in teaching. You just got your books out and read and read 'till four o'clock. Then righto, off you go." Other children remember going to the forge during their lunch break to watch the horses being shod, and also remember that Miss Walder would shut the very high windows in the classroom with a pole with a hook on the end which 'squeaked something terrible' to shut out the call of Harry Fielder who came round with his fish van, calling 'Fresh Herrings'.

As the years went on the girls would catch a bus into Storrington for cookery lessons; the school provided the ingredients and Mrs Goring would read out the recipe which the girls wrote down. From the late 1930s these lessons were held in the Girl Guides Hut on a Monday, which was slaughtering day at the Storrington slaughterhouse. There was great excitement one day when one of the cattle due for slaughter escaped and ran round the Hut in his bid for freedom!

Miss Gardner features frequently in the childhood memories of school in the 1930s; she was very strict, always wore her hair in a bun on top of her head, had dark clothes and a hat, and seemed very old, riding her high bicycle. She cut such an unusual figure that the first day she came to school all the children laughed at her. She was deeply religious and in her way generous too, one or two older people still have the books and the Bibles she gave them. For one lesson the girls used to take their socks in to school so that they could learn to darn them nicely. This good idea came to grief when Miss Gardener started bringing in others' socks for the girls who were quick and nimble to darn; the problem was that these socks were not always washed first! Meanwhile the boys went by taxi to Pulborough for woodwork.

Mr Dixon ran a Young Farmers' Club just after the war and most of the boys at school were members. It was the only night out for many of them as there was no Youth Club at that time. He had bought New Barn Farm from Mr Code, followed by Commonland Farm, then he bought Smugglers. He farmed them all himself and was a better landowner than he was a teacher. He had people running all the farms.

Exhibition at Cowdray Park – 1938
From left: Maisie Stoner, Mrs Dixon, Joyce Sturt, Mr Dixon, Gwen Humphrey, Lily Knight

Many of the girls remember the 1938 Cowdray Park Exhibition and 1939 Royal Windsor Shows; Mr and Mrs Dixon kept angora rabbits for their fur; four girls from the school were picked to go to the Show to demonstrate. At Windsor Joyce Sturt (now Duffin) did a lot of the spinning, while Joan Hawkins, Pam Thirkettle and Pat Winton took it in turns to weave, and to groom the rabbits by using the bellows to puff the fur up so that it could be plucked off more easily.

Ewen Steele recalls his schooldays of 1934 - 43: "The school had a playground front and back; girls at the back, boys at the front. The three bucket toilets were outside in the playground, one for boys, one for girls and infants and one for the teachers, and there was no hot water laid on. I remember a big dog called Bruce, who used to come and wait for a ball to come flying over the wall. Then he would take it back to his kennel and we had to take risks to go and get it. When it got to five to one, we used to throw the ball over on purpose so that getting it would make us late back to school and we'd have a bit longer to play. There were games of marbles and hoops - wooden hoops for the girls and iron hoops for the boys were bowled along. The marbles were put on the old stone pillars of the school wall and you had to see how far they went. The girls had hopscotch, rounders, skipping, and netball matches, and they used to trek to the rec with their stoolball, bats and wickets."

Every Wednesday after school the school became the library.

After 1940 older children were no longer taught in West Chiltington School; they went on to senior school. Built on the site of the old Workhouse, Rydon School, which opened on 3 June 1940 was first known as Storrington Council Senior Mixed School or Thakeham Senior. In 1952 this was changed to Rydon County Secondary School, named after Henry Walter Rydon, the chairman of the Rural District Council, and was what became known as a secondary modern school, teaching the technical rather then the academic subjects to those children who had not gained a grammar school place after the eleven plus examination had come in. The school boasted domestic science, needlework and crafts rooms for the girls and woodwork and metalwork for the boys, with a science laboratory, five standard classrooms, art room, gymnasium and assembly hall. In 1969 the local system changed to a three-tier system with junior, middle and senior schools, so the name was changed again to Rydon Intermediate School in 1969, but to the locals it is just Rydon School, and takes children from 10 to 13 years of age.

Pat Steele explains: "I went to Rydon when it first opened; those children who lived over three miles away had brand new bicycles and sou'westers given to them so they could cycle to school. There were Currys bikes and Hercules bikes, and people came to the village school to measure us for them. The children at the Common had to buy their bikes at 6d a week, as they were under the three miles limit, but once they left school the bike was theirs as they had paid for it. We, over the three miles, had to give ours back when we left school."

Grammar School places were offered at Horsham High School for Girls; or at Collyers in Horsham, or Midhurst for the boys. Just after the war the boys would cycle to Pulborough station and catch the 'Midhurst Matchbox', one of the Stroudley Terrier 0-6-0 tank engines and its single carriage. This used to travel through Fittleworth and Petworth to Midhurst, leaving at 7.45am and returning at 4.45pm which made quite a long day for the children This was the regular service, not just a school train, but at these times there were mostly children on it. These engines are now in the Bluebell Railway. Later on, perhaps about the late 1940s or early 1950s there was a bus service from West Chiltington to Pulborough where the boys would pick up a No 22 bus to Midhurst.

Teachers' accommodation could be then, as now, a problem: Miss Walder lodged with Joy Adams' grandmother (Mrs Pullen) at The Haven on the Common. She started teaching at the school as the infants' teacher when she was first qualified and stayed there until she retired. She had one brief, three week, period when she left to teach in Rusper, but returned in despair at the rudeness and unruly behaviour of the children! She, like all the teachers, was paid by West Sussex County Council, who would send someone out once a week to check the school register. If a child was found to be absent without a note to explain why, 'the truancy man' would go and see the parents for an explanation. A later teacher Miss Horner lived on the family farm out at Wiggonholt, and Miss Wilmer (the older sister of Perce Wilmer who owned the radio shop in Pulborough) lived outside the village. Miss Gardener lodged with Mrs Faires at the shop.

Wartime brought big changes to the school. The village took its share of evacuee children, and their teacher Babs Wallace was the teacher who controlled them all; she came with the Peckham group, arriving on 1 September 1939. She moved into various addresses around the village, ending up in Harborough Drive in 1946. In 1947 Bill Carver built her a bungalow in Finches Lane where she lived until 1989, making her wartime evacuation to the village fifty years long! She taught in the school and also helped out in Pulborough until she retired. She was particularly interested in art, music and country dancing, as well as teaching the more academic subjects. "It was thanks to Mrs Wallace that we children had a grounding in anything at all," said one child, now in his late sixties. It seems that although she was strict, she was well liked and respected. By the spring of 1940 there were three classes at school, the beloved Miss Walder was the infant teacher, and the children stayed with her for two years, then they moved up to Standard 1 & 2 with Mrs Wallace, who had replaced Miss Gardener who had gone to Fittleworth in 1943. Miss Margaret Walder retired in March 1967 with much sadness on both sides and was presented with, among other things, a retirement book inscribed with the names of the pupils she had taught over the years.

The arrival of these extra children disrupted village education to such an extent that, in effect, the school was divided into two: one week the village children had the school for lessons in the morning and spent the afternoons being taught in the Old Comrades Hall, while the evacuee children spent the mornings in the Hall and the afternoons in the school. The following week the positions were reversed. The winter of 1939, when the evacuees first arrived, was bitterly cold, and The Old Comrades Hall had just one tiny coal fire in it, and no real equipment. The children sat cross legged on the floor, not only for the singing classes, and for reading, but for writing, too. The situation was helped when Rydon School opened and the evacuee children integrated with the village children more, all going to the same place at the same time.

Ron Noble, one of the evacuees says: "I can remember more of the walk to school in the 1940s than of the actual schooling, we walked to school in all weathers and I can say I enjoyed every moment, chasing each other up the hollows and dodging the mud thrown by others from the high banks. Each day was a new adventure, we had satchels packed with the odd book or two, a wad of sandwiches and sometimes in the winter a huge potato - baked potatoes never tasted so good! My teacher was a Miss Beckworth who was very good, keen on art and maths. Mr Dixon kept us fit with sport and with boxing and we often helped out on his farm, which was much better than sitting in a classroom, except when dealing with the 'cows'; I was driving these cows along and whacking them with a stick when Mr Dixon said 'I wouldn't do that if I were you, he's a bull!'. We helped on many farms in the area, harvesting, weeding and lifting crops, mainly potatoes and peas which was necessary there being a war on. The farmers usually paid us, although one farmer where we went pea picking, was a bit reluctant, and with our earnings we would go to Storrington to shop."

The wartime children remember collecting acorns for the local pigs that were kept, and foxgloves, hips, coltsfoot and nettles to be made into medicines for the war effort. These were dried and stored in the upstairs of the old school house. Collecting was not only for others, though, many children remember collecting the hot cartridges that fell from the skies as the Battle of Britain was fought over their heads; it was a race to see whether they could get to the trophies before the police and Home Guard! The children also collected wood for the stove. So many children remember the cold of those early winters: when they got too cold, the teachers would send them out into the playground to jump and run around for a bit until they were warm; one of the teachers took some of the children for walks round the village, even in the snow. It was warmer walking than sitting still! The village looked wonderful in the cold, with frost on all the bushes. Monkmead pond froze over and Mr Kerr allowed the children to go sliding and skating on it. During those bitter winters of the war there were memorable occasions when Miss Gardener took the schoolchildren to Monkmead pond; once a Czech refugee who was a skater entertained them all afternoon with her skating demonstration.

The cane was still used, and Brian Ruff recalls one incident from his schooldays in the late 1940s or early 1950s, "One morning on our way to school they were thrashing at Churchfield Farm. My father was there, he had been a carter originally but was working with Jim Bacon from Gay Street who had a steam engine with a fly wheel that drove the belt for the thrashing. We were all watching this and forgot about school. I eventually wandered in to class and Mr Dixon asked where everyone else was - he was a good one with the cane and when the others arrived he caned them all." There was also the kindliness of some people, "there were two men who did a lot of the restoration of the Stone House, and one of them was really kind; he gave a fishing rod as a prize to the one who won the cross-country run at the Fayre. I think it was a family called Hayes who moved into Old School House first, and they were generous, too, because every Christmas for some years they would give a present to the children, the 6d that went on the plate underneath the slice of Christmas pudding that Mr Dixon served for our Christmas dinner at the school."

On 3 September 1939 a ten-year-old girl in Croydon, Barbara Owen (now Mrs Fordham) was listening to the radio with her parents. They heard, at 11am, that war had been declared. Within an hour she found herself being taken to West Chiltington, to Peri's Bower, now called Bracken Cottage, a Wells cottage in Bower Lane that was owned by her father's employer who had offered the family safety there until they could make other arrangements. She stayed there for about a week until she found herself with Mr and Mrs Larby at 15 The Birches. Because these arrangements had been made on an individual basis, she was classed as a Private Evacuee, and the Larbys received a small payment for her accommodation. It was strange that the school evacuees should also have come from Croydon with their teacher, but from a different school.

Although 'Private', Barbara was treated no differently from the other evacuees, and found no discrimination in the village. The Larbys were kindness itself; an early memory is of being taken into Storrington by bus to have a present bought for her. She decided upon a small doll, and on learning that she was fond of knitting, Mr Larby bought her wool and needles. She chose bright orange wool, and knitted the doll a substantial wardrobe of clothes, in orange.

She stayed with the Larbys for 11 months before returning to Croydon, in time to start a new term at a new school. During her time with the Larbys she walked to the school with the other children, eating apples and playing in or over the ditches. Many of the fields in the parish had ditches around them, partly to prevent waterlogging and encourage drainage and partly to provide a reservoir of water that would seep into the many wells in the village. So many of the children of those times remember playing in the ditches; as Barbara said: "it gave us an excuse to get wet without being told off!" She adds "one of the houses just before the Mill used to put out apples for us children to take to school, and no-one ever passed the wishing well without wishing and stamping in the water."

School dinners had been started in 1943; the first cook was Mrs Fred Slater who was assisted by Mrs George Cox. Harvie Steele says: "I can remember when I was in the top class in 1957, every Friday at lunchtime Geoff Lawson and I used to take the dinner money, of a shilling per day for each child, to the Westminster Bank in Pulborough on our bikes; well, Geoff had his and I borrowed his sister's. We used to cycle down Stream Lane and out that way with the money and the account book, and on the way home would call in to Geoff's farm for a drink of milk and to see his mum! I can't imagine children these days being allowed to cycle out of school with a bag of money! The Green brothers used to supply the vegetables for our school dinners, which were cooked by Mrs Cox and Mrs Pavey, and very good dinners they were, too. When I went on to Rydon, the headmaster there said that he always knew which were the West Chiltington children as they took sandwiches to school rather than have Rydon dinners, having been spoiled by the village school's excellent meals!"

Sue Overton-Smith (née Slater) also remembers this period in the life of the old school: "As I used to play with older children I couldn't wait to go to school, in 1952. I used to catch the early bus which came to the Common bus stop at about 8 o'clock which meant that I arrived with my teacher. In the winter she wore enormous fur gloves which were soft to touch. There were three teachers at the school: Miss Walder, Mrs Wallace and Mr Dixon, and about seventy five children.

In the Infants class we each had a little blackboard, a piece of chalk and a little square felt rubber before we progressed to books and pencils. We used the Old Lob reading scheme which was about a farmer and animals such as Percy the naughty chick, and Willie the pig; we learned to do joined-up writing and to spell words such as 'telephone'. Malcolm Knight, from the Queen's Head, used to come and press his face against the glass of the door when he was little because he wanted to see what we were doing and he wasn't old enough to come to school. On one occasion I can remember Christopher Manley from Nutbourne catching chicken pox and having to be dabbed with Calamine lotion.

Dr MacWhirter used to come to the school to give medical examinations; to enable Mrs Wallace's room to be used for the purpose, her pupils used to join Mr Dixon's.

For lunch, the Infants remained in their classroom and covered the tables/desks with blue and white checked tablecloths, but the top two classes went into the canteen where Mrs Pavey (the dinner lady) used to say 'Cabbage makes your hair curl and gives you rosy cheeks'. Sometimes we had the most delicious home-made biscuits and the story went around that the School Inspector liked them so much he ate ten!

In the Infants cloakroom we had a large tray on legs for sand or water play and two beds in case anyone was sleepy; we used to fold our arms and rest our heads on the desks for a short while after lunch each day.

The transition from the Infants to Mrs Wallace's was made easily enough even though she did have a reputation for being very strict. We had a system of Honour Marks and Black Marks and three of the boys were called The Terrible Trio because they were always getting black marks for one reason or another; it certainly made life interesting! Mrs Wallace used a ruler on the hand as a punishment whereas Mr Dixon used the cane, but only for boys! I remember one boy having the cane because he's made some tins of powder paint fall off the top of a cupboard; such punishments were always witnessed in horrified silence but they were few and far between.

I remember one winter walking to school along Mill Road, past Gentle Harry's Farm with the snow reaching high above my head; it was most exciting. Once at school we could hang any wet clothes over the railings surrounding the fire in the corner of the room. We were allowed to wear trousers in extremely cold weather, and the little bottles of milk would have chunks of ice in them so the milk crate was put by the fire, too; at playtimes in the winter we made icy slides on the slope which was fun. We played 'Fivesticks' and another favourite game was 'Horses' using skipping ropes; there were several singing games such as 'The Farmer's in his Den', 'Poor Jenny is a Weeping', and 'The Big Ship Sails on the Alley Alley Oh'. In the alleyway between the two playgrounds some people used to play Kiss Chase but it was usually stopped quite quickly.

In the summer we were allowed to use the high jump stand in the boys' playground, leading to fierce competition between the boys and the girls. Baseball was always a great favourite, too; this was most exciting as it was sometimes possible to hit the ball into the girls' playground or, even better, to knock it over the fence (and wall) down the hill to the pond! This counted as six. Thursdays were looked forward to because the ice cream van came and we were allowed to buy one; I can still remember the tingling sensation in my mouth after eating a long triangular shaped lolly.

We were learning to write in ink by this time; dipping our pens in the inkwells and trying to master the scratchy nibs. We had tables tests, and tried to see who could be the first to read all the one hundred or so books in the cupboard.

The whole school used to go to a service in the Church every Ascension Day; it was held by Rev Williams who was deaf and who therefore sounded strange to us children as we didn't understand fully the reason why. After the service he used to ask us questions and tell us about the church; we used to do sketches of the architecture.

At Christmas the people who lived at The Stone House gave a big box of oranges to the school - one for each child. Two regular events stick in my mind: we had to go on a walk round the village each year and on returning to the school, had to draw a map of where we had been, and the second event was that whenever there was a Meet we would all be taken to the cross roads where the whole village was gathered to see the hunt go off in their Hunting Pink or a lady in black with a bowler hat and hair in a net. The horses seemed enormous and the hounds were excitedly walking round, eager to be away.

Every day school began and ended with a prayer or reading; one regular one was 'When I was a child I behaved as a child…..but when I became a man I put away childish things' and another was the Prayer of St Richard. When we left we were allowed to choose our favourite hymn and sometimes sing a solo."

An 'adult's eye view' of the school in 1972 is given thus: "there were 102 children on the school roll then, they left their parents at the gate and walked round the building onto the playground at the back; if parents or visitors called into the office in the winter, all the heating would escape onto the playground.

The office was a small room shared by the Headmistress and the School Secretary, and contained a small round rug which the children sat on to

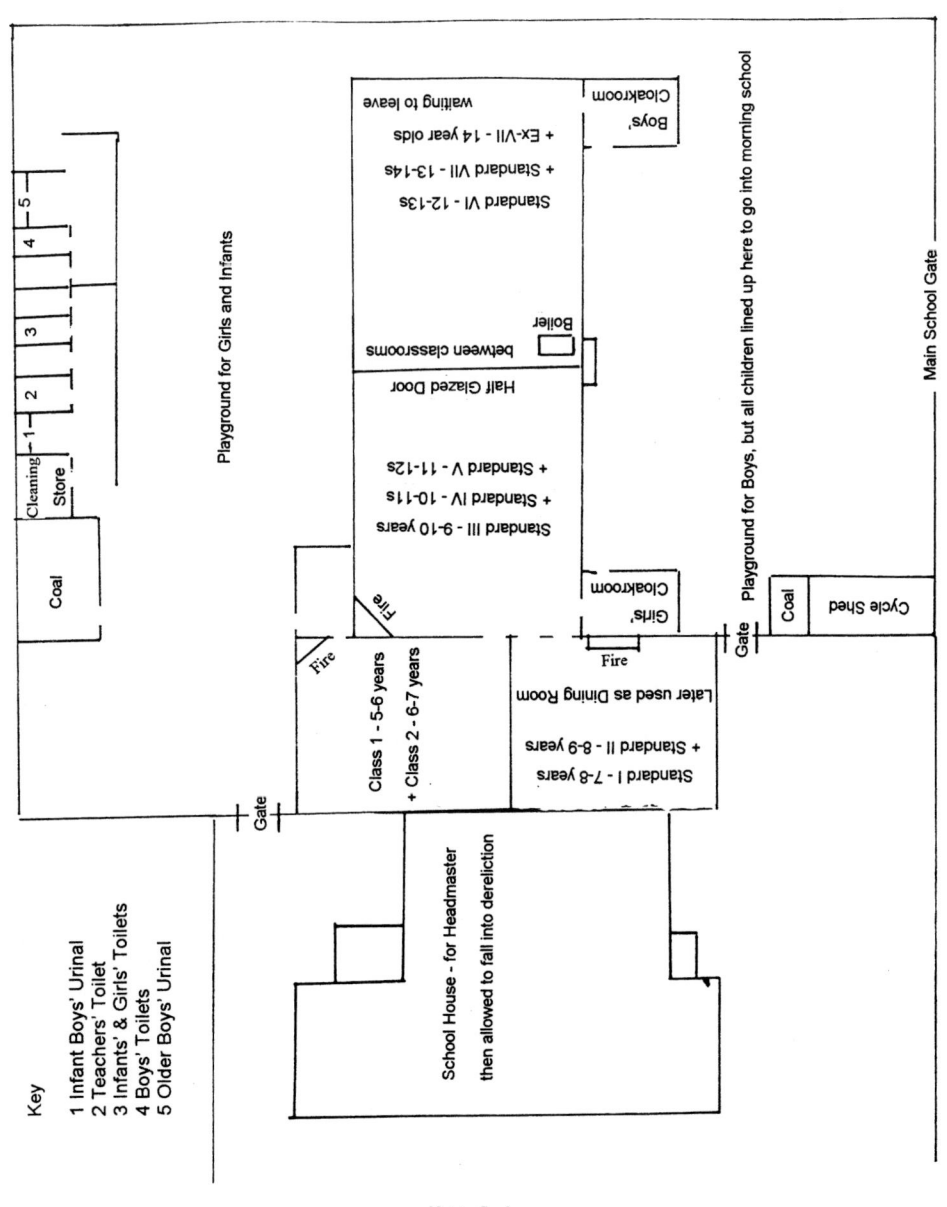

Not to Scale
Plan of the School

practice recorder and French. The room extended forwards on the east side of the building and had a door into the playground and another into the school. On the back of this door there was a cane which everybody knew was there, but no-one remembers it being used. This door led into the classroom for the oldest children.

West Sussex Gazette

AND SOUTH OF ENGLAND ADVERTISER

No. 6,224   Thursday, April 25, 1974   3p

Maypole Dancing – 1974
The last May Day celebrations at the 'old' school

    Walking along the front of the building one came to a glass and wooden partition with a door into the next classroom, beyond that was the kitchen. To the rear of the kitchen was another classroom for the youngest children. There was a small corridor along the back of the school leading to some newly built inside toilets. Off the corridor were double doors and steps down into the playground, which had outside toilets and a wooden-framed, blue plastic lined swimming pool, one of whose panels, one memorable day, gave way and flooded the playground.

The windows were high, the ceilings very high, and there was a very large, noisy oil-fired boiler for the central heating. The floors were boarded when the building was converted into a house, following its sale, and a display cabinet in the new entrance hall contains an assortment of the oddments lost under the floorboards over a period of nearly one hundred years.

The small room extending onto the front playground opposite the office was the cleaner's store cupboard and staff toilet; this front playground was used to practice maypole dancing in the summer. There was no school hall, the Church Hall down the road was used for PE, with Games being held on the present-day sports field. The children walked to these venues in line, taking all their kit and equipment with them. If anything was dropped, the adults had to pick it up as no child was allowed out of line or onto the road. There may be a relic of this rule even today as children will not go into the drive or road outside the present school to retrieve anything. As there was no hall all children had to clear away everything from their tables prior to lunch and all the tables and chairs had to be cleared to the side of the oldest children's classroom so that they could all meet for daily assembly and tables could be laid for dinners in the other classrooms. Every child had a school dinner and most children had school milk.

There were cycling proficiency courses, with road markings being painted on the playground and hand-operated traffic lights, but the courses ceased when it was decided that the village roads were too dangerous for training, and the training continued only when the children moved to Rydon.

Every year a Nativity play was performed in the Church. These plays were beautiful, but this tradition, too, had to be abandoned due to the increased number of children at the school and the number of parents who wished to see the performance. Parents would get to the Church 45 minutes before a performance in order to make sure they would get seats!"

The village school moved to its new premises on 3 December 1974 and the old site was sold for a private house. The Parish has to thank Mac Steele for his work to 'rescue' the old school bell: in 1988 when he heard that Mrs Davis who had bought the Old School House was moving, he approached her about the bell which she had had as a feature on her sitting room hearth. She had intended taking the bell away with her, but he persuaded her to consider selling it to the Museum; in the event, she donated it. The bell is inscribed Mears and Stainbank London 1876 and it

School Nativity Play – 1960 or 1961
Picture taken in the school. Angels from left: Mary Gumbrell, Janet Pavey, Christine Steele,
Vivien Bale
Front row: Trudi Shotnik, —, Charles Stone, —

used to hang in a small tower on the school building. The house changed hands in 1992; the new owners John and Amanda Vance say "we are both teachers and wanted to retain as much of the original character of the school as possible during renovations and improvements. The whole length at the rear of the building had had a concrete-floored, flat-roofed corridor added while it was still a school; the additions were stripped away and the concrete floor dug up and replaced with floorboards fashioned from old pine baulks from a dismantled Royal Navy building in Portsmouth, making our 'new' floor older than the original one. We altered the angle of the main roof to bring it out over the replacement construction which was almost the same footprint as the original; one part was constructed with a first-floor addition and all the existing skylights were changed into dormers. The brick garden wall, originally the back wall of the outside lavatories, was sandblasted to remove many coats of whitewash and paint; was raised by several courses and the tin roof was replaced by tiles, making a pleasing garden shed. Finally, the large front room with its high, stepped window (formerly a classroom and then the school kitchen) together with an original cloakroom was converted into a granny annexe."

Even before the war there were pre-school teachers, Peter Penfold remembers going to Miss Meeten whose house was on the south side of Big Hill, about half way down. Unfortunately he misbehaved so had to be removed, he then went to Miss Bolwell on the corner by the windmill. In both cases he was the only child there and was taught on his own, remembering the experience as being a bit lonely, particularly as he was so young. As his father had about four properties that he rented out, his mother was the rent collector, so it might be for this reason that she was unable to have him at home.

However in recent years pre-school education has become more organised and its importance recognised; various playgroups serve the 3-5 year-olds and mother and toddler groups have operated in various halls. In 1998 state-funded nursery education for four year olds commenced.

The village has at times boasted at least four private fee paying schools; Ivan Pullen remembers that Mr Dixon ran a school at New Barn, where his wife used to teach. He says "My wife and her sister went there; it cost a bit but Granny had a bit of money and she used to say it would be well spent". Later on, Mrs Gladys Dixon acted as a governess for a group of about six children in the house now called Tycanol in Haglands Lane. Liz Burgess (née Van Tromp) remembers going there from about 1936 when she was six until she was about nine. She says "Mrs Dixon kept goats, Petal and Pepper, and a donkey which would give us rides to and from its field, which was where Hindle Close is now. I remember the field had a black gate with Private written on it, and the animals were tethered in there; Mrs Dixon had had permission to use the field for grazing and the animals loved the brambles and jungle that there was. She also kept chickens and rabbits, and other small animals. We learned reading and writing, sums and needlework, but we all loved the animals which were the highlight of our day. When war broke out, Mrs Dixon decided that she could no longer run the school, and I went on to Mr Freeman's until I was fifteen. There was a whole group of us that went: Mary Law, Peter Cellier, Tony Ayling, Ralph Eames (Dr Eames' son), Ann West, Michael Wise and John Pickard." It seems Mrs Dixon had a boarding kennels in Commonland Farm and also kept hens for the eggs. Later she took up photography and turned her lounge into a studio; a woman of many parts.

There was a school at Little Thatch, a thatched Wells house in Monkmead Lane which was run by Mrs Hilda Barnes, a tall exuberant woman with her hair in a bun on top of her head. This was a small school where approximately fifteen to twenty children from about five were all taught in the L shaped sitting room. The children began at the 'little ones' table' and then when they were ready moved slowly round the room to end up with their own desks at the back; she taught up to, and possibly beyond, the 11+ level. There was also a huge round table, (which must have been Mrs Barnes' dining room table and did duty as such at lunchtime) a blackboard, a piano, and always a vase of dead flowers! She also had one of the first television sets in the village and the children remember watching The Lambeth Walk as one of the test programmes. Mrs Barnes had been a teacher before she was married and was a strict disciplinarian, but was a good teacher who, when necessary, employed a special tutor for the less able pupils. It is thought she started the school in the early 1930s, but it was certainly still going in 1965. About 1967 she had a stroke and died, and the school was closed, but a group of parents thought so highly of it that they thought about starting another, but the idea never got off the ground.

Richard Van Tromp who went to the school as had his brother, remembers that the first child to run up the drive from the road and touch the doorstep was the milk or ink monitor for that day. Packed lunches were taken, and sometimes there was a Milky Way at breaktime. Mrs Barnes' children had grown up, so the schoolchildren were allowed to play with the Lego, including a model complete with lights that her son Richard had made. Carol Cox' memories are slightly different; she remembers the riding. Mrs Barnes' daughter Penny, who ran a small riding school, would give her weekly riding lessons in the paddock beside the drive. This land has now been built on (the house is called Red Wyn Byn) but in those days had quite a few horses on it. Penny was a marvellous teacher, like her mother, and wonderful with both the children and the horses, which because of shortage of space, grazed on many a spare patch of land in the village, being collected every morning and taken to Little Thatch. The children also played rounders in the drive. A slightly less enjoyable aspect, however, was the school milk because in the winter the bottles on the doorstep would freeze and the milk tasted horrible to everyone except the blue tits who made holes in the metal bottle tops to get at the cream! Carol used to go home for lunch and enjoyed the walk up Sunset Lane through the trenches of ice.

It is Mrs Barnes' patience and caring attitude for her pupils that is most remembered, she gave help to the slower children and never allowed them to feel inadequate. Homework was sometimes given, but if a child was struggling, Mrs Barnes would ring the parents to discuss the extra work that would be sent home to enable that child to catch up, and would give extra tuition at weekends if she thought it would help to sort out a particular problem.

Mrs Barnes also ran a chicken farm at the house, and many recount how they used to go up to the house to buy her eggs: they were given a basket, and told to go and find as many eggs as needed which were sold on a 'per egg' basis. When the weather was sunny, the front door was left open and the chickens frequently wandered into the classroom.

A third school was run by Mr Stephen Freeman, an Oxford don, and his two spinster sisters in their house, now called Larch Hill, in Fir Tree Lane. He had a schoolroom built onto the house which he bought in 1936, being the first owner of this Wells Cottage; this school, like the others, catered for the upper echelons of the village, children from Roundabout and from Thakeham. This group of between twelve to twenty four children were taught in three classes; they grew up quite separate from the village children, who were having to manage in the village school which was overcrowded by the influx of evacuees. This school also took children from about four years old and it is thought that they could stay there until they were old enough to take the scholarship.

Elva Lipscome (née Johnson) went to Mr Freeman's school for ballet lessons on Friday afternoons with Miss Eileen Bellamy (who later married Van Tromp, see Chapter 6). There was a building on the right of the garden, a cross between a garden shed and a cricket pavilion with a wooden floor, where the ballet lessons were held for about a dozen girls and boys, who danced to music from a piano.

At the beginning of the War Felix Eames started a small school, in yet another Wells cottage, Myntwell, Spinney Lane, for some children who had been evacuated with their parents to West Chiltington. He was the husband of Dr Althea Josephine Eames whose practice was in Storrington and he started the school because his wife's patients asked her where to send their children to school. The Kelly's Sussex Directory for 1938 records the Eames as living at 99 Roundabout, Spinney Lane, so the school was called '99' after the house (remember when your doctor used to ask you to 'say ninety-nine' as part of their diagnosis?). Classes were held in the heather-thatched studio in the garden (Felix was an artist by profession) and there were swimming lessons in the garden pool; tuition continued until the children had found places in other schools. One of the half dozen or so boy pupils was Bill Pertwee of 'Dad's Army' fame, another was the son of Babs Wallace, the evacuee teacher, and a third was the son of Mrs Barnes who ran the school in Monkmead Lane. There seems to have been only one girl to the five boys. The school continued for perhaps a year.

Yet another school was housed at Ireton House in Common Hill. The late Mark Ogle wrote the following "About twelve to fifteen boys went there, as far as I can recall. I was there during the years 1957-58 after the family returned from the Far East and before I went on to preparatory school. I used to cycle to the school from Enderby Thatch where we lived. We were taught in one large room, and we had lunch at the school. The curriculum was pretty traditional: English, Maths, History, Geography, Scripture and a bit of Latin. The gardens bordered on fields at the back of the school, and we played football and other games. We were also often sent on cross-country runs: up to the Common, out to Smock Alley, back past The Elephant and Castle, through the village, and back up to the school. At that time there were very few, if any, houses on the other side of Common Hill, and I remember a very wild bit of woodland with rusting water tanks and dilapidated buildings in the middle of it.

Mr Wadman was the head teacher, perhaps the only teacher. I remember him as a large man with white hair and a loud voice, a kindly man and a

The New School – 1974

good teacher. My two best friends were Roy Dean, and Malcolm Knight who was the son of the landlord of the Queens Head."

The activities of the present village school during the last quarter of this century have been well documented in the school scrap book. The new building was officially opened on 24 March 1975 by Sir Edward Briton, the General Secretary of the NUT who had once taught the Headmistress. Various dignitaries attended and, to the amusement of the children, one appeared to go to sleep during the proceedings! The school had been on the County's building programme for some time, but the plan eventually agreed upon had to balance the needs of the school and its staff with the available budget, so was the usual British compromise; one example was that the new low level cisterns fitted to the children's toilets were removed one day and replaced by high level old fashioned cisterns with chains instead, presumably because they were cheaper. Due to the high water table on site, extra drains and soakaways had to be constructed which further ate into the budget so that the hoped-for new furniture and piano could not be provided.

The new building was universally welcomed; the apprehensions about its new semi-open plan were unfounded. The classrooms were light and airy, and dinners were served from the kitchen hatch to tables laid in the

Opening of the School Swimming Pool – July 1976
Norman Wisdom at the microphone, Chairman of the managers Stan Gooch sitting on his right, Headmistress Miss Shirley West on his left

tiled area in the centre of the school. The Friends of the School Association were not allowed to rest on their laurels, though, as the next project was the construction of the swimming pool, which was opened on a very hot day in July 1976 by Norman Wisdom. Six children went into the pool as part of the ceremony, but all the children had previously been in, the summer was too hot to have kept them out until the grand opening.

The school has developed and expanded and events have been celebrated: for the Queen's Silver Jubilee in 1977 the children participated in a sponsored walk for the Queen's Silver Jubilee Fund, from which a greenhouse was bought. A small pond was made under whose liner are sheets of newspaper which had been brought to the school, and named, by the pupils. Now the pond is established it is a wonderful environmental area with a pond dipping platform and a variety of trees. The delightful playhouse called Rainbow Lodge was purchased for the children, and a new office has been built so that the staff now have a staff room for their breaks and the office personnel have space to work. Two temporary

Arial Views July 1987
View taken by some of the fathers who took to the air to photograph the school and its surroundings

classrooms have been added to the south side of the school as the roll now numbers 181 children (in July 1999), and now a new hall is needed.

Recently, Year 5 children have had the opportunity to participate in residential educational visits, sometimes this is their first time away from home. This is a great step towards independence and the children always return with a mass of tales to tell, even if everyone is exhausted.

Mrs Muriel Astley, the School Secretary remembers the many school outings: "some when it rained all day, the sun only coming out once we were on the return journey and having to steam nicely all the way back to school. Other times when it was so hot we had to find drinking water and shady trees with or without midges and ants! Some children would always bring unsuitable food for the picnics, chocolate and sticky things and sweet and sticky drinks, guaranteed to attract every wasp in the vicinity and to ensure almost a wash down at the next toilets! Some children had exquisitely packed lunches, complete with garnish, and others were weighed down with sufficient food to satisfy a 20 stone manual worker. Many children were so keen to eat their food they would have liked to start lunch on leaving school on the outward journey! There have been visits to the theatre, often the first time a child has been in a theatre. The children have always enjoyed the outings, and the moments when a child discovered something new and interesting were pure magic.

The greatest challenge for me was the Local Management of Schools; in 1992 the school became computerised and was responsible for its own finances. At last we knew exactly where we were financially, although the budget is never enough."

The children at the village school in 1999 have compiled a collection of their memories of school; they say "We have a school uniform with a windmill on it because we have a windmill in our village." "When I was in Green Class (the reception class) I remember when a new person came we were allowed to play all day. So when Jonathan came we were playing and he told me one of the little bricks was a chocolate bar so I tried to eat it, then he said it was a little brick so I spat it out and Mrs James saw me so I got told off. Then I told Mrs James what Jonathan had said and he got told off and said 'sorry' to me." "I travel to school in my Mum's car, down the hill and through the hollows to school. It would be too far and dangerous to walk to school like they did in the olden days. Most of my friends go to school by car, but some who live near the school just walk to school." "I walk to school every day with the flowers on my way. I have a good week unlike the olden days where the people were afraid to speak because the teachers were fierce." "Every day I come into red class (Year 5, the top class) classroom, get out my books and look around. On the walls are displays and Times Table sheets, on units are more displays and boxes of school books, and dotted around the classroom are plants in pots. On every table is a tray with pots and pencils and pens in it, and the board we copied or looked at to tell us what to do." "There is an age here from 4-10 years. The early years' play area has been improved by a sand tray and a play house" "The school has been extended by two mobile classrooms and a bigger office. The mobile classrooms have names Pond Room and Garden Room." "As our school population has grown we've had to have lots of new teachers. We have just got a new head teacher. We have lots of new furniture coming to our school, and a new group room is going to be built too, we are going to use it for playing musical instruments/library/and lots of group things." "In the new classrooms we've got CD computers and lots of CD games that are good for the days we are doing maths or history." "We have got new gas central heating so in the winter the two new class rooms don't get cold and the heating goes right through the school and even into the mobile classrooms." "Outside the office they have a new security system with locks on the doors so no-one can just walk into the school" "We come to school at 8.45am have registration and usually have two lessons before Assembly. We have Assembly every morning except Monday, on a Monday we have Assembly in the afternoon because it's a whole school Assembly. Every day we have an hour of literacy and an hour or numeracy and every week we have one PE lesson. We have 9 subjects they are:- English (literacy), maths (numeracy), science, RE, art, DT, PE, history and geography." (RE is religious education, DT is design technology and PE is physical education). "Not long ago we went to Shoreham harbour and we did lots of geography." "School finishes at 3pm and we have lots of after-school activities like football and basketball and music and art lessons." "We have had lots of school events recently like Macmillan Coffee Morning and a May Fair and Sports Day."

This is indeed our history for the future.

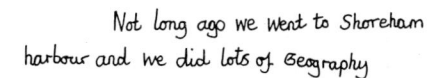

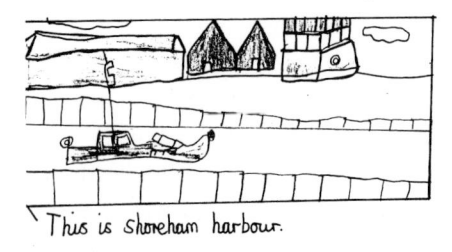

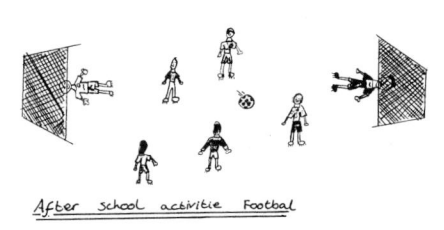

Children's Drawings 1999

Chapter 11

The World of Work

When asked "without television and modern distractions, what did you do in the school holidays?" the universal reply was "Work!" Even in the better-off families the children were expected to do their fair share: Elsie Cattell remembers that during the summer holidays she would go picking blackberries for Mr Barnes, the farmer at Palmers Lodge, who would take them to market in Brighton. The children were then paid for their work, and some of this money would go towards family expenses such as school shoes for the winter. Picking blackcurrants and strawberries at Naldretts is also remembered but in this instance the money went towards the school and Sunday School annual outings.

Gwen Smith was born in Pulborough in 1924, the eldest of five children; but went to live in the Birches in 1926. When she was a girl of about eight, she remembers that a horse-drawn mobile shop (described as a sort of chicken house on wheels, very clean but unmistakable!) would come and park on the Common where the transformer now is behind the garage. The front of this shop would be opened up, and there would be the empty punnets for the children to tip their freshly-picked blackberries into, to be sold. The children were paid 2d per pound for the fruit; they were also paid for the primroses they picked; this was their pocket money. After leaving school at 14 she started doing domestic work for 7/6d a week from 8am to 5pm for a Mrs Bateman at Roundabout, who also employed a cook and a nanny. She continues: "Shortly after I started I was greeted by a row of shoes to be cleaned, I was most indignant as that was a man's job, no matter that she was paying me! At thirteen I had had to run a house and look after six people: I had a mother in poor health, a disabled sister and two young brothers plus my father, so I used to do all the cooking, washing and ironing and I wasn't cleaning shoes. So I left and took three other jobs to fill up the day. Then the war came and I worked on the land, from 7am to 5pm, often with overtime, Saturdays as well and sometimes Sunday mornings, and that was when I was fifteen. It was called Work of National Importance and everyone over sixteen had to do it; we worked with Land Army girls at Linfields where we were raising food, and being near home it suited me very well." (AG Linfield's was a family business until the 1980s when it was taken over, and taken over again by the Thompkins Group which had a wide portfolio of interests including Smith and Wesson, the firearms manufacturer. In the early 1990s Thompkins sold the mushroom growing part of the business which is now known as Chesswood Mushrooms; there has since been a management buy-out.)

"My father worked with his father on the thrashing machine, so we were truly local, and I didn't want to move away. Dad used to take this machine wherever they were wanted with the main demand being in the summertime, so during the growing period when they weren't wanted so much he went into labouring for the building trade, and he helped to build a lot of those houses at Roundabout."

Ivan Pullen had a paper round in the 1930s and he remembers that a Mr Dodd gave him a £1 Christmas box, which compared very favourably with the 2/9d he earned for doing the round six days a week. However, he had mixed feelings about this particular house as they used to have *The Times, The Daily Mail, The Bystander,* and books delivered, quite as much as he could carry! But the folk in Roundabouts always gave a £1 tip. At fourteen he left school; in 1942 "They" at County Hall told you where to go and work. He received a letter which told him to go to Linfield's, but not liking the idea, he went and got a job at Haglands Farm which had a milking herd. As he says: "I worked there until about 1950 and when Smith that owned Haglands sold up when the war finished and went to Australia, we was all looking for jobs again then, and I went to Brinsbury Farm. I kept moving around all the seasonal jobs, there was plenty of work in them days. They say now 'It's not the sort of job I'm looking for' but if you're looking for a job you make it the sort of job you're looking for. To me life has always been like that. When you get into a job you don't say to yourself 'I'm fed up with this' you just keep doing it and when you do leave, you want to go back to it and say 'Can I have my job back!'"

Peter Penfold recounts how his father left Monkmead in the 1930s to be a Caddie Master at the West Sussex Golf Course. "You don't have Caddie Masters now," he says "but Father was in charge of all the caddies, and my brother and I learned to play there. As caddies we were paid 6d per round if we were under 12, increasing when we got to 14, so with tips and hard work I could end up with between three and five bob."

As one of a family with a limited income, and ten children, Elsie Willmer was working by the age of ten, fitting in her job around her school time. She describes her day: "I lived up at Woods Hill with Mr Coles and I used to get up and clean the front porch, the smoke room, the cloakroom and the dining room and hall with its brick floors before I went to school. This was in 1935 when Mrs Coles was in South Africa with her daughter, so I was left alone with Mr Coles and I had to do everything. In the morning I used to go to his room at a quarter to eight, to wake him up and open his curtains, then go back downstairs to finish my jobs and cook his breakfast. Then at half past eight I would go in and say 'it's half past eight now, sir, I've left your breakfast all ready, I'm going to school now'. I used to leave his trolley with bread and cheese and water for his lunch; he used to spend all day in the woods. I used to go home to have lunch with mother after morning lessons, and after school at night I went back to Woods Hill to cook a meal for him and do all the day's washing up. This was for five days a week, so I didn't have time to go out and play with the other children after school. I didn't get paid at first because I wasn't on my own, but then when I looked after him on my own I got 2/6d a month. There was no electricity in the house but they used to make their own gas, and no piped water, all the water was pumped from the woods where it had been dammed. There was a big wheel on one of the sheds, and Mr Russell the gardener, used to stand and turn this wheel to pump the water into the house. Sometimes, later, I used to cook for Mr Coles and for Mr Morgan from Nyetimber, as they were friends."

As well as looking after Mr Coles she was expected to do her share around her own home, which sometimes included getting the coal. She tells the story of this task "I remember carrying quarter of a hundredweight of coal, on my back for my mother, from the coalyard, up the hill, over the fields, through the twitten, and it was bloomin' heavy and a long way ($1/4$ cwt = 28lbs). On another occasion when my mother asked me if I would go twice to get two loads, I tried to be clever and get them both at once. I built myself a truck to carry it on; I got some wheels, an axle and a wooden box, and off I went with my younger brother Perce. After we had collected the coal, half a hundredweight this time, we dragged the truck across the fields, and, at the top of the hill the handles break, the coal and some apples we were given by someone, goes over the bank and spills everywhere. (We had taken our own sacks to put the coal in, there were scales in the coalyard to weigh out the amount.) By this time we were about half way home, so I sent Perce home to get the old pushchair, a wooden one with a back, and gathered up the apples which had all rolled out everywhere and put them back into the truck and the coal back into the sack. When Perce arrives back with the push chair we strap the coal sack on and I take the chair with the coal and Perce manages to bend down and push the truck with the apples as we had no handles. Coal was delivered for 7½d a quarter hundredweight, but if we collected it it was only 7d and my mother gave me the halfpenny so I could go and buy an ounce of sweets. Mother never made us help, she was a kind and gentle woman, she just asked us if we would."

There was a light side to this arduous life, though, and most people had the ability to laugh at some of their troubles. Elsie continues: " Even though I had left school and was fourteen, I still had to be in by 9pm. One night we were all having a wonderful time at a dance in The New Hall and I realised it was after my deadline, so I grabbed my bike and cycled as hard as I could up the steep hill to Woodshill. Just before I got to the drive, I let my back tyre down so that when I was asked 'wherever have you been?' I could reply that I had had a puncture!" Times, and excuses, don't change much with the years!

To the question "what did your father do?" would often come the reply "well, anything and everything". Pat Steele recalls that everyone knew her father, 'Old Charlie Winton' who used to be a farmer, but in later life,

Charlie Winton – in his cap, with his dog

amongst other things, was allowed to shoot on Bill Wadey's land. However, Bill used to have a rabbit shooting syndicate from Worthing come up to his farm, and one of the syndicate complained that someone was taking their rabbits and that he was going to wait and catch the offender. He caught him taking the rabbits out of the snares, and marched him off to George Skinner the foreman, triumphant. He was somewhat deflated though, when George replied to the "Do you know this man?" question with "It's old Charlie, everyone knows old Charlie!" Village communities bred characters, a trait which seems to be lacking these days. It is said that Charlie was the first person in the village to have a lorry, used to take the flowers to market. He also used to wassail the apple trees, and at one place where he was not given a tip, nor a glass of ale, he chanted the 'curse' "Donkey-Do, Apple now, Someone I know won't get no apples now", except that he mentioned the name of the ungenerous man! As he has already had quite a lot to drink it sounded completely incoherent! Ena Howard has written the words of a wassail song her father and friends used; the music to the song being produced by blowing down the spouts of watering cans:

> Here stands a good old apple tree
> Bear well, top.
> Every bough - apple now, every twig - apple big
> Hat full, lap full, four and twenty sacks full
> Hip and holler again, boys
> Hip and holler again - Hurrah!

Much of the farm work was seasonal, and accommodation could sometimes be found for the workers in tied cottages. When the job was finished, the cottage had to be vacated, the children taken out of school and the family moved on to find other work. There was little security because there were no unions, no contracts, and one could be sacked on instant dismissal, with a queue of others waiting to take your place. If no work was found, with no safety-net of Social Security, you just managed as best you could; those in this dilemma in the village resorted to staying with their families, but there were real difficulties for the migrant workers that came in. Joan Penfold says that she moved to the village when she was nine, and the family rented one of the Hatches Cottages. They had been there six months when John Duke, the landlord, told them he wanted them out by Friday as he was getting married and wanted the house for himself. Joan's father rushed everywhere to try and find the family somewhere to live; eventually they ended up in a tumble-down cottage at Finches Cottages while later he got a job two days a week with Albert

Mustchin, the coal merchant. Meantime, they went hungry. It is with this background that the 'crime' of poaching can be more sympathetically understood, although even the farm owners sometimes found it hard to make ends meet and felt that they needed the pheasant or rabbit shooting rights.

Joy Adams (née Pullen) adds her story of 1936 to this picture: "Dad was out of work for a long time after he had his appendix out, I suppose I was about ten or eleven. He had worked for the Council, but they had cut back, and I can remember one winter when he used to cycle miles and miles to try and find work. Then the rector, The Reverend Hall, who had just moved from the old rectory to the new rectory, asked Dad if he would like to trim the privet hedge all round his garden, for a shilling a day. Dad was very willing to take it. There was no help, except sometimes the parish would let you have a few coppers if you were lucky. We survived with what we could grow on the allotments, and a few rabbits. I was working at Rosebank on The Common, as a delivery girl, while I was still at school. After school I would go to the shop and pick up a small basket with two loaves in and deliver it to the Barkworth's maid Rosie. Then I went home for tea, and was back in the shop from 5pm to 9pm; on Saturdays I worked from 9am to 9pm, and all for one and sixpence a week! It was quite a lot of money in those days, I suppose, but we worked hard for it. We used to walk from The Common to a house opposite The Queens Head to get an order, come back to the shop to make it up, and then walk back with it. I remember two gallon of paraffin was always on that order (and that was heavy) and a tin of Compton's gravy powder. I had my bike one day and someone told Mrs Cozens at Rosebank that I was using my bike to go up the village to get the order, and she told me off about it. I never did see the sense in that, but I didn't dare use it again. After I left school I worked for a lady in Roundabouts for 2d an hour, but soon gave that up to go to Linfield's for $4\frac{1}{2}$d an hour but that was really hard work. They grew carnations, tomatoes, onions, strawberries, potatoes and chrysanthemums; a lot was grown under glass, but quite a lot was grown outdoors, too. They employed quite a few of the village girls, and in the summer of 1941 three of us worked down the rows of tomato plants breaking off the unwanted shoots. The juice from the stems stained our dresses, girls didn't wear trousers and dungarees as they do now, and dresses, like everything else, were on ration. We worked, bending over, in that hot summer so my neck became burned very brown and my mother tried to scrub it off with a scrubbing brush thinking it was stain."

Most of the girls went into service; the boys had the option of working on the land or for Mr Slater. Joan Penfold, however, went to work at High Bar Nurseries in Thakeham when she was fourteen, in spite of opposition, and stayed there for 43 years. They grew carnations for Covent Garden market and, after she was married, her husband Charlie, who was also employed by the nursery, would drive the horse and cart full of the flower boxes to Billingshurst station to catch the early train to London every morning. In the summer the boxes were packed all day, three dozen to a box, and hundreds of boxes were sent off.

Reg Slater had been helping in the family building business of P Slater and Sons Ltd while still at school, and at fourteen joined the business full time. He was born in the house that used to be called Warriors Rest (now Richmond Cottage) in what used to be called Sandy Lane (now Lordings Lane). His parents lived there after they were married but moved up to Palmers Lodge opposite the Queens Head after the Mustchins, who were the landlords, wanted the bungalow back for their daughter who was getting married. In those days, the 1920s and 30s, there was very little privately owned property and most houses were rented.

Reg says: "The family can be traced back to the 1700s; a Slater made the village stocks and whipping post in 1651 for 18s.0d in the same premises in Church Street that the family used until recently, and perhaps they go back even further. The records of the Overseers of the Poor state that in 1751 Thomas Slater was a carpenter at Hobjohns, and the company also made the wooden cart wheels for the blacksmith to tyre. The land has been in and out of the family; it belonged to the Greens at one stage, the market garden family, and we rented it until we bought it back Originally my great-grandfather built in stone and flint with local materials from quarries at Beeding and Woodshill, this latter quarry yielded not such good quality so was used less often, but the site is still there and is called Quarry Woods. The stone was dressed on site although some random stone was just built as it was dug, being carted up to the works by horse. At the turn of the century the Geal family lived at Dennis Marcus Farm and their sons had teams of horses and carts and did the local stone carting. They carted all the stone for Little Thakeham in 1901 when it was built. The wood was bought as trees which were sawn out at Bourn Saw Mills at Timberlands during the Second World War, or bought ready-prepared from Wenban Smith in Ashington, or from Benzleys now called Jewsons. In those days they were all family firms but Wenban Smith is the only one that has not been taken over by one of the big companies, and has dealt with Slaters for over 70 years.

Great-grandfather Slater (known as Old Ned) and Grandfather, his only son, each had a horse and cart which they used to transport bits and pieces and to take them to work, and I remember hearing that there was an old white horse called Tom who used to graze on the common at Herongate. When I joined the business at the beginning of the war they had a couple of little vans and it gradually built up until they had lorries. I had my first car in 1958 or 59 when I was nearly thirty - they didn't think I needed one! A push bike was enough for a boy; the elders were the ones that drove the vans; we put our tools on the handlebars of the bikes and off we went! The jobs were all local so we often just took the hand truck and the wheelbarrow. The uncles didn't have to take a driving test in those days, but we didn't travel far - Uncle Albert lived up at Harbolets bungalow in Broadford Bridge Road and had a yard up there, Grandfather had a yard opposite the Village Hall and we had the one in Church Street, so we used to cycle to the nearest yard, pick up materials in the van and go off to the jobs; larger loads were moved by Mustchins.

In the early days there were very few planning restrictions; you had a piece of land, drew a picture of what you wanted, took it to the Council offices in Storrington, and then built!"

War broke out in 1939 and many of the company employees were called up; when Reg left school at 14 in 1942 and entered the business there were only nine men but the numbers swelled to about forty when they all came back. They were the biggest employers in the village doing restoration and repairs; all the odd work and one-off buildings as opposed to housing estates. The workshops were on the site where Wheelwrights in Church Street is now: looking in to the estate, the offices were all along the left hand side with a workshop at the far end. In the centre was a timber store, and where the bungalows are was a paint store, the plumbers store, the lime store, the garage for the lorry, and scaffold racks, with sand, ballast, bricks and tiles being stored around the yard. The only work they sub-contracted was the electrical work which went to Tony Gocher and his father before him; he was a mechanic but took up electrical work when electricity came to the village in 1934. Reg became a director in the family business in 1964 and Funeral Director in 1967 on the retirement of his Uncle Albert.

Brian Ruff was born in the village in May 1938 and is Reg Slater's younger cousin, his mother and Reg's father being brother and sister, and he adds: "We probably only built one house a year but we did all the maintenance work - when I joined the main work was painting and decorating. We would start one end of Roundabout and whitewash every house and start again when we got to the end! Nearly every house had only cold water and there was little central heating so our three plumbers didn't have life too complicated. When I joined the company my three uncles ran it and I went to night school for two years. I didn't want to be a carpenter as my brother was, and I hated metalwork so wouldn't be a plumber, so I became a bricklayer; it pleased everybody that another bricklayer was going into the family business.

I went to Rydon School and on to Horsham Technical School; unfortunately the tech didn't last long which was a shame as it gave the youngsters a grounding in building skills. I left school at 15 but I insisted on an indentured apprenticeship; I was the first Slaters had had and it was years before they had another! My uncle thought that my first day at college was the only one - he didn't realise I had five years of it! I went one day a week for two years and then three nights a week, it was pretty hard as I had to walk from Horsham Station to Roffey. The Council paid my travelling expenses but my mother paid the fees as my uncle didn't realise that the company was supposed to. The Slater family owned Hobjohns in Church Street and one day Uncle Ernest suggested that if Sheila and I got married we could have the cottage for a nominal rent, so we did! Couldn't leave it standing empty! Sheila first came to the village when Mustchins sold the coal yard to Tyne Main as her cousin's husband was the first manager there. I stayed with the company until the end."

The building climate was changing as the 1980/90 recession was beginning. The company started to look for other outlets and worked for a while with a Swedish company called Scandiahus that made Scandinavian timber framed houses. There were further serious problems when Slaters built Wheelwrights; it was their first development, a sheltered housing scheme built on their land. They built in phases and the houses were snatched up as quickly as they could be built, but the prospective owners then found difficulty in selling their own property as the housing market collapsed, so they relinquished their options and did not move. The company then borrowed money to finish the project, but the bank asked for the loan to be repaid and the company had to be wound up in 1990. Sadly Slaters is no more, although Wheelwrights is its memorial.

As was traditional, the builders doubled as the coffin makers and undertakers with Albert Slater, Reg's uncle, looking after this side of the business. Brian expands on this "My mother was the eldest girl from a big family, she was called Aunt Sis although her proper name was Kathleen Sabina Slater, and when people called in the midwife they would call Aunt Sis as well. Equally, she was called on to lay out the dead; a goodwife I think the term used to be, and each district nurse had one they could call upon. The tradition goes back centuries and I was well used to being woken up by someone who needed her services, and although she often did the job for nothing she sometimes got a glass of sherry or a couple of pounds. When I used to get up in the morning, if her apron was in the scullery I'd know she'd been called out; the gentry would pick her up in the car otherwise she'd walk to where she was going. When I was about sixteen she suffered from angina and I thought it was time she stopped doing it, particularly after one time when she got up in the morning and found a couple of pounds in her pocket, she was so tired she hadn't a clue whose house she'd been to the night before. The last person she laid out was her husband in 1968. I helped her, it was a sort of tribute.

After a while it became too expensive to make the coffins ourselves so in the 1960s we started to order them from London and I used to collect them from Pulborough Station late at night; they would come down in a hessian stocking ready made up. We would collect the body from the house in one of our two carrying coffins and take it back to the yard where we had a chapel of rest. Originally the chapel of rest was attached to my uncle's house at Broadford Bridge, but when he retired from the business we created a new chapel of rest in the yard. Then we would take the body to the church, or wherever. We gave a personal service, we knew the families we were dealing with, and really were funeral directors, advising on church and hymns, but we didn't do the catering like they do today. In the 1940s we had had a bier, a wheeled cart, to take the coffins to the church, but often we simply used to carry them; it wasn't far. People didn't want, or couldn't go to the expense of a hearse which we had to hire in." Stan Gooch's funeral is remembered by Meg Judd: "the coffin came along the evening before in Slater's little green van. They were so much cheaper than Tribes in Worthing who would charge perhaps £400 to Slaters £250." Funerals are also remembered by the children who used to view them during school time from the boys' playground, standing quietly by the wall and watching the men in top hats and tails.

Brian continues: "People used to want the coffin in the church before the congregation went in, so we would light a remembrance candle and the rector, or one of us would stay. Once the coffin is received into the church a remembrance candle is lit and stays burning until the service is over; sometimes it was overnight. It's strange to tell a funny story about this but I remember once we had scaffolding in the church and the vicar was unable to take the service inside the building so he suggested we went either to Thakeham or had the whole service at the graveside. The relatives said that they would prefer the service at the graveside as the man had never been into church in his life and there was no need to start now!" Brian's wife Sheila adds "He and Reg got called out anytime; I remember once we were going to a dance, it was a RAFA do and I was all dressed up in a long dress when there was this knock on the door, and away he went to collect the body, then he came back and collected me! He got called out one Boxing Day when we were at my mother's, but it's the way things were."

Bill Carver also ran a building company in the parish. He was born in 1934 at Naldretts in East Street, in a house owned by his grandfather, and went to local schools, leaving at 15 to learn the building trade. His grandfather had come to West Chiltington in 1914 to be the landlord of the Elephant and Castle. When Bill's father (another William also known as Bill) grew up and got married, grandfather allowed the couple to live at one end of Naldretts. When Bill was three the family moved to the Common.

Bill's father was called up in 1918. By the time he had finished his army training the war had ended but he remained in Germany with the Army of Occupation, returning home in 1920. He worked as a bricklayer for the Council for some years and then found a job with the Storrington building firm of Walter Dean.

Bill takes up the story: "By 1935 Dad had decided to start his own house building company. There were a lot of men working for Walter Dean and Reginald Wells who

Carver's Yard

chose to come and work for father so he started off with a skilled workforce. David Thomas worked in the office and did Dad's plans and designs.

The first property Carver's built was a little bungalow called Jubilee Cottage, opposite Tudor Close entrance in Pulborough; this has since been demolished and a large house erected on the site. The next five houses were built on land backing onto the recreation ground running up to the old cottage called Mawkins. They were built for £500 each. I'm not sure how my father financed it all because when he left Dean's in 1935 I shouldn't have thought he was earning more than £3 a week. I expect he worked on a stage payment basis: first payment at damp course level, second at plate level, third at plastering and the rest on completion, and there were times when things were tight. Dad had left school at 13, my grandmother had left at 11 but had given herself a wonderful education through reading; there wasn't anything she couldn't talk about, and her determination to succeed was obviously transmitted to my father. He built up a terrific business; the men used to try and remember all the houses Carver's had built but they lost count because in those days Carver's did all the building in the area. If an architect put plans out to tender we were nearly always fortunate enough to get the job.

My father built several houses in Tudor Close before the Second World War including one called The Well House for Sir Harold Derbyshire who had returned from India I believe, and another large house called Grey Oak. (During the war the remaining land at Tudor Close had to be planted with potatoes, corn or whatever to comply with the war effort). There are also two architect designed houses on The Common which Dad built during 1935 and 1939; they are Windways (now in 1998 a retirement home) which looks as if it had been built hundreds of years ago with its solid oak doors, windows and beams, and Haslewood down Common Hill.

When the war broke out Dad wasn't called up and there was just enough work for him, and a few older men to do during the war years. When the younger men returned there were a lot of council houses to build; in 1946 Carver's built The Juggs, and other estates in Ashington, Storrington and Pulborough, requiring a workforce of about 60 men. Materials were difficult to obtain and timber was on licence until 1952 - this meant only a certain quota of wood was allowed per dwelling. However, as private house building hadn't really got started at that time, building Council houses was ideal as once you'd agreed your price the money was guaranteed!

We weren't really in competition with Slater's, because they didn't build a lot of houses, doing mostly jobbing work. Dad's first car was an old Austin; during the war he had a Singer which was used like a truck - the things he used to carry on the back seat! This car had a sunshine roof so he could carry the timbers sticking out of it. Mustchins the coal merchant used to move most of our materials though, and years later, when clearing out the office I found old receipts from Mustchins 'to move sand and ballast-12/6d'! We also used another man in the village, George Cox who was a haulage contractor.

Later on, after the company was incorporated in May 1951 as Carvers (Builders) Limited, we trained quite a few apprentice carpenters. They would come to us to work and on one day of each week they would attend college in Roffey to get their City and Guilds Certification; this had to be fitted in with the National Service, which men had to do at that time. We sub-contracted out electrical work but had our own plumbers and painters.

Our yard was between Foxfields and Harborough Drive on The Common. It was $\frac{1}{2}$ to $\frac{3}{4}$ acre in size with a house called Templemead, which Father had bought for about £500 in 1937. As you drove into the yard the office was on the right - attached to Templemead - and you could stop there on the way in with the workshops beyond the office. After some time Dad bought the land across the road opposite the yard, this was for storage of materials mainly. As West Chiltington began to change, people began to complain to Chanctonbury District Council about the yard's untidiness but the Council's answer was that Dad had been there too long for them to be able to do anything about it! My mother and the Company purchased several strips of land which combined to make Castlegate Estate which we developed over several years.

We had various gangs of men, one would be building properties on the firm's land, following plans drawn up by David Thomas, and another gang would build houses designed by a well known Storrington architect Peter Eddolls, and other architects, for clients on their privately owned land. In the 1950s you could buy a plot of land for a few hundred pounds; I remember a lady who used to come down to Sussex from London at weekends with her caravan suddenly coming to my father and asking him if he wanted to buy her land, she asked £250 for the two plots!

As well as buying land opposite the yard Dad had previously bought adjoining land from Hugh Penfold in Lcander, to extend the yard. In 1957, when I got married, we were able to build a bungalow, Hennies, behind the yard in which my wife Carole and I could live. In 1966 my father built another bungalow next to us for him and my mother to retire into. At this time, my sister Eileen Hobbs stayed in the old family home Templemead, with her family. Sadly, my father died in March 1970, a month before his 70th birthday, and I carried on the business.

We always had an eye to the future and maintained our land bank, we did our homework and usually got permission to build eventually. For example, we knew that one day the house next door to the yard, Foxfield, would come up for planning when it sold because of the size of its garden. There was a little cottage called Elfins which ran right alongside Foxfield, and one day I saw a sale board being put up so I dashed back to the office, telephoned the agents and bought it. Now we had the key to the development of Foxfield and its land because planning permission would only be given to the site if the access visibility was good, and the garden of Elfins gave the extra area needed. We waited a few years and Foxfield came on the market - we got 16 houses in there whereas the previous owner had applied for planning and could only get permission for two. That's business. Incidentally, that house Foxfield was interesting in that it was renamed several times by Mrs Armstrong who lived there prior to our purchase - it began as Waldron Cottage, was changed to Mount Pleasant and finally to Foxfield. She also owned Elfins at one time, which was called The Cabin originally. Finches Lane was another development of ours, off Little Hill.

We realised our way of working would have to change when mass-produced kitchen units and bedroom furniture, bookshelves etc came on the market. We used to make all these things in our workshop as we had all the necessary machines and tools to prepare the wood ourselves, and three full-time men in the workshop and about five other men who worked in there as well as on site - roofing, second fixing and that. Customers would be asked what they required in their kitchen and bedrooms and a carpenter would draw up a sketch and make exactly what was wanted, but it became impractical to do that when the units could be purchased ready-made.

I carried on the business until 1991. By this time house building had become too competitive for the small builder and, with large companies like Bovis and Berkley Homes moving into West Chiltington, I decided to call it a day. Land is so expensive now that much of the cost of your property is actually the land value, things have got silly and costs out of proportion. There is also much more bureaucracy. For instance my father did have some insurance but now that a man can, rightly, claim for redundancy, for accidents and so on, premiums are becoming unrealistic and that's another cost we have to carry. The men need security both in the workplace and job security; it's not like the old days when you took a man on, in the middle of the week sometimes, and paid him by the day to the end of the week, in cash, and if he was no good you could say 'sorry' and he would go. Father used to go down to the bank and draw a case full of cash, none of the men had a bank account so if you had paid them a cheque they would have had to go to a shop to cash it. When I gave up, one man's wages was as much as Father used to pay his whole workforce! I sold the yard and the rest of the land bank to other developers and bought a property in Pulborough, which has some acreage, and have happily retired as a small farmer!"

From builders to an electrician's story: Peter Penfold explains: "When I left school I got work as an apprentice electrician at Gocher's in Nutbourne until I went into the Air Force in 1938 where I continued the trade, until I came back to the village at the end of the war. Eventually I ran Penfold's Electrical Service in Storrington, Billingshurst and Pulborough, basic electrical work and repairing radios, as I had in the Air Force. Television was invented by John Logie Baird in 1926 and I put up an early television aerial before the war for a man at the bottom of Harborough Hill; I thought it was a wonderful thing, this picture in this big box. The first one after the war, on the new system, must have been for Carver the builder because I remember he came into the shop to buy a set; we all helped put up the aerial which was attached to a long pole attached to the back of the workshop. We all crowded round to see. I worked as an electrical contractor until 1975, when I decided to do something else and just keep the electrical business part time, running it from Field House, our home in Broadford Bridge. Field House (it has a different name now, next to the shop) was rather a derelict old place when we took it over so we did it up and made it habitable; we had cesspool drainage, water and a telephone but no electricity so I had to use a generator. If I needed more space and power I used the workshop at my father's house on the Common called Leander; the house is still there although it has been extended and altered. Father also owned the building that became Carver's workshop, and a little building called Redroof in Harborough Drive, which has also been rebuilt. No-one took over the business when I finished."

Church Close has been built on the site of Mustchin's old coal yard, and there was talk, at planning time, of calling the road Mustchin's or something similar, to retain the link with the past. Unfortunately the developer had, unbeknownst to the Parish Council, already named the road and the first house had been sold; the new owners were reluctant to have the name of their road changed so soon after moving in. At the entrance to the coalyard stands Lakerscroft, which was also owned by the Mustchins, but in the last century this plot was owned by Jimmy Norris, the carrier. When Lakerscroft was repaired about 1910 it is said that the workmen found that wooden crosses from the churchyard had been used to repair the rafters; in 1972 more were discovered during further renovations.

Coal was one of the major commodities in the village in the early days and Albert, or Squeaky, Mustchin's Coalyard features in many accounts of village life. Albert was born at Southlands Farm and started the coal business in 1921

Doug Golds recounts: "when I worked there in 1957 coal came to the yard from coal trucks coming into Pulborough Station from the mines in Wales or elsewhere. The company had four trucks, one was a small Austin called a doodlebug, and we used to take it to the station to collect the coal. It was quite fun, actually. Mr Mustchin sometimes used to ring the station to find out whether the trucks were in, but generally you went in your own time and they at the station would tell you where the truck was situated, down the siding or wherever. There was one line on the right and two on the left, and sometimes you would have to wait until the shunters had shunted the truck into the right position so you could get the lorry in. Pulborough was quite a busy station, used for freight because everything was sent by train in those days, and by other coal merchants. With the truck

Albert Mustchin with grandson Nicholas – 1960
Photograph taken in the coal-yard

positioned you would back the lorry up to the truck door in the side, open the doors and then there was a terrific rush of coal into the lorry, the lumps of coal were huge, some were 18" big and if they got stuck in the door and wouldn't come through you had to get a great sledgehammer and smash them up so the coal would flow. You had to wedge coal sacks around the sides and edge of the lorry where there might be cracks to stop the coal falling on the ground because it was your job to sweep up spills, but if you were careful the doorway was the same width as the rear tail board so you should be all right. Sometimes you would fill the lorry sideways on. Sometimes the trucks were left in the siding and you had to do it all yourself: walk up the track and take the brake off the truck, hold the brake, let the truck roll down the hill to the buffers and put the brake on, then position the lorry. When we got the coal back to the yard we had to shovel it off because Mustchin didn't have tipper trucks, the chap I worked with shovelled right handed so I had to learn to shovel left handed and we did the job between us. The coal was shovelled into the various bays which were made of railway sleepers covered in corrugated iron. Then we made up the orders for people, put it on the lorry and delivered it, mostly to West Chiltington. Sometimes we delivered out of the area, but each coal merchant tried to stick to his own area, particularly as delivery was included in the price.

Real good coal is anthracite, it is not a composite, it is real coal. Then you have house nuts which is the house coal, and then comes the range of 'made up' coals: furnacite which is made from the dust of anthracite, ovoids or ovals also made from coal dust, then various stages of coke: small coke which is partly burned anthracite, then gas coke which is a bigger coal partially burned, just enough to take the gas out of it. Grains, which were very, very fine, about a quarter of an inch long, and beans which were slightly bigger, these were all used for the boilers in the more wealthy houses. These magnificent boilers were often housed in underground cellars. Coke was the worst to deal with being lighter, one of those sacks was about four feet tall and you had to fill it to the brim to get a hundredweight in, one of those on your back was hard work if you weren't very tall. Mr Mustchin was a good employer, we had proper jackets, ribbed to protect us, and he didn't expect us to do anything he wouldn't do himself. He was a good worker and set a good example, it must have been hard for him too as he was shorter than me."

The noise from the coal yard finally drove Mr and Mrs Johnson out of Kings and Princes; Mrs Johnson even went round asking people to sign a petition about the noise, and the comings and goings from the coal yard, but her reception was mixed. Some people said that the yard brought jobs to the village even though, on one memorable occasion there were five coal lorries which blocked every exit from the village.

In front of Lilac Cottage was Mrs Hornsby's laundry; she took laundry in from the village and from Roundabout. Hector Hornsby's grandfather was called 'Loppy' Clements because of his limping gait, and he is remembered collecting the laundry in a wicker contraption on wheels from all the big houses, and taking it back to Lilac Cottage. Prior to the Hornsby's laundry, Harry Guy is said to have had a laundry at Lakers Farm.

The laundry is described by Ron Noble who came to the village as an evacuee during the war, and stayed with Barry Lenharth's family at Lilac Cottage (Barry was Mrs Hornsby's nephew): "There were three main buildings built of brick and stone, with a galvanised roof. You travelled the path from a gate with a lilac hedge on your right and the buildings on your left, and round the corner the first building on your left was the boiler room or wash room. This had a big boiler, or copper (which was actually made of cast iron) in the centre which was fired with a wood and coal fire underneath in a brick surround and all

Mr Clements – born about 1845

the water was carried to it by hand. Not only was the water ladled in, but when the clothes had been washed with soap, the water had to be ladled out as well. The operation was repeated for the rinsing, which I can't remember much about, but I can remember the mangle. It was a massive thing and took us two boys to manage it, it must have been over 3' because it took a single sheet, flat. The centre room was large, being the garage for the horse and trap, for the laundry was collected by horse in the early days. Eventually the horse was replaced, but Mrs Hornsby always collected and delivered, I think as often as two or three times a week. During the war she used to do the personal laundry of some of the Canadians at the camp, and sometimes when we opened the laundry bags there would be coffee or something else you couldn't buy in the shops, like a cheese - we had Welsh rarebit that night! The last room was the laundry room which had a long bench running round three sides for ironing, and a pot-bellied stove in the centre which supported a type of hot plate with about fifteen flat-irons on it. Immediately opposite this room was the well from where all the water had to be pumped by hand, and behind that and to the right was an area of high ground which was used as a drying area, lots of clothes lines and clothes props. In the 1930s this was built on

Mrs Caroline Clements – born in 1846

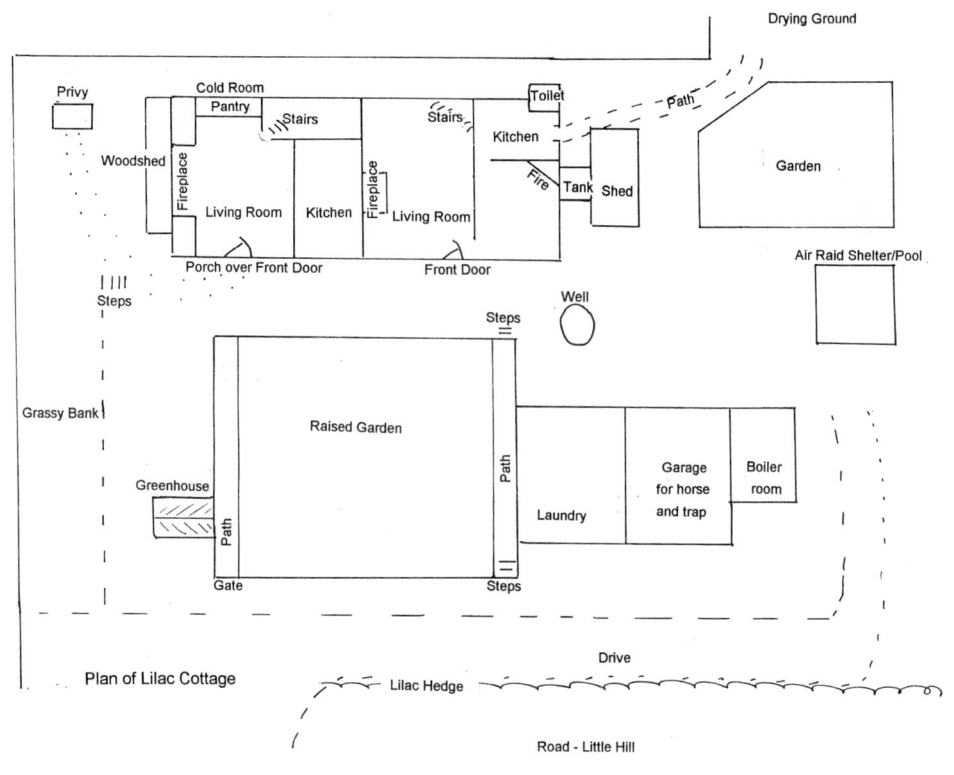

Plan of the Laundry and Lilac Cottage

and the houses Flowerdown, Trees and Woodstock have taken the places of the clothes lines." (The land was sold to Arthur Johnson who divided the plot into three, keeping one and selling the others to Mrs Duke and to the builder.) The plot of land on which Lilac Cottage and the laundry stood was very large, and the level ground was used mainly as a vegetable garden, but in front of the cottage there were quite a lot of flowers. Brian Ruff adds: "As Hector's mother and my mother were friends I often got the job of pumping the water up from the well; about four or five buckets every night. I was about ten at the time, I suppose, about 1948, and I got half-a-crown a week which was quite a lot of money, but it took about an hour to get five buckets full and on Fridays I had to get double the amount plus a big bath full as it was Hector's bath night."

In September 1900 the Parish Council passed the following resolution: 'That the Parish Council make arrangements with the Postmaster General to establish a Telegraph Office at West Chiltington, the liability of the

Council as Guarantors not to exceed the sum of fifteen pounds in any one year.' The telegraph office actually started operating in May 1901, and during its first year it forwarded 600 telegrams. Winifred Johnson (see Chapter 2) wrote that when she was born in 1909 nobody had a telephone, but telegraph boys cycled out from Pulborough with telegrams, which were usually messages of some sort of disaster so they were viewed with apprehension.

The telephone arrived in the village in 1928 with the very first exchange at Gooch's Stores in the village, but it had very few lines. There were few private telephones at first, but the village did have public telephone kiosks; in 1936 one was installed in the village, in 1939 at Broadford Bridge, and there was one at the Common. In spite of repeated requests from 1954 onwards, one was not installed at The Juggs as the telephone manager at Brighton indicated that the takings from a kiosk would be too small to offset the cost. When the telephone systems were rapidly expanding in the 1930s the exchange moved to a room built on the front of Oakmere (a thatched house in Mill Road next to Daux farm); this system was entirely manual and was 'manned' by Connie Slater who had trained at Petworth. She also trained another girl, Winnie Meatyard from Storrington, to help her and during the war they and Daphne Golds worked from 8.30 to 5.30 with a half hour for lunch. Mrs Luckhurst and her daughter Doreen lived at Oakmere so she was the night telephonist and caretaker with evening help when necessary. Also employed at various times were Olive Bale (née Slater), Ray Winton and June Warren. The area covered was large including Roundabout, Nutbourne and Broadford Bridge so the girls were kept busy. Connie was teased by some people in the village who could see her working through the window, pulling the plugs and lines; they wondered if she had been listening in, and could she tell them any good gossip! Actually, one resident remembers her mother winding up the telephone and commenting on the heavy breathing of whoever it was eavesdropping; Connie adds "they could always tell if we were listening!!" During the war it was a very busy exchange, handling calls from Abingworth Hall where some of the Canadians were billeted, and Coolham where the Polish Airforce was situated, as well as all the civilian calls.

In 1947 The West Chiltington Telephone Exchange was relocated to a building next door to The Chapel in The Common. In the 1960s the Post Office, which ran the telephones in this country at the time, realised that the exchange at The Common would soon run out of space to install any more equipment for expanding the service, so they built a very much bigger building behind, with access from Nyetimber Lane. This new building was, in fact, never used, other than for housing an emergency generator which came into its own after the hurricane of October 1987, for the annual party of telephone personnel in June, and for some months in the early 1980s to pack emergency food parcels!

In 1990 when the digital electronic telephone equipment came into being the site was sold for a house called Pinecroft, and for two houses with access from Nyetimber Lane called Holyoak and Willscroft.

In 1987 the Parish Council applied to have the telephone kiosk in the Village listed as an historic building; this was refused but in 1992 British Telecom asked the Council which red telephone boxes in the parish it wished to retain, the alternative being to have them replaced with modern kiosks. It was agreed that of the three kiosks remaining (Broadford Bridge's kiosk having been removed in 1981), two should be retained: the one in the Village and the one at Haglands Lane, and that the one at Coneyhurst should go.

In the early days there were fewer Health and Safety Rules and Regulations concerning working practices. Meg Judd recalls of the 1950s: "It was Brucellosis you got, Bill Grey the vet died of it; it was pretty deadly. The tests weren't compulsory then, so perhaps we were tougher in those days. Tuberculosis was the killer, thousands of people died of that." Ivan Pullen adds a story about another vet: "Charlie Mant was the vet from Storrington who was called if things were desperate, he was also the fire chief. On Haglands we had a Hereford cow with a white face and horns, my, she was vicious, you only had to rattle a bucket a bit and she used to lash out and you'd go flying; God Almighty I was frightened of that thing and I used to keep out of her way! One day she had a lump on her knee and we called old Charlie out and I said 'Be careful Charlie, she's a bit vicious, she lifts her leg out' and he said 'Oh, it's all right', goes in and gives her a pat on the backside and she goes bang, and he's out the door! The favourite in those days was black Iodex ointment, no matter what you had you rubbed that in; you keep rubbing and it goes dark green; well, he gave us this great big tub of it, I never rubbed it in but the cow kept on for years!" It has also been noted that, at the turn of the century over 75% of the local vets' work was with farm animals, whereas now the figures are the other way round with only 25% being farm work, the rest being with recreational horses and domestic pets.

Sir Peter Mursell, bought Churchfield Farm (see Chapter 2) in 1965 from Mrs Champ and ran it in tandem with another farm at River, both being satellites of the main farm in Wisborough Green which concentrated on fruit growing. At first they planted 15 acres of apples, 4 acres of strawberries, and blackcurrants which were sold to Beecham's for Ribena, and dug a reservoir. The light sandy loam of much of the farm is hungry and thirsty land but the water is not only used for irrigation but for frost protection as well. In those few critical weeks when the flower buds have burst, sudden spring frosts can cause the total loss of the crop, so there is an alarm system which alerts the farm to the falling temperature and James goes down to the reservoir to switch on the irrigation pumps. A fine mist settles on the flowers, and on the twigs and blades of grass around, which freezes generating a tiny rise in temperature on the flower; as long as the misting is kept up the temperature around the flower will not sink below zero and the future crop will be saved. The pumps are only turned off when the sun is up and the beautiful scene of the sparkling orchard, blades of grass and strawberry plants all coated in a thick coat of ice is beginning to melt.

Geoff Lawes from Billingshurst is a local apiarist who leaves his bee hives on the farm; before the varroa mite wreaked such havoc in our bee community he had 16 hives, but is now down to 7. They are useful pollinators but not the only ones: wind, birds, butterflies and other insects also do a good job.

Before the war fruit from the other farms had been sold in the markets of Brighton. Between 1965 and 1985 some strawberries were sold to the supermarkets through a co-operative with the remainder going to London and Brighton markets. The supermarkets were a fraction of the size they are today; then the fruit could be put in punnets, labelled and sent on a lorry to the depot. About 1986 refrigerated lorries for transport became compulsory, as did white coats, hats and boots for those handling the fruit, so as the overheads were so great for the farm's four acres of strawberries they gave up the supermarket idea and concentrated on wholesale and Pick Your Own.

James joined his father in 1985 when changes were beginning to speed up; by 1996 it ceased to be viable to sell in the wholesale markets and the current plan is to concentrate on PYO but also to supply local shops and roadside stalls. Even the thirty-five year long-standing arrangement with Ribena will end by the end of the century as Ribena can buy blackcurrants from Eastern Europe, frozen, packed and delivered when and where they want at less than the price they can buy fresh from Churchfield Farm. By the end of 1966 there had been a 45% drop in the price offered by Ribena over a five year period.

The other big change is in the apple market: three or four years ago James had 32 acres of apples, now he has six. The EEC designed a scheme to pay farmers to grub up apple trees as there was a surplus of fruit in the Community. In spite of local opposition, James says that it was one of the best decisions he has taken as the returns on his farm apples had been poor and if the EEC was offering to compensate him, his decision was made. The apple industry in this country seems to have had problems since we joined the EEC and left our protected market arrangements to face competition first from France, then the rest of Europe followed by almost the rest of the world. Add to this the rise in the power of the supermarkets to produce ever tighter specifications, and top fruit production becomes very difficult. In this country we cannot produce only grade 1 apples, and the supermarkets are not interested in anything else, so there will always be between 20% and 50% that they will not buy but could be sold to wholesalers. Because the supermarkets have put many of the small greengrocers out of business, the wholesalers that used to supply them have also declined. It is possible to use the second class apples for juice but a lot of juice is made from a small number of apples, and even there the standards have become ever tighter so that only about two thirds of what is sent to Kirdford Growers (an apple packing co-operative) is actually used, and there are substantial overheads in a 'processed' product.

So for these reasons, and the fact that James enjoyed the PYO on his brother's farm at Wisborough Green, he decided to make that his main enterprise. When the scheme first started it was considered the cream on the top of the business of farming, but now it is recognised as a system in its own right. There are standards here, too, but imposed more by the customer; if the farm produces good quality fruit the customers will come, if they don't, they won't. There is a Pick Your Own Association with an accreditation scheme, concentrating on providing a good service. The fruit is randomly tested and James is notified by post to tell him when and what was bought, and how well it did in tests. The soil is fed with 60 lorry loads of mushroom compost a year, the strawberries are sprayed, although most of the vegetables are not. In time it will be possible with genetic engineering to grow strawberries that are resistant to moulds, but on a commercial scale organic fruit farming is considered unrealistic. James is not only looking forward to new varieties of strawberry, but is planning to grow new products such as cob nuts, cherries and Christmas trees. He hopes that the nuts, being in the centre of the farm and rather exposed, will be too far away to be raided by the squirrels which, with luck, will feed from the surrounding hazel trees instead which, with the alders provide a wind break. A Phytophthora disease is attacking alders but so far has not been seen at Churchfield Farm. Not being subsidised at all he is constantly having to evaluate what the market wants and respond to its demands.

No longer do girls go into service or boys work on the land; agriculture and its supporting industries has diminished in size and importance and many of the farms and smallholdings have been sold. Now the residents commute to work in London and elsewhere; when one family moved into the area in 1988 someone said "welcome to Gatwick married quarters". Within a radius of five houses they knew seven people working in airlines or for the airport authority, and within the village as a whole, many more similarly employed. However, there is one job, still done in the village, which has not changed in the century; Roger Watts' interest in coppicing and all things related to it started during the war, before he went to school. He continues: "In East Sussex where I lived at the time, the countryside was very wooded and coppicing (cutting a broad-leaved tree down to the stump so that it re-grows to produce multiple stems called poles) was an important part of the rural economy. I spent hours watching the cutting of the underwood and the conversion of it into palings, posts, stakes and hurdles. When the coppicing season was over any hedges at the end of the cants (area of coppice felled in one block) were always laid, and I found this the most interesting part of all. As I grew up I learned all the skills needed, as part of my country life; then I went to work at Plumpton Agricultural College where I continued to learn. Unfortunately during the years between about 1950s and the late 1980s there was little demand for either the skills or the associated products and as I had to earn a living I moved over to general agriculture. However, interest has revived, perhaps due to conservation programmes and television gardening series, and the business is now going from strength to strength.

We have been at Si-Clare in Sinnocks now for 25 years, and I work mainly in the woods of Sussex, as and where the hazel is available, mostly in the summer. I sell the products to the public, and garden contractors; in fact to anybody who needs them. Then the hedge laying is carried out between November and March for landowners, so it's a full year's cycle.

It is satisfying to think that skills which were learned in the last centuries are being carried forward into the next, and into the next millennium."

A Mangle

Chapter 12

The War Years

Most of the stories and memories in this chapter actually concern the period of the Second World War. The problems of the Depression seemed either to pass over the head of the Village, it being a rural community too remote to be disturbed by such economic swings, or the children of that time were too young to realise the problems; those children are now in their late seventies, and there are few in the Village who can remember much further back than that. However, there are some writings which give an insight into earlier times; Winifred Johnson has written that she can remember men coming to the village in the 1914-18 war to commandeer all the spare horses as they were needed to pull the gun carriages. Barry Lenharth recalls that his father, Billy, (who lived in Lilac Cottage, Little Hill) had enlisted for the Great War as a runner when he was only fifteen because he could not find any work elsewhere. He was obviously interested in entertaining even then because at the end of the war he was presented with a tankard, which Barry still has, in recognition of the concert parties he produced, and the entertainment he provided. Although he survived the war, he was gassed and suffered thereafter.

Mick Greenfield has copies of letters from the First World War written by his grandfather, W Greenfield of the 10th Royal Fusiliers. One, *An Episode of the 14-18 War* reads: 'We were in the trenches at the tip of the well known Loos Salient. A salient is a projection in the line of trenches made necessary owing to the lie of the land, being always a somewhat isolated and precarious position to hold. The Head Quarters required information as to the strength of the enemy's artillery opposite this position and decided to draw their fire by putting down a smoke barrage which would be taken for gas. Orders were that the trench was to be evacuated during the operation with the exception of a sentry post. What this post were to do, or what use it would be, was difficult to see, but that was the order. I was the unfortunate corporal on trench duty at the time and

I was told to remain with the sentry post during the operation which was timed to last an hour. A Royal Engineer joined us with a supply of smoke bombs. His orders were to throw one over the parapet at five minute intervals. He was pretty jittery, not being used to front line trench duty. When zero time arrived I told him to get rid of all his bombs as soon as possible and then lie down on the bottom of the trench as I had had enough experience to foresee what would happen. The smoke started and the enemy, presumably suspecting gas, opened up with everything they'd got. The others and I just laid on the bottom of the trench and hoped for the best. By extraordinary luck or call it what you will, no shell landed in our bay of the trench, although the other sections were severely damaged. After about an hour the smoke cleared, the enemy fire gradually ceased and we breathed again. The remainder of the company then returned expecting to see us in bits and pieces and commenced forthwith to repair the damage. What the idea was, leaving us there during the turmoil is difficult to imagine but there it was. In any case we saw nil and could have in any circumstance done nothing.'

A second letter is entitled 'A Reminiscence of the Battle of the Somme July 1916 more particularly as it concerns the 10th Battn Royal Fusiliers and myself STK 991 Private W C Greenfield, 14 Platoon D Company' and reads: 'The Battalion spent the afternoon and the night of 14th July in a captured German trench near the village of La Boiselle (which was then only a heap of rubble) and quite close to the huge crater of a mine which was exploded on the morning of the first of July at the commencement of the battle.

Early on the 15th, a lovely summer morning, we were paraded and told we were to take part in an attack on the village of Pozceries. We were to be in support of troops in front of us who would pass through the village and were to follow up and occupy it. Alas! The best laid schemes etc, It was many days before the object was attained. We marched till we came to a sunken road, then we turned right, climbed over a low bank and proceeded to advance in what is known as extended order over flat and quite unsheltered ground. We at once came under intense machine gun and shell fire and casualties began to occur. I carried on till I came to a line of barbed wire entanglements and could see the troops we were supporting held up in front of it. I took cover in a shell hole and just at that moment my platoon officer (Lieut. Bevir) fell into the same shell hole, shot through the head. He was quite unconscious and died soon after. There was no movement of the troops in front so I could do nothing except wait. The fire continued all day but nothing fell in my 'hole' or I should not be writing this. What a place to spend a fine sunny July day!! As dusk fell my platoon sergeant (Sgt Samson) appeared and said the Battalion, or what was left of it, was going back. I joined him and helped carry our Company Commander (Capt Shurey) to the nearest casualty clearing station. He was badly wounded and died later. A small party of us made our way in the dark to our 'assembly' point on the road where a few details of the battalion had been left to form a nucleus, in military parlance, a cadre.

I was nearly at the end of my tether with fatigue, thirst and hunger but managed to make it. My platoon sergeant (Sgt Lindsell) who had been left behind, was there and I remember he handed me a tin of bully beef and a <u>pint</u> mug of rum. I wolfed the bully and drank the rum and collapsed to the ground where I lay till late the next afternoon. There was then a parade of the remains of the battalion and a sorry sight it was. My platoon went into action about 40 strong. When we paraded the strength consisted of <u>three</u> ie two who had been left behind and myself, in other words of those of the platoon who went into action, I was the only one to come out.

The Battalion was never the same again. It was sad to think that the great majority of the pals and comrades who had been together through nearly two years of training - The Tower of London, Colchester, Andover and finally Salisbury Plain - were in the space of an hour or two on a glorious July day either killed or wounded.'

A PS adds that this was written a while after the events, but that Private Greenfield would never be able to forget that day.

Another letter which Mick has, arrived just after the Great War had ended; the widow of a batman wrote a very critical letter asking how her husband had been killed, because all she had had from the War Ministry had been a letter simply saying he was dead, with no details. Old copies of The Tatler show page after page of officers who were killed, and it is hard to realise the carnage. When men fell in battle, it was the duty of the Commanding Officer or his deputy to notify the relatives but in cases like the above there was such slaughter that often the officers themselves died and wives and mothers did not know what had happened to their loved ones. The letters show how unaware those at home were of the dreadful conditions in France; there were no counselling services available in either war: men were men and supposed to get on with it, but for the families the waiting was harrowing.

Bill Hampton, now in his 90s, remembers a lighter moment from the First World War: "One Saturday afternoon (all farm hands worked a full day Saturday in those days) the estate carpenter up at Hatches Estate, George Hawkins he was called, locked up his shop and was going home to his Hatches Cottage the back way. There were about four of us boys playing in the meadow and he shouted at us to look and pointed, and right away, through Apsley we could see this airship falling steeply to the ground and a little fighter plane diving back down here. Well, it appeared that this was an observation balloon that had broken away and the fighter plane had had to shoot it down. We thought it had come down in Park Wood, so away we goes, four of us tearing along, then George came running as well, through Park Wood, into Danhill big field, still couldn't see it, still carried on and when we got out to Danhill cross roads and Apsley entrance, there were people running from all directions so we joined in. As Mr Freeman from Hatches had to oversee the farm at Apsley we knew it well, so we went right through the farm, out into the next field and there she stood, away behind Laybrook brickworks, what's now called Ibstock at Goose Green, about 100' up in the air because she still had some gas left in her. She had come down in a little wooded place, but being heavier one end as they'd shot some of the gas out of her, she was standing on end. I don't know how many people are left who would remember that, now. After all that excitement, we had to walk all the way back to the village, but it was worth it!"

Bill explained that Apsley Farm is recognisable by its white gate at the Danhill crossroads (B2133 and B2139).

Even isolated rural communities were reached by officialdom; in the Parish Council minutes of September 1914 it is recorded that a circular had been received from the Clerk of the West Sussex County Council concerning the Prince of Wales National Relief Fund. Subscriptions were collected and the sum of £7.16.0d was raised and sent off.

In peace too, the country was alert, for in June 1928 a letter was received from the War Office notifying that the Parish of West Chiltington, and practically the whole of West Sussex, would be used for military manoeuvres for six months from 1 August 1928.

In 1937 a course of lectures on Air Raid Precautions was arranged by Chanctonbury Rural District Council at the Comrades' Memorial Hall.

The arrival of the evacuee children was one of the first impacts of the Second World War on the village. The first wave came down from

Peckham on the Friday and from Croydon on the Saturday during what was called The Phoney War (between September 1939 and June 1940 which was an edgy seven-month period when nations were geared up for mass confrontation but seemed reluctant to start the fight on land) and quite a few went back again round about 1940/41. Some of those evacuees still keep in touch. There was some opposition to this influx of London children, but a combination of persuasion, the Parish Council, the local policeman and arm twisting forced people to accept them, as people went round the village saying 'you can take two, and you can take one because you have a spare bed.' When some children went back after Christmas tensions eased and the remaining ones were integrated and accepted, some more easily than others! Ewen Steele recalls: "They was little devils. They'd never been on a farm before. They didn't know what it was like. My mother used to clout me for what they did hoping they would take note and behave, but they were worse than ever 'cause they knew I'd take the blame! They broke the eggs in the chicken house, they let the calves out of the gate. I don't suppose it was all that serious, it just made more work."

Joy Adams recounts: "Mrs Kensington was in charge and we had to take these evacuee children to where they had to go; they were billeted on local families. They frightened us local children rather a lot, because they were Cockneys, they shouted and they hollered, and their favourite saying was "I'll slap ya darn". Us children was so used to quiet, we was honestly scared of these rough, tough, noisy lads. And the language! Some of the girls came with their hair all blond and permed up which was a shock to us little village girls. But they were full of head lice, so they were put into a sick bay to clean them off. And then they all came out in scabies, all these girls and boys, so back they went to the sick bay, the one in Storrington. I suppose there were just too many of them for us to be able to accept."

However Gwen Smith tells of a happier evacuee story: "There was this little boy, very young and a bit of a weakling who was evacuated to the Madgewick family at 12 The Birches. He hadn't been here long before he was ill with a severe chest infection, so his mother was sent for and stayed for about a month. She then said she was going back up to London to shut up the house and make arrangements to stay in the village with her son. The 'host' family invited her to stay with them, a true friendship was forged in spite of there being two women together in a kitchen, and the little boy flourished in the country air at a time when he really needed his mother. It seems that the war benefited someone."

People were undecided how best to secure the safety of their children: while some were sent from London to the countryside, others went to Canada or America. There were rumours that children at the village school might be offered places on ships going to Canada but following the disaster of The City of Benares, a steamer belonging to the Ellerman Line which had sailed for Canada in September 1940, the suggestion was dropped. 77 of the 90 children who were being evacuated on this ship, under the auspices of the Children's Overseas Reception Board, died when the ship was torpedoed by U-48 on 17 September.

A ten year old boy's view of life is brilliantly described by Ron Noble who arrived at Pulborough Station in 1940 as an evacuee. "The war was getting to a rather dangerous stage as far as German bombers were concerned and my mother and the nurse in our block of flats had discussed my evacuation. The nurse was a Miss Wheatley (who was the author Dennis Wheatley's sister) who had a cottage in the Roundabout area of West Chiltington and knew Mr and Mrs Lenharth who lived at Lilac Cottage, Little Hill, The Common, so after some discussion it was agreed to send me there as an evacuee until things in London were more peaceful. I arrived full of anxiety with a suitcase in my hand and a gas mask slung round my neck. I can remember the portly and jovial bus driver greeting me and walking me across the station car park to a single decker green Southdown bus that was to take me to Lilac Cottage, my home for the next few years. My first day was to be memorable for all the wrong reasons. After unpacking and having a meal I was to go out and play and be shown around by Barry Lenharth and the boys next door; in the woods the boys had a rope hanging from a high branch on one of the trees and the idea was to take the other end of the rope, climb a nearby tree and launch yourself into space, Tarzan style. This went well until my turn, when I touched the ground at the lowest point which had to have a large puddle of water that I put my foot into. With a shoe full of water I was taken home by Barry; his mother washed my sock and hung it from the oil stove weighted down by a tea caddy. After washing myself and cleaning my shoe, I thought my sock would be dry so I reached up and pulled it down, bringing with it the tea caddy which spilled a quarter of a pound of tea all over the floor, and this in the days of rationing! Day 1 finished - it must get better!

Lilac Cottage was divided into two homes; the left side occupied by Mr and Mrs Hornsby, who ran the laundry, their son Hector, and four boys who had been evacuated from Croydon. I was to stay in the right hand side with Mr and Mrs Lenharth and their son Barry who was eight years old;

Lilac Cottage

we were to become such good friends that the friendship has lasted right to now. Mrs Lenharth was Hector Hornsby's sister. Our half of the cottage had electricity and an indoor toilet, but all the water had to be pumped up to a tank which held 250 gallons which served the toilet and the kitchen sink; we had no bath and no hot water system, that's why there was always a kettle on the stove. This oil stove was a double burner Valor with a small oven, there was also a Baby Belling electric cooker which was a tiny thing; it amazes me now to think what wonderful meals were cooked on such a primitive set up. The most memorable thing though, was the smell of that stove, slightly oily and very cosy. The essence of home.

From the plan in Chapter 10 you can see the two cottages, in our half there were three steps down into the dining room, a small room with a table and four chairs, a corner cabinet with a radio on top and a cupboard near the window where Barry and I were to keep our toys and sweets. At that time sweets were rationed, but we were taught to share everything. The other downstairs room was the front room which had chairs, a settee, table and piano; Mrs Lenharth played the piano and Mr Lenharth played the violin, a one-stringed fiddle, and a carpenter's saw which he bent by holding the handle between his knees, his left hand holding the other end level with his face. He then bent it into an S shape and stroked it with a violin bow; he was quite an expert and could play many tunes on it. Upstairs there were two rooms, one of which Barry and I shared; I had never seen a room like it before with beams across the ceiling and walls.

Mrs Hornsby's half was kept in the same condition as when her mother lived there, I believe that would have been early Victorian, there were certainly pictures of Queen Victoria. No running water, all water was hand pumped from our end of the cottage. There was a well, actually in the cottage at the foot of the stairs, which for some reason had been filled in and boarded over. She used oil lamps and candles and the cooking was done on an old coal-fired stove in an enormous fireplace. At one side of this stove was a small chair that actually fitted into the fireplace, and we children would sit on that chair and look up the chimney to see the sky. The room contained a very old settee, an armchair, a dining table and chairs and a piano, all of which had belonged to Mrs Hornsby's mother. In the kitchen there were a table and chairs, a cabinet for storing food, the sink and an oil stove. The ceiling was beamed, as was the rest of the house, but the floors were very uneven being a dirt floor with cobbles forced into the soil. She had a carpet down, but when a cup dropped it never bounced! In the beams there were two hooks of about six inches where they used to hang the sides of meat in the old days and we kids used to swing on them when she wasn't around. The toilet was outside and had to be emptied when necessary, which, with seven people living there, three adults and four boys, was very often.

Interior of Lilac Cottage

The Laundry Room had a secondary use on Wednesdays and Fridays when it became our bathroom; out came the oval tin bath from the hooks on the wall, the water was heated from the copper, and a queue of five adults and six boys all took their turn. I can safely say it was no joke in the winter!

In the gardens around the cottage we grew vegetables and we all used to help in the garden, weeding, planting and generally keeping the place up together. We were all encouraged by having our own pieces of land to grow whatever we wanted; it's odd that my own potatoes seemed to taste the best, as did Barry's to him, it also taught us that the more you put into something the more you get out of it. As well as the vegetables there were quite a lot of flowers in front of the cottage, and Mr Lenharth had built a swimming pool, not a large one but big enough to accommodate his own family. This had been inspired as a result of his having worked for Mr Wells, building a swimming pool in Sunset Lane, but it was hard work as all the water had to be pumped into it. Ours was covered over with timber and soil during the war and used as an air raid shelter; we also used to grow mushrooms down there!

In spite of the hardships of wartime rationing, we always had a roast dinner on Sunday, served at the same time as 'Family Favourites' was broadcast on the wireless. On Sunday afternoon we went to the Chapel on The Common for Sunday School where we got a stamp to stick on our cards, before racing down to the army camp to find our friends and bringing them home for tea and a social evening singing songs around the piano, and charades. We were really well fed, well dressed and damn well-mannered. There was no favouritism because even though we lived in adjoining houses, we did everything together and shared all the chores, one day I did the washing up, the next day I did the vegetables, then cleaned the shoes, pumped the water, we all did everything in turns. I had never known a home and this was a real home for me.

Christmas was fun; we had a tree but it was never decorated until Christmas Eve, and I can still see Granny Hornsby hooking the decorations down on 5th January as we went to a pantomime, so that they'd be down by Twelfth Night. The tree was lit with real candles in flower shaped scoops - it must have been so dangerous. We put up holly and ivy and made our paper chain decorations and our cards; do you remember those potatoes cut in half for potato cuts? We used to dip them in the colour to make our cards."

Years later, Barry Lenharth took Ron Noble back to Lilac Cottage, which has now been made into one house, but the bedrooms have remained the same and 'the boys' could still see the same beams downstairs and pick out things as they had been. Barry lived in Lilac Cottage from 1932-1948 during which time he collected quite a lot of wartime souvenirs: bits of German aircraft, cartridge cases and the like. His father was a great 'bury-er of treasure' and had once buried a grand piano in the back garden of Lilac Cottage; he also buried Barry's tin trunk containing all his 'souvenirs'. When the new owners of the house excavated the ground for their extension they were sufficiently alarmed by Barry's trunk that they called in the bomb disposal squad!

Another early sign of the Second World War was the huge army encampment in Monkmead Woods which had a profound effect on the village. The site stretched from the corner of Heather Lane and Monkmead Lane, through the woodland area along Monkmead Lane to the sharp corner junction with Harborough Hill, but avoiding the marshy land adjacent to the golf course. On the other side of Monkmead Lane it went from Monkmead, up Nyetimber Lane on both sides of the road to about where Nyetimber Copse is now. There were few good roads in the parish

Presentation of King's Colours to 2nd Battalion
The East Surrey Regiment
The parade ground was created for the King and Queen to present the Winipeg Rifles with their colours about 1943. This presentation to the East Surrey took place on 30 November 1945

at that time, so the Canadians, who were the first arrivals, laid a road along Monkmead Lane for their vehicles, but Nyetimber Lane remained a sandy track. There was a perimeter fence of barbed wire with a guarded entrance near Monkmead, although with the road going through there must have been other entrances. Leonard Baker now lives in Worthing but was in the 3rd Division of the 17th Duke of York Royal Canadian Hussars, and describes the Camp "We were mobilised as the 3rd Canadian Motorcycle Regiment, but by 1941 were re-named the 7th Reconnaissance Battalion (17H) to form part of the 3rd Division. We came to West Chiltington, having enlisted as civilians from all walks of life, on 5 June 1942; the camp was a compact set-up consisting of Nissen huts for the men, with a scattering of brick built administrative buildings, stores and garages. The Parade Ground was where Silverwood is now, with the HQ and ablutions block on the corner of Monkmead Lane and Nyetimber Lane. There was never enough hot water, so if you got to the ablutions late, you got a cold shower! The NAAFI was across the road, to the left of the path down to West Sussex Golf Course, and their huts were in the woods to the right of the path. Other Divisions were in huts further up Nyetimber Lane; there was a vehicle compound and the dentist further along Monkmead Lane towards Pulborough. There were about 750 of us in the camp at a time. Training programs were set up almost as soon as we arrived; most of our time was spent training with each squadron having its own training area and field-firing ranges on the Downs. We would spend anything up to a week at a time living on those ranges.

I remember a night exercise when we had to get to Horsham without being caught; we went over the Downs and across the back ways to avoid the other troops. On another occasion a group of us were in Brighton saying goodbye to our girlfriends and missed the truck back to camp; we found a train that was going to Worthing at midnight (taking sailors back to Portsmouth) and walked from Worthing. We got back to camp at 5.30am and were lucky not to be found out! That day was track-vehicle maintenance, so we took the tracks off the vehicles, scattered parts around and had a sleep behind the trees, pretending to have gone to the stores for parts!

A chap called Lucas, the cook, used to dry used tea leaves in the sun on trestle tables at the back of the cook house, and sell them to the Queens Head, for his beer money! As I wasn't interested in the pubs, a group of us used to run round the golf course in the evenings. We threw a children's party on 23 December and each child received a toy from Santa while having their ice-cream - a real treat in wartime. For our own entertainment we went to various dances and played ice hockey at the skating rink in Brighton.

We left West Chiltington on 15 September 1943, but returned on 22 November 1943 for final training before we left for the marshalling area in Chichester on 9 June 1944 to take part in the Invasion of Normandy."

Gordon Chilton also now lives in Sussex, in Angmering; he was in the Royal Winnipeg Rifles, and adds to Len's story "We came to West Chiltington in the autumn of 1942 and stayed until June 1943; at New Year we celebrated by shooting our rifles in the air, and put the whole village in fear of attack! We also formed a bugle band which played the same tune every day for so long that everyone in the village was whistling it. We used water out of Monkmead pond for fire practice, which reminds me that we dug holes along the roadside to bury our explosives such as gelignite and 808, a very dangerous jelly which would explode spontaneously if allowed to get dry, so we had to keep it wet. After we left, I think our places were taken by the Canadian Scottish, and the Regina Rifles."

Alec Lawson, the milkman, lived in 'Lawson's Lane' (Nyetimber Lane); his farm and dairy (first called Fair View, now Ruffins) was the only house within the Canadian Army Camp. At that time the area was woodland frequented by nightingales, with no houses below Fair View; there was a water tower in the woods where Nyetimber Copse is now. A special pass was needed to get through the army encampment in order to go to the Roundabout Hotel; and the golf course was inaccessible; even Alec Lawson needed a pass to get in and out of his own home!

Many of the men married local girls, who then went to live in Canada; some of these marriages were not a success because of homesickness, misunderstanding of the Canadian way of life, or because the girls had been misled by the exaggerated claims of the soldiers about their wealth and prospects. Until those war years, travel was very limited, and the girls must have suffered a real 'culture shock' upon their arrival. The girls that went to Canada and the boys that never returned from the front have left a noticeable gap in the population, acknowledged by the generation that were young people at that time.

Joy Adams describes the soldiers as "a wicked lot", and there does seem to have been a certain amount of fighting and rough-housing amongst some of the men. Joy recalls one incident which took place at one of the dances held in The Old Comrades Hall by The Elephant and Castle: "You'd know when trouble was about to begin because the men would take those belts of theirs off, the ones with the big buckles, and they would start lashing around. So, at the first sign of a fight I would head for the door, grab my clothes from the cloakroom, and out. On this one night I got out and found I'd left my shoes behind, because I always changed into sandals at the dance, well, of course shoes were rationed on coupons so you couldn't afford to leave them. So I go back in, but my sister's trying to stop me, and I go back through flying fists and flying belts, and I'm ducking and jumping, up onto the stage, grabs my shoes, and rushes out through the fighting." The dances took place twice a week, on Wednesdays and Saturdays, with a further weekly dance in The New Hall below the forge. On Wednesdays there was a gramophone to dance to, lent by Hector Gocher to Connie Slater who organised these dances, but on Saturdays musicians from the camp would provide the music for nothing, in return for the dancing partners. Connie used to charge a shilling to get in, and all the proceeds went to the Red Cross after the hall hire of £1 was taken out. Very occasionally there would be dances at the camp itself, the gates would be open for the village girls to go to the dance, and trucks were also sent out to the smaller villages to collect the girls. That was a real treat because the soldiers laid on a wonderful spread of food to war-starved girls. The first taste of Pepsi-Cola came from the Camp; during one of the Camp dances there was a bomb dropped and the soldiers pushed the girls under the tables, under the furniture, anywhere, to get them out of the way of what might fall. The girls huddled, frightened, and distraught as the Cola bottles fell and crashed and all the food was ruined. All that wonderful food that was such a luxury! There was no food at the village dances because of the rationing. Following that incident, most of the girls were too shaken up to continue dancing and started to walk home, when one of the bombers came back and dropped another couple of bombs; the girls' escorts pushed them into a ditch under the hedge for protection and jumped in on top. Quite a surprise for the girls!

There are gleeful memories of the time the Canadians ended a heavy drinking session at The Elephant and Castle by filling the piano with beer and pushing it down the slope into the pond! Pianos seem to have featured prominently during the war; Pat Steele remembers that they sometimes used to borrow her family's piano for the dances at the Comrades Hall, wheeling it on a truck down the hill from Holly Close.

The troops were certainly lively, and there is another story of how the Welsh Fusiliers, who were stationed at Abingworth, were causing a bit of a rumpus in East Street. In those days the Police House was down at

Hatches, and PC George Plowden came out to see what all the noise was about. As he was in civvies the men thought he must be one of their sergeants, so he marched them all down back towards their barracks. However, by the time they got to the rectory, they realised he was only a civilian and they set about him, splitting his head open; he was off work for a long time. No one can say what their punishment was for attacking a policeman. It is also remembered that, in the days before the signposts were removed, they used to turn them all the wrong way round! Bill Van Tromp adds "One day a Messerschmitt 109 and a Hawker Hurricane were having a fight - they came down almost to ground level blasting away at each other, but then the German had to land as he was running out of fuel. He knew exactly where he was as he had been to school at Lancing - so much for removing the signposts! They used to dump a lot of their bombs here; between Threals Lane and Greenhurst Lane there were about six huge bomb craters which I had to fill in. I know that's not in the parish, but they came near!"

Barry Lenharth and Ron Noble who were eight and ten year olds at this time say that they were encouraged to meet the Canadians in the army camp, and they used to invite special friends from the camp to tea at Lilac Cottage where the men were made to feel very welcome. There was tea, of course, and musical soirees which sometimes had to be held in the laundry room as there were so many people to squeeze in. The Canadians were good singers and would group around the piano. In return they used to invite the boys and their families to the camp for cinema evenings, one of the Nissen huts was converted into the cinema and was decked out with bunting and flags, big trestle tables were laid with Pepsi, cakes and sandwiches which were such a luxury in the difficult days of rationing. Films with Bob Hope and Bing Crosby were shown. Ron adds "I used to save my pocket money to buy aircraft books. This was mainly because I got to know the Sandeman-Allens who lived at Daux Farm; I used to help out with their animals, cleaning out the rabbit hutches in the old barn, looking after the goats and doing various jobs, because she was on her own as her husband and son were away. One day when there was beer at the pub (because it often ran out during the war) the Canadians got into her garden and mixed all these beautiful angora rabbits together, some weeks later there were a lot more baby rabbits! I believe Mr Sandeman-Allen was a Wing Commander, and his son was also a pilot; I admired both men enormously, they were both tall and very striking in their uniforms. The son, I've forgotten his name, flew Typhoon fighters over France at hedge-top level, shooting up the German trains - it's called 'train busting'. He was returning from one of these missions when an enemy shell exploded just below his aircraft; although he was wounded and the plane was damaged he managed to fly home and landed safely. He was in hospital for a long time while they removed shrapnel and metal from him; he got the DFC for this and became the hero of the village, and Mrs Sandeman-Allen let me touch that brave man's medal."

Barry tells a wartime story of how he was sitting in class on 4 August 1944 when he heard the engine of the doodlebug cut out. All the children hid under their desks and it came down in Mac Steele's field at Park Farm below Knowetop. Barry remembers that the school was distempered at that time and all the distemper fell off the walls and ceiling with the explosion but no one was hurt except a cow, which the police, who carried revolvers during the war, had to come and shoot.

There were other memories from children of that time: of souvenir hunting for bits that fell over the village. As soon as they heard a plane come down they raced over to the place, before the police could stop them, to see what they could find. Someone picked up a glove with a finger still in it, but, in the way of children, she shook the finger out and kept the glove. They were too young, and too innocent, to realise the true horror of war although many have realised in later life how cruel the war years were. Someone in the army camp used to make rings out of the aluminium bits that the girls collected; one of the girls kept her aluminium ring for over forty years, a pretty thing because it did not tarnish. The boys collected bits of shell or ammunition. No one realised how dangerous it could have been with live ammunition lying around, and if one of the children did go home with a live bullet, someone would just drop a heavy stone on it to make it go off, and the child could then have the case. Another child collected the headphones from a plane wreck, but the police came and made her hand it back. The Germans used to drop very thin streamers of foil, rather like a metal audio tape of today, to interfere with radio communications, and the children used to walk across the golf course and collect pockets full of it. Brian Ruff remembers the excitement of the bagpipes when the soldiers marched along - aged about five or six he would 'march' with them, in the ditch as the regiment took up all the road.

Opposite the garage on the Common is an area now used as a car park, but it, and the land beside it was where all the metal was collected for the war effort. Pots and pans, old mowers, garden railings, anything made of metal was collected at this place and carted away to make some sort of munitions or military vehicle. Barry Lenharth, showing his hand says: "I was playing with friends among all that metal and I got hold of a mower blade. Someone turned it and it chopped my finger right off, but it was put back on, bandaged tightly in place and not even sewn back. It has served me for the last fifty years so they must have done something right! Ron and I got into such mischief in those days; we used to hide behind the butts on the Camp's rifle range and collect all their bullets which we would take to the Common. Just down Little Hill is a flight of steps which used to lead to the communal cess pit and we would lift up the manhole covers, put the bullet in there, hit the end of the cartridge and listen to the bullet flying around in the chamber. It backfired on us once though, as the cartridge split, and emergency surgery was performed by the girl across the road who had to extricate the bullet with a knife. Boys will be boys!"

But beside the philosophy of 'life as normal' there must have been apprehension. One man, working on Haglands Farm, was knocked right across the field by the draught from a doodle-bug that came down in the next field. He was lucky and was not hurt. During the Battle of Britain there were dog fights over the area, and that led to two fears, one, that if a German plane came down and the airmen saw you, they would machine gun you, and the other, that stray bombs could be dropped over the village. One dreadful event took place when three bombs were dropped, one over towards Wiggonholt. The village children grabbed bicycles and raced through the golf course to see, "and there was this field, and these seven beautiful horses. They were race-horses who had panicked and got into a huddle in the corner of the field. All dead. We just stood there and cried." What a waste, to add to the human waste.

Food rationing was introduced at the beginning of the war; the rations were universal and each week each person was entitled to: 2oz butter, 4oz cheese, 4 oz margarine, 4oz bacon, 2oz lard, 4oz sugar and 2oz tea. There were extra rations for children under 5 who got a pint of milk a day and 3 eggs a week, also free bottled orange juice was available for them at clinics. There was a point system for certain foods such as tinned meat, tinned fruit, dried fruit, syrup, whereby the 20 monthly points could be 'spent' on whatever was needed at the time, giving flexibility to the cook. Bread and potatoes were never rationed during the war, and there was a separate arrangement for meat, again to give flexibility, of one shillingsworth per person per week. It was possible therefore to have a small amount of expensive steak, or a larger amount of cheaper mince; offal and sausages were not rationed but were apt to be 'under the counter'! Fish, chicken, game and rabbit were not rationed either, so people in the country tended to do better than city dwellers.

A lot of food was imported so was therefore scarce; it came over by sea in convoys accompanied by naval vessels but these convoys were always vulnerable to attack by enemy ships, submarines or planes. Whenever there were bananas available there were never enough for everyone so the children got priority. It did not all go the children's way as sweets were rationed, too. Coal was rationed so fires were often lit just for cooking and then allowed to go out unless wood could be burned. Doctors could prescribe extra coal rations for their patients, particularly small children. Fuel had to be used to heat the water, so hot water must not be wasted and 5″ was the maximum allowed in a bath; hotels used to put a line on the inside of the baths at this height. Fuel was also used to create electricity so lights were to be used sparingly, and always turned off on leaving a room; rooms such as toilets and bathrooms had 5-watt bulbs.

Everything was what was called 'utility'; there was little choice, the amount of material in dresses or coats was limited, and clothes were rationed. Young people getting married borrowed from friends and the slogan 'make do and mend' was much used. However, things were not all rationed at the same time, butter and bacon, followed by sugar and meat were rationed as early as December 1939/January 1940 but the clothes ration did not come in until June 1941. In spite of all this, such luxuries as cakes could still be bought although the ingredients were limited, and hotels still served meals although they were limited to a maximum of three courses and a total cost of 5/-, but some of the expensive hotels got around this by adding a cover charge!

Although rationing was making life difficult for the city people, the countryside had a lot to offer: many people managed to supplement the rations with rabbits and pigeons. There were plenty of wild rabbits; they went into the pot with the home grown vegetables, and there was never a shortage of vegetables with all the farms round here. People kept hens as well, so there were eggs, and when the hens went off-lay there could be a fowl for the pot. If a cow calved and there was milk left over, it would be given to friends or family as an extra. There were problems if you did not own any land to grow on, and there was a certain amount of poaching. One family, whose father held the shoot for several farms to keep the rabbits down, seemed to live on rabbit, rabbit and yet more rabbit! It is interesting to note that a relative of that family still owns the rabbit shoot for some local farms. There were also double rations for the farm workers during harvest (referred to as Harvest Rations) of cheese, fats and sugar. Pat Steele remembers going to Mustchin's yard twice a week on Tuesdays and Fridays "to collect the Harvest Rations which were delivered there - terrible, dry, old, what-were-supposed-to-be, steak and kidney pies. The pastry was like chaff." People saved up their sugar ration to make jam, and, if none of a family liked one of the rations it could be exchanged with a neighbour for something else. For those in the village fortunate enough to have friends or relatives in Canada, rations were sometimes supplemented by food parcels from abroad, tins of luncheon meat or chicken, and on one occasion a bag of rice, a real luxury as little rice for puddings had been imported since the war began. Oranges and bananas were almost unheard of, but there was always corned beef to make up the meat ration, bones for soup and marrowbones for dripping when rendered down.

Some of the young men from the village joined the Territorial Army, whose headquarters were in Pulborough. One could choose which regiment one went into, but most of the local boys joined The Royal Sussex Regiment; Worthing recruited for the Royal Artillery and Steyning and Shoreham for the Royal Engineers. The Royal Sussex Regiment's symbol was a star and Royal Garter with a white roussllian plume out of the top; it is a French infantry plume and leads to an interesting history. In 1759 the 35th of Foot (later, in 1832 to become the Royal Sussex Regiment) was part of a British Force under General Wolfe at Quebec which was then held by the French under General Montcalm. During the attack on the Heights of Abraham the Regiment was engaged against the Royal Roussillon Regiment which at that time wore a white plume in their hats. As the Royal Sussex advanced the soldiers picked up the discarded French plumes and stuck them in their own headgear; to commemorate the victory the Royal Sussex incorporated the plume into its own cap badge.

THE ROYAL SUSSEX REGIMENT

Rousillion Plume

The Local Defence Volunteers – 1941 – later called The Home Guard
Front row from left: Walter Parrot, Fred (Nobby) Clark, George Bale, Sid Vincent, Nobby Crabb, Ron (Tiny) Parsons, Andrew Steele
Middle row: Mac Steele, —, Captain Dane, Kerr, Palmer, Sid Twichen, Billy Ayling
Back row: Gaskell, Freeman, John Steele, Parfitt, Ern Slater, Archie Steele, George Mansbridge, Charlie Rogers, Dick Cook, Bill Merritt, Fred Gumbrell, Boorer, Alf Crabb, Dick Daughtrey, Maurice Tree, Eddie Harris, George Curtis, William Voss

Everyone was expected to contribute to the War Effort, and those who were not on active service often found themselves in one of the volunteer services, such as The Home Guard. The Home Guard used to meet at what is now called Malthouse on the corner of Stream Lane; at that time it was described as "a tumbledown cottage reinforced with corrugated iron and wood." Mr Billy Lenharth was in the Home Guard and on some weekends half a dozen or so of them would go to Lilac Cottage to do some basic training very much in the manner of the television programme 'Dad's Army'. Their duties were vague says Billy's son Barry, and seemed to consist of fire-watching and waiting for the German army whom the six of them would see off! They also patrolled the village to check on blackout curtains and lights, to ensure that anyone out was about his lawful business and not spying. They practised firing with broomsticks and hoes, and of their two "officers", one had an old flintlock and the other had a First

World War rifle, both of which were used as props in the wartime concert parties! Drill was practised on the flat area in front of the laundry as there was plenty of room there and when the men had finished, Billy would drill his son Barry and Barry's friend Ron as well. Billy was either a Corporal or a Sergeant and had been given his initial instruction from a full time soldier who had arrived on a motor bike. There were regular meetings, perhaps once a week, for discussion and exercises, and a popular meeting in the pub every now and again, but two men were on duty every night at the hut. When Mac Steele had to be up early for the milking, his partner in the Home Guard, Tony Ayling used to keep watch for the pair of them, while Mac slept. However, one night they both fell asleep, and were awakened by a furious brigadier Hogsbristle - no-one seems to know who this was, but it is an amusing name, conjuring up just the right image! Elva Lipscomb (née Johnson) has written that "one night the chaps collected a red roadworks lamp and hung it outside Lakers Farm Cottage, where the elderly Miss Bolwell lived, so the Canadian soldiers returning to camp after going to the Queens Head thought they were on to a good thing. Miss Bolwell was not amused!"

The ARP (Air Raid Precautions) Wardens began their patrol as soon as it was dark to check on visible lights, and the story is told of one grandfather who had allowed his winter bonfire to stay smouldering overnight. A wind had got up sending a shower of sparks into the night, and the warden thundered on his door demanding that he get up out of bed, get dressed, and put out the flames before any German pilot saw anything which might give him an indication of whether he was over land or sea. The ARP Warden's other duties included organising stirrup pumps and sandbags in case of fire, maintaining a first-aid supply and ensuring that everyone had, and knew how to use, a gas mask. They were all volunteers who wore their own clothes but were issued with a black steel helmet with a white W on the front, and each carried a torch and his gas mask in its cardboard box slung over his shoulder.

Most of the houses had some sort of shelter dug in the garden in case of falling bombs, but sometimes the children would just be put under the kitchen table, particularly when the shelters had filled up with rain water after a particularly wet spell, as one or two of them did. Time was spent in the shelters however; although the village did not have an air raid siren, people soon learned the usual route for the planes to take to London, and the different engine sounds of English and German planes. A sensible precaution as well as the obligatory blackout material, was to hang heavy curtains at the windows or to stick a lacy fabric to the glass with flour paste to protect the household from shattering glass.

Pat Steele comments: "I remember the first air raid warning. A chappie came up the road with a handbell calling out 'Air raid warning. Take cover. Air raid warning. Take cover,' and some of my friends remember spending school time sitting under their desks! I also regret that I threw away the 'baby gas mask' that had been provided for the family as this type of protection is no longer seen. It consisted of an iron frame covered in a thick rubber material with a perspex window, and a drawstring. The baby was put right inside, and someone had to pump the handle on the side of the machine to keep the air flowing. Fortunately it never had to be used. I offered the contraption to the local museum, but, when they didn't want it, I took it to the dump!"

Another gas mask story is told by Elva Johnson who says: "Lennie Pullen and two other boys were making their way home after school with the gas masks that had been handed out that day. In the way of boys, they were kicking their boxes down the road, using them as footballs. I dared them to kick them into the stream, which they did, but my satisfaction was short lived when I heard Lennie being walloped for it!"

Before paid police forces developed, communities depended on volunteers and for the last 150 years Special Constables have had powers to support regular officers; at times of crisis this support has been essential. During the Second World War Cyril Hawkins and Mr Gumbrell were men who, because of their reserved occupation were not called up, and became Special Constables. Their duties included checking that there had been no enemy landings and reporting back; in this they used to walk for miles around the parish. Similarly, Bert Baker and Bert Slater patrolled the Broadford Bridge area.

The Italians were the first prisoners of war to arrive in the village. The farmers were responsible for those who worked on the farms; there was little desire to run away as they were fed, housed and looked after. They would arrive on the farms by truck every day from Nutbourne, Billingshurst or Kingsfold (the nationalities were separated) and be taken home again the same way after work. One of the children of the time remembers that they were allowed to talk to the Italians, but not to the Germans who followed later! The Germans were good and conscientious workers who got on well with the farmers; one or two of them even learned English. It would appear that the Germans almost ran their camp

Woman in a Gas Mask

themselves, and some of them used to sneak out, borrowing the guards' uniforms, to go to the dances at Loxwood. Even some of the local farmers were in on the plot and used to drive the men to the dance!

As farming was a Reserved Occupation some of the men stayed in the village, but the farms were still short-handed as men had been called up, so the prisoners, the old men and the children all helped, assisted by the Land Army girls. Because no-one could get machinery or spare parts, as the factories were making parts for the war effort, a lot of farms had to work by hand or borrow tractors and machinery from Brinsbury; it was the beginning of farm contract work. Brinsbury Farm was taken over during the war by War AG (agriculture); it was a large farm but was running with rabbits. The War AG people told the farm manager to improve food production or they would take the farm over; eventually this they did, and later it became Brinsbury College.

The Women's Land Army was created in 1939 to train women to take over the vital role of food production and delivery when the men were called up (in September 1917 it had been estimated that 200,000 women were working on the land in an unofficial land army). By the outbreak of the second war about a thousand girls had been trained and the numbers grew steadily. Many of the girls were totally unprepared for what they were letting themselves in for, for the hours were long and the animals unpredictable; the farm day could begin as early as 5.30am. Alma Steele explains how she ended up in West Chiltington: "I used to work in the control office of the Dorchester Hotel in London and one day I was walking along Oxford Street in my lunch hour and I saw this big poster of a girl sitting against something golden doing absolutely nothing and looking beautiful. The poster was in front of the headquarters of the Land Army, and was part of their recruitment drive; well it looked a lot better than a factory where a lot of my friends had gone after being called up, so I volunteered. I had no idea what I was coming to, I didn't even know that the golden stuff was stooks of corn! I arrived at this hostel at Brinsbury and thought how polite all the girls were as they all kept coming up and shaking my hand, until I overheard one of the girls say to another 'have you been over and shaken that girl's hand yet, go on, you can tell she's never done a day's work in her life!' These girls formed the gangs that used to go out onto the farms. There was another section there, to be trained not just to hoe, but to milk and to muck out, to be sent to farms where there were no men, except perhaps an old one, and to help in the day-to-day management. I joined those, and couldn't sleep for days for the pain in my wrists as I learned to hand milk, but I soon got over it. Eventually I had to leave the Land Army as I had a problem with my shoulder: I have an indentation there still where I used to have to carry great bales of hay, and the pitchfork left its mark!"

There were many Land Girls in and around the area, some were billeted at Little Thakeham and enlivened the scene with their parties. At Linfields they grew fruit and vegetables, and kept chickens both for eggs and for meat, and surprisingly they also concentrated on growing mushrooms which was a luxury product for wartime, selling for £1 per pound when a working man's wage was £2.5.0d a week. It was a mystery who bought them, but the place could not produce enough, and if the roof of the glasshouse had been damaged the local builder was urgently called in to make it watertight again. Gwen Smith remembers: "It was 1940 and we were doing the work of the men, lifting up bushel boxes of beetroot, onions, turnips. We also grew lettuce, leeks, cabbages, anything you can think of that was food. Every day it was collected and put on the big lorry and then they used to throw these boxes up onto the lorry for the driver to stack, and it all went up to Covent Garden. Linfields paid us, but it was a fixed rate set by the government, I think it was about 7d an hour with an automatic rise when you were 18 and then the adult rate when you were 21. There were hundreds of us there, did you know Jomo Kenyatta (a Kenyan politician of the Kikuyu tribe who managed the Mau-Mau and became the Prime Minister of independent Kenya) worked with us? I worked with him, he was a real gentleman, and he learned all he could about the work at Linfields. When work was over he'd go round schools and hotels and all sorts of places, lecturing, he was very clever. He was a biggish man and after we'd filled the boxes in the field he'd take them to the side for the tractor to come along to load up and take to the packing shed. The root vegetables had to be washed in huge tanks of cold water and you didn't have any rubber gloves in those days. We used to freeze in those cold packing sheds. Whopping great big iron tanks with the cold water running all the time, (Linfields is over a 200′ silt bed so they sank their own pumps and had plenty of water which, after use, simply sank back into the silt bed), no wonder it was called the war 'effort' but in spite of everything they were wonderful days - I was never so fit in my life! I used to work like a horse, and eat like a horse! And then back from work to run the house. My mother wasn't very strong but did what she could, so I got the coal in, and the water from the standpipe, and prepared the dinner for the next day; I also turned sheets sides-to-middle and when they were worn out again made pillowcases, and mended our clothes. We had advanced from our well to a standpipe by then, but it was more trouble than it was worth because it used to freeze up; and the men had to light a fire around it to thaw it out early in the morning before we women could get the water. That standpipe served eight houses; there were sixteen houses in The Birches so we had another one further down the road."

After the Canadians had left and the war had ended, the camp at Monkmead was used to accommodate the Displaced Persons: Poles, Romanians and Yugoslavs who found themselves the wrong side of the borders and had nowhere to go because the Russians had taken their homes. These DPs were sometimes families, not just the menfolk; some of these were absorbed into the community, getting farming jobs and accommodation, some of the men married local girls, some of the women got cleaning jobs and managed to stay, but a lot of them were thought to have been sent back forcibly to Poland when the Russians demanded it.

Eddie Shotnik's tale of how he found himself in West Chiltington is typical of the upheaval of war; his wealthy home in Poland had been overrun by the Germans who had taken him to Germany to work, but he had escaped through France and joined the Polish Army in Italy at Monte Casino in 1942. When the war finished, Europe was awash with people in the wrong place; many of the troops knew where they were trying to get back to, but the geography of Europe had changed and Poland was no longer as it had been. The Poles were given the choice: either go home and take a chance with this new communism, or leave your fate in the hands of the victorious authorities. Many of the older men went back; they had been regular soldiers for many years and they felt they had no choice, but as Eddie could make no contact with anyone from his family he decided to come over to England. (The older men who returned to Poland said that they would let the others know what the situation was like, but no one ever heard from them.)

The journey to Great Britain took seven or eight weeks and the group of two or three thousand soldiers, almost two brigades, ended up in Scotland; after a week in Glasgow docks they were loaded onto a train which stopped at Horsham and from there they drove to Kirdford. They stayed there for about three weeks before they were put to work at Seaford and along the coast, and on the Downs clearing unexploded bombs and ammunition. Although they had no tanks with them, they had brought lorries, bren gun carriers and full equipment. In the September they came to West Chiltington and met the Polish refugees who had been picked up from Russia, India and Pakistan, and were all settled into the camp at Monkmead, with the Polish squadron looking after the refugees. At this stage Eddie was still in the Polish Army; initially wages were paid and copious amounts of food supplied by the Americans, but when the British Government took over the wages were three shillings a day with limited rations. Deliveries were made every other day because there were hundreds of people at the camp needing food, laundry and equipment.

Eventually, though, disillusion set in: these fit men had little to do and less money to do it. Eddie explained that with a rock cake at the NAAFI stores costing sixpence and a daily wage of three shillings, things were getting tight, the plentiful supplies had dwindled and they were hungry; cigarettes were reduced and beer was out of the question. It must be said that the contrast with the supplies from the Americans was very noticeable, but Britain still had war-time rationing and food for everyone was scarce. At the beginning of 1947 he was entitled to six or seven weeks' leave and having met Joan Greenfield at a camp dance, she got him a job at Carver's builders as Carver was her uncle. Unfortunately he overstayed his leave and was picked up by the military police but when Mr Carver promised to give him a job for at least a year, he was demobilised at the age of 20.

Life on a builder's yard was very different from the luxurious life he had known as a child. Although he spoke Italian and German, he had arrived over here without a word of English, and being in a Polish community there was little incentive to learn, until he met Joan! The reception he got in the village was also a surprise; the villagers had learned to be wary after the boisterousness of the Canadians, and the English are naturally reserved. No one was ever unkind or abusive, just quiet. Add to that the rural simplicity of village life as compared with the wanderings and excitement that Eddie had experienced and he must have wondered just where he had landed up! In 1950 Joan and he were married, and lived in the Village before buying a piece of land on the Common and building their own house.

Before the wedding Eddie made great efforts to get in touch with his family which had been broken up and dispersed; his younger sister had left before the arrival of the Russians and ended up in Western Germany. His parents and older sister had stayed, but after his father was released from the salt mines in Siberia (which left him with a permanent disability being able only to shuffle along as the leg chains he had had to wear caused permanent damage) they packed up all they could carry and walked from Poland to Germany during the winter of 1949/50 to meet her. In 1953 Joan and Eddie met Mr Shotnik senior who was delighted to have a new family.

Joan had left school before she was 14 and worked in a house in Roundabout for fifteen shillings a week for a ten-hour day, six days a week. Of this sum she gave 5/- to her mother for her keep, 5/- to pay off her bicycle, and kept 5/- for herself. Eddie was paid £1 2s 6d in 1946 as a builder, but it soon went up to £2 because he was such a good worker. When they decided to build their own house, Eddie was earning £5 10s a week and the building work had to be fitted around his 10 hour day at Carver's. Two other Polish refugees were employed by Slater's builders for a year or so until they moved on, and others scattered to other parts of the country or to America.

When Peace was declared some of the Canadians were still in the camp and they and the villagers went from one pub to the next, dancing in the streets. Everyone shared what food they had and the Canadians contributed from their ration stores to the great party that was held in the Queens Head. There were flags across the street from Palmers Lodge to Step House and the shop, and there was dancing in the square.

High Barn is the highest part of the area and on VE night many people went up there to see all the bonfires; you could see to Queen Elizabeth Park at Meon in Petersfield in one direction and to Lewes in the other. Mustchin's had the biggest bonfire in their coal yard and when that had died down the young lads cycled into Storrington to join in the dancing in the streets there, and the general celebrations. There were far fewer people in the village then, all the men, and many of the women were away, leaving a population of about 1,600 old men and women, young people and children. On the 50th anniversary of the Armistice in 1995 the beacon bonfires were lit again but there were not so many.

In March 1949 clothes came off ration. In February 1953 sweets, which were about the last thing rationed, also came off and the country looked forward to 'Life back to Normal'.

The Second World War ended in 1945, and yet over fifty years on there are still repercussions; a letter arrived on the doormat of the Clerk to the Parish recently from a woman in Krakow in Poland seeking information. She wondered whether he could put her in touch with her old school teacher from West Chiltington, a Mr F C Belok. Eventually the Clerk received a letter from Mr Belok explaining "In 1946 there were two camps in West Chiltington; one belonged to the Third Polish Regiment and the other Nissen hut camp was occupied by the Polish Grammar School for Girls. The girls came from two areas: the main one was the Middle East where a Polish Army was formed under General Anders and the girls were the dependants of the service men who primarily volunteered from Russian POW camps. The other stream came from German POW camps where young girls landed who participated in the Warsaw uprising. The class rooms had only one cast iron stove and consequently were cold, and rationing was in force; the winter of 1946 I remember as the worst this century with heavy snowfalls. The following year, 1947, the school moved from West Chiltington to Stowell Park in Gloucester.

This Department of Education scheme was a complete success; we received the girls and boys in similar camps with no English and no educational background, and after six years or less we competed on equal terms with all other British Grammar School pupils in what are now called the A level examinations. Only a few months ago I met four sisters who had been pupils at West Chiltington Camp and all of them were graduates; one a dentist, two were A level teachers and the fourth was a civil servant.

Polish Grammar School 1946

Your correspondent had had a successful career as a graphic designer before marrying a professor of medicine at Krakow University.

I remember West Chiltington as a friendly village with a patient shopkeeper when our pupils used him to practise their newly acquired language!"

Polish Grammar School 1947
F C Belok the English Master with pupils in the hut classroom

Chapter 13

"Spare Time!"

For many years, of course, no-one had any *spare* time but it is surprising how many activities seem to have been fitted into so little time. It is now, when we have so much more leisure, that some clubs and societies are struggling, not so much for members as for officers. It is perhaps a reflection of the fact that the higher expectations of the end of the century bring more stress, materialism and tension, longer working hours and an exhaustion that cannot cope with the added responsibility of giving one's time to charities or social occasions.

Colonel Kensington's daughter Enid was the Lieutenant of the Girl Guides and Doris Coles was the Captain when Elsie Cattell was a girl in 1918. Meetings were held in the old Rectory garage before new premises were found in The Juggs field. Miss Milligan followed as leader, and was succeeded by Mrs Helen Rawlinson. The local group must have folded because when Sue Overton-Smith was ten in 1957 she had to join the Pulborough Guides as they were her nearest group. Joan Theis (who later remarried and became Joan Campbell) restarted the company at West Chiltington with herself as Captain, and Mamie Jones the Rector's wife, as Lieutenant, and asked Sue, and Anthea Bendall to become Patrol Leaders and help form a new company. They met in the Church Hall, and their first camp was held in the garden of Mrs Rawlinson's bungalow at Apsley. They participated at the annual Gymkhana where they had a Lucky Dip and hot dog stall.

By 1985 Pam Strong was Brown Owl and Janice Tomsett was Tawny Owl of the 1st West Chiltington Brownies when they entered the Brownie and Guide Tea Challenge. The Tea Council had given a million tea bags to Brownies throughout the country to raise money for the Save the Children Fund; the garden at the windmill was opened and 24 Brownies served tea to visitors, raising £80.

In about 1995 a local branch of the Rainbow Group was started in the village; the national association having begun about 1987 as a pre-Brownie organisation. It is a club for girls between five and seven years old; meetings are held in the Church Hall after school every Tuesday for an hour, where there are songs, games and crafts, and occasional outings. The girls have a distinctive blue tabard 'uniform'. At seven, the girls move on to Brownies until they are ten; there are two Brownie packs in the village at present, and one Guide group, all of which meet in the Church Hall. Unfortunately the boys are not so well served; a lack of dedicated leaders has meant that there is no Scout Troop in the village at the moment.

Peter Penfold was a member of the Scouts in the 1930s: "we started off as Cubs at the old Rectory; they used to keep a car or two in the stables and we had our meetings in the room above. Later they built a Scout Hut where the Juggs houses stand now but that was agricultural land then. We used to go on camping holidays, all packed into the back of a truck."

The children played games between working, and sometimes there was very little difference between either activity. Joyce Gibney remembers that in the 1920s she used to play paper chase all over Willetts Farm, and adds that it was quite safe for children to go anywhere in those days. When she lost her red hair-ribbon, which she often did, Uncle Tom would come and find her with her ribbon decking the end of his pitchfork. There were primroses and bluebells to gather in London Copse, and ditches to hide in.

In the 1930s things had not changed much and the children still played outside; one girl remembers playing with her friend in the pig pound. There were conker fights with the conkers they had gathered from the Churchyard; they would plague relatives who were baking for a fresh cake or biscuit; and they would pick kingcups from around the pond and collect tadpoles. There was also watercress growing wild there which the children would cut for their tea.

Sue Overton-Smith says of the 1950s that their games were much the same: "I remember walking across the fields with my family and hearing the frogs croaking in the marshy area beyond New Barn Lane; and it was always a treat to go and see Gill Lawson and her animals, particularly the piglets or chicks, and Arabella her horse. We also used to walk along Haglands Lane where we would pass Old Nell Short who would be sitting in a sort of shed plucking chickens, with feathers everywhere. There was also a goose-lady (Mable Figg) who used to drive the geese along Mill Road; she always wore wellingtons and held a stick - the geese would hiss

Castlegate

and it could be scary. It was even more scary to be confronted along that same road by a line of Teddy boys, stretching across the road. Older children used to say that they had 'knuckle dusters' and tell frightening tales, but fortunately we always passed them without incident. We used to roam across the fields and woods and play in the old railway carriages which were in the field where Castlegate has now been built. We used to go there and play 'house', taking small empty paste jars to fill with wild flowers, and decorate the inside. We also played in a little clearing in the in the woods by New Barn Lane, on soft green grass which we called 'mossy common', and I remember suddenly having to be very quiet as three baby badgers came across the grass very close to us. I shall never forget it."

Of the more formally-organised clubs and societies, Connie Slater remembers a concert group called the XYZs, run in the 1930s by Billy Lenharth and his wife from Lilac Cottage in Little Hill. Hector Hornsby, who lived in the other half of Lilac Cottage, was not involved in this, but his sister Gladys used to give Connie and her sister piano lessons, and when they were very young they were in a group of eight chorus girls who would go round entertaining. They entertained the old people in the workhouse at Thakeham, and around the villages of Pulborough,

XYZ's Concert Party – 1930s
From left, starting with the eldest: Elsie Manvell, Enid Daughtrey, Connie Short, Joyce Cox, Joyce Short, Eileen Tyrell, Rollie Manvell the youngest

Storrington, Thakeham and West Chiltington, performing music, dance and a pantomime, which ran for three or four nights. Connie remembers the workhouse as being a cold, dilapidated place with stone walls and long damp passages; the only light from candles as there were no oil lamps; and the whole place like a prison. Avera Denham, who was a professional dance teacher connected with the theatre in London and who used to live in Roundabout, voluntarily taught them ballet and tap. Costumes were made by Connie's mother, and Connie memorably recalls one performance when they were all dressed as pierrots in bright tangerine with big black collars, black shoes with tangerine bows and with tangerine and black bows in their hair. Their name was put up on the curtain, *West Chiltington XYZs;* a local man made all the scenery, programmes were printed and rehearsals took place twice a week in the New Hall. There was a full cast for the pantomimes, Connie remembers *Robinson Crusoe* and *Sinbad the Sailor* in particular, with the chorus and adults; performances were in the Old Comrades Hall, front seats 1/6d, the back rows were a shilling. As if this was not enough, there was also a summer revue of skits and sketches! After all the expenses were taken out, the money raised was given to the local hospitals and, during the war, to provide Red Cross parcels for the troops. Billy was versatile, making scenery, making and playing instruments and entertaining; he is remembered in a baggy coat and baggy trousers with a big, floppy bow tie dancing on the ends of his incredible shoes - these had caps which projected about 8" beyond the squared ends of his shoes upon which he would stand to dance; a clowning version of ballet's pointes. No one has ever seen this done before, or since. Both he and his wife were musical, Mrs Lenharth played the piano and Mr Lenharth played the violin, a one-string fiddle, and a carpenter's saw - he bent it by holding the handle between his knees; his left hand holding the other end level with his face, he bent it in an S-shape and stroked it with a violin bow; he could play many tunes on it.

Elva Johnson, a girl at that time, remembers watching Princess Elizabeth's wedding in 1947 on Hector Hornsby's television which must have been one of the first televisions in the village. Many other men remember being invited to watch the sports programmes.

Doug Golds is at present the chairman of the West Chiltington Silver Band, which was started on 8 July 1908. Doug's father moved the family from Thakeham to West Chiltington, possibly because the family was getting bigger and needed more space, and Doug joined the band when he was twelve in 1945. He takes up the story: "They were the main social force in the village and used to practice at Nutbourne at first, and have practised for many years now on a Wednesday in the Reading Room. This was also used for our meetings and became very smoky having only the old tortoise stove for heating; and in those days everyone smoked cigarettes. In a way, it was Slater's band - if you were a Slater you were in the band and if you were in the band you were almost a Slater! The band was actually started by Edmund Talbot Pullen (Ivan Pullen's great-grandfather); Grandfather Slater and his eldest son Albert were founder members, and there were four other Slater sons who also played. The conductor in the early days was Mr Chatfield. Edmund Pullen did not play but walked in front of the band with the flag. I was taught to play by Albert Slater; if you wanted to play you were given an instrument to see if you could get a note out of it, they taught you about embouchure (how to form your mouth) and theory (what the notes were). They gave you a tutor, with the lines and spaces written in, and told you to play a scale, then you could take the instrument home to practice.

The Silver Band – 1910

The Silver Band – 1910
1 Charlie (Speckie) Chatfield. 2 Bert Slater. 3 Frank (Mussell) Pullen. 4 (Soldier) Johnson, 5 Norman Ayling. 6 Maurice Tree. 7 Phil (Ned) Slater. 8 Bailey Parsons. 9 George Gumbrell. 10 Harry Howard, 11 Billy Ayling, 12 George Hayler, 13 Tom Gumbrell, 14 Jack Pannell. 15 Bill Rodgers. 16 Bill Cole. 17 Sid Short. 18 Harry Short. 19 Jack Parsons. 20 Norman (Ted) Slater. 21 Billy Pannell. 22 Philip Slater. 23 Sid (Bunk) Burchell. 24 Johnnie Barnes

When I first learned, there were so many of us that we had to share instruments; I shared a cornet with Jimmy Weeks and got so annoyed that I couldn't practice enough that I asked what else I could play, so I was given a tenor and have been playing it ever since! In fact I joined the voluntary band when I went into the RAF, and when I left the RAF I came back to the village band and picked up the tenor again. Obviously our musical knowledge was very limited and we were all self-taught. The only instruction I had was from another member, Billy Ayling whose daughter went to Horsham High School and was learning the violin there, so three or four of us went to his house in Gay Street and she used to teach us theory. It must have been a good grounding because what she taught me has stuck, the flats and sharps were B E A D G C F and I used to remember them by Beautiful Elizabeth Ayling Doug Golds CF, but I couldn't think of a word for the C or F! There was talk of the band folding a few years ago and in the rules it states that it must close if there are less than six members, but I was determined we would survive so I went round Rydon and the secondary schools; I don't think the band room is right for young children. I got five youngsters interested, but as homework, exams and boyfriends came on the scene, they drifted away. Once they leave they don't come back, and I did get a bit disheartened but I hope they have benefited from what they have learned; after all any learning is good and not wasted. However I'm teaching my nine year old granddaughter at the moment, so I hope she will carry on." One or two members play at Petworth now.

From the age of ten in 1938 Reg Slater played trombone in the band, and played for fifty years. He was also Secretary for a number of years and adds to Doug's story: "The purchase of instruments was a problem but we pooled the money we earned by playing, it was £3 in the beginning but went up to £25 or even £50 at the end, and this money went to buy instruments. (In her teens Elsie Cattell used to help run the dances and whist drives in the Comrades Hall which were held to raise funds for the band). Initially somebody went up to London with ten shillings and bought a load of instruments, and we just made a lot of noise! The next expense was the uniforms but in 1937 Mr Morgan from Nyetimber supplied the money for these; the first one we had was gold and red and modelled on the Hussars uniform, although its replacement looked more like a busman's outfit, and the last one was blue.

We played almost every weekend and sometimes in the week; on a Sunday evening at the cross roads by the Queens Head where the villagers used to congregate to listen; Pulborough, Storrington, Coolham; all round. Billy Reynolds had been in the theatre so he used to organise the concert parties. We were very well thought of and used to go to functions and carol singing in the village and up at Roundabout, and in other villages, even as far afield as Steyning. Someone held the clothes prop with the light attached to it, and the money we collected went into our funds. We used to march round the village and the Common on Flower Show days and finish up in the Flower Show Field. If we found we had a spare day in the

The Cup Winners – 1936
After the celebration march, there was a celebration dinner

The Cup Winners – 1936
1. Bert Ruff. 2. Bill Hammomd. 3. Tony de Fean'e. 4. Charlie Woods. 5. Bert Slater. 6. George Bale. 7. Michael Thorpe. 8. Eric Gartrell. 9. Henry Streeter. 10. Billy Pannell. 11. Phil Slater Jn. 12. Alec Parry. 13. Sid Johnson. 14. Hector Hornsby. 15. Jim Standen. 17. Norman (Ted) Slater. 18. Charlie Russell. 19. Ern Slater. 20. Norman (Jack) Cattell. 21. Tom Gumbrell. 22. Billy Ayling. 23. Walter Larby. 24. Fred Ruff. 25. Billy Lenharth. 26. Bert Stamford. 27. George Mitchell. 28. John Hampshire. 29. Rev George Hall. 30. Ron Streeter. 31. George Crabb. 32. Alf Crabb. 33. Lawrance Larby. 34. Fred Slater. 35. Bill (Dickey) Dixon. 36. Charlie Hare-Winton. 37. Arthur Johnson. 38. Charlie (Speckey) Chatfield

summer we would play outside the pubs: The Rising Sun at Nutbourne, The White Horse at Mare Hill, The White Lion at Thakeham or in the square in Storrington by The Anchor, and the village used to come out to listen. We went on our bikes with our instruments on our backs! It was a big band and in 1936, the year the football club won the cup, we won a cup on the same day; the teams telephoned each other and arranged to get off the coach at Hatches so that the band could play the football team down through the village. There was a celebration dinner at the Elephant afterwards.

During the war every village had a dance at least once a week; a tradition that carried on for many years after the war ended, with dances on bank holidays and on Wednesday or Saturdays. There was always something going on: the band practices on Thursday and Monday, and concerts on Saturday or Sunday, sometimes both. Even after the war the band was in demand at all the fetes." They also used to play for social evenings, and one evening is particularly remembered when there was a fancy dress competition; Pat Steele's brother was a terrible tease and told her he was going to dress her up as a dog's dinner for the fancy dress, as she was so fond of dogs! Everyone in the village had a dog, which all used to run lose in those days, so when she set off, with a crown of dog biscuits and an old coat decorated with bits of biscuit and a big bone in the middle, she was followed

WEST CHILTINGTON PRIZE BAND 1937

by three or four of the village dogs. Needless to say, she won a prize.

It is recalled that there was also a fete with a Punch and Judy show in the garden of the Mill House which was owned by Richard Page, that the Steele family used to give a display of Scottish country dancing at the village cross roads periodically, and that the Salmons from Harborough Drive used to hold square dancing evenings in their garden for friends in the late 1940s and early 1950s.

Bob Thornton writes: "The West Chiltington and District Branch of the British Legion was formed on 30 August 1921, but in spite of many searches and enquiries our records only go back to the AGM on 19 February 1935 when Colonel Kensington was the President and the Chairman was Albert Mustchin. Meetings took place in the British Legion Comrades' Hall; in 1958 the members 'marched in style from the old (Hall) to the new' Village Hall where a room was to be held in perpetuity, free of charge, as their headquarters.

The Royal British Legion (the Royal Charter was granted in 1925) helps ex-Servicemen and their families by raising money for, and awareness of, their needs. Initially they held fund-raising activities such as whist drives in the Comrades' Hall; a Dinner with an entertainment was held in 1957 and by the 1980s social evenings and entertainments were held annually in the Village Hall. In 1984 General Bob Foote formed the Legionnaires Golfing Society which raised money through its annual raffle, and by 1999 some £14,000 had been distributed to local RBL branches in aid of the Poppy Appeals; the Branch's network of Officers and helpers has raised many thousands of pounds over the years for this cause.

In 1960 falling numbers had caused discussion to take place concerning amalgamation with the Pulborough Branch, but this came to nothing so, to boost flagging funds and image, Major Guy Peace proposed that a Fête be held. In 1988 local membership had risen to 108 but by the early 1990s the membership was falling again and age was taking its toll. The West Chiltington Branch is, at the end of the second millennium, trying with the Grace of God to keep going because:

If not for them who fought and fell
What would life hold today?
That we might live in peace and love
They gave their Yesterday."

The Women's Section of the British Legion was also started in 1921 to help ex-Servicewomen, widows and orphans. Before the days of the Welfare State they had a large number of schemes providing allowances, children's homes, clothing and domestic items. On 21 March 1945 an inaugural meeting was held to start a Women's Section branch in West Chiltington; 36 members attending the first meeting on 5 June. Meetings were held in the Old Comrades Hall, and from 1958 in the new Village Hall. The early minutes are very business like and formal but occasionally end with a homely comment such as "It was generally agreed we should have a cup of tea" or "This ended a very jolly meeting". Strangely, no mention is made of the war, nor its end, only arrangements for a Victory Tea for the children in conjunction with the WI.

Dedication of the British Legion Women's Section Standard – 20 July 1947
The procession is led by the county standard bearer, followed by Kitty Coles (in white hat and spotted dress) with Mrs Palmer on her left. The West Chiltington standard bearer is Mollie Crabb with attendants Mrs Soffe and Mrs Slater. The Inman sisters are standing beside the school wall, while Valerie White skips along beside the procession.

Fund-raising is the main object as the Legion is able to help in so many ways with those who fall through the welfare gap, and the Women's Section concentrates on widows' allowances, welfare, grants and convalescence; in general improving the quality of life. The first bazaar was held on 4 December 1945 and raised the creditable sum of £67.9s 8d; one has been held every November since and now makes over £1,200. Smaller fund-raising events such as coffee mornings, table top sales and so on are also held from time to time, and the Women's Section is indispensable in doing much of the house-to-house collecting for the Poppy Appeal run by British Legion. The money raised helps all ex-servicemen and women, and the widows who would otherwise find life financially difficult; it is perhaps forgotten that the second world war did not end the world's fighting and that there has been a conflict every year but one since 1945 in which British troops have been involved.

The early connection with the residents of Gifford House, The Queen Alexandra Hospital Home for disabled ex-servicemen in Worthing, has continued, and every year a party comes for tea and an entertainment; an occasion enjoyed by guests and hosts alike. The original gifts of cigarettes however gave way to sweets some years ago! Gifford House was 'adopted' by the local branch even though it is an independent charity in its own right, because there was no local Legion home.

In 1971, on its fiftieth anniversary, the prefix Royal was added to the title of the British Legion, and on 21 March 1995 the fiftieth anniversary of the West Chiltington Women's Section branch was celebrated by a Thanksgiving and Re-dedication Service in St Mary's Church followed by a special tea.

The Women's Institute movement originated in Canada when a farmer's daughter, Adelaide Hoodless, from Stoney Creek in Ontario, lost a child. She believed her child had died through her ignorance of hygiene and child care, so she set up domestic science classes in rural areas. From these small beginnings the WI movement evolved and the first WI in the United Kingdom was formed in 1915 in Llanfair PG, Anglesey, North Wales.

West Chiltington WI was formed in 1921 and monthly meetings were held in fairly primitive conditions in the Old Comrades' Hall. In 1947 it is recorded that "we have demonstrations on 'lampshade making, soft toys, make and mend'. Classes are held from time to time on slipper and glove making and a year or two back the cookery classes were well attended. The Grannies' Tea which takes place in March always draws a full house… the Annual Fête which is held in the first week of August has flowers and fruit, jumble etc and the proceeds go to funds which are happily in a very healthy condition…….the June meeting is held in the delightful grounds of Voakes, and in August a garden party is given at Heathfield." As times changed, so has emphasis; when the Village Hall was built WI members were instrumental in getting a weekly doctor's surgery opened in the Hall, and have successfully campaigned for a 40 mph speed limit in the village.

The earliest memories West Chiltington Institute has are those of Eve Warren who came with her husband to farm at Palmers Lodge in 1937. In her 85th year she wrote that in those far off days one woke to the sound of the blacksmith's hammer on his anvil and in the evenings, nightingales sang in The Hollows. One of her happiest WI memories was appearing in a pageant held at Little Thakeham, then a private house. She also recalled the war years when members assembled several times a week at Gorse Place, off Harborough Hill, to make jam and bottle fruit donated from local gardens and orchards. Sugar was supplied by the Ministry of Food and everything was subject to inspection by its officials. The produce was then sold to local residents and at the Storrington WI market.

The interesting WI scrap book history of the village, now in the West Sussex Records Office, contains much on drains as the year the scrapbook was written was the year main drainage was put in; but it is a record of the changes in the village over the years. The local WI has demonstrated an artistic and musical flair; from its earliest days it has had an enthusiastic choir, and a successful Drama Group; when in 1962 the National Federation of WIs decided to publish a book to be called Twenty Poems, two members submitted a poem apiece and both were accepted.

In 1969 the WCWI entered the South of England Show at Ardingly in the craft section and won a Golden Certificate for the entry 'Trends and/or Traditions' in which comparisons were made between the old fashioned, in the form of the nanny, and the modern, in the form of the au pair.

Nowadays, apart from the monthly afternoon meetings, which include a speaker and either a competition or exhibition, there exists a Discussion Group, a Craft Section, and a luncheon club known as Focus on Food to which members bring an offering of food based on a theme, and recipes are exchanged. There are outings to places of interest, and trips to Europe have been organised.

In 1948 the annual subscription had risen to 3/6d. It is now £14.50. In

The WI Competition Entry – 1969 'From Nanny to Au Pair'
'Bassinet to carrycot, Wallpaper to Fablon, Sampler to collage, Seed cake to 'Danish pastry – but rice pudding and stewed rhubarb are timeless – and Victorian blouses are back.'

the 1960s the number of members had risen to 150 plus a waiting list, so it was decided to set up a second Institute which is also still running.

The West Chiltington Hayling WI was formed in October 1967, and its name was adopted from Hayling Pond. It was agreed to hold monthly meetings in the evenings, so that working mothers could attend, at the Church Hall. Founder member Mary Eames remembers when twelve rather apprehensive members met for the first time; fortunately one of their number had served in an East Sussex WI and was immediately voted President. A piano player was sought and found to accompany Jerusalem, the WI's national signature tune.

The new Institute, with great enthusiasm, plunged into WI competitions, displays and exhibitions. Their first effort was a model of Nigeria and members soon learnt what a high standard the County Federation required. At that time one of the members had been employed making glass eyes and her talents were soon put to good use! There is an active singing group, and after thirty years of singing, acting, dancing, learning new skills, playing and working together for the village, members are now looking forward to spreading their wings into Europe with a trip to Paris in 1999.

With the advent of working wives, and other factors, membership numbers throughout the country have begun to decline but fortunately this trend has not shown itself to any great extent in our village. In conjunction with 255,000 members in the UK, both West Chiltington Institutes are in full accord with the official purpose of the WI which states 'The WI offers opportunities for all women to enjoy friendship, to learn, to widen their horizons and together to influence local, national and international affairs'. In 1999 the WI released a report *The Changing Village*, which calls for government action to improve life in the rural communities by increasing the police presence; improving rural transport, housing, medical facilities and shops; by repairing old cottages; and by encouraging the government to build on brown-field sites in urban areas, so that green-field sites may be preserved for agriculture.

The WI's activities included a handbell ringing team, with an interesting history. No-one seems to know where the bells came from originally, but a letter claims that the bells were bought in 1922/23 through an advertisement, and that they came from Norfolk, or thereabouts. The letter continues: 'My mother, Mrs Sinclair-Burton, trained a team of bell ringers and they met regularly at Ireton House on Common Hill where she lived. In the autumn of 1925, after the death of my father, we moved to Bournemouth and I suppose this is when the bell ringing lapsed for lack of anyone to carry on.' The bells were eventually found in the loft of the village post office by Mrs Gooch in about 1925. In 1938 a group of WI members heard about the twenty bells and a team of six ringers was formed. They played until at least 1957, and were conducted by Mrs Cordery; the group only disbanding after the death of one of the members. When not in use the bells were kept by Mrs Warren in an out-house on her farm, and after the group disbanded they remained there, forgotten. In 1968 they were brought to the notice of Miss F Sharp, a musical member of the WI, and again a team was formed. In 1970 minor repairs were made, and over the years new bells, and members, were added, so that the team undertook engagements, were interviewed on Radio Brighton and were in much demand, particularly at Christmas time. In 1982 Miss Elizabeth Taylor retired as leader of the Handbell Ringers and the team was taken over by a member of Sullington WI.

The Handbell Ringers – about 1975
From left: Elizabeth Taylor, Paddy Holman, Nell Burley, Anne Owens, Frances Sharpe, Nora Heffer, Dorothy Bown

The West Sussex Federation of Women's Institutes formed a croquet section at Storrington recreation ground where the facilities were fairly basic, and they had to store their equipment in an empty telephone kiosk! In 1977 it was decided that it would be better to play at West Chiltington recreation ground and the Parish Council gave their permission. For the next eighteen years the WI ladies continued to play here. However on one particular day in 1989 when the sun shone brightly the players found to their astonishment that their croquet lawns had been taken over by cameras, lights, reflectors, generators, refreshment vehicles and mobile dressing rooms - the BBC had decided to take some film shots for the series *Ever Decreasing Circles*. There was some spirited discussion but even after it was established that the BBC had changed the day that they had arranged with the Parish Council, the film makers won the battle for the lawns!

In 1995 it was mutually agreed that the Croquet Club would no longer be an adjunct to the WSFWIs, and that it would function as an independent club with its own management and membership.

Over the years as new people moved into the village, other clubs and societies have come, and some have gone. Here are contributions from some of them, starting with one of the oldest and moving on to the more recent.

Stoolball is still played in the village, being a particularly Sussex game somewhat like cricket with eleven players fielding in cricketing positions, but there are more balls per over and they are bowled underarm. The bat is like a large oval table-tennis bat, and is held in either hand to defend the wicket which consists of a one foot square board on a pole. It is played primarily by girls and generally had its heyday during and just after the Great War although it is still played with enthusiasm in West Chiltington. Before the Second War the girls played stoolball at The Nabbs (the field between the Old Rectory and Church Grove). There was a West Chiltington team that played all the surrounding villages, being transported by van, and Elsie Cattell, a very keen player, recalls that the team was run by Mrs Dougharty.

The Cricket Club is also one of the older organisations still running in the parish having been formed in 1920, although it is thought that it was played in a more ad hoc way for many years even before that. From about 1920 it has had a regular venue at the recreation ground, and it is believed that some matches even took place during the war years. The first cricketers were the Barnes family from Palmers, the Shorts, and the Greenfields from Kings and Princes; all were market gardeners and all their labourers played; often they played against each other. The Club is very active and quite successful, and sometimes runs two teams in conjunction with the Elephant and Castle; in 1998 for instance there were 57 fixtures arranged, of which thirty were played on home ground.

   A regular fixture going back for forty years is with the Kenya Kongonis, a colonials' club from Nairobi which has an annual cricket tour when all the old members get together to tour Sussex and Hampshire. Sir Armigel de Vere Wade who used to live at Farthings had worked in Kenya and it was he who used to organise it; there was a marquee on the cricket ground where the players had lunch, and a reception in his garden in the evening. It was an all-day match, as was another annual fixture played against Colonel Kensington's team on one of the Bank Holidays. He used to run a regular cricket XI of his friends and their sons, and the club match against them would also start in the morning and include lunch in a marquee and supper in the garden of Voakes in the evening. The Club was also the first opponent ever to play The Cricket Society. It is a prime object of the Club to encourage the younger players, a task made harder by the fact that many schools do not now play cricket, so free 'nets' are run on a weekly basis. There has always been a lot of family involvement in the Club, where successive members of a family have played or given support either on or off the field.

The Club has, over the years, been lucky to find some very enthusiastic benefactors and supporters who have organised, cajoled and often kept it going financially through their efforts, one such being W J Watson who was an umpire to be reckoned with, and prior to him, Alf Crabb, an umpire and groundsman who was amazingly active in spite of having an artificial leg due to service during the war. As they say, they play behind the hedge and out of 'sight' but are happy to welcome spectators and supporters - you might even be converted!

Keith Tomsett writes: "The village had a football club inspired, run, organised and cherished by Hector Hornsby, in the 1930s. Although it has been disbanded and restarted on numerous occasions since its foundation, it has experienced much success over the years. The team used to play in the field that was at the end of Holly Close and had a changing room in Curbey Close, then they played at Nightingales before moving again on to the recreation ground. Alf Crabb the Verger was a great supporter of the football team and did a lot for them in the early days.

In the late 1950s the Club was regarded as one of the strongest sides in the Horsham and District League, consistently challenging for league and cup honours. It also contained many players prominent in village life today.

Winning the Division 4 Championship in 1984/5, scoring a hat-trick of honours in the 1986/7 season, winning the Division 3 Championship and Cup, and the Tony Kopp Cup, taking the Division 2 Championship in 1987/8, was crowned by winning the much-coveted Premiership double as Champions and Malcolm Simmonds Cup winners in the 1989/90 season.

There have been many occasions when sons have followed in the footsteps (or should that be bootsteps) of their fathers and grandfathers, and brother has played alongside brother. However, there can have been no greater example when, in the early 1960s, four Stepney brothers, Gordon, Roy, Ivor and Neville, joined forces to score 101 goals between them in one season. The first major trophy for the Club is thought to have been awarded in 1966, the year England won the World Cup, which puts

The Football Team – late 1950s
Back Row from left: Doug Rowlands, Fred Pavey, Brian Ruff, John Horlock,
Bob Penfold, Ken Johnson
Front Row: Gordon Stepney, David Charman, George Jackson, Stuart Bell, Den Norgate

The Football Team – 1998/9
Back Row: Keith Tomsett (Manager), Bruce Woodford, Callum Tomsett, Des Stepney (Capt),
Mark Hunton, Rin Tomsett, Simon Howard, Lea Durant, Ryan Durant
Front Row: Kevin Stevens, John Tomblin, Lorne Andrews, Paul Benham,
Phil Lewis, Dave Matthews

our boys in the very best company. As one club official remarked: 'Let's hope we don't have to wait for England to do it again before we win our next one!'

More than thirty years later, the team of the early 1990s has had a hard act to follow, but they achieved fame as Division 3 Champions in the season 1995/6. They are taking village football into the new millennium, led by Captain Des Stepney (yes, it's that name again). With four pairs of brothers in the side, including the Tomsetts who are following in the footsteps of their father, grandfather, great-uncle and several cousins, how can they possibly fail?"

Hermin Daley's account of the West Chiltington Dramatic Society gives an amusing picture from when it was formed in 1949 by Sylvia and Felicity Williams, the daughters of the Rector, and their brother Michael who, on moving to the village found that there was no existing form of entertainment. They went around the village accosting anyone who looked 'theatrical' or 'interesting' and soon had a growing number of enthusiasts (this was, of course, pre-television) who performed in The Old Comrades Hall. This was a very basic building with a solid-fuel boiler halfway down one side of the hall, ensuring nearby members of the audience were roasted whilst those at the back froze, a tin roof which made hearing all but impossible when there was a heavy rainstorm, one dressing-room with a curtain down the middle, and no toilets, which resulted in the girls using the churchyard - in twos as it was so dark! Despite all this, there was a wonderful camaraderie and great support from the village. The first production was *Cuckoo in the Nest*, directed by Sylvia Williams who had had acting experience in Nottingham; the scenery was built in Slater's workshop (every time the workshop door opened the scenery would wobble it was so flimsy) and the whole company was drawn from within the village.

They continued to grow in numbers and entered the County Drama Festivals, winning in 1956 with *Seagulls Over Sorrento*. This was then performed on the famous Glyndebourne stage to determine the Sussex Winner, but they lost to East Sussex.

The Society moved to the New Village Hall when it opened in 1957, and the first play there was *The Poltergeist*, which proved very dramatic as on the first night they fused all the lights when the curtain went up, due to overloading the electrical system by using power in the kitchen! They continued, without further electrical problems, to produce a variety of plays plus four pantomimes until in 1971 the Society was joined by Caroline and Tim Spicer who proved to be the most valuable assets so far. Tim had never acted in his life but from the moment he stepped on stage was declared by all, including the press, as a 'brilliant natural actor'; Caroline was a professional actress able to sing, dance, act and direct. Thus began a very active period of fifteen years seeing *Salad Days, My Fair Lady* and *Guys and Dolls*. Sadly this talented couple had to move to London and the Society moved on to other plays presenting, among others, *Under Milk Wood, Noises Off* and *The Exorcism*, to much acclaim.

In 1999 the Society celebrated its 50th anniversary by holding a Golden Jubilee Supper. This was an event of much merriment and more than a little nostalgia, attended by more than a hundred of the members past and present, including three of the original founder members. Through the years the Society has played a full part in the life of the village, providing dramatic entertainment, supporting good causes, being involved with an annual jumble sale, and running a number of stalls at the Village Fayre. It looks forward to an active future, and many more productions, in the enhanced Village Hall.

In February 1959 The West Chiltington Boys Club was officially opened by the Duke of Richmond and Gordon, who was President of the Sussex Association of Boys Clubs. Richard Page, who was the Club Chairman, explained that the Old Comrades Hall had been bought by the club from the British Legion (which would in future hold its meetings in the New Hall) for the boys; previously they had met in an old hut that had housed French-Canadian soldiers, then in the New Hall. A canteen, kitchen and toilet facilities had been provided at a cost of £2,000; the stage had been converted into a reading room; and the main hall was used for sporting activities such as table tennis, billiards, darts and boxing, this latter activity to be coached by the Rector, the Rev Raymond Morgan Jones. In his speech the Duke said that he was encouraged by the number of people who had turned up for the opening and hoped that they would continue their interest; the boys were to run the Club for themselves so that they could learn about the problems of running an organisation. He hoped that the boys would attend the adjustment-to-industry courses that were such a popular feature of the Sussex Association. By 1961 the club had admitted girls, who enjoyed using the four snooker tables.

The demise of the Boys' Club came in 1971 with the sale of the Comrades' Hall to the Clee family for the erection of their house,

Brookside Lodge. However, the sale of the hall provided the deposit for a new youth club building, although much fund-raising was also needed. At this point the Church tried to buy the old school, which was diocesan property, for the Youth Club when the lease to the County Council ran out in 1975, but it was too expensive and it too was sold for private housing in 1976.

It took until the end of 1980 for the new youth club building in Church Garden Meadow to be completed; although Duncan and Janet Green ran the youth club in the Church Hall in the interim. Duncan and Janet tried to steer the club away from the disco image of youth clubs, and provided table tennis and billiards, and a wonderful fortnight's summer camp. The new youth club flourished from the very beginning; the 20-30 founder members had first met on 8 February 1976. Soon there were about 100 members and three meetings a week; by 1981 there was a membership of 160 which, even though the meetings were on Wednesdays and in shifts on Fridays, had been a bit of a squeeze in the Church Hall. A friend of Duncan Green's, John Fox, took over Duncan's splendid legacy when he left the village to become a priest; and he has been succeeded by many wonderful leaders over the years. Currently there is a Junior Club for 8-12 year-olds on Thursday evenings, and a Senior Club for 12-18s on Monday evenings. The clubhouse boasts table-football, pool tables, a multigym, a computer Play Station, TV and video, as well as outdoor games of football and basketball.

When the new youth centre was opened in 1981, Richard Page, who had started the youth activities in the village 33 years before, relinquished the chairmanship of the club and was elected president. Some of the early youth club committee had consisted of Colonels Kensington and Drabble and General Ramsden, who had been the youngest member of the committee, at over 50! The village did not seem to mind the influx of military weight that got itself organising things; perhaps they were glad of someone to take charge and get things done.

The West Chiltington and District Rural Preservation Society, founded in 1965, encourages the care, signposting and preservation of the miles of footpaths in this, and adjoining parishes, and endeavours to foster a sense of pride on the part of civic and private enterprise in order that development shall be of a high standard and not detract from the beauty and character of the district. To this end it checks all planning applications and challenges developments which, in its opinion, would destroy the environment. Obviously there has to be some development, but there must be sympathetic regard for the existing feel of a village; we are not a town. A few examples might illustrate this: a high density planning application behind Gentle Harry's Cottage was opposed successfully; a would-be developer illegally felled wood on land beside Threals Lane and was fined £1,000 - he had hoped to be given permission to develop high density housing. This saga finally closed in 1997 when the Department of the Environment upheld opposition to any housing on the east side of Threals Lane.

The integration into West Chiltington Parish of an outlying area of Pulborough Parish which intruded into West Chiltington was the subject of much correspondence and publicity in the local press. One councillor remarked that the desire to be included in our parish was purely snob value, but the reply came back that West Chiltington was the most friendly village in West Sussex, and that we had no snob, having to take our footwear to one in Storrington for repair! The new boundary was approved.

A newsletter is published and coffee mornings are held in the Village Hall with guest speakers whose subjects are wide ranging: bridleways, the changing country scene, The Weald and Downland Museum, and a talk from the chairman of local Sussex Branch of The Council for the Protection of Rural England.

The Hayling Art Group, whose current secretary is Mrs Peggy Minor, meets every Wednesday morning in the Church Hall. Peggy and her husband had moved here after he retired. After she had had a couple of years of art tuition, one of which had been less than satisfactory, she and Mary Eames decided to organise an art club in the belief that the time was right for some independence. So in 1983 nine interested people became founder-members of a club with neither money nor equipment, but a lot of talent and enthusiasm. Their first exhibition was a great success, rather to their surprise, even though the advertising posters were hand printed, and the art stands held together with string! The club has continued to flourish and now has a membership of 18 who produce work of a high standard, in various mediums and of various subjects, helping each other where needed. The exhibitions produce between 150 and 200 paintings, the majority of which are for sale; there is an annual garden party and buffet in August, and a lunch some time in the New Year.

The West Chiltington Horticultural Society was founded by A E Grimsdale, who was its first Chairman, in 1970. It has monthly meetings, summer outings, and summer and autumn Shows, staged in the Village Hall and judged by experts, when members compete with the fruit, flowers and vegetables that they have grown. The winners receive National Society Awards, or one of the trophies donated by members, or presented in memory of loved ones. Speakers at the meetings cover many and varied subjects, from Soil Types to Water Gardening or even Gardening without Water, often illustrated with slides; there is a small monthly competition often ensuring much discussion, and a sociable coffee break. Membership includes corporate membership of the RHS and visits are made to their gardens at Wisley either as a group or independently. Other trips have been made to gardens whose owners have been the monthly speaker first, thus giving the group a unique insight into the problems and creation of that particular garden. The Society also has a stall at The Village Fayre where plants are sold, and members make a huge contribution to the Fete and Flower Show every year. Gardening is one of the nation's most popular hobbies but it still requires skill and knowledge which the Society hopes to impart.

The Probus Clubs are an association of retired, or semi-retired men who join together purely for social purposes. Part of a non-political, non-sectarian, non-profit making and non-fund-raising organisation they meet in autonomous clubs, with no central organisation. Although the name is an abbreviation of the words Professional and Business men, membership is not restricted to those two groups and any man who has had some measure of responsibility in any field of endeavour can join. West Chiltington's club was founded in 1989 and meets once a month for lunch followed by a speaker, and there is a monthly coffee morning at which members' wives are welcome. Visits are arranged to organisations and places of interest, and there are other social activities to which ladies are invited, including a Christmas Dinner.

The game of Short Mat Bowls has been a recent import into the leisure activities taking place in the village. In February 1990 a demonstration of the game was given in the Village Hall by two representatives of the Horsham District Council's Leisure Link Department, which was so enjoyed by the thirty people attending, that later that month a committee was formed to start the club. By the end of March there were treasurer and secretary, and a set of rules.

It says much for the enthusiasm of its early members that in so short a time the Club could progress from an idea to a functioning organisation with its own rules and equipment. While still in its infancy, the West Chiltington Short Mat Bowls Club has been remarkable for its rapid growth and, true to Sussex tradition, an acorn has grown into a sturdy oak.

The Table Tennis Club is one of the many local organisations that uses the Village Hall as its venue. Founded by Daphne and James McCree, and awarded a £200 grant by the Parish Council, the club was launched in March 1991. The main problem in the beginning was the acquisition of table tennis tables: one was bought from the Leisure Division of Horsham District Council (who had it stored in a freezing shed in the middle of a frosty field), one was borrowed from Daphne herself, and a third was bought from the Badminton Club. Later a fourth came from Mac Steele, who trundled it along to the Village Hall on his tractor and trailer. Notices were posted around the village to announce the club's presence, and the West Sussex Gazette wrote a piece. In spite of this there were only thirteen people at the first Friday morning meeting, but numbers have risen sharply and the current membership of 30 now comes from far as well as near, having five tables in play each week. Fees have fallen to £5 for 12 mornings, and the orange juice that had to be purchased at 20p is now free! A Friday evening club was also started for those who could not attend during the day, but closed after a few months due to lack of support. Following the refurbishment of the Village Hall, a storage room at ground level was made available for the Club, so three 'wheelaway' tables were purchased in kit form and assembled; prior to this trestle tables had had to be man-handled up and down the steps for storage at the side of the stage, with risk of injury to life and limb. Accidents while playing were, apparently, covered by the Village Hall insurance!

The Walking Group is perhaps the newest group, born in 1992 - Joyce Firkin has now left the village but has written: "Whilst living in Watford I had been involved for five years with a most enjoyable church-based rambling group. In moving to this lovely village in beautiful Sussex I longed for something similar here. There were plenty of 'official' rambles, but I felt there was scope for something more informal and slightly less rigorous.

Following a very successful Parish Walk, in 1992 I think, ably led by our then Churchwardens, I appealed through the Parish Magazine for support from anyone who knew the district well, since I was a comparative newcomer. As a result, Elsie Pullen and John Price contacted me, and with supporting friends from Keep Fit, Church and WI, slowly our small group emerged and grew, the leadership being shared. Now in the very capable hands of Graham and Elizabeth Cutler (founder members) we trust it will go on well into the 21st century to give much enjoyment to many. A pub lunch is part of the pleasure."

In 1987 Mary How from Cherry Tree, Sunset Lane, died from cancer at the age of 43. On the night she died, her husband and her doctor founded The Mary How Trust, dedicated to early detection of malignant disease. Over the following years The Big Red Bus was bought and equipped to screen, test and advise the local population, initially for malignancies but latterly for non-malignant disease which would affect quality of life; the results are integrated into the local health services so that patients can receive appropriate treatment. Now the geographical area has increased, so the bus visits outlying rural areas on a regular basis, where some 2,000 people will be screened during a year. Payment is not obligatory, so those of limited means are not excluded; however, the Trust requires an annual income of £100,000 to cover costs so there are various fund-raising events across the locality such as whist and bridge evenings, fairs and rallies, and the Special Evening two days after the Fete and Flower Show. The village also benefits from the Mary How Cinema which shows films in The Village Hall once a month (except July and August). The Hall is convincingly transformed into a cinema with a large screen, professional equipment and the raffle, without which no English meeting can function effectively, for about 160 patrons. With free and copious car parking, and up-to-date releases it is a regular fund-raiser which is well patronised.

Many of the above clubs and societies have been organised by the enthusiasm and inspiration of individuals, but the Parish Council has also played its part. It installed swings in the Recreation Ground in 1938, but they were destroyed by age and misuse during the war, and no longer existed by 1946. In 1955/6 a start was made on the construction of a children's playground because a lack of facilities for the children was causing a hold up of subscriptions to the Village Hall Fund and unpopularity for the Recreation Ground Committee. Three swings were installed at the northern end of the ground during the summer of 1956 but letters of complaint were soon received concerning the nuisance caused by the children at that site, so the swings were moved to the area of the tennis courts. By the summer of 1970 Worthing Art School had built an adventure playground at the northwest corner of the Recreation Ground; part of a special project by the senior students. Unfortunately it was not wholly successful so by 1979 the new children's playground, built with financial aid from the District Council, was completed at its new site on the reclaimed land opposite the pavilion.

In November 1992 a skateboard ramp was installed for the older children. Following comments by the judges of the Best Kept Village competition in 1996, the Parish Council decided to go ahead with a programme of improvements to the children's playground. Obsolete equipment was replaced by more modern and attractive fixtures, a new safety surfacing was laid, and separate toddler and junior play areas were created, with new fencing and gates to keep the children in and the dogs out! The three phases of work were finished by the summer of 1999.

A Tennis Club was also formed in 1946. Space was made at the Recreation Ground for two hard and two grass courts at the west end of the ground; the two grass courts were laid out and ready for use by the summer of 1947 but the hard courts never materialised, which may explain why the Tennis Club folded in 1952 due to competition with hard courts elsewhere. An attempt was made to revive the tennis club in the late 1950s but the Parish Council decided that too few people would want to play to make it an economic proposition.

In 1962 permission was granted to the owner of an adjoining property for a 20 year lease on a piece of the Recreation Ground on which he proposed to erect a hard tennis court, and in 1982 this lease was extended. In the September the West Chiltington Tennis Club was re-formed and the Parish Council provided the money for the renovation of the old court and the provision of a second court. Work began in 1987 and by September 1991 there were three hard courts and a new pavilion.

As well as the organised arrangements of clubs and societies, people in the village have, and have had, many interests: several well known personalities who have not already been mentioned have been associated with the parish: in Gay Street the artist Claude Muncaster, whose real name was Grahame Hall, was born in 1903 although he later moved to Fittleworth. He was a Member of the Society of Sussex Painters, Sculptors and Engravers (which was formed in 1924), and specialised in marine and landscape painting, lecturing and writing. He was the father of Martin Muncaster, the television personality. The portrait painter Augustus John used to stay at Lakers, and further back in the century the author Herman Cyril McNeile (who wrote under the nom de plume Sapper) died at Kings and Princes. Sapper created the fictional detective 'Bulldog' Drummond who was the patriotic hero of a series of thrillers written between the wars. Edward Ertz, the painter and wood engraver, was born in 1862 in Illinois, USA, but in 1940, having moved to Pulborough, he bought The Grange on The Common, although it is not established that he ever lived there.

Robin Adler (see chapter 4) is one of Britain's foremost photographers, perhaps being best known for his 1960s television series *Robin Adler's Camera Club* and his weekly photographic feature in *The Observer* called *Portrait Gallery*. Famous personalities of the day would sit for him in his photographic studio in fashionable London, among whom were Harold Wilson and Pandit Nehru, Enid Blyton and Somerset Maugham, and Yehudi Menuhin, but the most famous were his many photographs of Royalty including both the Queen and Prince Philip, Prince Charles and the Princess of Wales.

There are also people with interesting hobbies: there are model train enthusiasts, lacemakers, owners racing Jaguar cars, woodcarvers, a silversmith and many dog breeders. Mick Sell has horses. He did his National Service near Storrington, where he met and married Audrey who was a Washington girl. After a sojourn in Essex, where Audrey could not settle, he got a job as cowman at Nyetimber Farm which kept him in the neighbourhood. When his daughter was young, she had a pony, as many daughters do, and his love of horses was born. Some time later he had to take a pair of ponies to The Maple Stud at Ewhurst in Surrey to have them broken in, saw these strange dun coloured horses there, and determined to have one. He bought his first Norwegian Fjord horse some time later from The Maple Stud.

The Fjord is one of the oldest pure horse breeds known, having come to Norway and Scandinavia from Mongolia when the whole of that area was joined together in the ice ages, some 20,000 years ago. It bears a close resemblance to the original Wild Horse, or Przewalski, named after the eponymous Colonel who discovered it in the nineteenth century. The Vikings bred and worked these horses, and a few are said to have been brought over to this country by them because they are capable of hard work pulling loads in harsh conditions on frugal rations. Fjords were brought into Scotland in recent times by Mrs Jean Bruce in the 1930s, and by the Hon. Mrs Janet Kidd at The Maple Stud in the 1960s when she used them for driving competitively. They live for about thirty or forty years. There are a few of these rare Przewalski horses in Marwell Zoo which is undertaking a conservation breeding programme.

Nowadays, over here, they are mainly used as recreational horses, and Mick's pair, called Maple Benji, born in 1982, and his true brother Maple Hank born the following year, have given great pleasure to the whole village. Mick has been fortunate enough to have been offered the use of the two fields behind the Old Rectory, first by General Balfour, and later by the Conways who bought the Old Rectory recently and added another field. So the future of the fields, for both the ponies and the village is secure for the time being. Hank and Benji are featured in the WI collage, and have been the centre of attraction at many a wedding celebration. When Edith Green retired from the village shop after twenty four years service, the post office owners, Molly and Alan Wyle, wanted to repay her for all her loyalty so asked Mick to collect her from the shop in his trap and drive her and her mother home through the village. The horses are kept fit between star appearances by being both ridden and driven around the village, or exercised on a rein. They have appeared at Storrington Carnival and at Churchfield Farm's charity day, as well as winning Audrey first prize in a photographic competition held by *The West Sussex Gazette*.

While Mick has horses, Alan Room has birds: Alan came to live at Green Acres, Little Hill, with his parents in about 1993 from Croydon. He had always wanted owls and the move to the countryside was the ideal time to start, so, after reading up about them, he set about building an aviary. With dimensions of 24' x 8' x 8' the smaller barn owl occupies an 8' cubed section leaving the rest for the larger European eagle owl. There is a solid dividing wall between the two sections so the larger owl will not frighten the smaller one, and it has appropriate furnishings: for the barn owl there is a hay bale, oak beam and old garden gate, and for the eagle owl there are three clumps of bamboo, pine poles and space to cool off in hot weather. The sand on the floor of the aviary had to be specially washed as the salt that is normally present in sand forms a corrosive acid when wet which would burn the bottom of the owls' feet, which are gnarled to maximise their grip when asleep.

Alan took the eagle owl, coming up to its first birthday, to the village school for the children to see, but for both the owl's and the children's security they were not allowed to touch the bird. The children's thank you letters delighted Alan because they included birthday cards and a name for the owl: Amber, because of his beautiful orange eyes. When Alan has to take him out to a school, the owl goes upside down into a cardboard box in the car; he rights himself in the box, but putting him in this way prevents him opening his wings and damaging their fine bones.

 A wild European eagle owl in Scandinavia would be born in a shallow bowl-shaped nest on the ground, the owlets learning to run to escape predators before they learn to fly up to the trees, whereas the barn owl would be born in a tree, often in a nest vacated by a woodpecker the year before. In the wild the eagle owl, with his wing span of 4'6" could kill pigeons, or even a small deer, and when Alan lost his 8 month old female European eagle owl some time ago he was relieved to hear that she was welcomed by the farmer at Shipley, on whose land she was living. She was hunting the rabbits that had been eating his Christmas tree plantation; she would kill and only eat the best bits, then kill again. It is interesting to speculate how this female has managed to survive two years in the wild having been born in captivity, and what will happen if she ever does return. Alan is hoping that when his male starts the hooting calls associated with the mating season in February, she will hear him and may return; the calls can be heard up to four miles away, and the owls have hearing that is infinitely better than human hearing. Their eyes are also specially developed, with two sets of lids; each eye blinks independently so that they are constantly on the alert; and it is because the eyeballs cannot move from side to side that the owl has developed the ability to move its head so far round for maximum vision and can see for three miles distance. At the point of impact when killing their prey, the owls' eyes are shut to prevent damage to them from the struggling prey, and a slow-motion film of Amber shows him upside down catching the prey with his foot and eating it whole. Alan's owls may be seen at the Tent Service.

Alan took his owl to the school but the schoolchildren went to Shepherds Cottage in Mill Lane to see Sue Godsmark's animals and birds; the ducks and wildfowl had a pond and there were baby birds and owls. The children would divide into groups, some drawing a duck, some pond dipping, others examining a feather. Sometimes Sue would take the barn owls to the school for the day, going from class to class, where after a talk to the children about the birds, some of the lucky ones were allowed to hold them and stroke their soft down, feeling the warmth coming from it; in passing they learned about the heat retentive qualities of down.

For some years Sue had a buzzard called Shenade, which she bought as a youngster which had been bred legally in captivity, and who was therefore close-ringed and registered with the DOE. It took time for Sue to win her confidence by encouraging her with food; for a month Sue carried this large bird round on her arm, with the jesses on its legs, to familiarise her with the house (which with those beating wings never had a speck of dust settle), until she was comfortable and tame. When she had been trained to stay on the wrist, she was taken into the garden, and one day she was placed on a gatepost with a long creance or fine lead, and Sue backed a short distance away. She called, and the bird came. Gradually the distances were increased until the bird had confidence and strength, and Sue then took a deep breath, took off the creance and called the bird to fly to her, free. Free, but hungry because food was the training aid, and she would always fly for food. Although Shenade's aviary was big, Sue always used to try and fly her whenever possible because she felt Shenade needed the exercise; buzzards have a tendency to be laid back and lazy!

It is Sue's two African Grey parrots that whistle and talk to passers by along the footpath beside the hedge, and there was a time when the human walkers would hoot to her owls in the garden as well. Her object with barn owls was to breed a few and have them returned to the wild in suitable areas that would support them. Along the way she has also reared and repaired our native birds that have been brought to her as foundlings. One fact she feels strongly ought to be better known is that owls leave the nest at four or five weeks old, long before they can fly, and they live for a few days looking rather helpless on the ground. The parents are not far away and the birds should not be picked up and given into her care but, unless they are in danger from a cat or the road, should be left where they are for the parent birds to look after; placing the owlet high up in a hedge will keep it safe from Charlie Fox. Most of the owl casualties are from road accidents, or from being hit by trains, because apart from foxes and other ground hunters they have no predators. She, like Alan, feeds the birds on day-old chicks which can be bought frozen, from the pet shop, then thawed, and it is on these that the baby owls practice their hunting skills, pouncing on them and tossing them around, as a kitten would.

Sue has had other interests: she has bred rare wildfowl whose young went to Arundel Wildfowl Trust, before being reintroduced in their native Italy. It might only have been a few eggs at a time but, as she says: "every little bit helps the reintroduction programme." She also kept Angora goats; there was a shortage of Angora stock for breeding, so a complicated breeding programme was set up. The nannies of more usual breeds were artificially inseminated, or the fertilised eggs were transplanted from Angoras, to produce pure Angora kids to increase the stock more rapidly. But birds are Sue's real love, and who knows where her interest will lead her next?

A modern interest is The Lottery, and one of the winners of the jackpot the very first week, were Mark and Kathy Williams from Lakers Farm. Mark used to visit the disco in the Cellar Bar of the Roundabout Hotel; he so liked the area that, when he came to buy a property, he and his wife decided to purchase here and they have lived at the farm for about nineteen years.

Mark, having been made redundant three years previously, had invested his redundancy money to start his own company selling office furniture, and the business was hardly doing well enough to cover the cost of the mortgage. They managed to struggle to the end of each month, but the situation had got sufficiently desperate for them to decide one day to sell some things at a car boot sale; they had never been to one before and were so awed by the efficient organisation of the other sellers who had come armed with tables and calculators, that they never even unpacked, and came home!

At 8pm on the Saturday evening of the first lottery draw they thought they might have won; the jackpot was nearly £6 million. By 9pm, when the numbers were shown again, they were convinced, but by now, apprehensive, for what were they to do with the ticket? Someone might break in and steal it; if they put it on the mantleshelf it might fall in the fire; if they put it in a pocket it might fall out, perhaps down the toilet; if they put it on a window sill it might blow away! Perhaps there had been a mistake and all the tickets had been printed with the same number! They put it beside the bed in the end, and hardly slept all night, checking to see it was still there. It was eventually confirmed that their prize money was £839,254.00. and that there were five other winners.

On Monday morning they set off for Camelot (the lottery organisers) headquarters in Rickmansworth to collect their winnings having instructed the company repeatedly that they did not want any publicity. Camelot, however, had other ideas as they needed the publicity, particularly for this first win. To Camelot's surprise Mark said that he could not spend the day there as he had to get back to work; the sum was a great help in paying off the mortgage, and reinvigorating the business but not enough to enable them to retire! By the time they arrived home on Monday, journalists from *The Sun* newspaper were knocking on the door. Mark rang Camelot and asked for advice; they said he had two options: talk to the press, or let the neighbours talk to them as they would be sure to ferret the information out of someone as they had a £10,000 gift for anyone who would give information. As it happened, there was another Mark Williams in the village who Camelot telephoned; they telephoned all the Williams in the village, and anyone else they could think of. Finally Mark and Kathy gave up and allowed the man from *The Sun* an interview, but only on condition that they gave £5000 to the charity Children in Need. This was followed by local newspapers and Meridian television interviews, and finally the hullabaloo died down. With hindsight it is quite amusing the lengths *The Sun* went to, but at the time it was very stressful, particularly as both Mark and Kathy were concerned about the security of their two daughters.

In those early days there was no advice as to what to do with the money, nor how to handle the publicity. Life has now settled back into routine; holidays, school fees, a new car and maintenance of the house can now be afforded, and a flat was purchased in London, but the secretary who took over Kathy's work in the office left to have a baby so both Mark and Kathy work at the business almost as they used to do before.

The Walking Group – winter 1998

Chapter 14

Future Fortunes

This cannot be entitled "Conclusion" nor even "Epilogue"; like the god Janus after whom January is named as his two faces look both backwards and forwards, this chapter is both looking back over the last century and looking forward to the next.

In this past one hundred years we have seen the introduction to the village of the motor car, and of flying abroad for holidays, we have seen washing machines and refrigeration, the vacuum cleaner and the steam iron, processed foods, a loss of community spirit, the Tesco bus and the failure of public transport, the decline of the village shop and blacksmith, but the rise of recreational riding and domination by European Community rules and regulations. What a mixed bag! It can perhaps best be summed up by Gwen Smith thus: "Family life was a togetherness, it was belonging, security. It didn't matter how poor you were. I loved my old Dad; I would follow him around and copy the things he did. If he was digging in the garden, I would go and dig beside him, he taught me lots, not only gardening, I learned by watching him and helping him. We had family meals together, no trays on your lap and watching television. We talked to each other and the family was all in one village, all together and supportive of each other. We also all kept in line because we knew we'd be seen doing wrong as it was such a small place, but we respected our parents and teachers and were happy in spite of the apparent hardship."

Keeping a helpful eye on village affairs is The Sussex Rural Community Council, an independent charitable organisation that has been in existence for sixty years providing advice and assistance to village communities. Examples of the issues that continue to concern them are: how to keep the rural bus services; provision of reasonable cost housing to keep young people in the villages; community care provision; a parish council service to assist perhaps with the optimum use of the village hall ensuring its financial viability. Their brief is thus to support and assist in most aspects of rural life, in keeping the villages alive. Part of their funding comes from the government via the Rural Development Commission and the local authorities, and they liaise with the government, being the rural voice for Sussex, and lobbying on our behalf. They are not in a position to hand out funds to the communities, but they can show parish councils and others where to go to get the funding they require for a project, and are consulted by the people with the money (say West Sussex County Council) about the appropriateness of different applications. They are not an environmental organisation as such, but if a village shop is threatened with closure because of a big supermarket development in the locality, they will oppose the development if it means that more cars will be on the roads and the sustainability of the village is threatened. They will also push for a better local bus service, using the environmental argument amongst others.

During elections they lobby prospective MPs so that if they are elected they will recognise the importance of the countryside and its way of life. As an example, they are demanding a mix of housing in rural areas, because if no low-cost housing is provided for local people the whole structure of a village will change, into a dormitory for rich families working in the towns with no commitment to village life. The builders say that in West Chiltington the price of land is too high for them to make a profit on anything other that large executive housing, but if this is allowed to go on, employers in the village cannot employ local people, and the school will find it difficult to attract teachers who cannot afford the housing. The SRCC helped with the housing needs assessment when Steele Close was built, and are now trying to encourage landowners to be interested in the future of their community, and to sell land for building at a price that would make social housing possible. This would be a real turn-round in philosophy from that which prevailed at the end of the last century!

At the moment, and looking towards the future, the organisation is harnessing the computer and Internet systems to encourage casual visitors into the villages. West Chiltington could not cope with a massive influx of tourists, but if people already staying in towns in the area could be encouraged to call into our pubs for lunch, to PYO at our local farm, to buy postcards from our village shops 'and while we're here, that jar of local honey looks nice', our village economy would be stimulated. Leaflets have been produced showing just such local attractions, and these leaflets are available at tourist centres in the area and on the Internet. The Parish Council and local businesses are involved in the discussions, and in the assessment of the results. The Computer Centre, set up in the Village

Post Office has not been an overwhelming success, partly because the local shopkeeper did not have the time to teach people how to use the equipment while running the village shop, and partly because the cost of home computers has come down so fast that many people now have their own machines. This negative lesson has a positive side in that the computer will now be used, perhaps, as a touch-screen type, to serve as a database for local clubs, organisations and functions, as an events-calendar, or even as a living history with pictures and sounds, perhaps even re-sited in the Museum. The SRCC is driven by its tremendous enthusiasm and commitment to keeping the villages alive by looking forward with new ideas.

The previous thirteen chapters give a view of the village over the last century, but for all that this village is remote, hidden by its hollows from the rush of the A24, A29 and A23 as they tear towards Worthing, Bognor and Brighton, we are still influenced by world affairs.

It was in 1997 that Hong Kong reverted to the Chinese, precipitating an exodus of British families after the hand-over, the time of migration being governed in many cases by the educational demands of the ex-pats' children. Robin and Nicky Williams decided that a home in the UK was preferable to life in Hong Kong and they came here to settle having known of the area through Nicky's stepfather who used to come to a Wells cottage here before the war. To their delight they discovered that living in Sussex was very much cheaper than life in Hong Kong and they have also been encouraged by the welcome they have received from neighbours and from local shops. The story does not end there, though, because when the Hong Kong economy trembled and the Hang Seng Index crashed, once again world affairs intruded: Robin was recalled to Hong Kong with his family as his Hong Kong employer could no longer afford to pay him in sterling, so the family is packing up again and returning.

This book contains the memories of men and women of the parish who can recall what village life was like when they were children. Reference has also been made to Domesday Book, the first thorough survey of all the lands in England. In 1985, to celebrate the 900th anniversary of Domesday Book, the BBC organised a nationwide survey of the British Isles. West Chiltington WI helped in this survey by being allocated a block to the north of the village, and during the very wet summer of 1985, six members spent many hours tramping along muddy lanes visiting at least 30 farms and houses. They obtained information on farming life, crops, livestock, social problems, changes occurring and the effect of the EEC. They also gathered information on the local flora and fauna, as well as local interests and personalities. The Village School was allocated the village and Common area to survey; each block being a 4 x 3 km square. This was not an historical survey, but dealt with contemporary life as the original Domesday Survey did; it only becomes history later.

This also applies to the wonderfully detailed contemporary collage of the village made by the WI and finished in April 1994 hanging in the Village Hall; some of the people and places mentioned in this book can be seen in it (see photo on the dust jacket). The idea began, as Elizabeth Anderson, of the WI, explains: "The first collage we saw was at Wisborough Green, made in cross stitch, and then we learned of other cross stitch ones where people sat together and worked on it; a bit like the old sewing bees. The WI was running competitions for hand and needlecrafts at that time, and we had some very skilled people in our WI, so we decided to try our hand at a collage, just to be different. Bob Orme, the husband of one of the members was a cartoonist amongst other things, so he did us a lot of these beautiful little cartoons. The work is so detailed that you really need to stand on a stool to look at it: look at the expressions on, for example, the golfers' faces where one of the women is so smug because her husband has miss-hit. The black cat by the police station used to belong to Steve Leal the policeman; the cat had had an accident and only had a stub of a tail. There are two WI members playing croquet; one of them was rather broad, so we did it just like that. I'm there with Fellah, and Roger Harrison is there with Pedder and Percy to represent the dog walkers in the village. You can see the dogs were very friendly, but there's one going off after a cat. As I walked Fellah we used to see incidents which went into the collage; there was a dog in the orchard staring up at a squirrel in the tree, or a little boy playing by the lake. The sheep, which used to be in the field behind the recreation ground, were made from a pair of old leather gloves I had which were lined with sheepskin. At the borders of the picture are all the flowers, birds and butterflies that were actually seen here in the village, and as space was limited I've only put in all the old houses, although Heathfield, the one down at the bottom is probably the newest, but it marked the boundary nicely! There are over two hundred items in all, and ten yards of road, all of which is fringed. It's a shame that it has had to be covered with glass, but you have to, of course, because of the dust, but we didn't cheat and glue the items on hoping the glass would hold them in place, every item is stitched on. There are cheats though: one was behind the bus; I ran out of road fringing and when I went for some more they'd changed the colour and the join was very obvious, so I put the bus in to hide the colour change. Actually the bus used to go along there anyway, and stop at Peacock Tree, and while we're talking about Peacock Tree, do you see the two people there, well, one is the past president Jean Orme handing over to the new president Maxine Mott; both were involved with the collage.

We built the collage as we went along with each person interested doing an item, at first at home, and then our sewing it on. It first lived in Daphne Harrison's house, but then outgrew its space and so ended up in my spare bedroom. Towards the end we used to work here together, but not all thirty of us at once! Something funny happened when it was in my room: because we were working all around it I put the compass on upside down, so had to get it back from the framer and correct it. It's right now, so no one knows, except the old villagers who were in on it!"

When the century opened the village was a very inward-looking, self-reliant community, where everybody knew everyone else. The remnants of that community mourn its passing; the old village as it was, is dying out. It used to be that a true 'villager' is one who went to the village school, grew up in the village, and in their turn, lived and worked here. This pattern was disrupted first by the wars; war brides going overseas, young men who never came back from the front, families broken up and dispersed. So often nowadays it is the rising and unrealistic house prices that force village children to find jobs and houses elsewhere, in less expensive places; and the school, although full to overflowing, is not educating 'future villagers'. Those children will not leave school at fourteen to work on the land, or in Slater's yard, but will go on to further education, will get jobs, marry and have children elsewhere. The old fabric of a close-knit community is all but gone and times have changed. It has become the responsibility of the newcomers to maintain and cherish the values of village life and to prevent the village turning into just another town dormitory, or scrap of suburbia. When asked whether there is a sense of community here now, the consensus of opinion is that there is a good community spirit in West Chiltington but that it is entirely different from the old one. We still have shops, post offices and our garage, and people still stand in the road and gossip. The framework required to keep a big village together is similar to that required for a smaller one but needing more people to arrange the clubs, societies, outings and services that bind people together, and it is part of this village's strength that these people have been found and that a spirit of community, of belonging, does exist. It is this appreciation that makes village life so special, this sense of community that makes even an in-comer feel welcome, that we have to preserve; at the same time being careful not to disregard the achievements of 'the old village'.

Elizabeth Anderson wrote: "We came to Westward Lane in 1958, and walked our two dogs all round the village, particularly in 'the glade' in Monkmead Woods (which were fairly open then and in some places very marshy) and in the woods and fields along Nyetimber Lane, where the only existing dwellings then were Heathfield House and the old chapel.

When I joined the WI in 1965 I helped to compile a list of local plants for our records, all seen on these walks and along the River Chilt and other footpaths. My list of plants eventually reached over a hundred, and included some quite rare flowers, such as Blue Flax and Chicory, Bog Pimpernel, Marsh Helleborine, Early Purple and Spotted Orchids, Wood Spurge, Ragged Robin and the Fly Honeysuckle which is found only in Sussex. There was also plenty of wild-life about in those days, from barn owls and pipistrelles, water-rats in ditches (since filled in), herons, wrens, nuthatches and chiff-chaffs, flocks of siskins and, only once, the electric blue flash of a kingfisher. In two successive years there were noisy gatherings of crossbills which quickly stripped all our pine cones, but we have seen none in the twenty years since. There used to be skylarks and lapwings, but these are now gone, replaced by magpies and crows. However, collared doves and pigeons are still abundant.

I have endearing memories of three foxcubs playing with their mother in spring twilight and vanishing without a sound as if by magic; a tiny dormouse sitting fast asleep in the sun on our living room carpet one February morning; an elegant weasel standing upright, still and bright eyed under low brambles; a badger seen skulking in a wet dawn; a crèche of baby slow-worms beneath a flat stone; a rare White Admiral butterfly by a stream; and - most cherished memory - glow worms in the garden, radiating green light like lanterns and mesmerising our two dogs.

This wonderful variety of growth and greenery, colour and sound, animal and bird life, surrounds us and has enriched our lives in West Chiltington for forty happy years. Once, while walking through the Glade, we came across a woodsman working among the trees. He was frying eggs and bacon on a spotless polished shovel over a fire of twigs. The fragrance of his cooking is with me yet. Poachers were about in those days, too; one

Sunday morning while walking the dogs very early in Monkmead Woods, a shot rang out and a wild duck fell dead at our feet. My husband snatched it up and hurried home - it made a wonderful meal! Such happy memories."

So how long does a newcomer have to live here to be accepted as a true villager? Perhaps it is nothing to do with length of time but with attitude: Col Kensington, Col Drabble, Douglas Andrews, Elizabeth Anderson, Gerald Evans and many unsung people have all arrived here from somewhere else and have put effort and concern into the village and its activities. There are good and bad in both the old and the new village, and a lack of appreciation of the other's problems; perhaps it is time with the new century, to put the differences behind us and let us all be West Chiltingtonions.

Some of the changes are not so great as at first supposed: grocers no longer deliver from Storrington but Eismann and Tesco (via the Internet) deliver to one's house; the coal delivery for the stove has been replaced by an oil delivery for the central heating; the milkman does not come from the local farm but now supplies bottled water, garden compost, and chocolate biscuits as well as milk; the postman's bike has been replaced by a van, and parents (fathers as well as mothers now) still chat by the school entrance, even if through their car windows!

In the months before December 1999 West Chiltington Parish Council discussed many ways to celebrate the millennium. Horsham District Council will put on a firework display on the Downs so the village's more modest display has been postponed until the summer - at perhaps the Fayre or the Fete. The Parish Council is celebrating in the time-honoured way by issuing the school children with a commemorative mug. Louise Mursell is organising, with others, a tea party in the Village Hall on Sunday 2nd January 2000 for children between 5 and 11; she hopes to include songs and games and the making of craft mementoes so that in years to come the children will remember this special New Year. The Church hopes to participate in the national campaign to have all the country's church-bells ring in the New Year; the problem is that the ringers might have been out at parties so the national-ring was re-scheduled for mid-day on New Years' Day. There is to be a new pictorial village sign designed by Terry Copping, erected by the Village Hall. Finally there was this book: a looking-back through the last one hundred years to the way village life used to be lived, with all its hardships and joys, its ways so changed, and its hope for the future.

As Doug Golds says: "You have to advance. I have been asked by some of the new people who have come into the village if I would join the organisation to preserve the village but I have said 'No' because I didn't stop them coming and so I feel they shouldn't stop others from coming too. You as new people have come in and been accepted; and taken away some of the beauty of the village; and it's not up to me to say you shouldn't be here; it's not up to me to say something new shouldn't be here. We should go to great lengths to preserve, but people still need to live; they still need a home and they still need the support that the older villagers can provide. Take a new road for example: what a scar it puts on the landscape at first but look at it in a couple of year's time and you can't see the problem; it's all been landscaped, it has all softened and nature says 'you won't kill me!' Take The Hollows; that leafy lane was just a track once and now it is surfaced with tarmac, that's progress. It's the same thing on a larger scale. Advancement."

There is an old Sussex saying "We won't be druv" and it is very evident in West Chiltington. As this book is compiled we are on the verge of a long-term shift of political emphasis; we are inundated by rules and regulations emanating from Brussels; social fabric is changing, and yet the gentlemen of the village still raise their hats as they bid 'Good morning'. We may have parties and fun as we face the new millennium, but the manners and attitudes of the village change only slowly and We Won't be Druv to do anything we don't approve of. May our independence of thought and character live long into the next century!

The Cross Roads in the Village 1999

Glossary

Billhook - a hooked bladed tool with a sharp inner edge for cutting or pruning.

Binder - a reaping machine that binds stalks of grain into sheaves.

BSE - Bovine Spongiform Encephalopathy - a fatal disease of cattle involving the central nervous system.

Chaff - the seed coverings and other debris separated from the seed during threshing.

Copper - a large metal vessel for boiling water, for laundry, bathing or domestic use.

Coppicing - the hazel poles are harvested every 8 years and converted into a wide range of products, such as hurdles, fences and screens. It is the oldest form of forestry; woven hazel fishing screens have been dated back to 5,000 BC, and the south's semi-natural woodlands have developed under the coppice system.

Currency - in February 1971 decimal currency was introduced. The old system used 4 farthings ($^1/_4$d) or 2 halfpennies ($^1/_2$d) to a penny (1d), 12 pennies to a shilling (1/-), and 20 shillings to a pound (£).

D-Day - the opening day, 6 June 1944, of the Allied invasion of Europe in World War II.

Draw Knife - a two handled knife, used with an upward motion towards the handler, was used to shape wooden wheel spokes which were finished with a spoke shave. The Felloes were the wooden curved pieces round the circumference of the wheel next to the rim.

Faggots - bundles of wood about six feet long and nine inches in diameter which were tied in the middle and had many uses on the farm. In the kitchen two or three faggots used to be burned in the oven until they became only red hot ashes at which moment the bread dough was put on top and cooked for about 20 minutes in the bread ovens.

Form - the wooden bench children sat upon, usually in school.

Lammas Day - 1 August. Originally observed as harvest festival in England.

Land Measurement - At the beginning of the century land areas were measured in acres, roods and perches; a rod, pole or perch is 16½ feet, a rood is 40 square rods approximately, and an acre is 4 roods.

Mangle - a wringer where two cylinders were turned by a handle to squeeze water from the clothes.

Michaelmas - 29 September, the feast of St Michael the Archangel. One of the Quarter Days when magistrates were elected, the university terms began, and rents were collected.

NAAFI - Navy, Army, Air Force Institutes; an organisation for providing canteens for servicemen and women, hence, one of the canteens.

Rick - a stack of hay, corn etc built into a regular shape and usually thatched, and in the open air.

RNAS - Royal Naval Air Service.

School Classes - in West Chiltington School the Reception Class is Green Class, Year 1 is Purple, Year 2 Yellow, Year 3 Orange, Year 4 Blue, and Year 5, the top class, is Red.

Scythe - a long pole farming tool with a long curved blade attached used for mowing and reaping. It was swung over the ground by two short handles coming from the pole.

Sickle - a short handled farming tool used for cutting corn, lopping or trimming, with a semicircular metal blade.

Stooks - a group of sheaves of grain stood on end in a field to dry.

Thresher or thrasher - a power-driven machine for separating grain/seeds from the straw or husk.

TVO - Tractor Vaporising Oil, a paraffin-like fuel used on old tractors such as the Massey-Fergusson, after starting with petrol. Phased out in the 1960/70s when the diesel-engine tractor was invented, but can still be obtained for classic vehicles.

Utility - severely practical belongings produced during the war, with no embellishments or ornament, and very little choice of colour, style or fabric.

VE-Day - Victory in Europe Day, 8 May 1945, when Germany surrendered unconditionally at the end of World War II.

VJ-Day - Victory over Japan. Although on 14 August 1945 Japan had unconditionally surrendered, it was not until 2 September that the forces capitulated to General MacArthur in Tokyo Bay. Surrender of the forces in SE Asia to Mountbatten on 12 September finally brought the Second

World War to an end.

Weights and Measures - the Imperial System used 16 ounces (oz) to a pound (lb), 14 lbs to a stone (st), 2 st to one quarter (qtr), 4 qtrs to one hundredweight (cwt), 20 cwt to one ton.

A farthing

Bibliography

Chambers Twentieth Century Dictionary - New Edition 1972

Chief Constables' Reports published by the Home Office

Chronicle of the 20th Century, published 1988 by Longman Group UK Ltd

Encyclopaedia Britannica

English History 1914-1945 by A J P Taylor

Ham, Joan - Storrington in Living Memory, published by Phillimore & Co Ltd - 1982
Storrington in Georgian and Victorian Times - 1987
Sullington: Domesday to D-Day - 1992

Neale, Kenneth - West Chiltington: The Decennial Census of 1851, in Sussex History Volume I, Number 5, Spring 1978.
An article in Sussex Archaeological Collections, on Smock Alley Village Blacksmiths and their Home, West Chiltington, Sussex

Parish Council Minute Books

Saunders-Jacobs, Sylvia - West Chiltington in West Sussex published by WC Parish Council

Sotheby's World Wine Encyclopedia published by Dorling Kindersley 1988

The English Poor Law 1780-1930 by Michael E Rose published by David Charles

The Mond Legacy by Jean Goodman published by Weidenfeld and Nicolson 1982

The Oxford Companion to Local and Family History 1996

Who Was Who - 1961-1970

The Windmills of Sussex by Martin Brunnarius 1979 published by Phillimore & Co Ltd

Various Press Cuttings, often anonymous, but including The West Sussex County Times, The West Sussex Gazette, The Worthing Herald, and others.

Various Reports of the West Sussex County Nursing Association

West Sussex as seen through the eyes of the Women's Institute 1975, edited by Elizabeth Anderson for the West Sussex Federation of WIs, Chichester

West Sussex within Living Memory 1993, Countryside Books, Newbury, published by West Sussex Federation of WIs, Chichester

Windmills of Sussex by Brian Austen 1978 published by Sabre Publishing

Index

Adams Joy *31, 131, 274, 310, 338, 363, 370*
Adler Andy & Robin *65, 415*
Adsett Gladys *62*
Anderson Elizabeth *132, 425, 427*
Andrews Albert *112*
Andrews Douglas *iii, 428*
Annis Karen *239*
Appleton Paul & Liz *278*
Archer-Wills Anthony *94*
Armstrong - Marie & Bernard *180*
Arunvale *100*
Ascoli John *153*
Astley Muriel *330*
Ayling Billy *394*
Ayling Elizabeth *394*

Bacon Jim *195*
Baker Leonard *369*
Baker Margaret *175*
Balance Nurse *242, 308*
Balfour General Sir Victor *227, 255*
Barclays Bank *129*
Barkworth Terrence *128*
Barkworth WT *126, 273, 274*
Barncroft *35*
Barnes Brian *76*
Barnes Hilda *325*
Barnes Penny *326*
Barnes Walter and family *61*
Barrow Gladys - see Adsett
Beattie Geoff *117*
Beasley Nurse Lorna *242*
Belok F C *385*
Bessant Mrs *32, 59*

Bicknell Vivienne & Alan *174*
Bluebell Railway *120, 121*
Bolwell Miss *274, 378*
Boyd Winifred - see Johnson
Broadford Bridge Post Office *91*
Broadford Bridge Stores *89, 91, 97*
Brown Stephen & Pam *69*
Brownies *294*
Bryder Brenda - see Ridpath
Burgess Liz - see Van Tromp

Caldecott Rev Andrew *13, 227, 279*
Callaway Mr *35, 221*
Cannell Jim *257*
Carver Bill & Carol *343, 384*
Carpenter Dave & Terri *91*
Cattell Elsie *75, 105, 274, 304, 388*
Cattlestone Farm *95, 97*
Chad Mr *310*
Champ Mrs *355*
Chatfield Mr *393*
Charman Mercy *38*
Charman Ted *37*
Cherilyn *117*
Chilton Gordon *370*
Church Hall *287*
Churchfield Farm *47, 355*
Cinema *219, 413*
Coles Doris *388*
Coles Mr & Mrs J *82, 275, 335*
Collett Millie *160*
Coulson Clive *75*
Community Minibus *266*
Cox Carol - see Fisher
Cox George & Mrs *317*

Cozens Mr & Mrs H *109, 338*
Crabb Alfred *214*
Crowhurst Ted *57, 60*
Cub Scouts *389*

Daughtrey Bernard *177, 305*
Davis Don *115*
Denham Avera *391*
Denham Steve & Lynda *119*
Dixon G W *176, 308, 310*
Dixon Mrs Gladys *312, 324*
Dougharty Frank & Madeleine *95*
Dougherty Roger & Gillian 102
Douglas-Home Robin *158*
Downer Tom *39, 62, 119*
Drabble Lt Col Peter and Mrs Eve *186, 214, 217, 227, 428*
Drabble Timothy & David *186, 188*
Duffin Joyce *45*

Eames Dr Althea Josephine *327*
Eames Felix *327*
Edwards Bill *183*
Elinson Iso *69*
Elliott Teddy *138, 264*
Ellis Billy *107, 110*
Ellis Daisy *107, 110, 242*
Engledow Gladys *279, 297*
Evans Rev Gerald & Sheila *278, 296, 428*
Evershed Tom & Alice *92*

Faires Ted & Lily *107, 114, 117*
Faulkner Max *76*
Field Angela *223*
Fisher Carol *326*
Fisher Jeremy Carol *154, 163*
Fitzgerald Michael *155*
Fjord Horses *415*
Fooks Tim *66, 277*
Ford Dr John *85, 228, 245*
Fordham Barbara *316*
Forge Cottage *57*
Forge The *57*
Freeman Albert *52*

Freeman Edith - see Pettit
Freeman Stephen *326*
Fuss Fairy *159*

Garage The *107, 110*
Gardener Miss *311*
Ghost stories *88, 163*
Ghurkas *258*
Gibney Joyce *92, 101, 389*
Gifford House *399*
Girl Guides *294, 388*
Gobles Farm *78, 88*
Godsmark Sue *417*
Golds Doug *348, 392, 428*
Gooch Stan *27, 30, 287*
Gooch's Stores *26, 247, 353*
Gould Joan *183*
Green Cis *42*
Green Duncan and Janet *277*
Green Edith *27, 40*
Green George and Dick *40, 280*
Greenfield Mrs *62*
Greenfield Michael *61, 306, 359*
Greenfield Percy *57, 61, 169*
Griffiths Dave *47*
Grigor Alastair *262*
Gumbrell Bill *37*
Gumbrell Ernie *214, 257*

Hall Rev George *282, 338*
Hampshire Elsie *113, 165*
Hampshire George *151*
Hampshire John *214*
Hampton Bill *26, 51, 82, 170, 251, 303, 362*
Hare-Winton Pat - see Steele
Harrison Roger *246, 425*
Hatches Estate *51*
Hawkins Cyril & Sybil *47, 379*
Hawkins Joan - see Marlow
Hayling Art Group *410*
Heath Air Marshall Sir Maurice *162*
Hobjohns *35, 339*
Hobjohnscroft *36*
Holloway Wendy and Steve 115

Hornsby Hector *277, 350, 392, 405*
Howard Ena *337*
Huntleys *75*

Johnson Colin & Kathryn *68*
Johnson Elva - see Lipscome
Johnson Winifred *24*
Jones Rev Raymond Morgan *286*
Judd Meg & Gerry *31, 164, 354*

Kensington Enid *193*
Kensington Lt-Col Guy Bellfield *131, 191, 218, 228, 251, 255, 428*
Kensington Memorial Hall *287*
Kensington Mrs Lillian Mary *13, 37, 54, 119, 191, 212, 240, 249*
Kenyatta Jomo *274, 382*
King Mr & Mrs *276*
King Nellie *274*
Kings and Princes *61*
Knag Renee - see Knight
Knight Renee & Bill *113, 231*
Knowles Peter & June *259, 275, 278*

Larby Mr & Mrs *316*
Lawes Geoff *355*
Lawson Alex *180, 370*
Lawson Geoff *317*
Leal Steve *235, 425*
Lenharth Barry *359, 364, 372*
Lenharth Billy *377, 390*
Lipscome Elva *47, 277, 327, 378, 379, 392*
Llewellyn Mr *114*
Lottery The *419*
Lucas Rev Kenneth *247, 277, 289*

Manfield Peter, Roy & Sheila *173*
Mant Charlie *354*
Manvell Elsie - see Hampshire
Manvell Renee - see Knight
Marino P *111*
Marlow Joan *47*
Mary How Trust *229, 413*
Mathieson Don & Peggy *28*

Melrose Stores *107, 111*
Meeten Henry *66, 67*
Meeten Lucy *290*
Mills R W *280, 304, 310*
Morgan John Junius *197*
Moore Aidan & Jenneth *161*
Moss Stuart & Sandra *202*
Mursell James & Louise *355*
Mustchin Henry *182*
Mustchin 'Squeaky' *338, 340, 349*
Mustchin Dennis & Rosemary *133*
Mustchin Nick *117*
Mustchin's Coal Yard *66, 347, 385*
Myram Robert *98*

New Barn Farm *186*
New Hall *44, 219*
New House Farm *35, 47,*
Newman Bob *291, 295*
Nicholas Ken *200*
Noble Ron *315, 350, 364, 372*
Northridge Rev JGR *288*
Nyetimber *14, 197*

O'Donnell Rev Kevin *278, 299*
Ogle Mark *327*
Old Comrades Hall *216, 279, 314, 391*
Overton-Smith Sue *228, 276, 278, 317, 389*
Owen Barbara - see Fordham

Palmers *71*
Palmers Lodge *71*
Pannell James *39, 123*
Pavey Fred *89*
Peace Major Guy & Jean *165, 221, 244, 265*
Peacock Maurice *124*
Penfold Joan *337, 339*
Penfold Peter *134, 324, 334, 347, 389, 164*
Pertwee Bill *149, 327*
Pettit Edith *25*
Phillips Jack *59, 75*
Phillips Lou *60*

Plowden George *117, 235, 372*
Police *235*
Probus Club *411*
Pullen Edmund Talbot *393*
Pullen Elsie *32, 193, 228, 335*
Pullen Ivan *131, 147, 264, 311, 334*
Pullen Joy - see Adams
Puttock Bill *35, 60*

Queen Mary *254, 255*
Queen Victoria *251, 366*

Railway Carriages *107*
Rainbow Group *388*
Rawlinson Major & Mrs Helen *285*
Recreation Ground *211*
Reeves Rev Jim *292*
Ridpath Brenda, David & Muriel *113*
Ridpath's Stores *113, 115*
Riley Nurse *241*
Rogers Phyllis *107, 118*
Room Alan *416*
Rosebank *109*
Rowland William Knight *209*
Royal British Legion *397*
Royal British Legion Women's Section *398*
Ruff Brian *276, 316, 340*

Salisbury Ann *97, 162*
Sanson Mrs Margaret *150*
Scouts *389*
Sell Mick & Audrey *415*
Shaw Billy *184*
Shotnik Eddie *383*
Short Connie – see Slater
Short Herbert *103, 106, 111*
Short Mat Bowls Club *411*
Sims Colin & Maureen *201*
Slater Albert *184, 340, 393*
Slater Connie *106, 353, 390*
Slater Elsie - see Cattell
Slater Fred & Mrs *317*
Slater Old Ned *105, 340*

Slater Reg *212, 339, 394*
Slater Sue - see Overton Smith
Smith Gwen *111, 149, 254, 307, 308, 333, 363, 382, 422*
Smith Jim *122*
Smither Roger & Bertha *197*
Smyth William *301*
Snook Mr *180, 221*
Southlands Farm *51, 222*
Stead Nurse *242*
Steele Alma *78, 80, 381*
Steele Ewen *77, 81, 190, 312, 363*
Steele Harvie and Ramsey *86, 317*
Steele Mac *78, 80, 222, 255*
Steele Pat *233, 312, 336, 376, 379, 396*
Storrington Sawmills *95*
Strudwick Ted *120*
Sturt Joyce - see Duffin
Summers Mr & Mrs David *277*
Sussex Rural Community Council *422*

Table Tennis Club *412*
Thomas Captain *180*
Todd Clara *217*
Tomsett Jan *388*
Tomsett Keith *405*

Vance John & Amanda *324*
Vassall William *161*
Van Tromp Bill *55, 157*
Van Tromp Eileen *156, 159, 327*
Van Tromp Elizabeth *157, 325*
Van Tromp Richard *325*
Village Hall *216*

Wade Sir Armigel de Vere, & Lady *176*
Wadey Bill *337*
Wadman Mr *327*
Wakeley John *180*
Walder Miss *305*
Walking Group *412*
Wallace Mrs Babs *117, 314, 318*
Walter Angela & Brian *224*

Walter Colonel *68, 74, 217, 221*
Warren Peggy *71*
Warriner Frank *218, 223, 260*
Watts Roger *357*
Webb Mervyn & Pauline *169*
Wells Reginald Fairfax *138, 140*
Wells Pam *278*
West Chiltington & District Rural Preservation Soc *409*
West Chiltington Boys' Club *408*
West Chiltington Cricket Club *222, 404*
West Chiltington Croquet Club *403*
West Chiltington Dramatic Society *218, 285, 406*
West Chiltington Football Club *222, 405*
West Chiltington Golf Club *77*
West Chiltington Horticultural Society *411*
West Chiltington Silver Band *227, 248, 392*
West Chiltington Tennis Club *414*
West Sussex Golf Club *77*

Willetts Farm *87, 92*
Williams Felicity *277*
Williams Mark & Kathy *419*
Williams Michael *136, 259*
Williams Robin and Nicky *424*
Williams Rev W Harold C *285, 319*
Willmer Elsie - see Pullen
Windmill The *66*
Wing Nurse *241, 242*
Winton Charlie *39, 47, 182, 336*
Winton Ray *310, 353*
Wisdom Norman *222, 329*
Women's Institute *225, 228, 294, 399, 424*
Women's Institute Handbell Ringers *402*
Woodshill *78, 82, 335*
Woodshill Farm *82*
Wright-Warren Nurse Patsy *242, 244*

XYZ Concert Party *390*

Youth Club *224, 409*